Archaeology and the M3

Hampshire Field Club and Archaeological Society: Monograph 7
General Editor: Kenneth E Qualmann

Archaeology and the M3
The Watching Brief, the Anglo-Saxon settlement at Abbots Worthy and retrospective sections

by P J Fasham and R J B Whinney

major sections by

J P Coy, J G Evans, C A Keepax, J M Maltby, M A Monk and D Williams

contributions by

W J Carruthers, S M Davies, N Digby, A B Ellison, P F Fisher, H C M Keeley, B Meddens, K E Qualmann, I Riddler, M Robinson, D F Williams and P Wilthew

illustrations by

J Cross, S C Garrett, C M Hearne, S E James, K M Nichols and R C Read

cover illustration by

J Cross

Published by the Hampshire Field Club
in co-operation with the Trust for Wessex Archaeology

HAMPSHIRE FIELD CLUB MONOGRAPH 7
Published by the Hampshire Field Club and Archaeological Society.

This monograph is published with the aid of grants from the Historic Buildings and Monuments Commission (England), Hampshire County Council and Winchester City Council, which bodies deserve the grateful thanks of the authors and publishers. Crown copyright is reserved in respect of material in the volume resulting from central government expenditure.

ISBN 0 907473 07 5

Produced for the Society by
Alan Sutton Publishing, Stroud, Glos.
Printed in Great Britain

CONTENTS

LIST OF ILLUSTRATIONS
All photos, Trust for Wessex Archaeology unless otherwise indicated.

LIST OF TABLES

Introduction

This volume is in two parts. Chapters 1 and 2 record and describe the results of the watching brief during the early construction period of the M3 extension from Popham in central Hampshire, to Bar End, Winchester, when the topsoil strip occurred in the spring and summer of 1983. Included in that programme was the further work done on various contractors' compounds at Easton Lane which have been published with the rest of that excavation (Fasham *et al* 1989). Chapter 1 is concerned with the small sites discovered or investigated during the construction period and Chapter 2 puts on record the chance discovery of the Anglo-Saxon settlement at Abbots Worthy.

The rest of the volume is a retrospective view of the entire M3 project with major contributions by the principal environmental archaeologists who have been involved with the project. It is a rare opportunity to be able publicly to examine and review one's work and to see just how far our approaches, concepts and techniques have developed. I would do it differently if starting now.

I am grateful to Martin Biddle and Collin Bowen, the only Chairmen of the M3 Archaeological Rescue Committee, who have always been strong supporters of the project. The project has always benefited from the support of Geoff Wainwright and his colleagues in English Heritage (formerly part of the Department of the Environment).

The timing of this paper could not be more opportune as it forms the last piece of work that I shall do on the M3, and almost the final report I shall produce in Wessex, before moving to Gwynedd. The M3 seems to have been with me for most of my life but fortunately it is associated mainly with happy memories of discovery and of the many individuals who endured the extremes of the weather in all seasons. Above all there is one person who has both endured the project and me and so I dedicate this volume to Sally.

Peter Fasham   February 1988
Salisbury

Acknowledgements

Watching Brief

The watching brief and the preparation of the material and the post-excavation work for the watching brief has very much been a collaborative venture. The fieldwork team included Robert Read, Wayne Cocroft, Chris Hudson and Debbie Spaulding, assisted at Abbots Worthy by Graham Scobie and at Popham by Duncan Walters. The preparation of the data in the post-excavation stage was done by Mark Lewin-Titt and particularly Nick Digby. The specialists who have contributed to the report are fully acknowledged by their contributions. Sue Davies managed to find time between her other commitments to organise and collate the finds section of the Abbots Worthy report. The illustrations were all prepared in the offices of the Trust for Wessex Archaeology under the able guidance of Robert Read and also drawn by Serena Garrett, Carrie Hearne, Liz James and Karen Nicholls.

The fieldwork was a joint project between the Trust for Wessex Archaeology and the City of Winchester District Council and the substantial contribution in kind of the latter organisation must not be allowed to pass without remark. The field archaeologists were shown every consideration by all concerned in the construction of the motorway. The Department of Transport's consulting engineers Mott, Hay and Anderson, through their resident engineers Messrs Robins and Kale, greatly facilitated the archaeological work and it is a pleasure to record our appreciation of the cooperation received from the main contractors Mowlems and Nuttalls and the earthmoving contractors Blackwells.

The project was funded entirely by English Heritage and their support is once more warmly recognised, as is the encouragement of Dr G J Wainwright and Messrs S Dunmore and P Gosling.

P J Fasham and R J B Whinney

I am grateful to staff at the Plant Science Laboratories, University of Reading, for allowing me access to their reference material and to Frank Green for giving me details of his unpublished work and for his useful comments. I would also like to thank Andrew Jones at the Environmental Archaeology Unit, York, for his work on the mineralised concretions.

W Carruthers

We would like to thank Annie Milles for help with the multivariate analysis and Pete Wardle for writing the computer programmes for calculating the diversity indexes. Useful discussions with a number of people, and especially David Evans and Mark Pollard, have helped us get closer to understanding the problems of dealing with large quantities of data. The work was supported by grants from the Department of the Environment and English Heritage.

J G Evans and D Williams

Retrospective

It is with great pleasure that I record my thanks to those environmental archaeologists who have contributed so much to the entire M3 project and have again produced the goods for this volume; Jennie Coy and Mark Maltby for their work on animal bones, John Evans for his interpretation of the landscape history, Carole Keepax for examining so much charcoal and Mick Monk for his contribution to the agrarian history of the area as seen through carbonised seeds and weeds.

Georges Vicherd kindly provided most of the information about autoroute archaeology in France.

I am grateful for the comments of many colleagues who made the effort to read this report in its draft stage : M Biddle, H C Bowen, S M Davies, J W Hawkes, D A Hinton, A J Lawson, S J Lobb, E Morris, J C Richards, R Whinney, P J Woodward and the staff of English Heritage although I must remain responsible for the contents.

During the lifetime of the M3 Archaeological Rescue Committee the secretarial base was with the Hampshire Council of Community Service, with Vic Emery and John Allen respectively as Honorary Secretary and Treasurer. Hampshire County Council and Winchester District Council always supported the scheme and gave freely of assistance in kind and sometimes with finance. The final acknowledgement for this report lies with English Heritage who supported the project throughout and enabled this review to be written.

P J Fasham

Abstract

Archaeological investigations on the M3 through central Hampshire started in 1972 and were still in progress eighteen years later. Between 1972 and 1983 archaeological fieldwork was primarily under the direction of one person who was also responsible for arranging the post-excavation work. In 1983 the 17 kilometres of the M3 between Popham, just south of Basingstoke, and Bar End, just east of Winchester, were constructed.

This volume falls naturally into two main parts: the results of the watching brief and a retrospective of the whole project.

Chapter 1 puts on record the smaller sites discovered by the watching brief of which the most striking is a Roman aqueduct along the north bank of the River Itchen supplying water to Winchester. Chapter 2 describes the Anglo-Saxon settlement at Abbots Worthy which probably extended along the north bank of the River Itchen. Where intersected by the M3 it was only 700m away from its cemetery at Worthy Park.

The rest of the volume is a retrospective of the whole project with major sections on archaeo-botanical studies, animal bone, land molluscs and charcoal. The C14 determinations from the entire project are listed, as are all the archaeological investigations and their places of publication.

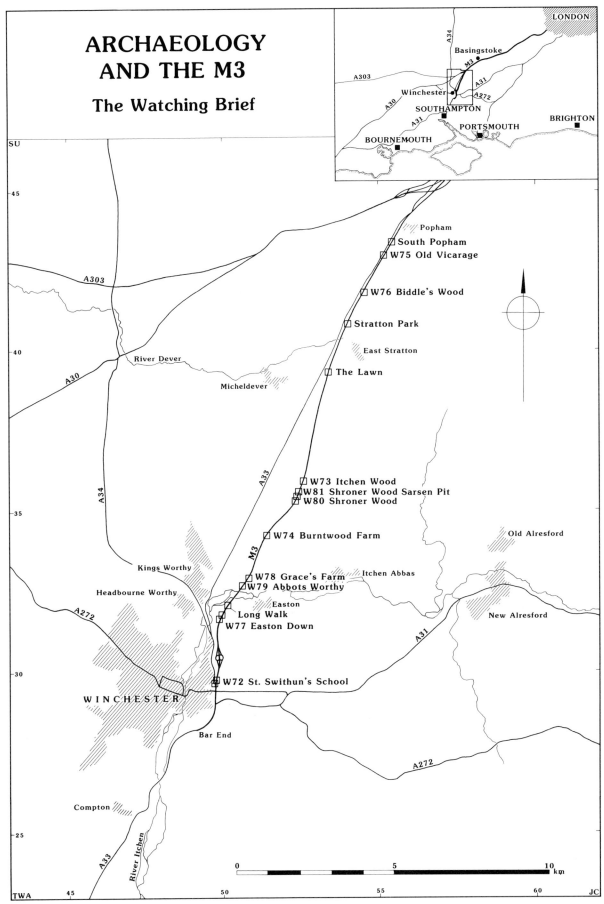

Fig 1. General location plan and positions of sites recorded during the M3 watching brief. See Fig 44 for location of all archaeological investigations on the line of the M3.

Chapter 1

The Watching Brief – Small Sites
by P J Fasham and R J B Whinney

The location of all excavated sites is shown on Figs 1 and 44 and they are listed in Table 23. The small sites from the watching brief are described from south to north and the headings usually contain the following information: a common name for the site, parish, grid reference and the Trust for Wessex Archaeology site code (a number with a W prefix). Sites investigated by the M3 Archaeological Rescue Committee have a number with an R prefix.

St Swithun's School, Winchester, SU 49682750, W72 (Figs 2 and 3)

Machine clearance by contractors in advance of their main works enabled limited manual cleaning and excavation to take place. The main site was a ring-ditch, identified previously from aerial photographs, but there was also a linear ditch (Fig 2). There was no trace of another ditch, discovered during a geophysical scan by the staff of the Ancient Monuments Laboratory using a fluxgate gradiometer, which approached the site from the south and then veered to the east (Clark 1974). The site, on a north-facing slope, was located just below the crest of an east-west chalk ridge, itself cut by the valley of the River Itchen.

The circular ring-ditch, F7125, had an internal diameter of 24m, whilst the ditch itself was about three metres wide. In the time available it was possible to excavate four opposed trenches, each 1m wide, across the ditch. The sides of the ditch were steep and the flat base was some 1.3 to 1.5m wide.

Three features were located within the area enclosed by the ditch. The first, F7119, in the centre, measured 1.73m long, 0.66m wide and 0.22m deep. It contained no finds. The second, F7123, was a small circular feature, 0.35m in diameter and 0.10m deep. It was located about two metres to the south of F7119 and also contained no finds. The third, F7121, about three metres northeast of F7199, was a shallow circular feature, 0.40m in diameter and 0.10m deep.

The linear ditch, F7104, ran approximately north–south on the southwest side of the ring-ditch. A 30m length was exposed in the top-soil clearance. It was 1m wide, 0.35m deep, with rounded sides. At the north end it appeared to cut an earlier, parallel ditch, F7117, and the recut visible in Section E may reflect this sequence. Further traces of the earlier ditch were seen in other sections across F7104.

About 15m north of the ring-ditch an east–west lynchet was discovered. It was observed only when the motorway cutting was well advanced, and it proved impossible to record in plan or section.

The pottery, by A B Ellison

The broad identifications of the pottery are summarised in Table 1.

On the nearby Easton Lane site, in general, A7-type fabrics could be correlated with Neolithic (early) and Late Bronze Age forms (Fasham *et al*

Table 1. St Swithun's School (W72). Broad identifications of the pottery from ring-ditch F7125.

Context	Section	Ceramics
7128	F7125A	Early Iron Age
7137	F7125B	Iron Age? (and later)
7167	F7125D	Early Iron Age
7163	F7125C	Iron Age and Romano-British
7163, 7164	F7125C	Prehistoric (pre-Iron Age fabric A7) – 16 sherds, 3 large, from a single vessel, including small finds 364, 365, 366 Beaker? (fabric C5) – one small body sherd, not worn M/LBA (fabrics A5, A9) – three sherds, all different vessels, all indeterminate

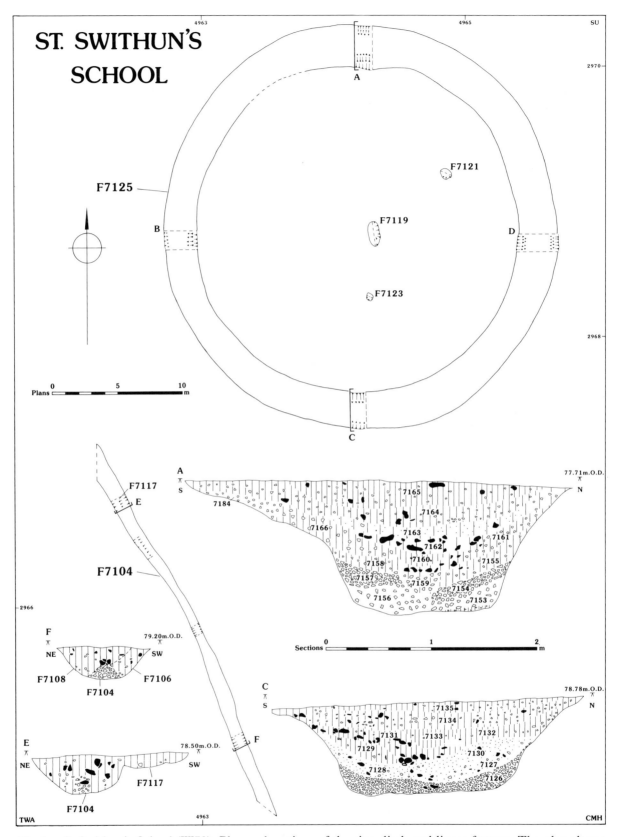

Fig 2.   St Swithun's School (W72). Plan and sections of the ring-ditch and linear feature. The plan shows the two features in the correct position relative to one another.

Fig 3. St Swithun's School (W72). The ring-ditch is in the foreground under the spill from the topsoil clearance. The line of the motorway under construction can be seen running north. The site of Easton Lane, Junction 9 on the M3, is on the first crest where the slip road is clearly visible. Scales are 2m. Photo: P J Fasham, Trust for Wessex Archaeology.

1989). The base looks as though it might be rounded, and therefore Neolithic, although the fabric and treatment are rather rough. A fragment with a possible lug does not help with the identifications. Given these uncertainties, it is safest to identify the ceramics as Neolithic or Bronze Age

Easton Down, Itchen Valley Parish, SU 44593119, W77 (Fig 4)

Archaeological features were observed in drainage ditches cut along both sides of the motorway after the initial clearance of the topsoil by contractors. Conditions for recording were not good.

Easton Down forms the west end of a chalk ridge which is cut by the valley of the River Itchen. The major archaeological feature of the Down was a ring-ditch relating to a Wessex-type burial which had been excavated in 1974 (Fasham 1982, 24–40). Little was visible of the ring-ditch during the construction works, but a series of ditches and lynchets were observed and recorded over a distance of some 500m.

F7205, obliquely cut by a drainage ditch, was not visible running across the motorway. The oblique section recorded a width of 10m and a depth of 0.50m for this feature, which was positioned on the side of the Down, just above a dry valley.

F7282 and F7283, observed in the drainage ditch on the east side of the motorway, were the remnants of positive and negative lynchets respectively. They appeared to have been cut through at an oblique angle by the drainage ditch and were discernible only as subtle variations in the depth of the unploughed soil in their fill. They covered a total spread of 10m. F7282 was 0.24m high and F7283 was 0.14m deep.

The best section of lynchets was recorded on the east side of the motorway, in F7207 and F7209 (Fig 4). F7207 was 9.10m wide and 0.25m deep, whilst F7209, 1m up the slope, was 4.60m wide (oblique) and also 0.25m deep. These lateral dimensions do not provide the basis for an accurate assessment as they were again cut through at an angle. It was originally believed that they formed positive and negative lynchets, but it now seems more likely that they are both the negative lynchets of a field boundary that had moved downhill.

F7313 was an irregular feature of shallow profile on the west side of the motorway.

F7211 was a shallow feature running east–west across the motorway. A single section, 1.00m wide was excavated, and showed the feature to be a ditch, 3.70m wide and 0.23m deep, with sides sloping

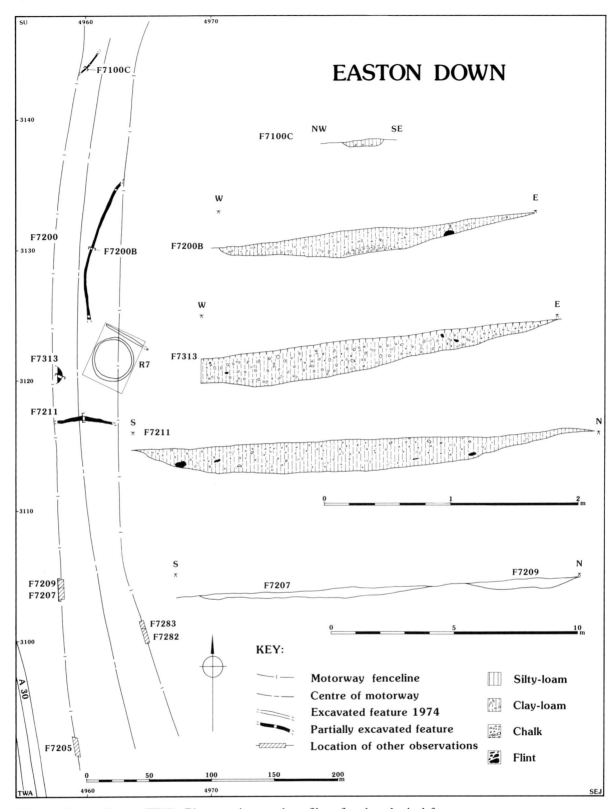

Fig 4.   Easton Down (W77). Plan, sections and profiles of archaeological features.

gently to a broad, flattish bottom. A similar feature was excavated adjacent to the ring-ditch in 1974 (Fasham 1982, 30).

F7200 was recorded running for 90m northeast to southwest along the motorway. It was 2.70m wide and 0.12m deep, and although it had the profile of a shallow ditch, it may have been a natural feature.

F7100 ran northeast to southwest across part of the motorway. It was slight, only 0.40m wide and 0.09m deep. For most of its length it had probably been truncated or reduced by the machine clearance.

Long Walk, Itchen Valley Parish, SU 49863189, no site code

A number of ditches, possibly prehistoric boundaries, and a probable lynchet were exposed by contractors' machine clearance on the north-facing slope of Easton Down, immediately above the valley of the River Itchen. These three or four linear features, cut into the chalk, were recorded in plan only.

Grace's Farm, Itchen Valley Parish, SU 50603286, W78 (Figs 5–9)

Discovered during topsoil clearance by contractors' machinery, a 70m length of a linear feature, F7350, was recorded. It ran east–west across the gentle north slope of the valley of the River Itchen. Five sections, each approximately 1m wide, were excavated to reveal a feature with a width of 2.00 to 2.70m where it was exposed at the surface of the chalk subsoil. The sides of the feature were very steep or almost vertical, and the base was 1.30 to 1.40m in width. The general surviving depth was 0.65 m. At the bottom of two of the excavated sections, thin bands or lenses of water-lain silts were discovered (Fig 5, sections B and D).

The soils, by Helen C M Keeley

This feature contained four layers. The upper 0 to 0.50m (context 7407) consisted of homogeneous fine sand which contained a few gravel-size stones; 0.50 to 0.55m was a layer of gravel (context 7406). From 0.55 to 0.60m (context 7405) there was fine sand, which overlay stones and gravel. The sediments contained very little organic matter (loss on ignition range 1.13–1.82, mean 1.62), had slightly alkaline pH (7.32–8.03, mean 7.64) and contained molluscs.

The molluscs, by Beverley Meddens

Editorial Note: In order not to prejudice the interpretation of the mollusc data the archaeological interpretation of the feature was not disclosed to the author and the report was initially produced without prior knowledge that the feature was interpreted as an aqueduct.

Of the various samples taken by Dr Keeley three contained molluscs. Each sample was nearly 5kg, air dried weight. The samples came from the upper fills, layers 7407 and 7406.

Extraction of the molluscs was done following the method described by Evans (1972). All three samples were processed with ease through a 500 micron sieve. The molluscs were generally poorly preserved and identification, which was difficult in some cases, was done using a ×10/×20 binocular microscope and several reference works (Ellis 1969, Beedham 1972, Evans 1972, Ellis 1978, Kerney and Cameron 1979). I am grateful to Dr Kerney for checking and correcting the identifications. Identification to species of the Sphaeriidae was not pursued, because of of the poor condition of the samples and the expertise of the author, however Dr Kerney identified *Pisidium nitidum* in all three samples, *Pisidium amnicum* in sample 1189 and *Pisidium subtruncatum* in sample 1188. The Sphaeriidae were counted by counting the left and right valves and a minimum number of individuals was taken to be the largest of the two. Numbers for the Arionidae may be too low because I do not feel all the specimens were retrieved.

Table 2 lists the numbers of specimens recovered; taxonomy is according to to Walden (1976) and Kerney (1976b). These assemblages are made up of at least two components, freshwater and terrestrial. Some of the terrestrial molluscs could be intrusive modern specimens, and these are marked in the table. The occurrence of *Cernuella virgata* is very interesting but almost certainly modern (Kerney pers comm). Most of the species present in these assemblages are living there today.

The freshwater aquatic fauna is characterised by *Bithynia tentaculata* and *Valvata piscinalis*. The requirements of the species in this group are fairly homogeneous and indicate a particular environment. *Bithynia*, in large numbers, requires abundant vegetation and calcareous water, and *Valvata piscinalis* requires eutrophic slow-moving water. *Pisidium amnicum* also prefers well-oxygenated flowing water, and the other Sphaeriidae also have similar requirements. *Lymnaea palustris* is a species of small overgrown pools and ditches, and although *Lymnaea peregra* is ubiquitous it is typical of slow-moving clean freshwater. *Lymnaea stagnalis* and *Armiger crista* however are not tolerant of fast-moving water. The requirements of the species in this group are fairly homogeneous and indicate a eutrophic, well-oxygenated, slow-flowing body of water with plenty of vegetation growing in it.

The terrestrial assemblage can be broken into at least two components as well as a group of species with catholic requirements: species that demand dry open grassland and those that more often than not occur in marshes. The dry grassland element is characterised by *Helicella itala*, which is particularly specialised, *Pupilla muscorum* and *Vallonia excentrica*. The wetter environment is characterised by the marsh species Succineidae, *Zonitoides nitidus*, *Carychium minimum*, *Vallonia pulchella* and *Ashfordia granulata*. Although these species are present in

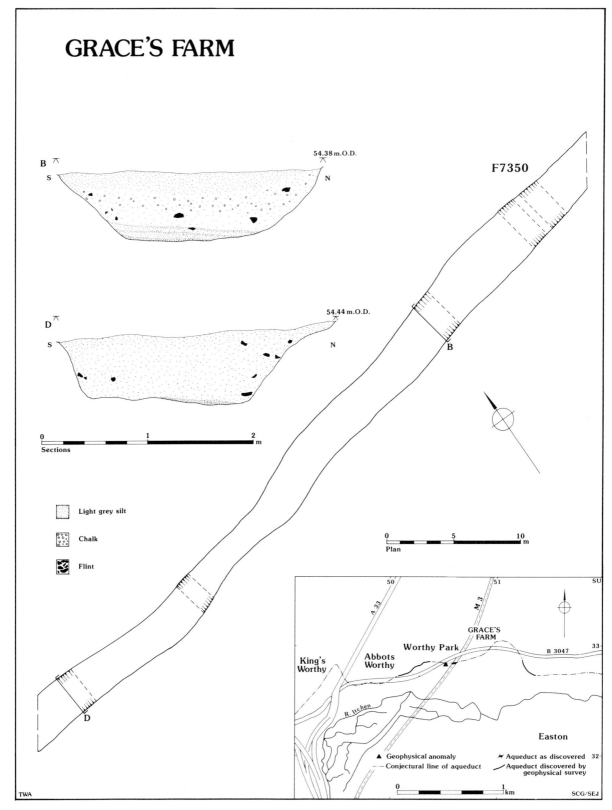

Fig 5.   Grace's Farm (W78). Plan and sections of the aqueduct. The inset shows the location of the site and of the recorded geophysical anomalies.

Table 2. Grace's Farm (W78). Molluscs.

Species	Context/Sample No:	7407–1188	7406–1189	7406–1190
	Depth:	0–50cms	50–55cms	50–55cms
Carychium minimum cf.		1	–	–
Succineidae		1	3	1
Cochlicopa lubrica		1	1	1
Cochlicopa sp.		7	4	1
Vertigo pygmaea		4	5	4
Pupilla muscorum		20	9	4
Vallonia costata		14 (5)	3	4 (5)
Vallonia pulchella		1	– (1)	1
Vallonia excentrica		33	23 (1)	14 (3)
Vallonia spp. exc./pul.		42 (3)	77 (4)	56 (1)
Punctum pygmaeum		2	4	–
Arionidae		6	1	43
Vitrinidae cf.		1	1	–
Vitrea contracta		1	–	–
Nesovitrea hammonis		1	1	–
Aegopinella nitidula		–	1	2
Oxychilus cellarius		4	4	5
Oxychilus alliarius		1	–	–
Oxychilus helveticus cf.		1	–	–
Zonitoides nitidus		–	1	–
Milacidea and Limacidae		24	18	16
Ceciliodes acicula		(98)	(87)	(1161)
Cernuella virgata		– (1)	–	– (1)
Helicella itala		4	3	9
Ashfordia granulata		–	1	–
Trichia hispida		28	18 (1)	32
Valvata piscinalis		92	577	498
Bithynia tentaculata		3	14	7
Bithynia tentaculata (operculum)		115	91	57
Lymnaeidae		–	10	3
Lymnaea palustris		1	–	–
Lymnaea stagnalis		4	–	5
Lymnaea peregra		6	–	2
Planorbis carinatus cf.		–	–	1
Planorbis albus		–	2	1
Armiger crista		1	–	–
Sphaeriidae		44	54	20
Ostracods		19	34	19
Unidentified apices		20	32	4
TOTAL		387	901	753

Figures in brackets indicate specimens that could be modern, and are not included in the totals. For *Bithynia tentaculata*, only counts for apices are included in the total. Totals do not include *Ceciliodes acicula* which are certainly modern.

small numbers, they are present with a number of species which frequently live in marshes, for example *Cochlicopa lubrica*, *Punctum pygmaeum*, *Nesovitrea hammonis* and *Trichia hispida* (Evans 1972). The presence of *Trichia hispida* in conjunction with *Vallonia* as an indicator of plough-wash has been discussed by Allen (1985), but in this instance *Trichia hispida* is more likely to be associated with the other catholic species. Similarly, the other Zonitidae require damp, sheltered and undisturbed habitats, and therefore would not be out of place in an environment that could be provided by vegetation growing on the banks of a stream.

The feature has been interpreted archaeologically as an abandoned aqueduct and the analysis of mollusca can be seen as consistent with this interpretation, however the source of the material is a problem. Dr Keeley hoped that the examination of the molluscs would shed some light on the nature of the sediments. The deposits could be fluvial or slopewash with a reworked aquatic element. Although the assemblages seem to be consistent with the interpretation of the feature as an aqueduct or stream, there could be some reworking of material from unknown sources. The overall preservation of the material was poor, and there are possibilities that erosion and reworking of the more resistant elements such as the opercula of *Bithynia tentaculata* could bias the results, as discussed by Thew *et al* (1984, 115).

If the deposits are alluvial sediments various possibilities for explaining the origin of the molluscs present themselves. There are effectively three elements to the assemblages: the truly aquatic element, either reworked from elsewhere or representing a living fauna in a well oxygenated body of water; the open country terrestrial fauna characterised by *Helicella itala*, which could have been washed in from the surrounding landscape; and the wetter terrestrial and marsh fauna that would be happy living on the bank of a stream with its associated plant life. A similar interpretation was given to the mollusca from the Roman aqueduct at Dorchester (Sparey Green 1987).

Sample 1188 has a larger proportion of terrestial and marsh species than samples 1189 and 1190. However there does not appear to be a significant change in the nature of the assemblages, but there is an increase in the proportion of *Bithynia* opercula in the upper layer and this raises the question of reworking rather than changes in the local ecological conditions.

The evidence from the mollusca can be interpreted as consistent with the feature being an aqueduct, albeit slow-flowing and weedy, but well-oxygenated. There is added evidence for the local ecological conditions being quite overgrown in the immediate environs of the water, but very open, dry grassland conditions further afield. The wider environmental evidence is in accordance with other molluscan evidence in the area (Allen 1985, Mason 1981, 1982).

The pottery, by Susan M Davies

Ten sherds of pottery, in four fabrics, were found in context 7351 of ditch F7350. Nine are Romano-British, with a single sherd of grass-tempered, Early Saxon, pottery also present. The number and weight of each individual fabric are shown in Table 3. The fabric numbers refer to those described in more detail in the report on the material from Abbots Worthy (Davies, below 55).

The nine Romano-British sherds probably represent the remains of three vessels. No form can be attributed to the sherd in fabric 5.8, but the two sherds in fabric 5.4 are most likely to be from a

Table 3. Grace's Farm (W78). Number and weight (in grams) of pottery recovered by fabric.

Fabric	Rim		Base		Body		Total	
	No	Wt	No	Wt	No	Wt	No	Wt
1.1	–	–	–	–	1	10	1	10
5.4	–	–	–	–	2	20	2	20
5.7	2	100	3	110	1	10	6	220
5.8	–	–	–	–	1	5	1	5
Totals	2	100	3	110	5	45	10	255

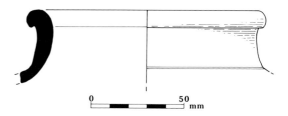

Fig 6.   Grace's Farm (W78). The Roman pottery.

necked and cordoned jar of late 1st-century date, though the rim is missing. The remaining six sherds in fabric 5.7 are all from one vessel (Fig 6). The best parallel appears to be from the Alice Holt potteries, form 3C.3 (Lyne and Jefferies 1979, Fig 29), a hook-rim jar dated AD 220–270. The fabric would be in keeping with such a source.

The presence of an Early Saxon sherd in the deposit is presumably indicative of the length of time that the postulated aqueduct took to fill up. No form can be identified, but the fabric is identical to material found at Abbots Worthy, where a series of small jars/cooking pots was recovered in this fabric.

General considerations

The overall shape of F7350 and the water-lain deposits within it are unusual in their geographical, geological and archaeological contexts. These anomalous factors, together with the fact that the feature apparently followed the slope at a consistent contour level (about 53.30m), suggest the possibility of a carefully designed, constructed and positioned, and thereby important, feature within the Romano-British landscape. The same contour traced to the east arrives at several springs above Manor Farm, near Itchen Stoke some six kilometres away (Fig 7). One similarity between this feature and the Dorchester aqueduct may be seen in their shape. Both are flat-bottomed with steep sides and the width to height ratios are both approximately 2:1, and their overall dimensions compare closely. The combination of all these elements, including the molluscan data, thus make it possible to suggest that F7350 was a segment of an aqueduct which supplied fresh spring water to Winchester.

Comparison with the Dorchester aqueduct, provides further information. The fall of the Dorchester aqueduct is 1:2400, or about 0.40m per kilometre (RCHM 1970, 585–589). If a similar fall is allowed here, then the aqueduct would arrive at Winchester at a height of 46.72m above sea level, or put another way, at a point just east of the northwest corner of the city. In general terms it is quite possible to allow at least 0.5–0.75m either side of the calculated height of arrival and still maintain a reasonable fall on the aqueduct.

In order to arrive at this point close to Winchester, the topographical conditions dictate a lengthy and at times circuitous route. From the springs in the Itchen Stoke area, along the appropriate contours, the aqueduct would cover a distance of 23.75 kilo-

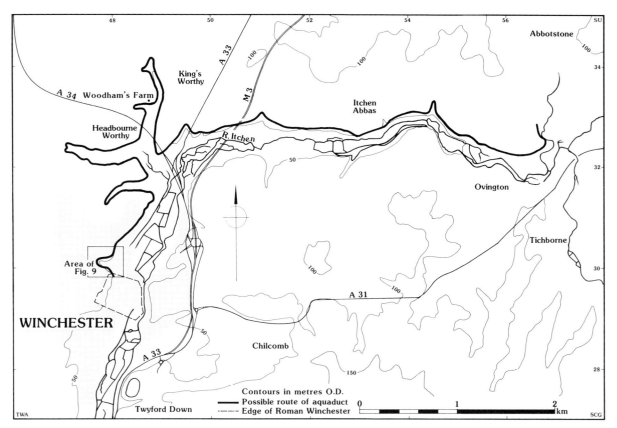

Fig 7. Grace's Farm (W78). Plan showing a possible course for the Roman aqueduct from its likely source to its arrival in Winchester.

metres. Between Itchen Stoke and Headbourne Worthy, the supposed route runs almost parallel to the River Itchen itself. However, from Headbourne Worthy, it would be necessary for the aqueduct to follow the contours along the slopes of three dry valleys before reaching Winchester (Fig 7), although a short bridge at this point would cut about ten kilometres off the length. Such a combination of straight lengths and more winding sections, resulting in a total distance of some 23.75 kilometres, is paralleled not only at Dorchester (RCHM 1970), but also on the continent, for example, between Uzes and Nimes (Musée archaeologique de Nimes 1986), approaching Arles, and with the numerous aqueducts that supplied Lyon.

It therefore seems that the feature excavated at Grace's Farm is an early Roman aqueduct, fed from springs in the Itchen Stoke area, which provided fresh, clean water to the rapidly expanding urban community in Winchester.

It is alleged that probably all Romano-British towns cities were provided with a supply of water by aqueduct (Stephens 1985a, Wacher 1974), as were many military establishments (Stephens 1985b). Most of the British aqueducts were relatively simple and were not, like most of their Gallic counterparts, in covered masonry channels. They were also apparently of comparatively short length. The Lincoln aqueduct shows some sophistication but does not reach the same technical level as the recently exca-

vated site of Aux Roches, Ars-sur-Moselle (Massy 1984), with its header tanks to assist the crossing of the river Moselle, or the syphon system at Lyon (Burdy 1985 is a useful small field guide). Stephens (1985a) has pointed out that Winchester has the only enclosed channel known in Britain but this is a channel feeding a very small part of the lowest area of Winchester. The value and function of this channel is discussed by Qualmann (below). It is unlikely that the chalk cut channels were not lined and traces of a clay lining have been found in the Dorchester aqueduct (Sparey Green 1987). Timber may have been used to line the channel, or the natural process of silting may have produced an adequate seal. The chance discovery of the aqueduct has added a considerable dimension to the Roman landscape of the Itchen valley and to the city of Winchester itself.

Fluxgate scan, by King Alfred's College and the Royal Commission on Historical Monuments (England)

Initial field work along the suggested course of the aqueduct revealed no evidence of the channel surviving as an upstanding monument in the areas visited. As part of its field training course the History Department of King Alfred's College, Winchester did some geophysical work immediately west of the M3, adjacent to the excavated section. An anomaly was detected. Subsequently in January 1988 the Royal Commission on Historical Monuments were able to examine further areas. Slightly further west, in Worthy Park, the line of the aqueduct was identified as a geophysical anomaly extending for about 300m and registering 1mA with the machine set at 30mAT/m. At this point a scarp underlying later earthworks, typical of medieval settlement remains, may be the aqueduct. A 200m length of ditch, reading 0.4–0.75mA with the machine set on 10mAT/m, was recorded by the fluxgate gradiometer to the east of the known exposure. These three observations of a linear feature on the anticipated line do seem to confirm the feature as an aqueduct.

An examination of available aerial photographic evidence suggests that one of the ditches adjacent to the Woodham's Farm site may be the aqueduct (Fig 8). It certainly is in the correct topographic location, though recent evaluation in advance of housing

proposals failed to provide confirmation (R Whinney pers comm).

The Winchester evidence, by K E Qualmann

An aqueduct approaching Winchester from the north in the way suggested would have met the Winchester–Silchester road (Margary 1956, 42a) just less than two kilometres north of the town. It would probably have run parallel to the uphill (western) side of the road, for some distance. Indeed, had the road been carried on an embankment over low ground, the water supply might have followed the road line directly to the town defences. Observations at 82 Hyde Street in 1954 (Collis 1978), confirmed by recent work on the same site, have however shown that the Roman road ran down into the Fulflood valley before climbing a steepish slope to the North

Fig 8.   Grace's Farm (W78). Aerial view of the Woodham's Farm site; south is to the top of the frame. Archaeological features have been highlighted and the curving ditch on the approximate line of the aqueduct has been marked. Photo: National Monuments Record, reproduced by permission of the Royal Commission on Historical Monuments England. Crown copyright reserved.

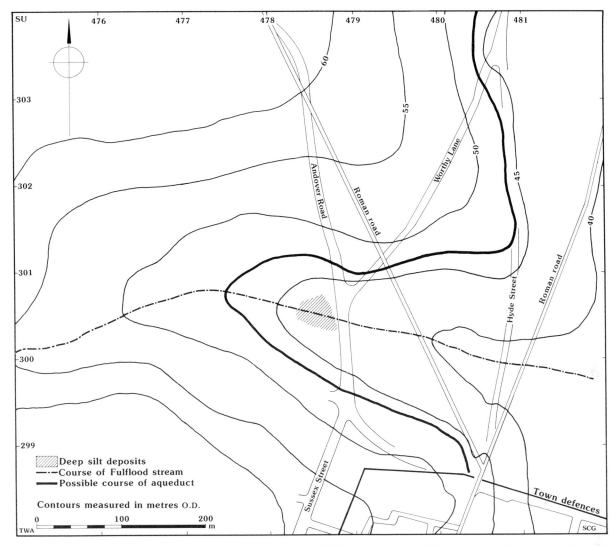

Fig 9.   Plan showing the area where the aqueduct would have arrived at Winchester and the potential site for a cistern. For location see Fig 7.

Gate. The aqueduct is therefore likely to have diverged from the road line to follow a more gently sloping course along the sides of the Fulflood valley (Fig 9).

The Fulflood was an intermittent stream, known from documentary sources (Biddle 1976) to have drained the valley to the northwest of Winchester in the early Middle Ages. Plotting of contours from exposures of natural chalk and occasional observations of water-lain silt deposits (Qualmann forthcoming), have enabled reconstruction of its course. The aqueduct would have crossed the valley bottom at about SU 47813005, an area today occupied by a railway yard northeast of Winchester station. Unusually deep silts were recorded less than 40m to the east during construction at 11–14 Andover Road in 1972. Silty light grey clays up to 4m deep were observed, with early medieval gritted pottery in the uppermost layer. The southern limit of the deposit was identified and a possible northern edge was seen 52m away on an adjacent construction site. The western and eastern limits of this deposit are not known.

While interpretation based on such limited evidence is hazardous, this deep, silt-filled feature may have functioned as a reservoir in the Roman period. It might also have served to raise the level of the water it held just enough to bring the supply into the town at, or just above, the North Gate. From this point, some 80% of the defended area of Winchester could have been served.

Stephens (1985a) has pointed out that Winchester had the only enclosed channel known in Britain, a channel which fed the bottom of the town. The evidence for this is the report of an 1849 discovery which states that 'the mouth (of the water conduit) was below the present level of the river' (Gunner 1849). While the mid-nineteenth century level of the River Itchen is not known with any certainty it is unlikely to have been much higher than today. Hence, the level of the Roman water supply at a point east of modern Eastgate Street was probably no higher than the present river bed. Such a supply could feed only a very limited area of the defended town. Indeed, Gunner's suggestion that the conduit supplied a single house or bath may well be correct.

Burntwood Farm, Itchen Valley Parish, SU 51173421, W74

Topsoil removal by contractors prior to the motorway construction revealed a number of linear features on a low southwest running spur. No new features were discovered as they had all been previously investigated by means of a formal excavation (Fasham 1980a, R5 and R6) and so are not illustrated here.

On Burntwood Farm (R6) a ditch, F7297, aligned approximately east–west, was shown in section to be some 0.25m deep, with steep sides and a flat base 0.24m wide. This ditch was excavated as Land Boundary Ditch 8 in 1974 (Fasham 1980a, 54 and Fig 17). Two further parallel ditches, F7301 and F7307, were exposed by the topsoil stripping to the north of F7297. These were the same ditches that defined the trackway excavated in 1974. F7301 corresponded to Feature 2, F7307 corresponded to Ditch 79, and at its northern end, F7309 was the same as Ditch 3 (Fasham 1980a).

To the north, where the line of the motorway passed to the east of the 1974 excavations at Bridgets Farm (R5), there was no trace of a linear ditch which was predicted to run eastwards from the excavations (Fasham 1980a, Fig 8). It seems most likely that this ditch had been destroyed as a result of excessive removal of the topsoil by the contractors at this point.

Shroner Wood Ditch, Itchen Valley Parish, SU 52073524, W80 (Fig 10)

Some 30m to the north of the access road to Shroner House, a linear ditch was recorded after topsoil clearance. It ran across the line of the motorway on a northwest to southeast alignment and was observed for some 75m. This ditch, F8078, was 3m wide at the top, and about 1m deep. The section, cut on the west side of the motorway line, showed evidence for a recut (F8082). No artefacts were recovered.

Shroner Wood Sarsen Pit, Itchen Valley Parish, SU 52163538, W81 (Figs 10–13)

The Shroner Wood sarsen pit was surveyed and excavated prior to the clearance of the wood. It lay on the eastern edge of the wood on the top of a low hill. Following an initial survey, the pit was excavated (Fig 11). It measured 12m by 10m. Below the leafy mould that formed the topsoil was a layer of redeposited clay, apparently the result of nineteenth century exploration of part of the pit which had suggested that the sarsens were part of a megalithic burial chamber. Under this was the natural mottled brown Clay-with-Flints.

Embedded in the natural clay were over 30 pieces of sarsen, which were clearly all part of one or two

parent rocks which had been split and broken by natural causes and agencies. There was no evidence of deliberate wedging or splitting. Subsequent machine excavation during construction work exposed a second layer of sarsens but it was not possible to determine the full depth of the pit, nor the total number of sarsen stones in it.

Observations, by P F Fisher

The significance of this feature is the quantity of sarsen pieces it contained, compared with the dearth of sarsens over much of the Hampshire Downs. Visual examination of 35 sarsen pieces led to the recognition of two types: a sandy silcrete (Clark *et al* 1967; Summerfield and Goudie 1980) and a less usual silcrete containing some blackened, rounded flints which are typical of Tertiary pebble beds (Summerfield and Goudie 1980, 73). Interestingly, both types occur in the same stone showing that they are in fact a single formation.

The sarsens are contained in a depression, probably a doline, filled by reddened clay (see soil description below), typical of the natural Clay-with-Flints in the area which was observed in a neighbouring excavation.

No evidence of working of the sarsens was observed. Even the surface hollows (suggested mortices) were probably natural, as they are common on sarsens found elsewhere (Summerfield and Goudie 1980, Fig 4). Split stones might have been broken by man, but because burning is the most likely process employed in such an exercise, the lack of charcoal in the pit argues against this.

As with all other sarsens, those at Shroner Wood are probably derived from Tertiary sands (attested by the incorporated pebbles). The inclusion of the sarsens in a natural depression is unexceptional, because the feature probably originated by gradual dissolution of chalk, allowing the overlying sarsens to be incorporated in the fill. In this way the stones would be protected from subsequent subaerial erosion or clearance by man. This location, in an area where only occasional sarsens are generally known, clearly demonstrates the likely extension of a former Tertiary silcrete surface over the Hampshire Downs where otherwise sarsens are a rare phenomenon.

Soil profile description:

L	−2–0 cm	Leaf litter composed of partially decomposed broad leaves.
Ah	0–7 cm	Dark brown (7.5YR3/2) silty clay loam with many roots and granular structure; smooth and abrupt, on:
Eb	7–27 cm	Brown to dark brown (7.5YR4/4) silty clay loam with many roots and with fine angular block structure; wavy and abrupt, on:
Bt1	27–47 cm	Reddish brown (5YR6/8) clay with many continuous discrete clay coats on angular blocky ped faces; uncertain boundary, on:
Bt2	47–107+ cm	Yellowish red (5YR5/6) clay with occasional dark reddish brown (5YR2.5/2) mottles, many continuous clay and manganese coats on fine angular blocky ped faces and in pores; local lens of yellow (10YR7/6) silt loam (probably rotted chalk).

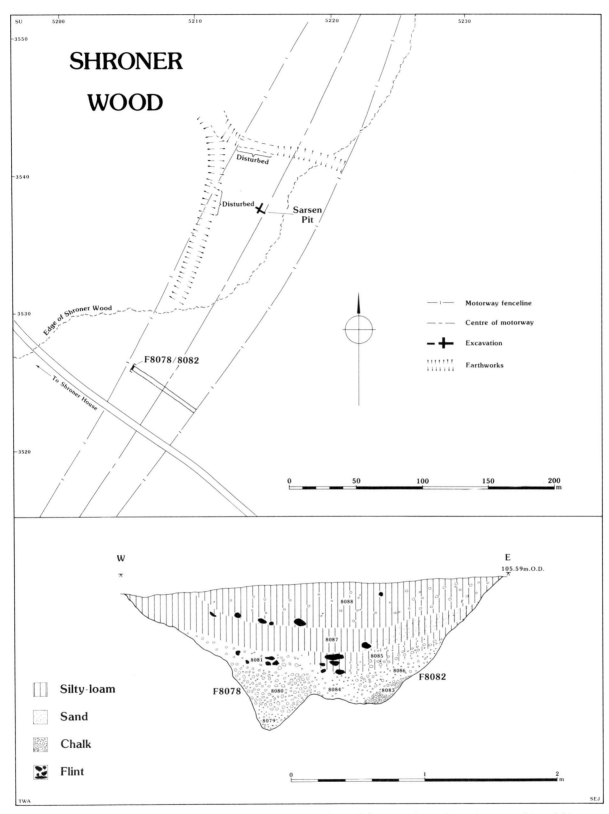

Fig 10.   Shroner Wood (W80). Plan showing the location of features in and on the east side of Shroner Wood. The section is of F8078.

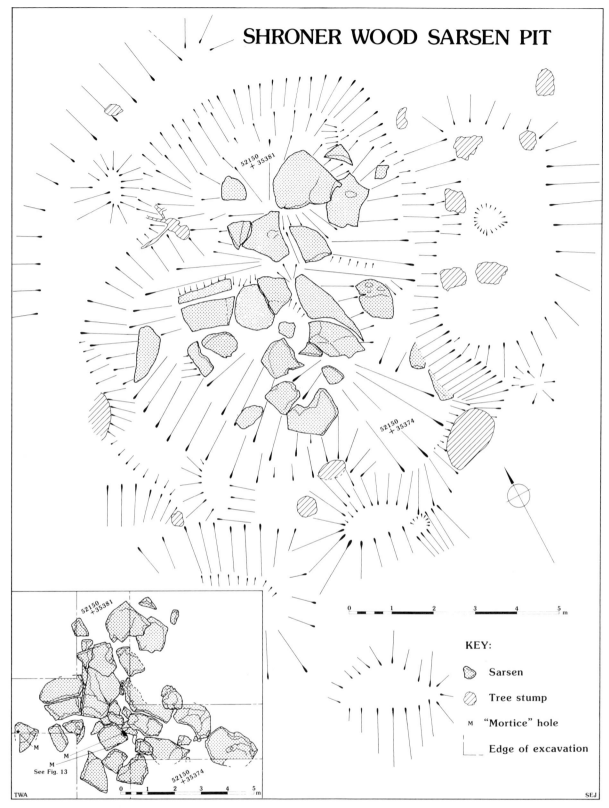

Fig 11.   Shroner Wood sarsen pit (W81). Plan showing the sarsen pit in Shroner Wood before and after (inset) excavation.

Fig 12. Shroner Wood sarsen pit (W81). View from north after the limited excavation. Scales are 2m and 0.5m. Photo: P J Fasham, Trust for Wessex Archaeology.

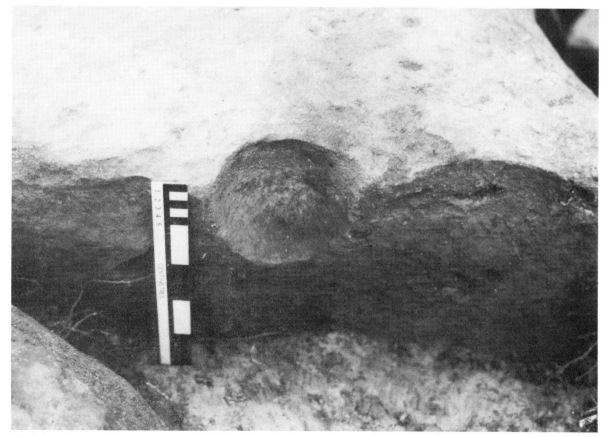

Fig 13. Shroner Wood sarsen pit (W81). Detail of a small natural surface hollow, resembling a mortice, on stone 9. Scale is 0.5m. Photo: P J Fasham, Trust for Wessex Archaeology.

Shroner Wood Earthworks, Itchen Valley Parish, SU 52123542, no site code (Fig 10)

Prior to the clearance necessitated for the motorway, earthworks within Shroner Wood, to the east of the modern A33, were recorded. They were situated in the southeast corner of the wood, north of the sarsen pit, on a low hill.

The earthworks consisted of two intersecting ditches, one of which ran approximately north–south for about 140m and the other east–west for approximately 100m. From their point of intersection they both ran northwest, but soon became untraceable. They were recorded only as earthworks since circumstances did not allow for the excavation of sections.

Because there were no finds it is difficult to interpret or date these ditches. They appear to predate the Shroner Wood boundary, for the northern ditch ran out of the wood to the east. It is conceivable that they may be outliers of the earthworks recorded in Itchen Wood to the north and Micheldever Wood to the northeast (Fasham 1983).

Itchen Wood Earthworks, Itchen Valley Parish, SU 52403200, W73 (Figs 14 and 15)

Itchen Wood lies to the south of Micheldever Wood, where other earthworks were excavated and recorded in 1974 (Fasham 1983). It is separated from Micheldever Wood by the Northington Road, which runs along the bottom of a shallow dry valley. During tree clearance prior to the construction of the motorway, a complex series of earthworks and other features was exposed. Hollow-ways, banks, ditches and pits were recorded in a strip some 70m wide over a length of 500m. Further earthworks were located and recorded before destruction by the Chilland Road diversion, to the east of the main motorway route.

All the visible features were initially surveyed after clear-felling, but before the disposal and burning of the resulting debris. Topsoil clearance followed immediately after removal of the felling trash. This made the survey operation extremely difficult with a large number of felled trees and piles of brushwood on the ground. A limited number of features were then mechanically sectioned and recorded in more detail. The location and alignment of the trenches was determined more by the felled trees, roots and stumps than by archaeological considerations. Trenches were not therefore at right angles to the features. Only those features actually sectioned were given context numbers and these are used in the following description. To facilitate description, letters have been assigned to the unexcavated features.

At the northern end of the complex was a small rectangular enclosure or Celtic field, identified on three sides by a series of earthworks. F7213, a lynchet, 1m high and 0.70m wide, was aligned east–west and ran for about 90m before turning south to form the east side of the enclosure or field. Parallel with F7213, and some 80m south, was a ditch and bank (F7227 and F7228, F7230 and F7231), which formed the southern side. Where sectioned, the ditch was 0.70m wide at the top and 0.60m deep with steep, straight sides and a flat bottom some 0.30m wide. The bank was about 2m wide, and survived to a height of only 0.23m. To the east, an extension of F7213 made up the third side of this enclosure or 'field'.

Within the enclosure were traces of four lynchets. F7222 and F7223 were sectioned to reveal a width of 19.50m and a maximum height of 0.75m. The two other lynchets, M and N were surveyed only, as was a low mound, P.

To the west of the enclosure was lynchet H which had been truncated by the later chalk-pit R. A similar chalk-pit, Q, was located to the east.

South of chalk-pit Q, a series of short banks and intervening ditches was recorded. All were aligned roughly northeast to southwest. Three, F7234, F7236 and F7241, were sectioned. V, A, B, C and D were surveyed only.

West of this group of earthworks was a further lynchet that developed into a ditch and bank F7249 and F7250. The ditch, F7249, ran to the west and was discernible for some 95m. To the north was another parallel ditch, E.

At the western end of F7249 was what appeared to be part of an oval-shaped enclosure, again defined by a ditch and bank, F7260 and F7256. The ditch was 0.90m wide, the bank was 2m wide and survived to a height of 0.20m. The oval was not complete, for the north side appeared to be formed by a ditch, F, which continued into the woods to the west. There was a further short length of ditch, G, inside the enclosure. There were no finds to date this enclosure.

On the east side of the motorway line, a 70m length of hollow-way was found aligned roughly northeast to southwest. This track, F7277, was 3m wide at the base with gently sloping sides up to the local ground levels. It was 0.80m deep at its lowest level.

From the southern end of the hollow-way there were no features for a distance of about 120m. At this point a substantial bank and ditch, F7264, extended across the cleared route of the motorway. From the east it ran southwest for 70m then turned at right angles to the northwest for a further 130m. The approximate width was 5m, and, although it survived to no great height, the overall width of the bank was suggestive of a boundary of some importance. Just to the south of the corner of F7264 was another chalk-pit, S, slightly smaller than those to the north and circular in plan.

Thirty metres further to the south, F7270 was a hollow-way with slight banks on both sides. It was aligned northwest to southeast, and was recorded for a length of about 70m. To the north, the bank was

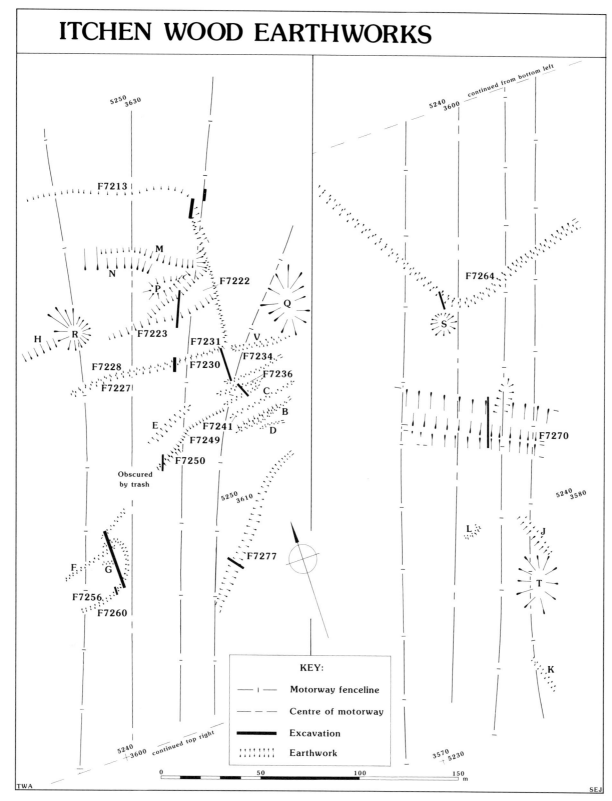

ITCHEN WOOD EARTHWORKS

KEY:

— I —	Motorway fenceline
— — —	Centre of motorway
▬▬▬	Excavation
⏐⏐⏐⏐⏐⏐⏐	Earthwork

Fig 14.   Itchen Wood (W73). Plan of the earthworks.

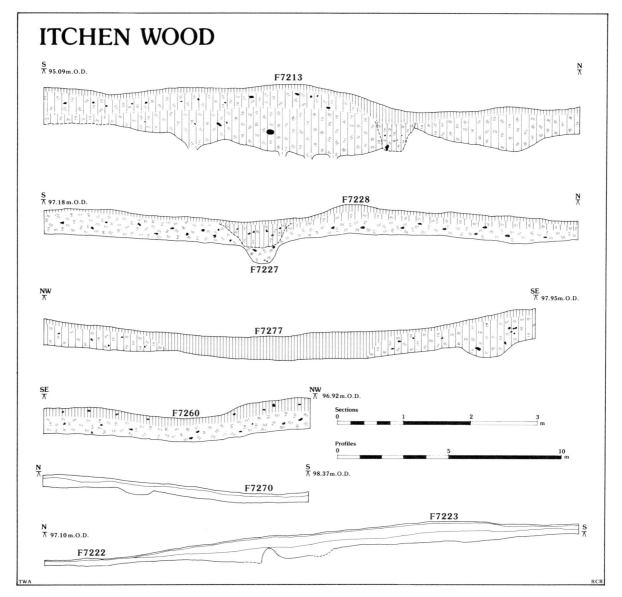

Fig 15.   Itchen Wood (W73). Sections and profiles of some of the features.

0.20m high, with a ditch 1.50m wide and 0.60m deep. The track hollow was 7m wide. To the south was a further ditch and low bank.

South of the hollow-way were several small features. The most obvious of these was another chalk-pit, T; the others consisted of lengths of a curved bank and ditch, L, a bank 30m long, J, and a ditch 20m long, K.

Interpretation of these various features is hampered by conditions relating to fieldwork: the necessity to attempt the survey after felling and with large and high heaps of trash and trees on the ground; the ability to section only a few of the earthworks and not to investigate large areas by excavation; the lack of diagnostic and datable artefacts and the restrictions imposed by the linear nature of the survey. This is in contrast with the survey completed in Micheldever Wood just to the north (Fasham 1983), where greater time was available in a less dense piece of woodland.

The rectangular arrangement involving F7213 and F7223, with a minimum area of 0.5 of a hectare, is probably more likely to be an enclosure rather than a Celtic field although parts of it are defined by lynchet-style features. Within the enclosure are lynchets from a field system which may well have pre-dated the enclosure as they do not extend to the east.

A further enclosure is represented by F7256, F7260 and earthwork F, which is associated with ditch F7249. Both enclosures are similar to prehistoric and Roman sites and probably are of that date rather than post-Roman. It is tempting to assume that the hollow-ways, F7270 and F7277, are post-Roman but the latter particularly is similar to the Roman hollow-ways in Micheldever Wood (Fasham 1983). The bank and ditch of F7264 resemble coppice boundaries.

It is to be hoped that the results of this hurried survey will be placed in a broader context when the rest of the wood is surveyed.

The Lawn, Micheldever Parish,
SU 53183936, no site code (Fig 16)

Two small pits were discovered following the removal of topsoil at The Lawn, just east of the A33. Both features were on the west side of the motorway in an area where landscaping was taking place: they were 14m apart.

The pits were both circular in plan. Feature A was 0.55m in diameter with gently sloping sides which curved into the base about 0.17m below the surface. Feature B had steeper sides and a flatter base, with a diameter of 0.61m and a depth of 0.18m.

Four undiagnostic sherds of pottery were found in Feature A. One ceramic sherd and other fragments were found in Feature B.

Stratton Park, Micheldever Parish,
SU 53654049, no TWA code, R1

A ditch, F7286, was recorded immediately north of Trench B of the 1974 excavations (Fasham 1981). It was flat-bottomed, with very steep sides and a step on the eastern side. It was 1.30m deep and 1.30m wide at the base. The ditch was not recorded in plan but was linear in nature, running approximately north to south. It was interpreted on site as a modern feature.

Biddles Wood, Micheldever Parish,
SU 54504210, W76 (Figs 17 and 18)

Biddles Wood, situated just to the east of the A33, lies within Stratton Park on a ridge which is aligned east-northeast to west-southwest. Along the west edge is the line of the Roman road from Silchester to Winchester (Margary 1973, route 42a), running from the north-northeast to the south-southwest. The site had been previously surveyed (Fasham 1981), and thus only observations and very limited investigations of the features revealed during the topsoil stripping were carried out. The remains of the Roman road surface survived and were exposed over a length of some 60m. The surface, F7435, was made of an orangey clay matrix, in which were embedded flints of all sizes. This surface was not sectioned. On the west side of the road a parallel ditch, F7431, was recorded and sectioned in two places. It proved to be up to 0.70m wide with sides steeply-sloping down to a flat base, some 0.15m wide. This feature was evidently a *fossa* or roadside drainage ditch, whilst F7435 was the *agger* or raised surface of the Silchester to Winchester Roman road.

A ditch and bank, F7425, cut across the Roman road some 35m to the north of the exposed section.

This feature was aligned east-southeast to west-northwest and ran for some 23m across the motorway line. The ditch was V-shaped in section, with a narrow rounded base, and 2.10m wide at the surface. The associated bank was about 5m wide, with a flat top. There were no finds.

This ditch and bank were clearly later in date than the Roman road and are likely to represent the remains of a medieval or post-medieval feature. Their proximity to Stratton Park, a post-medieval deer park, could suggest that F7425 originated as a deer-leap or similar park-land boundary.

Old Vicarage, Micheldever Parish,
SU 55092498, W75 (Fig 19)

The excavation of a trench for a diverted water supply revealed a ditch south of the road to Woodmancott. The field at this time still had a cereal crop thus making hand excavation difficult, but a small box adjacent to the water pipe trench revealed the west terminal of ditch F7288 apparently running east–west. It was a broad V-shaped ditch about 0.75m deep and 1.55m wide at the top.

A small trench was excavated by hand through the cereal crop and ploughsoil some 3m west of the terminal and exposed a 1.5m length of ditch, F7292, which was 1m wide and 0.4m deep.

The priorities and availability of sites elsewhere on the line of the motorway, particularly the pressing simultaneous need to complete work on the Abbots Worthy Anglo-Saxon settlement, meant that no more work took place on this site. After the topsoil strip even the archaeological features that had been recorded were not visible and thus no further information was recovered.

Ditch south of Popham, Popham Parish,
SU 55344337, no site code

Some 400m north of the road to Woodmancott, a linear ditch, aligned north to south and 1.5–2.0m wide, was observed as it was crossed by the motorway route. It was not possible to record this feature in any more detail.

Popham Village, Popham Parish,
SU 556439, no TWA code, R2

As part of the programme of observation during construction of the motorway, 'a controlled watching brief' was completed on the site of the medieval village at Popham. This has been published with the results of the 1975 excavations (Fasham 1987a).

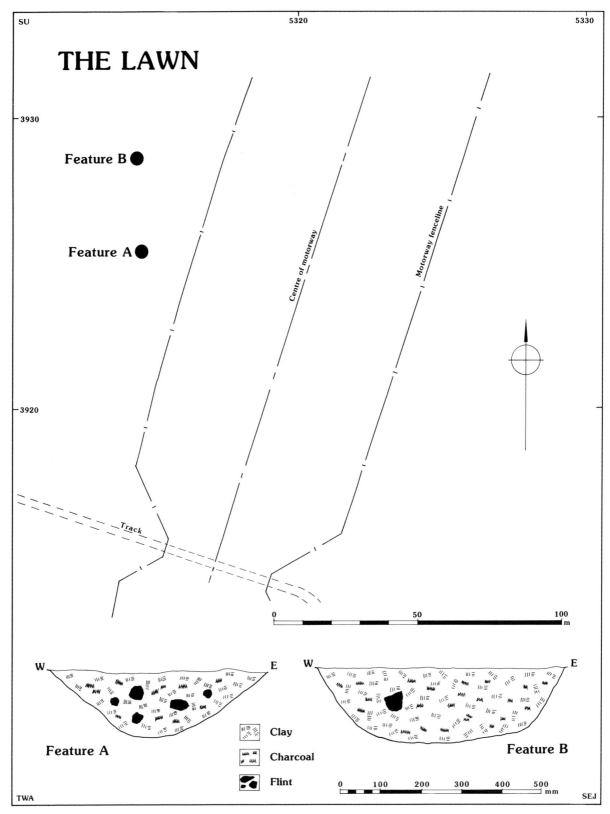

Fig 16.   The Lawn. Location plan and sections of two pits.

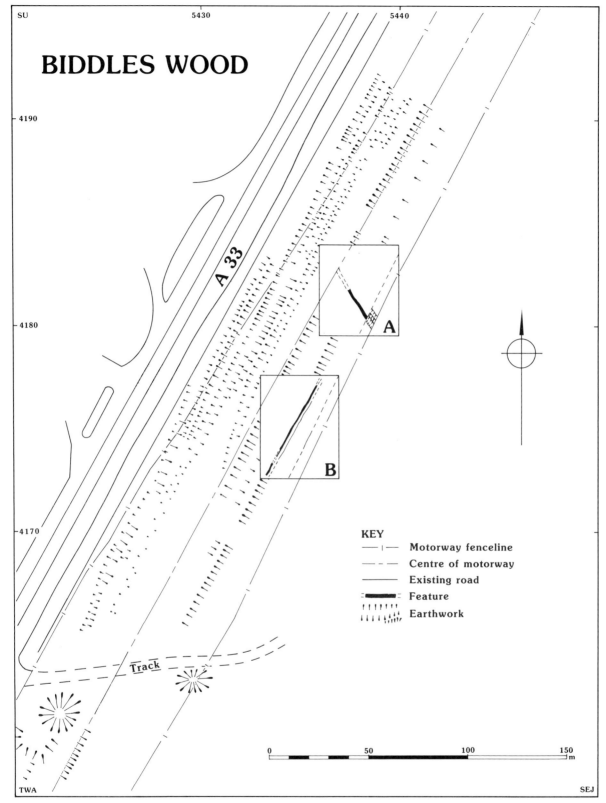

Fig 17. Biddles Wood (W76). Plan showing the location of fieldwork. Areas A and B are shown in detail on Fig 18.

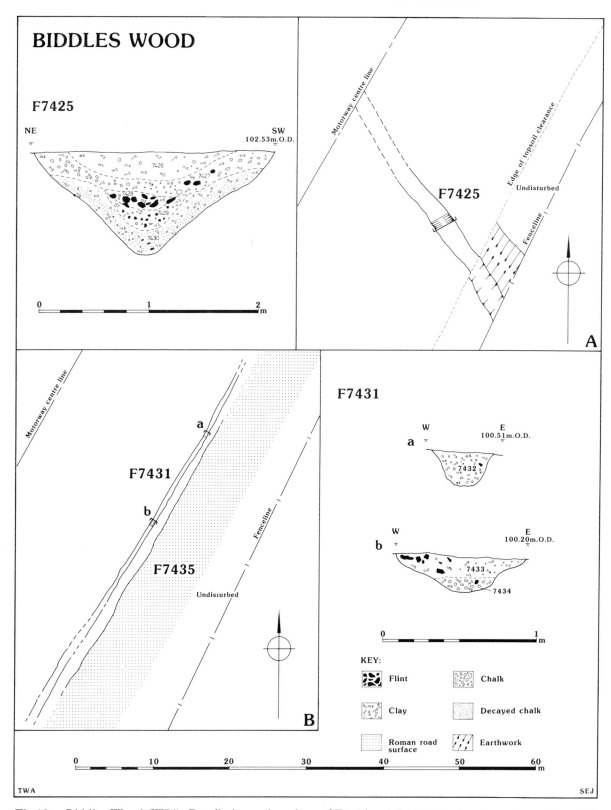

Fig 18.   Biddles Wood (W76). Detail plan and sections of F7425 and F7431. For location of areas A and B, see Fig 17.

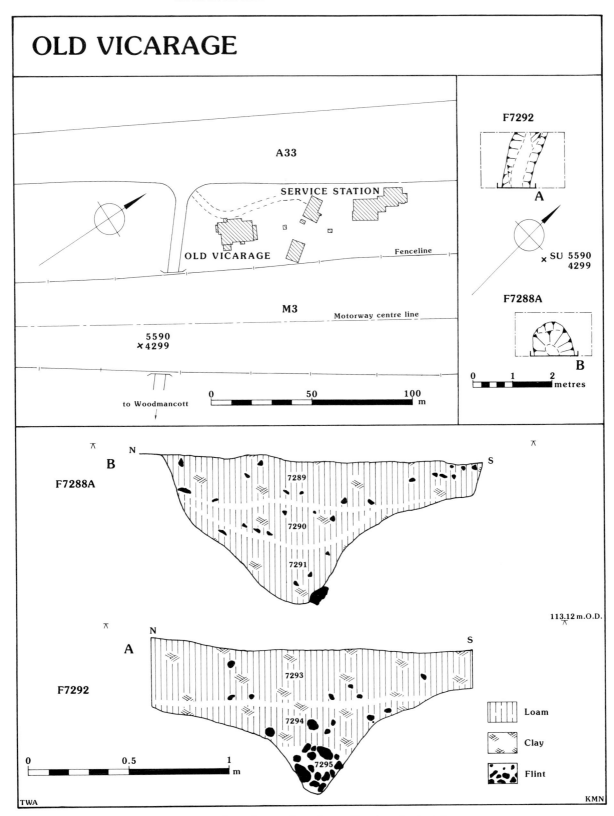

OLD VICARAGE

A33

SERVICE STATION

OLD VICARAGE

Fenceline

M3   Motorway centre line

5590
×4299

to Woodmancott

0   50   100
m

F7292

A

× SU 5590
4299

F7288A

B

0   1   2
metres

B

F7288A

N   S

7289

7290

7291

113.12 m.O.D.

A

N   S

F7292

7293

7294

7295

Loam

Clay

Flint

0   0.5   1
m

TWA   KMN

Fig 19.   Old Vicarage (W75). Location plan and sections of archaeological features.

Chapter 2

The Abbots Worthy Anglo-Saxon Settlement, Itchen Valley Parish

SU 50503266, W79 (Fig 20)

The Excavations, by P J Fasham and R J B Whinney

Introduction

In July 1983 routine observation of side ditches on the line of the motorway revealed features cut into the Coombe rock 70m to the north of the River Itchen at Abbots Worthy. The location of the site is shown on Fig 20. The features were recognised in the drainage ditches on either side of the road (Fig 21), buried beneath a colluvial deposit which was up to 0.40m deep. Anglo-Saxon ceramics were found in these features.

The colluvial deposits were not suitable for the road building and were removed, but more carefully than usual in order to minimise any damage to the underlying archaeological deposits. In accordance with standard procedures agreed between the Department of Transport and the Department of the Environment (Directorate of Ancient Monuments and Historic Buildings), construction work on the motorway was re-arranged to allow a thorough archaeological investigation of these deposits to take place.

This investigation lasted for three weeks. During the excavation the site was known as Itchen Abbas Road (IAR) but has subsequently been referred to as Abbots Worthy.

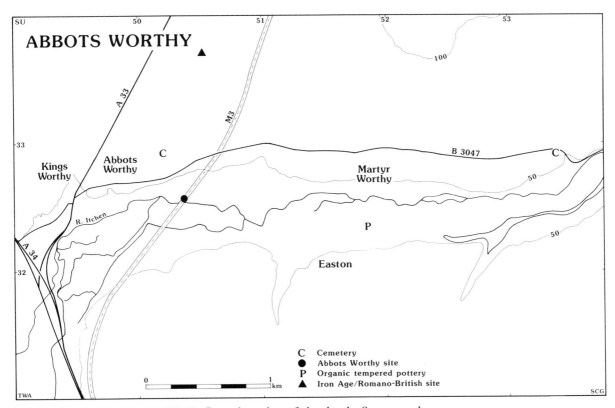

Fig 20.   Abbots Worthy (W79). Location plan of the Anglo-Saxon settlement.

Fig 21.   Abbots Worthy (W79). General view of the site from the north along the drainage ditch which first exposed the archaeological features. The spoil heap in the foreground is immediately north of sunken-featured building F7339. The crane and construction works are on the north bank of the River Itchen, starting work on the bridge over the river. Photo: W D Cocroft, Trust for Wessex Archaeology.

Archaeological Background

The best-known Anglo-Saxon site in the vicinity is the mixed inhumation and cremation cemetery in Worthy Park (Fig 20), 700m up the valley slope to the northwest. Partial excavation of the cemetery in 1961 revealed the remains of 45 cremation urns and 96 graves, some with more than one inhumation. The cremations are dated to the sixth and seventh centuries AD, and the inhumations to no later than the middle of the seventh century AD (S Hawkes, pers comm).

Another Anglo-Saxon cemetery has recently been discovered at Itchen Abbas, 3.25 kilometres to the east, where at least 20 inhumations were revealed during the laying of a new gas-pipe (Fig 20). Subsequent limited excavation has dated some of the burials to the mid-fifth century AD (Whinney 1985, 1986).

About one kilometre from the river, on the north slopes of the Itchen valley, a large complex of crop- and soil-marks has been identified from aerial photo-graphs, covering an area of 13.5 hectares (Fasham 1980a, 37). It is possible to identify a group of four ring-ditches, an isolated fifth ring-ditch, which has been excavated (Fasham 1982, 40–3), a hilltop enclosure of possible Early Iron Age date delimited by a ditch some seven metres wide and enclosing some 3.25 hectares, and a series of rectangular enclosures with associated streets. These latter enclosures, dated by unpublished excavations to the Romano-British period, cover an area of nine hectares.

Anglo-Saxon ceramics have been recovered during field-walking on the south bank of the River Itchen at Easton (Fig 20), about 1.25 kilometres to the southeast (M Brisbane, pers comm).

Geology and Topography

At the point where the site was discovered, the River Itchen flows east–west and has cut its valley through the Upper Chalk deposits of the lower escarpment formed by the uplift of the Winchester anticline. The north side of the valley slopes gradually down to the river, occasionally interrupted by broad, dry valleys, but in contrast the southern side of the valley is generally steeper, with more exaggerated dry valleys. The valley bottom is wider to the south of the river than to the north.

Above the chalk are deposits of valley gravels and fen peat. The full extent of these deposits is not known, but where the motorway line crossed the valley, the gravels and the peat seemed to be coterminous, and to lie above the Coombe rock.

On the lower part of the site, bands of gravel were present in the Coombe rock. Two of these ran parallel to the line of the river, but did not extend across the full width of the motorway. A third band formed a right-angle. A machine-dug trench revealed these bands to be natural features, presumably old water courses of some form.

A series of sections in the drainage ditch on the eastern side of the motorway line were examined (Keeley 1985), and revealed that a deposit of colluvium, up to 0.50m thick, had built up in this part of the valley since Anglo-Saxon times. This accumulation of material above the archaeological features explains not only their survival, but also the reasons why the site was not discovered during the initial field walking, geophysical and aerial photographic surveys.

The Soils, by Helen C M Keeley

The drainage ditch provided a section 130m in length through hillwash down to the river. The locations of the profiles, which were described at intervals along it, are shown in Fig 22.

The topsoil overlay a fairly thin layer of colluvium which filled undulations in the surface of the chalk. In the floodplain, closer to the river, the colluvium petered out and topsoil overlay a gravelly, sandy,

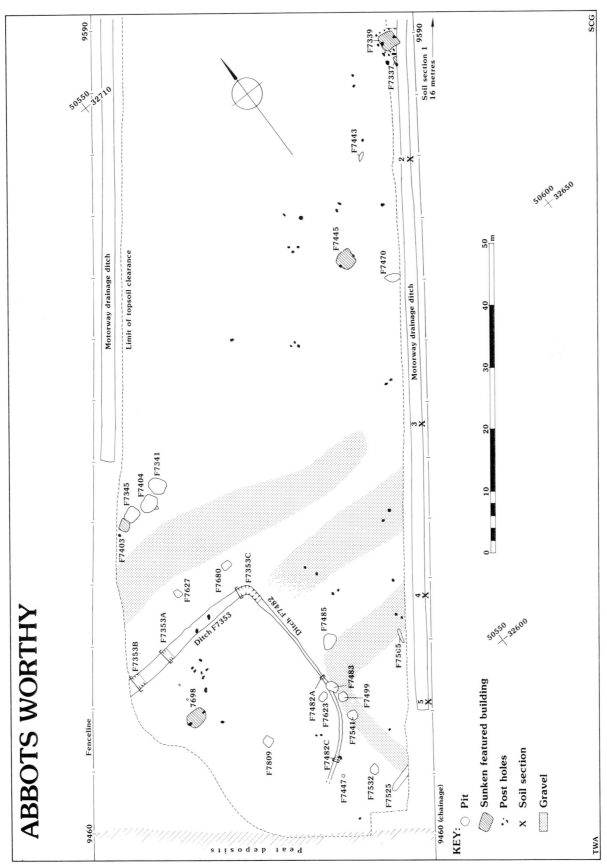

Fig 22.   Abbots Worthy (W79). General plan of the excavations of the Anglo-Saxon settlement.

chalky subsoil. Approximately two metres of peat occurred close to the river but this did not contain pollen due to the fluctuating water table (P J Fasham, pers comm). Various features were apparent in the colluvium and the top of the weathering chalk, and patches of Clay-with-Flints occurred over the site.

Descriptions of the sections

Section 1

The site was freely drained and on a gentle slope (c 4 degrees). There was a wheat crop in the field. Stones were mainly flint, with some chalk, and earthworms were present throughout the profile.

0–0.25m was dark brown (10YR3/3) moderately friable fine sandy loam with moderate medium subangular blocky structure. Stones were 10% gravel to large angular flints and chalk fragments; roots, common coarse to fine fibrous.

0.25–0.70m (colluvium) was yellowish brown (10YR5/6) moderately friable fine sandy (clay) loam with moderate medium angular blocky structure. Stones were 10% gravel to large chalk fragments and angular flints, increasing with depth to 30%; roots, few fine fibrous.

Below 0.70m was weathering chalk with many angular flints, containing patches of friable coarse to fine loamy sand with weak subangular blocky structure and abundant coarse distinct strong brown (7.5YR5/8) mottles.

Section 2

The topsoil was similar to that at Section 1. The colluvium, which had a stony layer at its base, had thinned to 0.20m, overlying about 0.20m of mottled, relatively stone-free weathering chalk.

Down from CH9560 the colluvium was more stony, thickening to 0.50m but with stones throughout, rather than at the base as seen further up-slope. Below CH9540 the colluvium thinned again to about 0.30m depth. The depth of topsoil remained relatively constant at about 0.25m.

Section 3

The topsoil was as usual (0–0.25m) but contained 15% stones. The colluvium (0.25–0.40m) contained 20% stones. Below 0.40m the weathering chalk contained 60% gravel to large stones (angular flints and a few chalk fragments).

The colluvium finally petered out around CH9500 and the profile consisted of topsoil over gravelly chalk.

Section 4

The topsoil (0–0.25m) was slightly more silty than previously and contained 10% stones. 0.25–0.70m was fine sandy loam with 70% gravel to large stones (flints and weathering chalk fragments). Below 0.70m was weathering chalk with 90% stones.

Three metres further downslope the subsoil was mainly fine gravel-weathering chalk with a few flints.

About 10m down from CH9500 waterlain material (the old flood plain) was encountered, which ran into peat near the river.

Section 5. Flat site.

0–0.30m was very dark greyish brown (10YR3/2) moderately friable fine sandy loam with moderate medium subangular blocky structure. Stones were 10% gravel to large angular flints and a few chalk fragments; roots common, medium to fine fibrous.

0.30–0.60m was dark brown (10YR3/3) friable fine sandy clay loam with weak medium subangular blocky structure. Stones were 30% gravel to large; roots, few fine fibrous.

0.60–0.80m: similar to layer above but mainly stones and weathering chalk fragments.

Below 0.80m was black (10YR2/1) firm, humic, fine sandy silty clay loam with moderate medium angular blocky structure. Stones were 10% gravel to large; roots absent. This material was interspersed with gravelly patches approaching the river.

Method of Excavation

The colluvial deposits were removed mechanically by the contractors, using a grader which pushed them into heaps which were then dumped into lorries and removed. This operation resulted in a hard, compacted surface, which became baked during the course of a very hot and dry spell. Because of these adverse conditions, it is possible that not all archaeological features, especially small post-holes, were discovered. However, the complete area was scrutinised with sufficient care during and after the machining to enable the excavators (PJF and RW) to be sure that any major timber structures, such as those discovered at Chalton (Addyman and Leigh 1973), Cowdery's Down (Millett and James 1983) and Winnall in Winchester (M Morris, pers comm) had not been overlooked. An area of 1.88 hectares was stripped and examined by a team of no more than six people in three weeks.

The features revealed were excavated by hand, and were planned by means of site co-ordinates related to the chainage distances along the motorway. This was the most convenient method of organising in situ recording in such conditions.

The site was located immediately adjacent to the extensive peat deposits in the valley bottom. Unfortunately the work involved in the construction of a bridge across the river meant that it was impossible to determine whether the archaeological features extended into these deposits. Analysis of the Itchen valley peat at Winnall Moors, 2.5 kilometres downstream, has shown that the top 1.20m of peat has been generated since the Norman Conquest (Waton 1982). Therefore, it is possible that the Anglo-Saxon features at Abbots Worthy might have continued both within and under the peat. However, the impression gained during the course of the excavation was, with the possible exception of ditch F7353/7482, that they did not.

The Excavated Features (Fig 22)

The archaeological features lay in two main groups, one occurring next to the peat and extending up slope for 70m, the other being centred 30–40m further away from the river. The significance of the open area between the groups is not known and, without the benefit of the full definition of the extent and plan of the site, it is not possible to be certain of its function.

Four different types of features were recorded: a ditch, sunken-featured buildings, pits, and post-holes. The northern cluster of features contained mainly sunken-featured buildings and post-holes. By contrast, all feature types were found in the group by the peat, although it was clear that they were not all contemporary.

The ditch F7353/F7482

The ditch was the largest feature recorded (Fig 22). It ran east–west from the western edge of the excavated area for a distance of 27m, where it turned south to follow a north–south direction for another 23m. From there, it gently recurved to the west for a further 16m before fading out.

The north part of the ditch, F7353, had steeply sloping convex sides and a flat bottom about 0.20m wide. The width and depth of F7353 reduced from 2.40m and 1.30m respectively at the west end (Fig 23), to 1.06m and 0.59m respectively at the corner. This gradual decrease in overall dimensions may have been caused by differential topsoil and hillwash clearance. The sections indicate that the ditch had been recut at least once.

At the point where the ditch turned to run north–south (recorded as F7482), it changed character quite dramatically. It became very shallow, about 0.20m deep, with fairly straight sides and narrowed to 0.40m in width. Towards the southern end, it remained fairly shallow, but broadened out to a width of about 0.80m where it was recut. There were very few finds from this feature: one sherd of

pottery, a fragment of antler and a small number of fragments of animal bone.

It seems likely that F7353/F7482 formed two sides of a sub-rectangular enclosure, the remainder of which lay beyond the western edge of the area available for excavation. The sections through the ditch yielded no artefacts to indicate a possible date, but stratigraphically it is the earliest feature in the group by the peat.

The sunken-featured buildings (SFBs)

Five SFBs were excavated: two were in the concentration of features by the peat, and three in the group furthest from the river. One of these latter three had been badly damaged by the motorway drainage ditch.

SFB F7698 (Fig 24)

SFB F7698, closest to the peat deposits, was

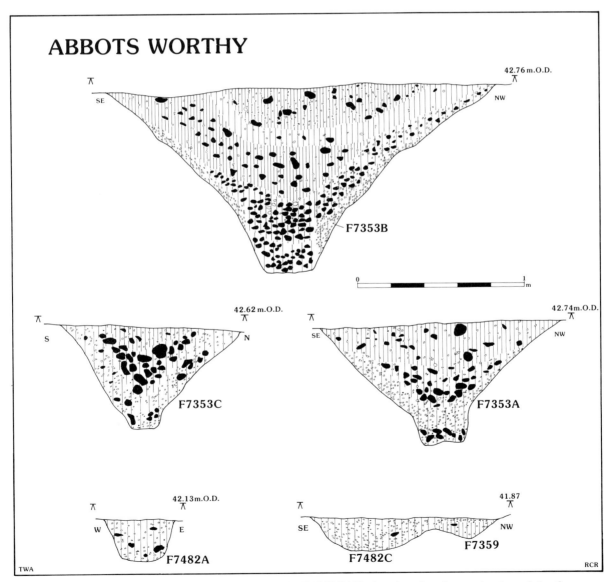

Fig 23.   Abbots Worthy (W79). Sections of ditch F7353/7482 showing the change in size of the feature.

sub-rectangular in plan with rounded corners, and aligned east–west within the area enclosed by ditch 7353/7482. It seems likely that the mechanical removal of the colluvial deposits caused some reduction in the archaeological levels, for the sunken area had a maximum depth of only 0.12m. The building was 3.60m long and 2.60m wide.

Two post-holes were found at each end of the east–west axis of the structure, suggesting that the original posts were replaced at least once during the life of the building. Post-hole F7823 was broader and shallower than post-hole F7825 by which it was cut. F7821 was also broader and shallower than F7827 and it is assumed that F7821 was contemporary with F7823. F7821 was 0.48m deep and 0.35m wide, F7823 was 0.30m deep and 0.30m wide, whereas F7827 was 0.52m deep and 0.23m wide and F7825 was 0.50m deep and 0.25m wide. No post-holes were found outside the sunken area, but three stake-holes were recorded on the northern edge.

One hundred and twenty stake-holes were found in the floor of the sunken area, but they showed little sign of regularity of pattern or grouping. An apparent gap in the general spread of the stake-holes in the centre of the south side could indicate an entrance or opening at this point, but this is by no means certain.

Finds from the fill of the building included 22 sherds of Anglo-Saxon pottery, 94 fragments of animal bone, a small iron spatulate-ended object (Fig 34.15) and a disc-shaped antler spindle-whorl (Fig 36.28).

SFB F7403 (Fig 24)

This feature was on the west edge of the area available for investigation, adjacent to a group of three large pits. Part of its eastern edge had been cut away by one of the pits. The removal of the hillwash deposits caused some denudation of the archaeological remains, but it was possible to determine that the structure was rectangular in shape, aligned east-west, and that the sunken area measured at least 3.10m by 1.75m. The sunken area survived only to a depth of 0.11m.

The single post-hole, F7369, associated with this building was on the main east–west axis, but beyond the west end of the sunken floor. The post-hole had vertical sides and a flat base and was 0.35m deep and 0.45m wide at the top. Its presumed counterpart at the eastern end of the main axis had been destroyed by the later pit.

Finds from the fill of the building included 28 sherds of Anglo-Saxon pottery and 24 fragments of animal bone.

SFB F7445 (Fig 24)

SFB F7445 was 55m east of SFB F7403 and was also aligned east–west. Sub-rectangular in shape, it measured 2.75m north to south and 2.90m east to west. Again it appears that the mechanical removal of the colluvial deposits in this area may have

reduced the archaeological remains, for not only were the surviving levels in the sunken area shallow, 0.15m deep, but the southeast corner of the building had also been damaged.

Two large post-holes were at the ends of the main east–west axis of the building, one inside and one outside. Both were sub-square in plan, with vertical sides and flat bases. F7536, at the eastern end, was 0.32m deep and 0.21m square; F7468, at the west, was 0.49m deep and 0.25m square.

Seventy-three stake-holes were recorded cutting the bottom of the sunken area. Twenty were regularly spaced around three sides of the floor area. Most of this group were concentrated in the northern half of the building; it appears that the removal of the hillwash may account for their virtual non-existence in the southern half. Because of the lack of further groups of post-holes outside the sunken area, it seems likely that the walls of this structure were supported in some way by the stakes around its edge.

Finds from the fill of the building included 44 sherds of Anglo-Saxon pottery, over 150 fragments of animal bone and two small fragments of undecorated folded copper alloy sheet (not illustrated). The pottery included a wide range of forms (below, Table 12).

SFB F7337 (Fig 24)

This building was 2.50m south of SFB F7339, and apparently on a similar alignment. The main body of the building had been destroyed by the cutting of the motorway drainage ditch, and only a small part of the western side and the northwestern corner was available for investigation. From the surviving evidence, its overall dimensions cannot be assessed, but it is likely to have been of much the same scale as the other four structures. It was at least 2.50m wide east-west, based on the evidence recorded as F7319 in the eastern side of the drainage ditch, which could not be excavated. A quarter of the hut lies untouched beyond the motorway drain at this point.

The bottom of the sunken area of this building was 0.12m below the present surface, and appeared to be dipping gently to the east.

A single large post-hole, F7757, was excavated in the sunken area, at the western end of what appeared to be the main east-west axis of the building. It was vertically sided, 0.40m deep, and sub-rectangular in plan, 0.30m by 0.35m.

A few post-holes surrounded the sunken area of the building. F7634 and F7636 were at the west and east ends of F7632, a shallow slot 0.76m long and 0.21m wide. F7629, a post-hole to the northwest, may be associated, and the function and association of the large post-hole or small pit 7479 is not clear. The fill of the sunken area was a mid- to black-brown silty loam with inclusions of charcoal flecks and flint nodules. No stake-holes were found cutting the bottom of the sunken area.

The number of finds from the fill of the sunken area was limited: nine sherds of Anglo-Saxon pottery, 12 fragments of animal bone, a dark green

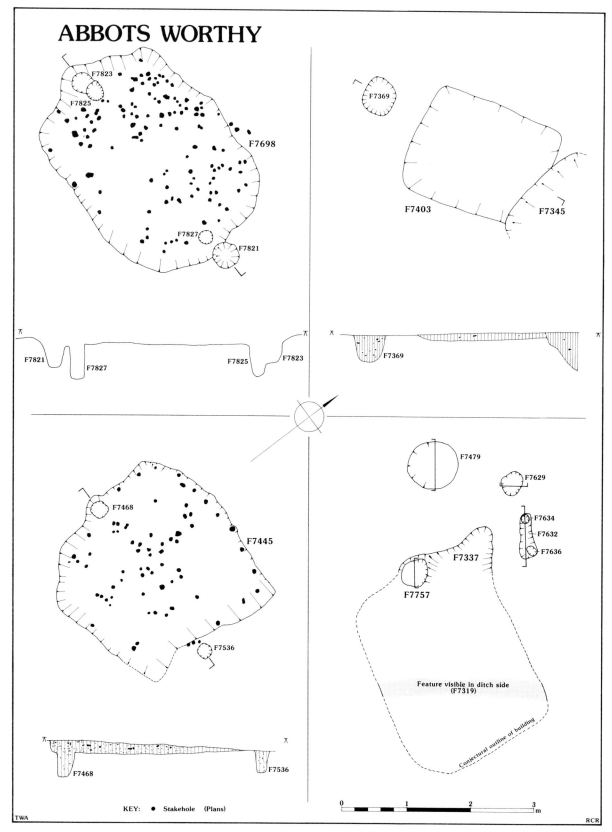

Fig 24.   Abbots Worthy (W79). Sunken-featured buildings. Plans and profiles or sections, where relevant, of F7698, F7403, F7445 and F7337.

translucent annular glass bead (Fig 37.43) and some small fragments of burnt flint and daub. This is probably a reflection of the limited amount of fill that was available for excavation rather than a measure of relative poverty.

SFB F7339 (Figs 25, 26 and 27)

This most northerly of the buildings was discovered on the extreme eastern limit of the excavated area. Although its southeastern corner had been partially removed by the motorway drainage ditch, it was by far the best preserved.

The sunken area was rectangular in shape and the longer north and south sides were about 2.75m long, while the east and west sides were 2.45m long. The edges of the area were almost vertical down to the bottom, some 0.95m below the surface. In the southwest corner, the floor was raised 0.16m above the general level, to form a roughly rectangular step which measured 1.20m by 0.40m.

Three large post-holes, F7625, F7527, and F7807, were at the ends of the main east-west axis within the feature. F7625 was 0.31m deep and 0.34m in diameter; F7527 had similar dimensions. This obvious similarity of size suggests that these two post-holes were contemporary. The third post-hole, F7807, although still substantial, had differing dimensions, being 0.40m deep, and 0.25m diameter. It therefore seems likely that F7807 was the surviving post-hole of an earlier pair, which was replaced at a later date by F7527 and F7625. The cutting of F7625 may have removed any trace of the earlier post-hole on the western side of the hut.

Cut into the floor of the sunken area were 24 circular stake-holes. Most were clustered in the eastern central part of the floor, away from the edges of the hut. They appeared in some cases to be paired.

Post-holes of very similar dimensions surrounded the sunken area. To the north, F7647, F7640, F7613, F7611 and F7609 formed a line. A single post-hole, F7638, was found to the west, and on the south, F7605, F7607, and F7619 also formed a row. The motorway drainage ditch had destroyed any features that may have existed on the east. Three further post-holes, F7615, F7617 and F7621, may also have been associated. All of these post-holes had fairly similar physical characteristics and thus may be regarded as being contemporary.

The fills of the sunken area may indicate the way in which the hollow was filled after the building went out of use. Burnt clay in layer 7511 might suggest the collapse of wattle walls which may have lined the area. A single Roman coin, of Constantine I (AD 330–37), was found in the building together with a quantity of residual Roman brick and tile, which suggests that at least part of the filling was made up from redeposited material.

The bulk of the finds comprised 345 sherds of Anglo-Saxon pottery and over 900 fragments of animal bone. Three worked bone and antler objects also came from the fills of the building. These were a double-sided composite comb (Fig 36.25), a pointed bone implement (Fig 36.30) and a crude point, fashioned from an antler tine (Fig 36.34). Together with these objects, comb tooth segments (Fig 36.35–39) and fragments of waste material of bone and antler (Fig 36.40–42) were also recovered.

Seven fragments of copper alloy were found in the fills of the building, comprising a pin (Fig 32.1), a pair of tweezers with suspension loop (Fig 32.2), a fragmentary ring (Fig 32.4), a carefully shaped strainer (Fig 32.5), and three small scraps of thin sheet (not illustrated). Of forty-seven iron objects from the building only the most significant have been illustrated and include two knife blades (Fig 33.7–8), an awl (Fig 34.12), a spike (Fig 34.14), a key-handle for a barrel padlock (Fig 34.16), a curved blade or fitting (Fig 34.18) and a flat strip (Fig 34.24). Iron smithing slag and fragments of two Mudstone whetstones (not illustrated) were also recovered.

The pits

Fourteen pits were excavated, two in the group of features furthest from the river and twelve in the other group. They displayed considerable variation in plan (Fig 28) and section. As pits occur so rarely on rural sites of this period they will be described in some detail.

Pits in the feature group furthest from the river

There were two possible pits in this group of features. Pit F7470 was elliptical with an irregular base and contained only one flint flake. It was regarded as being a natural feature. F7443 has been regarded as a pit although it is elliptical, 1.76m by 0.7m, and shallow, 0.17m deep. It contained one sherd of pottery and a strip of iron (Fig 34.24).

Pits in the group closest to the river (Figs 29, 30 and 31)

This group of features was dominated by two clusters of pits, one of which was east of SFB F7403 and comprised two oval pits, F7341 and F7404, and one sub-rectangular pit, F7345. The second cluster was more dispersed. Ten metres to the south of the first cluster were two sub-rectangular pits, F7627 and F7680, about 6.50m apart. Five more pits, F7483, F7485, F7499, F7541 and F7623, were around the southern section of the early ditch F7482. Pit F7532 to the south and pit F7809 to the west were isolated examples.

Pit F7341

This was the most easterly of the group of three large pits located close to SFB F7403, on the west side of the motorway line. It was sub-circular in plan, with a maximum diameter of 2.94m and a depth of 1.44m. Its sides were almost vertical and its base was flat. The lower fills were dominated by bands of chalk, probably from the pit sides. These

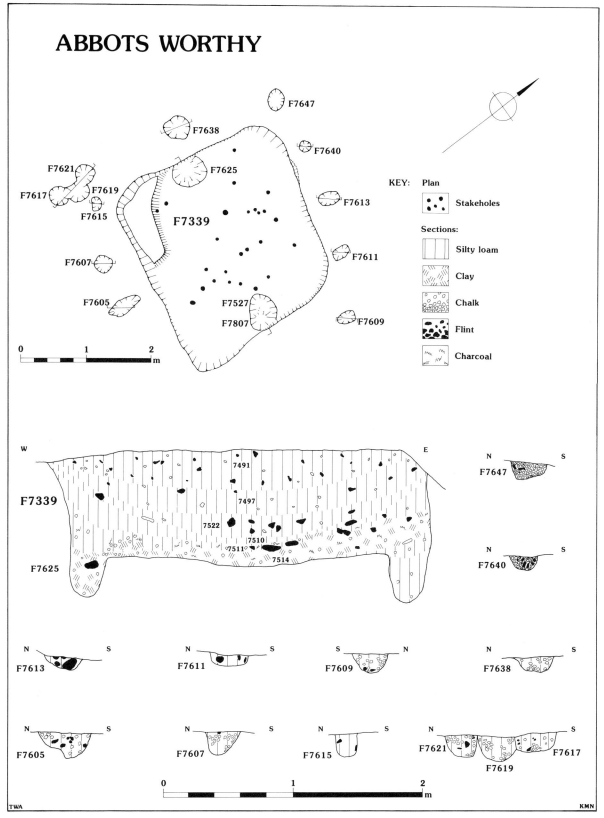

Fig 25.   Abbots Worthy (W79). Plan and section of sunken-featured building F7339.

Fig 26.   Abbots Worthy (W79). View from the southwest of sunken-featured building F7339 under excavation; the surrounding post-holes are quite visible. The motorway drainage ditch cuts the far end of the structure. Scales are 2m and 0.5m. Photo: R J B Whinney, Winchester Museums Service.

Fig 27.   Abbots Worthy (W79). Detail view from the northwest of sunken-featured building F7339 showing the internal gable posts and the ledge. The motorway drainage ditch is on the left. Scales are 2m and 0.5m. Photo: R J B Whinney, Winchester Museums Service.

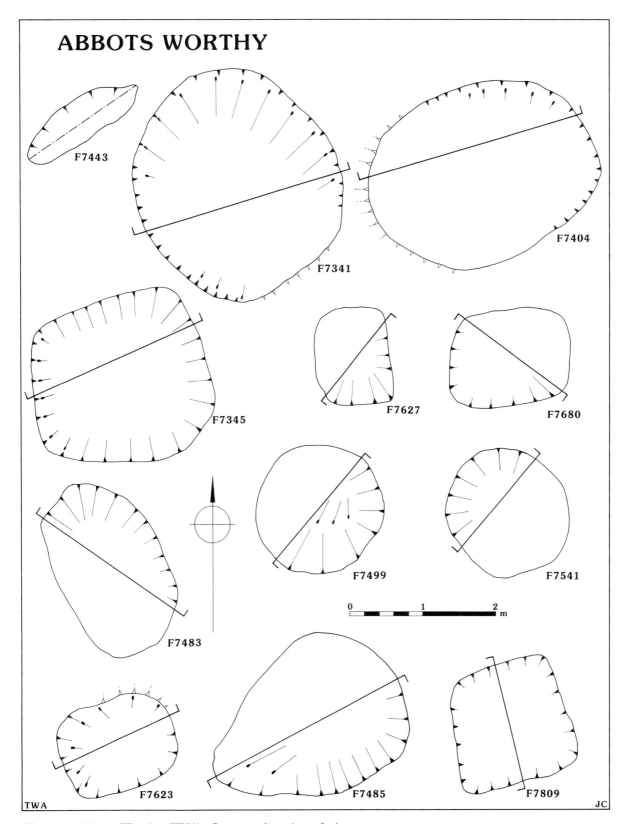

Fig 28.   Abbots Worthy (W79). Comparative plan of pits.

Fig 29.   Abbots Worthy (W79). General view of a pit complex in the western group of pits. From the foreground the pits are F7341, F7404 and F7345. Sunken-featured building F7403 extends from the ranging rod on the top of F7345 to the post-hole beyond. The general conditions under which the excavation proceeded can be seen. Scales are 2m and 1m. Photo: R J B Whinney, Winchester Museums Service.

were interspersed with bands of grey clay containing flint and chalk nodules of varying size. Over these on the southern side of the pit was ashy layer 7391, in which some fragments of slag contained impressions of straw. This was probably fuel ash, and had been dumped into the pit. Above this layer was a deep deposit of grey, gritty loam with pockets of redeposited chalk, flint nodules and some charcoal. The top fill was a very dark grey clay loam with flint nodules and pottery sherds. Several of the fills were indicative of waste and rubbish which had been dumped into the pit but there was no hint of any original use.

This pit contained 20 sherds of Anglo-Saxon pottery, 189 fragments of animal bone, a pair of iron tweezers (Fig 34.11), a bone pin-beater (Fig 36.32) and a bun-shaped loomweight (Fig 37.44).

Pit F7404

This pit was immediately west of F7341, and although also sub-circular, had a rather more oval shape, with the longer axis running east–west. It was 3.10m long, 2.00m wide and 1.30m deep. The

bottom was fairly flat, and turned sharply to meet the sides, which were slightly undercut. The lowest fills contained bands of chalk which had fallen from the sides, interspersed with grey clay loams with flint nodules and charcoal. In the middle of the pit was another grey clay loam, which was sealed by the upper deposits of darker grey clay loams with flint nodules.

As with F7341, the fills in the pit were suggestive of the dumping of waste and rubbish, and shed little light on its original usage. The finds included 17 sherds of Anglo-Saxon pottery, 39 fragments of animal bone, iron smithing slag and a single-sided composite bone comb (Fig 36.26).

Pit F7345

Immediately west of pit F7404, this pit cut the eastern edge of SFB F7403. It was sub-rectangular in plan, 2.40m long and 2.10m wide. It had a semi-circular profile, with a narrow flat base and gently curving sides and was 1.35m deep in the centre. The fills of the pit showed no signs of chalk collapse, but like those in pits F7341 and F7404, were very suggestive of waste and rubbish dumping. The environmental evidence indicated the presence of hay.

Finds from this pit included 37 sherds of Anglo-Saxon pottery, 162 fragments of animal bone and a number of iron objects which included a double-bladed knife (Fig 33.9), a borer (Fig 34.13) and a mount (Fig 34.22). A fragmentary amber bead, probably originally cylindrical, was also found in the pit.

Pit F7627

This pit, very similar to pit F7680, was sub-rectangular in plan, with the long axis aligned north–south. It measured 1.30m by 1.00m and was 0.57m deep. The sides were almost vertical and curved down to a flat base. The main fill was a very dark grey clay loam which contained flecks of daub and charcoal, as well as flint nodules.

The finds included 129 fragments of animal bone, two pieces of iron smithing slag, small fragments of flint, tile and daub from sieved samples and a fragment of an antler connecting-plate for a double-sided composite comb (Fig 36.27). No pottery was recovered.

Pit F7680

Very similar to pit F7627, this feature was sub-rectangular in shape, aligned east–west and measured 1.60m by 1.25m wide and 0.88m deep. There were two distinct fills. The lower, 7625, was a grey clay containing some chalk, and above that, 7624 was a dark grey clay with flint nodules as well as chalk. Carruthers (below) has suggested that cess was present in this pit.

Finds were not common: 49 fragments of animal bone, five pieces of pottery and small fragments of flint, daub, brick and burnt clay were recovered.

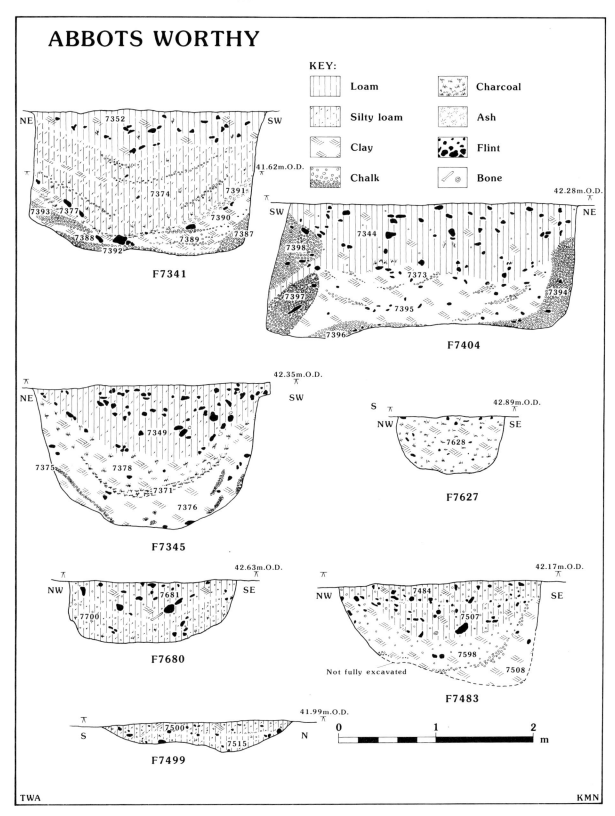

Fig 30.   Abbots Worthy (W79). Sections of pits; see Fig 28 for plans.

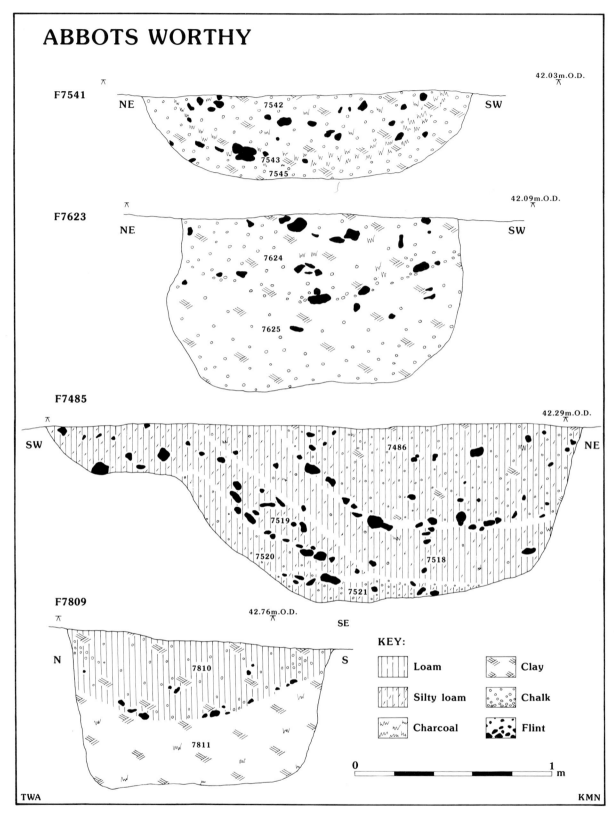

Fig 31.   Abbots Worthy (W79). Sections of pits; see Fig 28 for plans.

Pit F7483

This pit was at the centre of a group of five pits about 17m south of pit F7680. It cut the earlier ditch F7482. It was sub-oval in plan with fairly steep sides and probably a flat base, although this was not reached because of waterlogging problems. It was 2.50m long, 1.85m wide and had a depth of at least 1.05m. The fills were generally of a dark grey clay loam, with or without the presence of coarse components such as chalk and flint nodules. Once again, the environmental evidence suggests that cess was disposed of in this pit.

Finds included 233 fragments of animal bone, a badly corroded small copper alloy disc (Fig 32.3), a well-made and highly polished perforated bone awl (Fig 36.33) and only seven small sherds of pottery.

Pit F7499

Immediately south of pit F7483, this circular pit, with a diameter of 1.80m and a depth of 0.18m, was very shallow compared with the others in the area. It contained two main fills, which were silty loams with some flint and chalk inclusions.

Finds were limited to small fragments of pottery and animal bone recovered from sieved samples.

Pit F7541

This circular pit was two metres south of pit F7499 and had a diameter of 1.80m and a depth of 0.43m. Its sharply defined edges curved gently in to form a rounded base. The fills, suggestive of an even and gradual accumulation rather than of deliberate dumping, were generally of a dark grey clay loam, with or without flint and chalk inclusions.

An iron key-handle (Fig 34.17) from a barrel padlock, and a fragment of an iron ring (Fig 34.19) were found in the pit, together with two sherds of pottery and a piece of worked flint which were recovered from sieved samples.

Pit F7623

Situated one metre to the west of pit F7483, this feature was sub-rectangular in plan, 1.45m by 1.32m, and 0.83m deep. It had straight sides, slightly undercut, which turned sharply into a flat base. The two fills were both grey clays, but the upper one contained flint nodules and was more adhesive.

The pit contained over 160 pieces of animal bone, and a number of small fragments of pottery; flint daub and brick were recovered from sieved samples.

Pit F7485

This pit, four metres northeast of pit F7483, was originally circular, but had been extended to the southwest, to produce a final sub-circular shape. The main pit had a diameter of about 2m. The sides were steep and turned sharply into the base. The pit was 0.88m deep at the centre. On the southwest, the side was much less steep and led down to a step 0.50m long and 0.24m deep. The fills were of clay loams, with various amounts of flint nodules and chalky grit. Evidence for cess disposal was found in the botanical remains.

Finds from this pit were few and comprised fragments of pottery, burnt flint, daub, animal bone and tile. The pit also produced an angle-backed iron knife (Fig 33.10).

Pit F7809

This outlying pit was very similar in form to pit F7623 and was ten metres away to the west. It was sub-square with rounded corners, nearly vertical sides and an almost perfectly flat base. The sides were 1.33m long and sloped steeply down to curve into the flat base, some 0.75m below the surface. The fills, again based on a grey clay matrix, contained chalky gravel, flint nodules and patches of decayed chalk. The presence of charcoal in them might hint at waste dumping.

Over 140 fragments of animal bone were recovered from this pit, together with fragments of flint, daub, brick, tile and one sherd of pottery from sieved samples.

Pit F7532

This pit was six metres south of its nearest neighbour, pit F7541. It was very shallow, with a maximum depth of 0.15m. It was 1.55m long and 1.10m wide, with a very irregular plan and an uneven base. It seems likely that this feature was not a pit but a natural feature similar to F7470.

Only a few fragments of animal bone and an iron nail were recovered from the fill.

The post-holes

A number of the post-holes have already been discussed in association with the sunken-featured buildings, especially those surrounding SFB F7339 and SFB F7337 at the east of the site. The few other post-holes in the eastern part of the site were some distance away from those features. To the west there was a cluster of post-holes around SFB F7698. The full details of the post-holes are in the archive.

Other excavated features

Only two other features that have not already been mentioned were recorded.

Ditch F7525

The butt end of a ditch which was aligned east–west extended for some five metres into the site from the eastern edge of the excavation. It was one metre wide and contained one sherd of Romano-British New Forest Ware and a few fragments of animal bone.

Slot F7505

A shallow, narrow slot was recorded to the northeast of F7525, just inside the excavated area. It was aligned south-southeast to north-northwest, and was 2.25m long, 0.53m wide and 0.13m deep. It is not likely to have been a shallow ditch, but may possibly have been an isolated beam slot. There were no finds from this feature.

The Finds, by Susan M Davies

(Table 4 shows the distribution of object types by feature)

The Metalwork

Coin

A single Roman coin, SF 437, was found in SFB F7339, context 7497. It belongs to the period of Constantine I (AD 330–37) and bears *Urba Roma* on the obverse, and the Wolf and Twins on the reverse. Despite its fragile and powdery surface, the coin is complete.

Copper alloy objects

Nine fragments of copper alloy were found, seven from the fill of SFB F7339. Pit F7483 produced a thick disc (Fig 32.3) which the X-radiograph suggests has four central perforations set in a square, and which therefore could be a button. SFB F7445 produced two small undecorated fragments of folded sheet.

The objects from SFB F7339 comprised a pin (Fig 32.1); a pair of plain tweezers with suspension loop (Fig 32.2); a fragmentary ring or ferrule (Fig 32.4);

and a carefully shaped strainer (Fig 32.5). Three small scraps of thin sheet were also found.

These objects are not closely datable. The pin, of a form which does not seem to be easily paralleled, is not a type which occurs at *Hamwic* and is therefore presumably pre-eighth-century (D A Hinton, pers comm), perfectly in keeping with the other dating evidence. The plain tweezers are a type which occur commonly in Early Saxon contexts, as at the Portway cemetery, Andover, Hampshire (Cook and Dacre 1986, grave 26) or Winterbourne Gunner cemetery, Wiltshire (Musty and Stratton 1964, grave VI). There are also parallels from the nearby cemetery at Worthy Park, from graves 49 and 50, both men's graves of the late fifth/early sixth centuries AD (S C Hawkes pers comm). However, there are also many examples from later contexts, such as from Hamwic. The strainer can be well paralleled by examples found at the settlement at Old Down Farm, Andover (Davies 1980, Fig 8.6), in a sunken-featured building, suggested to date to the sixth century AD. The Old Down Farm example was postulated to be a residual Roman piece, but the occurrence of another at the Abbots Worthy Saxon settlement in an identical context, a *grubenhaus*, would seem to belie this suggestion. The function of such strainers remains uncertain, but the Abbots Worthy example was partially covered with powdery haematite (Fell, in archive), possibly a residue from some sort of heating.

The small number of copper alloy objects recovered is in keeping with other local settlement sites, and could be indicative of the care with which the metal was curated and collected for re-use.

Illustrated items (Fig 32)

1. Pin, sub-square-sectioned shank, with narrow groove defining head. Length 108mm. SF 439, SFB F7339, context 7514.
2. Tweezers undecorated but with suspension loop. Not closely datable. Length 52mm, ring diameter 11mm. SF 495, SFB F7339, context 7522.
3. Small disc, badly corroded. X-ray evidence suggests four perforations centrally, set in a square, as in a modern button. Diameter 17.5mm. SF 454, pit F7483, context 7507.

Table 4. *Abbots Worthy (W79). Distribution of object types by feature and feature type.* SF = Small Find. (* = illustrated object)

Material	Object	PIT SF	Feature	SFB SF	Feature	POSTHOLE SF	Feature	DITCH SF	Feature	OTHER SF	Feature	TOTALS
	Coin			437	7339							1
	Pin			439*	7339							1
	Tweezers			495*	7339							1
COPPER	Button	454*	7483									1
ALLOY	Ring			399*	7339							1
	Strainer			431*	7339							1
	Sheet/Strip			426								
				497	7339							3
				440								
	Fragments			414	7445							1
												10

Table 4, continued. Abbots Worthy (W79). Distribution of object types.

Material	Object	PIT SF	PIT Feature	SFB SF	SFB Feature	POSTHOLE SF	POSTHOLE Feature	DITCH SF	DITCH Feature	OTHER SF	OTHER Feature	TOTALS
	Knife			486★	7339							
				496★	7339							2
	Inlaid knife	541★	7485									1
	Folding knife	369★	7345									1
	Tweezers	382★	7341									1
	Key	519★	7541	523★	7339							2
	Point/Awl/Borer	386★	7345	448★	7339							2
	Hook					398★	7479					1
IRON	Spike			449★	7339							1
	Ring	518★	7541									1
	Rivetted and curved blade?			460★	7339							1
	Nails	(2)	7337	(8)	7339							
		(1)	7809	(1)	7403	(1)	7479					14
		(1)	7532									
	Door Fitting	389★	7443									1
	Rivetted Fitting	379★	7345									1
	Waste/Strip frags.	390	7445	391	7445	388	7415					6
				408	7339							
				436	7339							
				498	7339							
	Unidentified	377	7341	514★	7698							2
												37
LEAD	Waste	425★	7447									1
GLASS	Bead			392★	7337							1
AMBER	Bead	–	7345									1
CLAY	Loomweight	383	7341									1
	Single-sided Comb	371-375★	7404									1
	Double-sided comb	513★	7627	465★	7339							2
	Needle			– ★	7339							1
	Awl							453★	7483			1
BONE	Pinbeater	542★	7341							533★	Unstrat.	2
AND	Point			543★	7339							1
ANTLER	Spindlewhorl			488★	7698							1
	Buckle-mount									532★	Unstrat.	2
	Tooth-segment (unfinished)			441★	7339							
				464★	7339							
				487★	7339							5
				507★	7339							
				510★	7339							
	Antler tine	544	7541	420★	7339							
				504								
				505								
				506★	7339	553	7353					12
				546★								
				557-561 incl								
												27
TOTALS		23		47		3		2		2		77

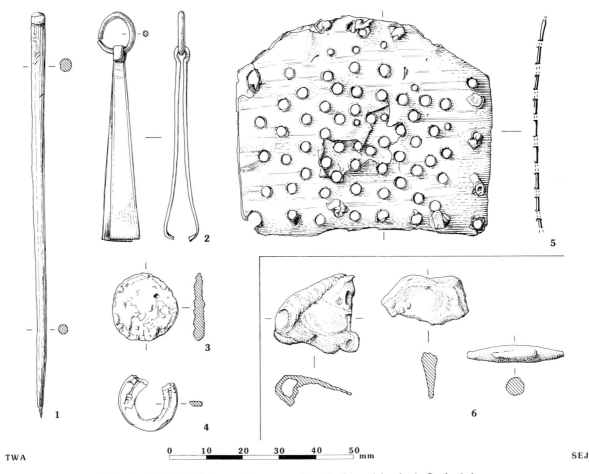

TWA

0 10 20 30 40 50 mm

SEJ

Fig 32.   Abbots Worthy (W79). Objects of copper alloy, 1–5, and lead, 6. Scale 1:1.

4. Fragment of ring or 'washer', slight traces of concentric grooves on both surfaces. Diameter (external) 16mm. SF 399, SFB F7339, context 7383.

5. Strainer; two thin sheets of copper alloy secured together by folding along the largest edge, and by nine copper alloy 'ties'. The regularly set perforations were made (?drilled) from the concave surface. The surfaces are partially covered with haematite. The piece appears to be complete. Length 69mm, width 56mm, thickness *c* 1mm. SF 431, SFB F7339, context 7512.

Lead

Three small fragments, a rod, a piece of folded sheet and a piece of melted waste, were found in pit F7447, context 7448 (Fig 32.6).

Iron objects

Some 82 iron objects were found, of which 48 (58%) were retrieved from the fill of SFB F7339. Apart from nails (18 examples) only rarely was more than one object recovered from any one category (Table 4). These included knife blades (4), keys (2) and awls/borers (2). However, among the range of object types, most of which are common enough items on any settlement site of the period, there are a small number of items worthy of further comment.

Knives

Of the four blades found, two (Fig 33.7 and 8)

were from SFB F7339, and are types not uncommon in the Early Saxon period, and which can be paralleled on many other, mainly cemetery, sites. The types also occur in later contexts, particularly Fig 33.8, which can be paralleled at Portchester (Hinton, in Cunliffe 1976, Fig 133.19 and 27), and are therefore not closely datable.

The other two knives are of rather more unusual character and both were recovered from large pits lying on the north side of the excavated area. The double-bladed knife (Fig 33.9) is less common. There is an example from Canterbury with a bone handle ornamented in tenth-century *Borre* style (Graham-Campbell 1980, no 473); and several more from the site at Thetford, in use from the ninth century onwards (Goodall, in Rogerson and Dallas 1984).

The angle-backed knife inlaid with a strip of twisted/beaten copper and silver (Fig 33.10) is clearly of workmanship of unusual quality, and its occurrence at Abbots Worthy suggests an owner of some status. Knives of this shape are not uncommon in Middle to Late Saxon contexts, occurring again, for example, at Thetford (Goodall, in Rogerson and Dallas 1984), but finely inlaid examples are not so frequently encountered. One is known from Winchester in a later Saxon context, and one from Netherton, Hampshire, which has been described by Leslie Webster as 'not much in use before the tenth

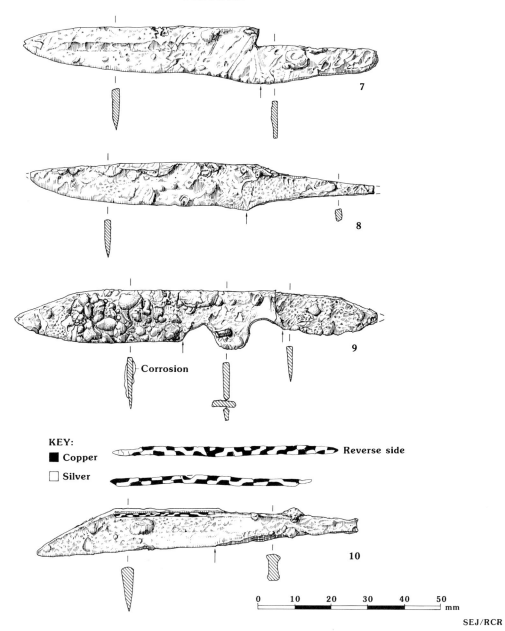

KEY:
■ Copper
□ Silver

Corrosion

Reverse side

TWA   SEJ/RCR

Fig 33. Abbots Worthy (W79). Iron knives, 7–10. Scale 1:1.

century' (D A Hinton, pers comm). Two examples have been found at *Hamwic*, both firmly in Middle Saxon contexts (P Andrews, pers comm). Such dates are early for the use of inlay, which is more commonly tenth century or later. However, in view of the context at Abbots Worthy and other associated artefacts, specifically the single-sided composite comb (Fig 36.26 and Riddler below) and the ceramics, taken with the evidence from *Hamwic*, it seems that the objects could well date to the eighth century AD.

Rivetted fittings

Another unusual item was also retrieved from the pits, the rivetted mount (Fig 34.22) made from a pattern-welded plate (re-used sword?). Such re-use

of material clearly shows the care taken to curate and salvage useful raw materials, a phenomenon observed elsewhere, as at West Stow, in the Saxon period.

The sunken-featured buildings produced a wide range of items, mainly fairly standard objects that would not be out of place in an Early Saxon (sixth-century?) context. The exception to this range is the unusual curved blade (Fig 34.18) with its copper alloy rivet(s). As yet parallels have not been found, but there is no reason to suppose that the object dates to later in this period.

In general the diagnostic iron and copper alloy objects, and the clay loomweight (below), find parallels in the later part of the Anglo-Saxon period. This is probably, however, because there are many more sites of the tenth and eleventh centuries, particularly

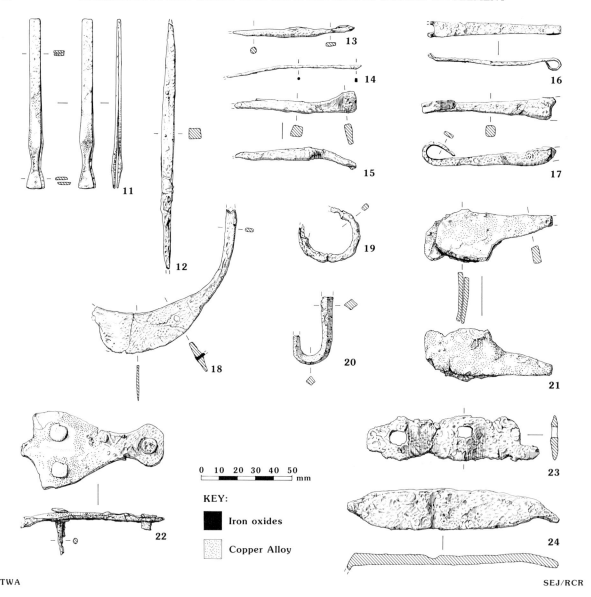

KEY:

Iron oxides

Copper Alloy

0 10 20 30 40 50
mm

TWA

SEJ/RCR

Fig 34.   Abbots Worthy (W79). Iron objects, 11–24. Scale 1:2.

urban ones yielding larger collections of artefacts, than there are sites of the eighth and ninth centuries. Comparisons with the Middle Saxon *Hamwic* site at Southampton are therefore particularly important, as they show that an earlier date is not precluded, and indeed might be preferred on the negative (and dubious) evidence of the absence of the ubiquitous hooked tag from Abbots Worthy.

Illustrated iron objects (Figs 33 and 34)

Knives

7. Blade with straight back and cutting-edge, both curving towards the point; 'knotched' tang with traces of mineralised antler (?haft). Probably Böhner type A. Overall length 95mm, blade thickness 2mm. SF 486, SFB F7339, context 7498.

8. Blade with straight back, and cutting-edge curving up towards the point. Traces of unidentified (possibly antler?) mineralised material on the tang. Broken at both ends in

antiquity. Böhner type B. Overall length 93mm, blade thickness 1.5–3mm. SF 496, SFB F7339, context 7522.

9. Double-bladed knife, with off-centre rivet, suggesting a multipurpose knife, showing many signs of wear and sharpening. The shorter blade has been bent in antiquity. The effect of corrosion on the blade has been to produce a heavily blistered surface, particularly on the larger blade. This corrosion lies within a layer of haematite which coats the original surface. The haematite possibly results from burning on a hearth (V Fell, pers comm). Overall length 99mm, blade thickness 1.2mm. SF 369, pit F7345, context 7349.

10. Angle-backed knife blade with straight cutting-edge, and an inlaid strip of twisted and beaten copper/silver, on either side. One strip is 28mm long, a single strand forming a regular 'chequered' pattern. The second, 31mm long, is composed of two strips and the wire has been reversed at the join, making an irregular pattern. Mineralised remains on the tang are probably of the bone or antler handle. Overall length 88mm, blade thickness <3.8mm. SF 541, pit F7485, context 7486.

Other objects

11. Tweezers (or possibly a binding strip?); plain and with the blades out of alignment. Again these show signs of haematite

partially coating the surface. Length 90mm, blade tip width 8.5mm. SF 382, pit F7341, context 7391.

12. Awl or drill, square-sectioned, with mineralised bone adhering to the lower end. The bone is probably debris rather than an integral part of the object. Broken both ends. Length 130mm, thickness 5–6mm. SF 448, SFB F7339, context 7497.

13. Borer, or point, crudely formed with tapering ends. Length 72mm, thickness 5mm. SF 386, pit F7345, context 7371.

14. Spike, with round section tapering to one end. Broken both ends. Length 74mm, diameter 1–2mm. SF 449, SFB F7339, context 7497.

15. Spatulate-ended object of uncertain use. Length 66mm. SF 514, SFB F7698, context 7699.

16. Key-handle for barrel padlock. Length 72mm. SF 523, SFB F7339, context 7544.

17. Key-handle for barrel padlock. Length 72mm, breadth (maximum) 9mm. SF 519, pit F7541, context 7543.

18. Curved blade or fitting with single copper alloy rivet and traces of two further rivet holes at either broken end. Possible remains of a plating or solder around the rivet. Function uncertain, possibly a leather-working implement. Length 102mm. SF 460, SFB F7339, context 7544.

19. Ring fragment, with circular section. Diameter (approximate) 28–33mm, section 4mm. SF 518, pit F7541, context 7542.

20. Hooked fragment with trapezoidal section, broken both ends. Length 36mm, thickness 5mm. SF 398, post-hole F7479, context 7480.

21. Fragment of incompletely welded sheet, with a crudely forged flat handle. Function unknown, probably a forging scrap. Length 71mm, width 26mm. SF 377, pit F7541, context 7352.

22. Mount with three large rivets, the surface of which when excavated was entirely covered with a thick haematite deposit. X-radiographic examination revealed a pattern-welded structure extending across the width of the plate (Fig 35) with composite rods arranged longitudinally to the length of the plate. Stereo x-radiography suggested a double construction of alternating composite straight rods and composite twisted rods, and subsequent metallographic sampling confirmed this. A similar microstructure to that of this mount was demonstrated in the pattern-welding of the Palace of Westminster sword (Anstee and Biek 1961, pl XIII). A full report on the metallographic examination, by Vanessa Fell, is in the site archive. Since pattern-welded objects are not common, and are almost exclusively swords, the possibility exists that this rivetted mount was made from a re-used sword blade. Length 80mm, width (maximum) 40mm. Rivet length (maximum) 23mm. SF 379, pit F7345, context 7398.

23. Strip, possibly door fitting, with two rectangular ?nail holes. Length 92mm. SF 389, pit F7443, context 7444.

24. Flat strip with tapered ends and slight groove across its width, set off-centre. Length 115mm, width (maximum) 24mm, thickness (maximum) 4mm. SF 498, SFB F7339, context 7513.

Technological material, by Paul Wilthew

The material examined (AM 852759 and AM Lab Report 4779) comprised over 50 samples which were regarded as being of possible technological significance. The individual samples were very small and the total weight of material was only about 1.5kg. Identifications of each sample are in the archive.

A large majority of the samples was fuel ash slag, which is the result of a reaction at high temperature between ash and silica-rich material such as sand or clay. It is often associated with high temperature technological processes such as metalworking, but it can be formed in any sufficiently hot fire, and there was no evidence that the fuel ash slag from this site was connected with any technological activity.

A few pieces of coal, most of which had been burnt resulting in coke, were present but there was no evidence to link them, or the burnt clay or the ferruginous concretion, with any technological activity.

The only samples which could be connected with metalworking were the dribbles of lead-tin alloy, which may have been waste from casting pewter, and

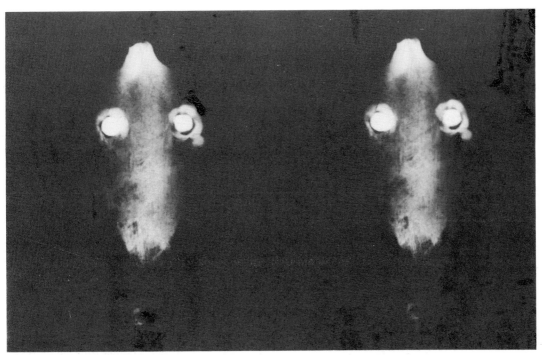

Fig 35. Abbots Worthy (W79). Stereo X-radiograph of pattern-welded fitting, iron object 22.

the iron slag. The former does not, in itself, prove that pewter was being worked on or near the site since it could also have been a (perhaps accidentally) melted pewter object or simply dribbles of solder. The lead-tin alloy was in F7447, an undated pit at the south of the site (Fig 22). The iron slag was almost certainly all iron smithing slag, which collects in a blacksmith's hearth, although one sample could not be positively identified. The presence of such a small quantity of iron smithing slag, although it was probably produced in the vicinity of the site, does not enable any conclusions about the nature of ironworking on or near the site to be drawn. The iron smithing slag was mainly in SFB F7339 but also in pits F7404 and F7627.

The Worked Bone and Antler, by Ian Riddler

Ten objects, ranging from combs to pins, were found in addition to some 27 fragments of waste material from the manufacture of objects. The majority of items were recovered from the sunken-featured buildings, in particular SFB F7339, which had a large quantity of associated waste material.

Objects

Combs (Fig 36.25–6)

Two distinct types of comb were present at Abbots Worthy. The double-sided comb (Fig 36.25) can be compared with similar undecorated double-sided composite combs from the Early Anglo-Saxon settlements of Sutton Courtenay (Leeds 1923, pl XXVIII, D and E) or West Stow (West 1969, Fig 10.6; West 1978, Abb 15.3.4), but it differs from these in having broad teeth (3/3.5–4 per cm).

The use of the comb is unclear. Combs from Early Anglo-Saxon graves have been found by the head of the deceased, as at Collingbourne Ducis, Grave 31 (Gingell 1975–6, 90), Harnham Hill (Akerman 1853, 260) or Kingston, Grave 53 (Faussett 1856, 52) and it is reasonable to assume that these were intended to comb hair.

The single-sided comb (Fig 36.26) is rather more unusual. The fragment of end segment allows the comb to be identified as a 'Winged' type, a reasonably common class of early medieval comb (Roes 1963, 19–21), but details allow it to be more closely defined. The end segments of 'Winged' combs can be separated into two principal types, depending on whether the transition from the back of the comb to the end segment is smooth or abrupt. The Abbots Worthy example belongs to the 'abrupt-end' type. A neat groove has been cut into the inner face of the end segment, and analogies with other Early and Middle Saxon combs suggest that this represents the vestige of a design for an inward-facing beast.

'Winged' combs occur initially in England in the seventh century, with examples from Kingston, Grave 142 (Baldwin-Brown 1915, pl LXXXVI, 1), Burwell, Graves 32, 83 and 121 (Lethbridge 1931, Figs 25.1, 34, 36.5), and from West Stow (West 1969, Fig 10.8). It is possible that they developed largely in the second half of the seventh century, but a date earlier in that century is implied by their occurrence at West Stow (Hawkes 1973, 198; West 1969). A recent attempt to link this particular group with a comb from *Hamwic*, and to extend it into the eighth century, is not convincing (MacGregor 1985, 88).

The Abbots Worthy example differs notably from these in its use of connecting-plates carved from large mammal rib – presumably cattle – and not from antler. As a result, combs of this type are noticeably thin in cross-section. The 'wings' formed by the end segments rise abruptly from the back of the comb, which often has a display side decorated with a diagonal lattice decoration. Examples of this group are now known from *Hamwic* (three examples), Ipswich (unpublished), York (MacGregor 1978, Fig 29.10) and Hessens (Haarnage 1959, Taf VII, 2). A connecting plate from another possible member of this group comes from Dorestad (Roes 1965, pl XXVIII, 210). The examples from *Hamwic* derive from contexts which extend from the middle of the eighth century to the first part of the ninth, and that from Ipswich is dated to the Middle Saxon period. A dating for the group as a whole in the later seventh and eighth centuries – with a possible extension into the first part of the ninth century – is confirmed by the Hessens comb, which is dated stratigraphically to the late seventh century. It is perhaps substantiated also by the particular decoration used, of intersecting diagonal lines. This scheme, for Frisia, has been dated to the period around AD 700 (Waller 1936, 232–3).

It would seem therefore that the Abbots Worthy comb should be dated to the later seventh or eighth century. It is notable that there is no evidence for the working of large mammal bone at Abbots Worthy, where all of the excavated waste material is antler. It is possible that bone was worked here, and this is suggested by the two pin-beaters, described below. Equally, however, it is possible that this comb was made elsewhere, conceivably at *Hamwic*, where there is considerable evidence for bone and antler working (Addyman and Hill 1969, 75–77; Driver 1984; Riddler forthcoming).

The spindle-whorl (Fig 36.28)

This type of antler spindle-whorl can be produced easily from the burr of a red deer antler, and the methods of manufacture can be seen from unfinished examples (Schoknecht 1978, Abb 12; Ulbricht 1978, Taf 42.6, 7). The form of the spindle-whorl is determined largely by the choice of material. The dense compact bone of this part of the antler makes this type of spindle-whorl heavier than those produced from the 'caput' of domestic cattle femur. The latter tend to be found more frequently on Anglo-

Saxon sites, but examples of antler spindle-whorls are known from Hamwic (Addyman and Hill 1969, Fig 29), Sutton Courtenay (Leeds 1947, pl XXII, m), Yelford (Leeds 1923, pl XXIX, 1) and elsewhere.

The buckle-loop (Fig 36.29)

This remarkable object appears to be a version, in bone, of a small oval belt-buckle loop frequent in copper alloy. The tongue for the buckle and any accompanying belt-plate – if they were originally present – are now missing. The size of the buckle relates it to those from Anglo-Saxon cemeteries of the middle or late seventh century, where the buckles tend to be smaller than the broader, heavier types of the sixth and early seventh centuries (Hawkes 1973, 194). The imitation in bone of a metal dress-fitting is rare in Anglo-Saxon England, although a few bone annular and disc brooches are known, and bone buckles with plates have been recovered from York (Meaney 1981, 139–140; MacGregor 1985, 102–105). The closest parallel for this object from Abbots Worthy lies however with the bone buckle loop from Volvic, Puy de Dôme (Werner 1977, 297, Abb 15).

The bone pin (Fig 36.30)

Objects of this type are commonly found on occupation sites of the Early Medieval period. They are produced by the simple modification of pig fibulae, and can be perforated or unperforated. Leeds suggested that they were a simple form of dress-fastener, and this interpretation has been widely adopted (Leeds 1923, 182–3; MacGregor 1982, 91–2; Graham-Campbell 1980, no 208). Others have related them, however, to textile production. It is clear that the expanded heads would considerably restrict their use in weaving, although they were possibly used in braid manufacture (Mann 1982, 10) or for mesh knitting (Ambrosiani 1981, 136). A recent survey of bone pins has indicated the range of their possible uses (Wilson 1983, 347).

The Abbots Worthy example shows a distinct horizontal wear pattern about the hole through the distal end of the bone. This is confined to one side of the hole and it lends support perhaps to the interpretation of this object as a dress-fastener. There is clearly some uncertainty over the use of this type of object, and a non-interpretative identification has been preferred here.

The pin-beaters (Fig 36.31 and 32)

Pin-beaters are common finds on Anglo-Saxon occupation sites. They were probably used to beat in the weft on a loom (Hoffmann 1964, 135–6) and their association with weaving is confirmed by their occurrence in Early Anglo-Saxon graves like Kingston, Grave 299, where two were found within a box of weaving implements (Faussett 1856, 93).

Those from Anglo-Saxon contexts are made from animal bone, though elsewhere wooden examples are known (Schietzel 1970, Abb 8.4). The bone examples tend to be produced from shaped sections of cattle metapodia and whilst some have recently been described as made of 'ivory' (Fell 1984, Fig 12), the use of this rare material for pin-beaters in Anglo-Saxon England is unlikely. It is based upon an eighteenth-century predilection for the term (eg Faussett 1856, 52).

The two Abbots Worthy examples were probably originally pointed at both ends, and they conform to the typical Saxon type.

The awl (Fig 36.33)

The function of this highly polished and well-made object is not clear. The channel cut into its end looks to be functional, and it distinguishes this object from decorative pins of the Viking period, which can be grooved and perforated (Schwarz-Mackensen 1976, Abb 1.5). There are no traces of wear on the object. Its flattened oval cross-section might have been determined by the bone used in its manufacture.

The few objects which may be compared with this example do not help to elucidate its function. A pointed bone implement from Arhus is longer, and although its end has been modelled, it does not include a channel (Andersen et al 1971, 110, CDU). A further general parallel is provided by an object from *Hamwic*, recovered from the Six Dials excavations (Riddler, forthcoming). A closer parallel however, is provided by a bone awl from Dorestad (Holwerda 1930, Abb 71.68). This lacks the channel of the Abbots Worthy awl, but it is of a comparable size (c 150mm) and it is also undecorated.

Waste material (Fig 36.34–42)

The waste debris from Abbots Worthy consists of 27 fragments of antler. It is assumed that these derive from the antler of red deer (*Cervus elaphus L*), and not from fallow deer, a species largely absent from Anglo-Saxon England. There are no diagnostic fragments of fallow deer antler, or of the antler of roe deer, which was a less suitable working medium (Ulbricht 1978, 22). The waste can be separated into the various parts of the antler (Table 5). The surviving waste represents only those fragments which were of no use in working. There are no sections of the antler beam, or fragments of the crown.

No antler burrs are present in the waste assem-

Table 5. Abbots Worthy (W79). Summary of waste antler fragments.

Tines	7
Tine ends	2
Core tissue	1
Segments of outer surface	1
Junctions of tine and beam	1
Shavings	15

blage, but one had been transformed into a spindle whorl (Fig 36.28). The seven antler tines show traces of sawing, combined in some instances with the breaking of the tine from the beam. The fragments were removed by sawing either along or across the line of the beam. The sample of antler waste is small, but it is nonetheless surprising that so many near-complete tines should be present, and so few tine ends.

A further tine from SFB F7339 has been sawn and shaped to a point (Fig 36.34). Its function is unclear. A similar worked tine from Flaxengate, Lincoln, has been interpreted as an unfinished awl or pin-beater (Mann 1982, 33). Saxon pin-beaters tend to be manufactured from cattle long bones, however. Elsewhere it has been shown that antler tines could be adapted as wedges for boneworking (Ambrosiani 1981, 112 and Fig 62). Similar modified antler tines are known from Hamwic and from Haithabu (Ulbricht 1978). The tine/beam junction (Fig 36.42) has probably been cut from the base of the antler, just above the burr. The beam has been split vertically after sawing. Sets of shallow lines on the upper and lower sawn surfaces represent either marking lines for splitting, or earlier attempts to split the beam closer to the junction with the tine.

The Abbots Worthy waste has been neatly sawn, and roughly worked with a knife. The various antler shavings from SFB F7339 are noticeably large and coarse, when seen against material from *Hamwic*, or from Haithabu (Ulbricht 1978, Taf 22). The exclusive use of antler at Abbots Worthy contrasts with the situation in contemporary urban centres like *Hamwic* and Dorestad, and also with smaller assemblages from West Stow, or from Munster, where animal bone was also worked (Driver 1984; Prummel 1983; West 1969; Winkelmann 1977). The presence of two pin-beaters, a comb with animal rib connecting plates and a worked pig fibula from Abbots Worthy allows, however, for the possibility that some domestic animal bone was also worked on the site.

The majority of the waste came from SFB F7339 in the northeast part of the site. A number of shavings were found in F7417, and the remainder of the waste was scattered amongst four other features: F7345, F7353, F7512 and F7623.

Unfinished pieces

SFB F7339 also produced five unfinished antler tooth segments, and a fragment of antler with rough knife working, possibly also intended to be a tooth segment (Fig 36.35–39). The segments are well-finished and show no traces of rivet holes, indicating therefore that they had not been assembled into a comb. Their sizes correlate well with those of the tooth segments from the double-sided comb (Fig 36.33).

Summary

The worked bone and antler objects from Abbots Worthy form a fascinating, if relatively small, collec-

tion of artefacts. The buckle loop (Fig 36.31), for its size, would fit readily into a seventh century context. The single-sided composite comb belongs to a type, identified here for the first time, which was current in the Middle Saxon period, and the bone awl has been compared to an example from Dorestad.

The implication is therefore that the objects of bone and antler from Abbots Worthy belong to a settlement of the seventh and eighth centuries, which was possibly associated with the incumbents of the nearby cemetery at Worthy Park, which is considered by the excavator to have been in use from the later fifth century down to the middle of the seventh century AD (S C Hawkes pers comm).

Illustrated objects (Fig 36)

Combs

25. Double-sided composite comb, virtually complete and lacking only a few teeth. The tooth segments are made from antler, and it appears that the connecting-plates are also made from this material. The comb consists of six tooth segments and two end segments, held together by two connecting-plates and secured by nine iron rivets. The comb is undecorated and although saw-marks have cut into the connecting-plates, they are not consistently applied and they do not seem to be decorative. Several details suggest that the comb is not very well-made. One of the connecting-plates shows how, in two instances, more than one attempt was made to create a hole for the reception of the rivet. A cross-section of the comb further indicates how it has not been precisely rivetted: the rivets are not perpendicular to the tooth segments. At one end of the comb the connecting-plates extend to the outside edge of the end segment; at the other, they do not. This aspect of the design of the comb follows possibly from the use of narrow strips of antler for the end segments. These are only a little wider than the tooth segments, whereas double-sided composite combs normally have wide end segments.

    The comb is short but wide, is symmetrical and has no display side. It has been heavily used, possibly to a point where it had become worn out, and the teeth are well-beaded. It is interesting to note that the pattern of tooth wear shows how the comb has been worn down about the middle: on both sides the teeth graduate out in length from the centre. Length 134mm, width 48.9mm. SF 465, SFB F7339, context 7544.

26. Single-sided composite comb, consisting of two incomplete connecting-plates, and a part of one end segment. The end segment is now displaced at an angle to the connecting-plates, which are no longer aligned together.

    The comb is decorated on one side by a series of intersecting diagonal lines, forming a lattice design. This is bounded towards the middle of the comb by two near-vertical lines. The middle section of the comb has been left blank, but traces of decoration on the broken edge of the connecting-plate suggest that the pattern was repeated at the other end. If both areas of decoration were the same length, the original length of the comb itself would have been *c* 155mm.

    Additional decoration is provided on the base of the connecting-plate by a series of tooth-marks. They are found on this side of the comb alone, where they are present along almost the entire length of the base. In this case, unlike the double-side composite comb 25, they do form an additional element of decoration for the display side of the comb.

    The presence of a fragment of an end section allows this comb to be identified as a 'Winged' type (Roes 1963, 19–21). Length 99.5mm. SF 371–375, pit F7404, context 7373.

27. Fragment of an antler connecting-plate for a double-sided

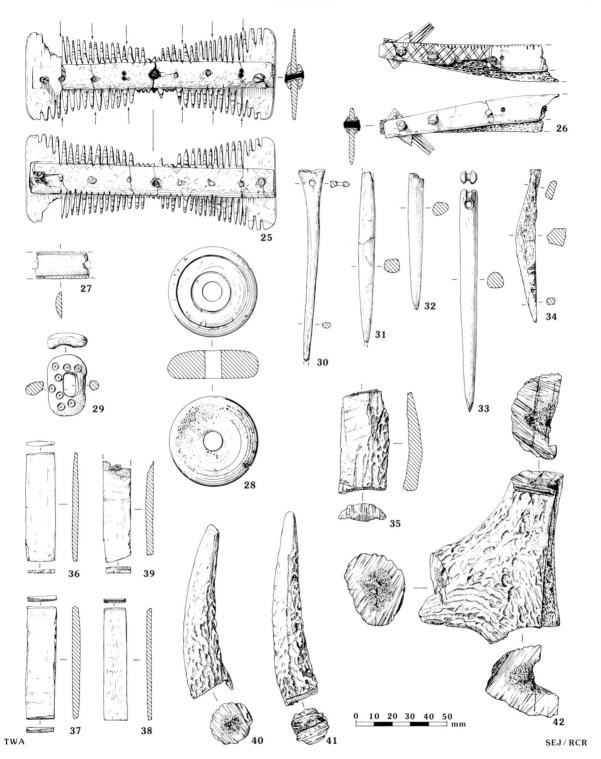

Fig 36.   Abbots Worthy (W79). Objects of bone and antler. Scale 1:2.

composite comb. Decorated with two parallel edging lines along each side. Saw-marks indicate that the teeth on either side of the comb were of similar widths. Length 26mm, width 14mm. SF 513, pit F7627, context 7628.

Other objects

28   Disc-shaped spindle-whorl, manufactured from an antler burr. Decorated on both sides by two concentric circles. Traces of apparent errors in inscribing this decoration are visible. Pierced by a cylindrical perforation. Diameter

48.5mm, diameter of perforation 10.5mm. Thickness 13mm. SF 488, SFB F7698, context 7699.

29.   Small buckle loop, produced possibly from part of an antler tine. Highly polished. Decorated on the display side by eight stamped ring-and-dot motifs, irregularly dispersed. Length 32mm, width 22mm. SF 532, unstratified.

30.   Perforated and pointed implement, incomplete, shaped from a pig fibula. Traces of wear around the perforation. Length 101mm, perforation diameter 3mm. SFB F7339, context 7522.

31.   Pin-beater, incomplete, now in two fragments. Both points

are missing, but most of the shaft survives. Undecorated. Length 90mm, diameter 13mm. SF 533, unstratified.

32. Pin-beater, fragmentary, consisting of one tapered end and part of the shaft. Undecorated, highly polished. Length 72.5mm, diameter 7mm. SF 542, pit F7341, context 7377.

33. Bone awl, highly polished, perforated. A channel runs around the end of the object, behind the perforation. Undecorated. Length 111mm, diameter 9mm, perforation diameter 3mm. SF 453, ditch F7483, context 7507.

34. Point, crudely fashioned from a tine-end. Length 81mm. SF 543, SFB F7339, context 7544.

Waste material and unfinished pieces

35. Unfinished tooth segment, crudely cut. Length 52mm, thickness (maximum) 8mm. SF 487, SFB F7339, context 7498.

36. Tooth segment, unfinished, probably for double-sided composite comb. Length 56mm, width 15mm, thickness 2.5mm. SF 510, SFB F7339, context 7514.

37. As 36. Length 60mm, width 16mm, thickness 4mm. SF 464, SFB F7339, context 7546.

38. As 36. Length 59mm, width 12.5mm, thickness 3mm. SF 441, SFB F7339, context 7516.

39. As 36. Length 54mm, width 15mm, thickness 4mm. SF 507, SFB F7339, context 7514.

40. Antler tine-end, sawn and snapped off. Length 93mm. SF 546, SFB F7339, context 7493.

41. Antler tine-end, sawn and snapped off. Length 103mm. SF 506, SFB F7339, context 7514.

42. Tine/beam junction of antler, sawn and split. 93mm by 69mm. SF 420, SFB F7339, context 7498.

Ceramic Objects

One bun-shaped loomweight, SF 383, with a single central perforation was found in pit F7341,

context 7391. It is 140mm long, 100mm wide and has a maximum thickness of 53mm (Fig 37.44). The clay is heavily tempered with chalk lumps and the object poorly fired. Its upper surface is partially burnt.

It has been suggested that bun-shaped loomweights were common from the ninth-century onwards (Dunning *et al* 1959, 24–25). At Abbots Worthy this example is associated with a single-sided comb (Fig 36.26), suggested by Riddler (above) to date perhaps to the eighth-century AD. A slightly later date cannot, however, be ruled out.

Brick and Tile, by Nick Digby

Thirty-two fragments of brick and 84 tile fragments were found, mostly residual Roman material. Again SFB F7339 was the most productive of all features, containing 88% of the brick and 33% of the tile (by number of fragments). The large pits on the west side of the site, F7341, F7345, and F7627, also produced quantities of material. No diagnostic material was recovered.

Glass and Amber Objects

A single dark green translucent annular glass bead, SF 392 (Fig 37.43), was found in SFB F7337, context 7338. Its dimensions are: diameter 14mm, perforation 4.5mm and height 4.5–5.8mm.

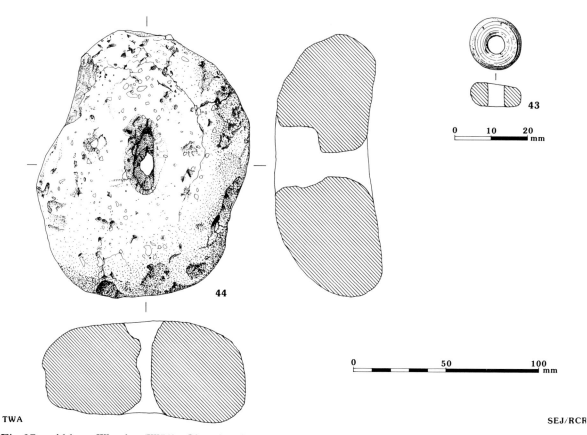

TWA   SEJ/RCR

Fig 37.   Abbots Worthy (W79). Glass bead, 43, scale 1:1. Clay loomweight, 44, scale 1:2.

Although such beads are common finds from Early Saxon graves, they are also common on Christian-period sites, such as Thetford (ninth-century onwards) and cannot therefore be dated with any certainty.

A fragmentary amber bead, probably cylindrical, was found in pit F7345, context 7345.

Finds of Stone, by D F Williams

Many of the fragments of stone are quite small. Some of them may well be from quernstones, but given their shapelessness it is difficult to tell in most cases. The majority are not local to the area of the site, while some pieces have come from the nearby valley gravels. The site at Abbots Worthy lies on the Upper Chalk, close to pockets of valley gravel and sand, about two miles north of Winchester (1" Geological Survey Map 299). The distribution of different stones by feature is shown in Table 6.

The Worked Stone

Though a large number of fragments of 'foreign' stone were recovered, only three appear to have been utilised, all as whetstones. None of the fragments is illustrated, as their condition is too poor. The stone was identified by Dr D F Williams, who suggests that although a likely origin is difficult to determine, all the whetstones have been fashioned from pebbles of Palaeozoic date, which could have been obtained locally from valley gravels. None of the whetstones is particularly attributable to a specific period, but all are likely to be of Early Saxon date. None are illustrated.

1. Central fragment of probably rectangular whetstone with only one face and part of the sides present. The extant surfaces are well-polished and smooth. Grey Micaceous Mudstone. Extant dimensions: length 56mm, breadth 38mm, thickness 15mm. SF 418, SFB F7339, context 7498.
2. End fragment from a sub-rectangular whetstone, again with only one face and part of the sides present, the object having

Table 6. Abbots Worthy (W79). Distribution of different types of stone by feature.

	SFB 7339	PIT 7341	SFB 7345	SFB 7403	PIT 7404	POST HOLE 7437	SFB 7445	PIT 7483	PIT 7485	PIT 7499	PIT 7623	PIT 7627	POST HOLE 7682	SFB 7698	PIT 7809	POST HOLE 7823
Quartz conglomerate (quern)	–	1	–	–	–	–	–	–	–	–	–	–	–	–	–	–
Malmstone	–	–	1	–	–	–	–	–	–	–	–	–	–	–	–	–
Pennant sandstone (South Wales/ Bristol)	3	1	–	1	–	–	2	1	–	–	–	–	–	–	1	–
Oolitic limestone (? Purbeck)	2	–	–	–	–	–	–	–	–	–	–	–	–	–	–	–
Shelly limestone (? Purbeck)	5	–	–	–	–	1	–	–	–	–	1	–	1	–	–	–
Shelly limestone with ooliths (? Purbeck)	47	7	–	–	–	–	–	–	–	–	–	–	–	1	–	–
Shelly limestone (Purbeck marble)	1	1	–	–	–	–	–	–	–	–	–	–	–	–	–	1
Sandy limestone	1	–	–	–	–	–	–	–	–	–	–	–	–	–	–	–
Brown sandstone (uncertain)	–	–	–	–	1	–	–	–	–	–	–	–	–	–	–	–
Grey sandstone (uncertain)	3	–	–	–	–	–	–	–	–	–	–	–	–	–	–	–
Grey sandstone fossil shell (uncertain)	–	–	1	1	–	–	–	–	–	–	–	1	–	–	–	–
Greensand	3	–	–	–	–	–	–	–	–	1	–	–	–	–	–	–
Ferruginous sandstone	1	–	–	–	–	–	–	1	1	–	–	–	–	–	–	–
Siltstone	–	–	–	–	–	–	–	1	–	–	–	–	–	–	–	–

split along a natural lamination in the stone. Surface well-polished and smoothed. Indurated Mudstone. Extant dimensions: length 62mm, breadth 44mm, thickness 24mm. SF 492, SFB F7339, context 7511.

3. End fragment of a flat, possibly rectangular whetstone. Surfaces and end well-polished, with several deeper striations across the end, diagonally to the faces of the stone. Calcareous Mudstone. Extant dimensions: length 60mm, breadth 52mm, thickness 10.5mm. SF 522, pit F7483, context 7484.

The Pottery

A total of 587 sherds, weighing 12.453kg, was found in a range of features across the site. The bulk of the material, however, came from the fills of SFB F7339 (Tables 7, 8 and 9). Most of the pottery (c 93%) dates to the Early or Middle Saxon period (sixth to eighth century AD), but some, presumably residual, Roman material was also found.

The pottery was sorted into fabric types by context, and then subdivided into diagnostic and body sherds. Each individual subdivision was then weighed and counted. Subsequently vessel forms were attributed where possible and recorded separately, with the decorated sherds. All details of the quantified record are held in archive; this report summarises the main results.

The fabrics

Four groups of fabrics were isolated on the basis of major inclusion types, using a binocular microscope and hand lens, with ×30 and ×10 magnification respectively. Groups 1 to 4 and Fabric 5.5 are Early to Mid-Saxon in date, whilst the rest of Group 5 comprises a number of recognisable Roman pottery types almost all of which are probably residual in the contexts in which they occurred. The validity of the fabric separations was tested by thin-section analysis carried out by Dr D F Williams, whose report is appended at the end of the summary fabric descriptions. The thin-section analysis was also intended to investigate the provenance of the pottery.

The total number of sherds and weight of pottery recovered, by fabric type, is shown in Table 7. Discussion of distribution across the site, correlation with vessel form and other aspects are presented in the appropriate period section.

Group 1: organic inclusions

1.1 Organic inclusions 3–6mm common to abundant; rounded glauconite 0.75–2mm moderately common; rounded quartz < 0.15mm common; rare dark grey iron ore <0.3mm, grog <3mm and mica <0.05mm. Hard. Surface voids frequent (burnt out organic inclusions). Section shows an irregular layering resulting from the number of organic fragments (up to c 70%). The outer surface of the sherds in this fabric has often broken away. Colour range (surfaces) dark brick red to, more commonly, dark grey-brown.

1.2 Organic inclusions as 1.1. Rounded quartz <0.15mm common; rounded semi-shiny black inclusions (probably glauconite) <0.15mm fairly common. Fabric soft and brittle. Surface voids common, but quartz grains also give a sandy feel and look to the surface. Colour range dark grey-brown throughout, margins occasionally reddish brown.

1.3 Organic inclusions <5mm fairly common; rounded quartz <0.2mm common to abundant, <0.45mm sparse; rare iron ore and grog <0.3mm. Surfaces usually well-smoothed. Hard to very hard. Colour range dark grey-brown to black.

1.4 Organic inclusions <5mm sparse; rounded quartz <0.15mm common, <0.45mm moderately common, <0.3mm sparse; sparse reddish-brown and grey iron inclusions <0.4mm. Soft. Colour range dark reddish-brown to dark grey. Frequently used for thick-walled vessels.

1.5 Organic inclusions <4mm sparse; rounded quartz <0.15mm common, <0.5mm sparse; occasional iron <0.3mm. Hard to very hard. Granular feel and look to surface. Colour range dark grey to dark orange.

1.6 Organic inclusions <6mm sparse; rounded quartz <0.2mm abundant, <0.6mm sparse; glauconite <0.3mm fairly common; dark grey inclusions <0.15mm (?iron) fairly common. Hard to very hard. Colour range mid-grey to greyish-brown. Surfaces usually well-smoothed.

1.7 Organic inclusions <7mm moderately common; rounded quartz <1mm common; red-brown iron oxides <0.15mm sparse; glauconite <0.75mm sparse. Hard. Colour range mid- to dark grey or grey-brown. Surfaces well-wiped but with irregular finish.

1.8 Organic inclusions as 1.7; rounded quartz 0.75–1.3mm common; rare chalk <4mm. Hard. Dark grey to dark brown. External surface heavily grass-marked with few visible quartz inclusions. In contrast the inner surface shows little grass-marking but abundant quartz.

1.9 Organic inclusions <7mm moderately common; angular calcite crystals 1–3mm moderately common; rounded quartz 0.15–0.45mm common; glauconite <0.15mm sparse. Hard. Dark brownish-orange to dark grey. Surfaces well-finished if slightly pitted.

Group 2: sandy

2.1 Rounded quartz <0.5mm moderately common, <0.3mm common; rare angular calcined flint <4mm. Hard, dense granular fabric. Dark grey throughout. Surfaces wiped carefully.

2.2 Sub-angular quartz 0.4–0.6mm abundant; angular calcined flint <1.5mm rare. Hard to very hard. Dark grey to dark pinkish-brown. Surfaces crudely finished with sandy texture.

2.3 Rounded quartz <0.3mm abundant; iron inclusions <0.5mm fairly common; rare shell, grog and flint. Hard to very hard. Dark brown to dark orange-brown.

2.4 Rounded quartz <1mm common, <0.1mm common; opaque dark grey inclusions (unidentified) fairly common. Hard to very hard. Usually mid-grey.

Group 3: flint

3.1 Angular calcined flint <2mm common; rounded quartz <0.3mm sparse, <0.1mm common; iron oxides and ?glauconite sparse. Hard to very hard. Dark brown to dark grey-brown. Surface crudely smoothed.

Group 4: limestone or chalk

4.1 Rounded off-white inclusions, probably limestone, <0.75mm common to abundant; rounded quartz <0.5mm fairly common; angular calcite <0.45mm and iron oxides rare. Hard. Brick red to dark grey-brown. Surfaces smoothed.

4.2 Ooliths <0.45mm common; quartz <0.5mm moderately common, <1mm rare; shell fragments <0.5mm rare; angular calcined flint <7mm sparse; iron oxides rare. Hard. Dark grey throughout. Surfaces well-smoothed.

4.3 Limestone grains <0.5mm moderately common; rounded quartz <0.5mm common; shell fragments <1mm, glauconite and ?grog sparse. Hard. Dark grey to black. Well-smoothed.

Group 5: miscellaneous

5.1 Central Gaulish Samian.

Table 7. Abbots Worthy (W79). Number of sherds and weight of pottery recovered by fabric.

Fabric	RIMS		BASES		DEC BODY		PL BODY		TOTALS		% OF GROSS TOTAL	
	No	Wt	No	Wt	No	Wt	No	Wt	No	Wt	No	Wt
1.1	14	261	6	650	3	78	127	1413	150	2402		
1.2	15	175	–	–	1	10	40	492	56	677		
1.3	21	444	–	–	–	–	81	4223	102	4667		
1.4	8	113	14	1018	1	14	64	862	87	2007		
1.5	5	88	–	–	5	64	14	117	24	269		
1.6	5	177	–	–	4	29	8	101	17	307		
1.7	1	14	–	–	–	–	16	173	17	187		
1.8	1	11	–	–	–	–	–	–	1	11		
1.9	–	–	4	84	–	–	–	–	4	84		
total	70	1283	24	1752	14	195	350	7381	458	10611	78.02	85.68
2.1	4	23	2	25	1	18	21	154	28	220		
2.2	–	–	–	–	1	16	16	165	17	181		
2.3	4	63	1	34	2	25	6	74	13	196		
2.4	–	–	–	–	–	–	1	34	1	34		
total	8	86	3	59	4	59	44	427	59	637	10.05	5.07
3.1	1	19	–	–	–	–	3	19	4	38	0.68	0.003
4.1	2	18	–	–	–	–	14	211	16	229		
4.2	–	–	–	–	–	–	1	20	1	20		
4.3	1	6	2	94	2	16	7	75	12	191		
total	3	24	2	94	2	16	22	306	29	440	4.94	3.53
5.1	–	–	–	–	1	10	1	19	2	29		
5.2	3	50	–	–	–	–	5	65	8	115		
5.3	–	–	–	–	–	–	2	28	2	28		
5.4	–	–	–	–	–	–	1	14	1	14		
5.5	–	–	1	138	–	–	–	–	1	138		
5.6	–	–	10	114	–	–	–	–	10	114		
5.7	4	136	4	112	–	–	5	47	13	295		
total	7	186	15	364	1	10	14	173	37	733	6.3	5.89
GROSS TOTAL	89	1598	44	2269	21	280	433	8306	587	12453		

5.2 Oxfordshire red colour-coated.
5.3 Romano-British oxidised coarseware.
5.4 Imitation Gallo-Belgic wares.
5.5 Micaceous buff ware: sparse white mica <0.75mm; iron oxides and quartzite rare.
5.6 New Forest colour-coated ware (Fulford 1975 fabric 1b).
5.7 Roman greywares, probably mostly products of the New Forest kilns.

Petrological examination of the pottery, by D F Williams

Seventeen sherds of Early Saxon pottery forming the macroscopically-defined fabric series were submitted for detailed examination in thin section under the petrological microscope. The small size of many of the samples ruled out the possibility of heavy mineral separation of the sandy wares. The main objectives of the analysis were to confirm the validity of a provisional fabric identification in the hand-specimen and to see if the pottery might have been locally made.

On the basis of the range of non-plastic inclusions in the pottery, a number of fabric divisions have been made. The original fabric numbering of the samples has been retained throughout.

1. Organic-tempered

Fabrics 1.1, 1.2, 1.3, 1.4, 1.5, 1.7, 1.8 and 2.1.

All the fabrics in this group display to a greater or lesser degree a number of elongate voids which probably once held grass or chaff. These voids not only appear on the surfaces of the sherds, but are also present in the paste, suggesting that vegetable matter was deliberately added to the clay at some stage of the manufacture.

Fabrics 1.1, the most obviously vegetable-tempered sherd in the group, 1.3 and 2.1 also contain a scatter of light brown grains of ?glauconite, set in a groundmass of frequent sub-angular quartz grains. Fabric 2.1 also contains a little limestone. Glauconite is commonly found in the Greensand, and also occurs in the Thanet Sands, Reading Beds and parts of the London Clay. In northern Hampshire it is apparently also to be found in the Upper Chalk (Jukes-Brown 1908, 23). Recent work on Glauconitic fabrics in the southeast of the country suggests that it may be difficult to tie down the Glauconite to a particular provenance (Freestone 1982).

The remainder of the fabrics in the group contain little else but inclusions of quartz and flecks of mica, with the odd piece of flint also present.

2. Sandy fabrics

Fabrics 2.2, 2.4 and 5.3.

All three samples are dominated by inclusions of quartz, with flecks of mica and occasional flint. Also visible in thin section of 2.4 are some dark brown rounded grains which might be altered glauconite, though further tests are needed to confirm this. There is a degree of textural variation in the size and frequency of quartz in the samples: 2.2 contains frequent sub-angular grains, average size 0.4–0.6mm, with a few larger grains; 2.4 contains a scatter of large grains <2mm across; and 5.3 contains frequent small grains, average size 0.1mm and under.

3. Flint-tempered

Fabrics 2.3, 3.1, 4.1 and 4.3.

As might be expected from a site situated on the chalk, a group of flint-tempered fabrics came to light. The fabrics also contain quartz grains and limestone (?chalk), a small amount of the latter in 2.3 and 3.1, with more in 4.1 and 4.3.

4. Calcite-tempered

Fabric 1.9.

In fresh fracture this sherd can be seen to contain glistening crystals of calcite. This is confirmed in thin section which shows large twinned angular fragments of calcite scattered throughout the fabric, together with some grains of quartz. The large size, comparatively fresh condition and angularty of the calcite present here strongly suggests that it was deliberately crushed and added to the clay as a tempering agent. The vessel represented by this sherd can be regarded as an import to the site, as the nearest available deposits of calcite are to be found in the Jurassic formations of Purbeck or those further to the west.

5. Oolitic-tempered

Fabric 4.2.

Thin sectioning shows that the fabric is tempered with crushed limestone and shell, amongst which distinct ooliths can be made out. The ooliths can also be seen in fresh fracture using a ×10 hand lens. The presence of ooliths suggests that like sherd 1.9, an origin is to be sought in the region of the Jurassic rocks, making this sherd an import to the site. Fabrics B and C at Cheddar also contained limestone, sometimes fossiliferous or shelly limestone, although ooliths are not specifically mentioned (Peacock 1979).

The Roman pottery

A small number of abraded sherds of late first to late fourth century date was recovered from the buildings, pits and a single gulley (Tables 7 and 8).

Table 8. Abbots Worthy (W79). Occurrence of fabric by feature.

Fabric:	1.1	1.2	1.3	1.4	1.5	1.6	1.7	1.8	1.9	2.1	2.2	2.3	2.4	3.1	4.1	4.2	4.3	5.1	5.2	5.3	5.4	5.5	5.6	5.7
SFB																								
F7337	–	★	–	–	★	–	–	–	–	–	–	–	–	–	–	–	–	★	★	–	–	–	–	–
F7339	★	★	★	★	★	★	★	★	★	★	★	★	–	★	–	★	★	★	★	–	–	–	★	–
F7403	★	★	–	★	–	–	–	–	★	–	–	–	–	★	–	★	–	–	–	–	–	–	–	–
F7445	★	★	★	★	–	–	★	–	–	★	★	–	–	★	–	–	–	–	–	–	–	–	★	–
F7698	★	★	–	–	–	–	–	–	★	★	★	–	–	★	–	–	–	–	–	–	–	–	–	–
PIT																								
F7341	★	★	–	★	–	–	★	–	–	–	–	–	–	★	–	–	★	★	–	★	–	★	–	★
F7345	★	★	–	★	★	–	–	–	–	★	★	–	–	★	★	–	★	–	–	★	–	–	–	★
F7404	★	★	★	★	★	–	★	–	–	★	★	–	–	–	–	–	–	★	–	–	–	–	–	★
F7443	★	–	–	–	–	–	–	–	–	–	–	–	–	–	–	–	–	–	–	–	–	–	–	–
F7483	★	★	–	–	–	–	★	–	–	★	★	–	–	–	–	–	–	–	–	–	–	–	–	–
F7485	–	–	–	★	–	–	–	–	–	–	–	–	–	–	–	–	–	–	–	–	–	–	–	★
F7499	★	–	–	–	–	–	–	–	–	–	★	–	–	–	–	–	–	–	–	–	–	–	–	–
F7541	★	–	–	–	–	–	–	–	–	–	–	–	★	–	–	–	–	–	–	–	–	–	–	–
F7623	–	–	–	–	–	–	–	–	–	–	★	–	–	–	–	–	–	–	–	–	–	–	–	–
F7680	★	–	–	–	–	–	★	–	–	★	–	–	–	–	★	–	–	–	★	–	–	–	–	–
F7809	–	–	–	–	–	–	–	–	–	–	–	–	–	★	–	–	–	–	–	–	–	–	–	–
OTHER																								
F7319	★	★	–	★	–	–	–	–	–	–	–	–	–	–	–	–	–	–	–	–	–	–	–	–
F7322	–	–	–	–	–	–	–	–	–	★	–	–	–	–	–	–	–	–	–	–	–	–	–	–
F7353	–	–	–	–	–	–	–	–	–	–	–	–	–	★	–	–	–	–	–	–	–	–	–	–
F7441	–	–	–	–	★	–	–	–	–	–	–	–	–	–	–	–	–	–	–	–	–	–	–	–
F7479	–	–	–	★	★	–	–	–	–	–	–	–	–	–	–	–	–	–	–	–	–	–	–	–
F7489	–	–	–	–	–	–	★	–	–	–	–	–	–	–	–	–	–	–	–	–	–	–	–	–
F7525	–	–	–	–	–	–	★	–	–	★	–	–	–	–	–	–	–	–	–	–	–	★	–	–
F7539	–	–	–	–	–	–	–	–	–	–	–	–	–	–	–	–	–	–	–	–	–	–	★	–
F7834	–	★	–	–	–	–	–	–	–	–	★	–	–	–	–	–	–	–	–	★	–	–	–	–
F7858	★	–	–	–	–	–	–	–	–	–	–	–	–	–	–	–	–	–	–	–	–	–	–	–

★ occurrence

– no occurrence

Wares included second century Central Gaulish Samian (fabric 5.1); late first-century imitation Gallo-Belgic forms (fabric 5.4); orange coarseware (fabric 5.3); and products of the late Romano-British kilns of Oxfordshire and the New Forest (fabrics 5.2, 5.6 and 5.7). Forms were not readily attributable, even to the Oxford and New Forest finewares, and the material is clearly all residual.

The occurrence of this relatively insignificant quantity of Roman material (6.3% by number, and 5.89% by weight of the assemblage) is unsurprising in an area where activity in the Roman period was as intense as around Winchester, and with a major settlement one kilometre upslope.

The Anglo-Saxon pottery

Five hundred and fifty-one sherds of Anglo-Saxon pottery were retrieved from the site, of which 345 came from SFB F7339 (62.6% by number, 55.8% by weight). This building also produced most of the other artefact types and faunal remains in quantity. In contrast, the other features on the site, including the other sunken-featured buildings and deep pits,

Table 9. *Abbots Worthy (W79). Comparative distribution of fabrics in totally excavated sunken-featured buildings and the large pits.*

| FEATURE | SUNKEN-FEATURED BUILDINGS | | | | | | | | PITS | | | | | |
| | 7339 | | 7403 | | 7445 | | 7698 | | 7341 | | 7345 | | 7404 | |
FABRIC	No	Wt	No	Wt	No	Wt	No	Wt	No	Wt	No	Wt	No	Wt
1.1	90	1717	3	29	21	113	3	16	2	24	18	308	2	19
1.2	28	415	4	15	2	17	8	52	2	8	3	28	1	29
1.3	93	1872	–	–	1	6	–	–	–	–	–	–	3	17
1.4	61	1701	7	70	5	131	–	–	3	15	2	30	2	17
1.5	13	197	–	–	–	–	–	–	–	–	3	30	1	6
1.6	15	395	–	–	–	–	–	–	–	–	–	–	–	–
1.7	6	75	–	–	4	22	–	–	1	16	–	–	2	46
1.8	1	11	–	–	–	–	–	–	–	–	–	–	–	–
1.9	1	38	–	–	–	–	3	46	–	–	–	–	–	–
Total	308	6421	14	114	33	289	14	114	8	63	26	396	11	134
2.1	10	72	1	35	1	4	5	27	–	–	2	14	1	15
2.2	3	7	–	–	1	7	2	28	–	–	2	55	1	16
2.3	13	266	–	–	–	–	–	–	–	–	–	–	–	–
2.4	–	–												
Total	26	345	1	35	2	11	7	55			4	69	2	31
3.1	1	11			1	4	–	–	–	–	1	4	–	–
Totals	1	11	–	–	1	4	–	–	–	–	1	4	–	–
4.1			9	139	–	–	1	7	1	9	2	18	–	–
4.2	1	20			–	–	–	–	–	–	–	–	–	–
4.3	5	36	4	65	–	–	–	–	–	–	–	80	–	–
Total	6	56	13	204	–	–	1	7	1	9	4	98	–	–
5.1	1	19	–	–	–	–	–	–	1	10	–	–	–	–
5.2	1	23	–	–	–	–	–	–	1	32	–	–	3	23
5.3	–	–	–	–	–	–	–	–	–	–	1	3	–	–
5.4	–	–	–	–	–	–	–	–	1	14	–	–	–	–
5.5	–	–	–	–	–	–	–	–	–	–	–	–	–	–
5.6	2	70	–	–	8	44	–	–	–	–	–	–	–	–
5.7	–	–	–	–	–	–	–	–	8	221	1	5	1	6
Total	4	112	–	–	8	44	–	–	11	277	2	8	4	29
Gross totals	345	6945	28	343	44	348	22	176	20	349	37	575	17	194

rarely produced more than 20 sherds (see Table 9 for examples). All the vessels are hand-made, with the surfaces smoothed to varying degrees of refinement.

Fabrics (These notes incorporate Dr D F Williams' discussion)

Eighteen fabrics were isolated, nine of which (Group 1) contained organic inclusions to a varying degree and which accounted for over 78% of the assemblage by number (85%+ by weight), as might be anticipated from ceramics of this period in this area. The other fabrics contained inclusions of sand (Group 2), flint (Group 3) or limestone/chalk (Group 4), with one micaceous fabric present (5.3). The overall quantities of each fabric recovered and the group percentage of the entire collection is shown in Table 7.

The range of fabrics is fairly extensive when compared to other published pottery of the period (Davies 1980), but the collection from Abbots Worthy is also comparatively large, and possibly covers a wider timespan. Since most of the pottery is likely to have been produced locally many of the variations could be explained by minor differences in source material and potting technique. Three fabrics, however, are not the result of local production: 1.9, which contains calcite inclusions; 4.2 which contains ooliths; and 5.3 with its large plates of white mica and totally alien clay matrix and finish. The nearest source for the first two seems to be to the southwest, possibly Purbeck. The source of the last is uncertain, but could be continental. None of these three fabrics appears to be a common find on Anglo-Saxon sites, at least in Hampshire, although a few sherds of calcite-gritted ware were found on another rural site of Early to Mid-Saxon date, at Meonstoke, Hampshire (Hughes 1986; Newing 1987, 10). There is insufficient evidence from the Purbeck area for the period to say that it is a very likely source area for the material.

The distribution of fabrics by feature type appears on Table 8, with a more detailed comparison of material in buildings and the deeper pits on Table 9. Seven of the fabrics only occur once, four in SFB F7339, two in pits and one in ditch F7525. There does not seem to be a significant difference in fabric contents between the different feature types, which might be indicative of a chronological or functional variation (but see vessel form discussion below). The assemblage is so obviously dominated by the accumulated rubbish in SFB F7339 that, other than on the basis of fabric alone, there is no reason to suggest that all the features form part of a single period settlement.

Vessel form and decoration

Vessel forms represented include a range of small and large jars, dishes and bowls – for the most part fairly crude and undecorated domestic material. Parallels can be found at Old Down Farm (Davies 1980), and Portway, Andover (Cook and Dacre

1986), Portchester (Cunliffe 1976) and *Hamwic* (Hodges 1981).

Eighteen simplified 'types' were defined on the basis of shape and size. The definitions cannot be absolutely rigid because of the crude and fragmentary nature of the pottery. In many instances it is difficult, if not impossible, to assign a type objectively and, for example, to distinguish jars from bowls.

The type series

1. Probable jar, for storage or cooking. Inclining, slightly expanded rim; shoulder ill-defined. May have perforation below rim for suspending the vessel (Fig 38.1, 2 and 3).
2. Large storage jar; upright or slightly inclining rim and neck stemming from a short slack shoulder (Fig 38.4 and 5).
3. Jar with upright or slightly everted rim and slack shoulder (Fig 38.6).
4. Everted rim jar or cooking pot; neck clearly defined and with rounded body (Fig 38.7 and 8).
5. Everted rim storage or cooking pot; rim usually plain and slightly rounded; short neck. Body fairly globular (Fig 38.9, Fig 40.39, 40 and 42).
6. Upright or slightly everted rim jar, no real neck, steep shoulder (Fig 38.10 and 11).
7. As 6, shoulder more upright, probably carinated.
8. Carinated bowl, probably with short upright rim. May be the same form as 7, but no rim profile available (Fig 38.12 and 13).
9. Small round-bodied bowl with everted rim (Fig 38.14).
10. ?Open bowl, with slightly everted rim and curving profile (Fig 38.15, Fig 40.37).
11. Steep-sided bowl with outward flaring, expanded rim (Fig 38.6).
12. Shallow open bowl, possibly with footring, rim usually slightly beaded, or at least defined by a shallow groove (Fig 39.17).
13. Steep-sided open bowl with plain or slightly pointed rim (Fig 39.18, 19; Fig 40.33, 38 and 41).
14. Upright-walled bowl or dish, with plain rounded rim (Fig 39.20, Fig 40.36).
15. Plain base angle.
16. Solid pedestal base (Fig 39.21).
17. Footring base (Fig 39.22).
18. Pointed base, possibly from a lamp or some form of amphora (Fig 40.43).

Decorative motifs and designs

The range of decoration is limited to two basic types: stamped or impressed (types 1–11), and incised or burnished linear (types 12–14). Most of the decorated sherds came from SFB F7339. Few specific forms can be attributed, but most are probably small carinated or shouldered bowls or jars of types commonly found in cemetery contexts. The correlation with Lady Briscoe's (1981) stamp categories appears in brackets following the description of the decorative type, as for example [A1i].

The decoration type series

1. Eight-part rosette [A5a]; (Fig 38.12 and 13).
2. Four-part rosette or cross [B1a]; (Fig 39.24).
3. Dot [A1a]; (Fig 38.12 and 13).
4. Ring [A1b]; (Fig 39.23).
5. Ring-and-raised-dot [A1a or 2b]; (Fig 38.12 and 13).
6. Segmented circle [A5d]; (Fig 40.34).
7. Horse-shoe [G1ai]; (Fig 39.24).
8. Fish-hook [?H]; (Fig 39.24).

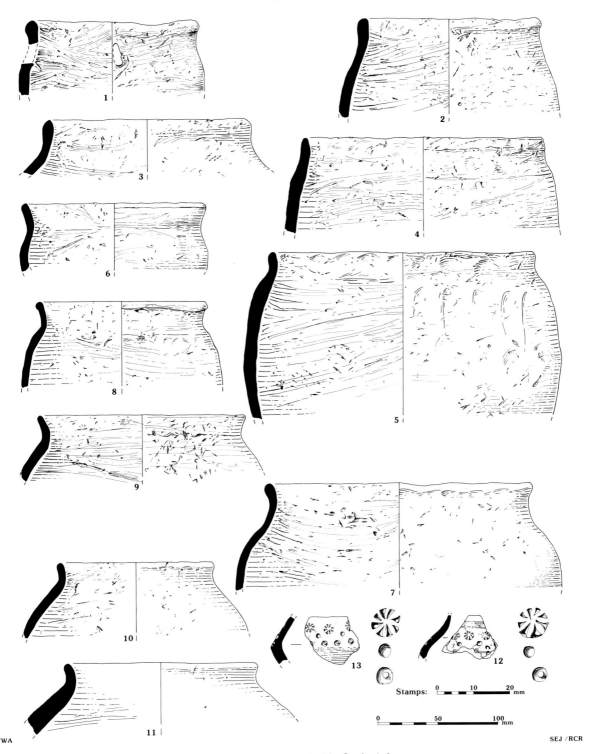

Fig 38.   Abbots Worthy (W79). Anglo-Saxon pottery, 1–13. Scale 1:3.

 9.   Subrectangular (Fig 39.24).
10.   'Maggot' [?K1b]; (Fig 39.24).
11.   Comb-impressed linear [N1]; (Fig 39.25–27).
12.   Horizontal linears (Fig 39.28–32).
13.   Diagonal linears (Fig 39.30).
14.   Miscellaneous linears (Fig 40.43).

The total number of occurrences of all motifs was 25. Apart from numbers 6, 11 and 14, the others all occurred in various combinations, shown on Table 10.

Many of the stamp types can be paralleled not only within the region and further afield, but also in the immediate vicinity at the Early Saxon cemetery at Worthy Park. The eight-part rosette, type 1, occurs on one vessel from Worthy Park (Myres 1977, cat no 1190, Fig 239), whilst type 2 is found on a further two (Myres 1977, cat no 1198, Fig 204, and cat. no. 1952, Fig 305). Type 10 is combined with type 2 on vessel 1952. Comb-impressed linear decoration also occurs at Worthy Park, on vessel 1199 (Myres 1977,

Fig 362), though it is much cruder than the example from Abbots Worthy (type 11). In view of the similarity of the stamped decoration between the two sites it is not unreasonable to suggest contemporaneity. The date range for the decorated material seems to lie in the sixth century AD, but the settlement seems to have been in existence until rather later.

Table 10. Abbots Worthy (W79). Combinations of decoration types on pottery.

Decoration Type	Combined with Decoration Type
1	3 + 5 (3 examples)
2	7 + 8 + 9 + 10 (1 example)
3	1 + 5 (3 examples)
4	12 (1 example)
5	1 + 3 (3 examples)
6	–
7	2 + 8 + 9 + 10 (1 example)
8	2 + 7 + 9 + 10 (1 example)
9	2 + 7 + 8 + 10 (1 example)
10	2 + 7 + 8 + 9 (1 example)
11	–
12	4 and 13 (1 example of each)
13	12 (1 example)
14	–

Illustrated sherds (Figs 38–40)

Abbreviations used in the catalogue: T, Vessel Type; F, Fabric; Dect, Decoration Type(s).

Numbers 1 to 30 inclusive were found in the fills of SFB F7339.

Fig 38
1.   T1 with suspension hole, F1.3. Context 7522.
2.   T1, F1.1. Context 7497/7498.
3.   T1, F1.1. Context 7497/7498.
4.   T2, F1.6. Context 7498.
5.   T2, F1.6. Context 7516.
6.   T3, F1.1. Context 7498.
7.   T4, F1.3. Context 7544.
8.   T4, F1.3. Context 7544.
9.   T5, F1.2. Context 7511.
10. T6, F1.1. Context 7498.
11. T6, F1.4. Context 7522.
12. T8, Dect 1, 3 and 5, F1.5. Context 7497.
13. T8, Dect 1, 3 and 5, F1.6. Context 7497.

Fig 39
14. T9, F1.2. Context 7522.
15. T10, F1.2. Context 7498.
16. T11, F1.2. Context 7498.
17. T12, F2.3. Context 7517.
18. T13, F1.1. Context 7498.
19. T13, F1.2. Context 7497.
20. T14, F1.4. Context 7510.
21. T16, F2.3. Context 7517.
22. T17, F1.9. Context 7522.
23. Form uncertain, Dect 4, F1.5. Context 7517.
24. Form uncertain, Dect 2, 7, 9 and 10, F1.5. Context 7516.
25. Form uncertain, Dect 11, F2.3. SF 573, context 7544.
26. Form uncertain, Dect 11, F1.6. SF 578, context 7522.
27. Form uncertain, Dect 11, F1.6. SF 566, context 7522.

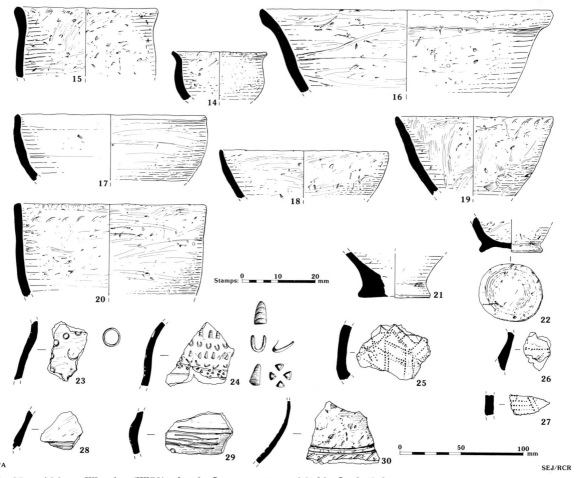

Fig 39.   Abbots Worthy (W79). Anglo-Saxon pottery, 14–30. Scale 1:3.

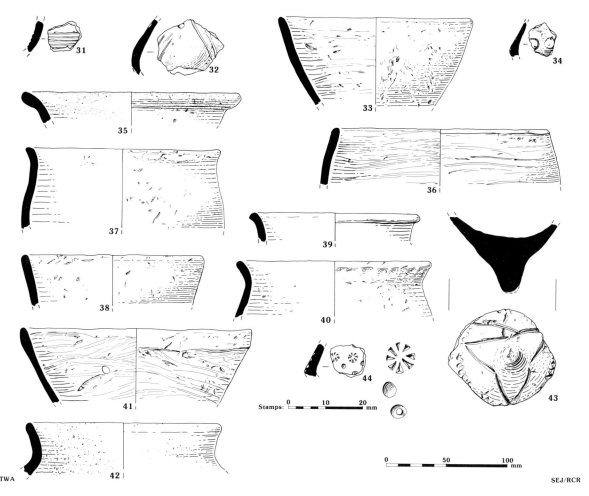

Fig 40.   Abbots Worthy (W79). Anglo-Saxon pottery, 31–44. Scale 1:3.

28. Form uncertain, Dect 12, F1.3. SF 564, context 7514.
29. Form uncertain, Dect 12, F1.4. SF 572, context 7544.
30. Form uncertain, Dect 12 or 13, F1.1. SF 567, context 7493.

Fig 40
31. Form uncertain, Dect 12, F1.2. SFB F7445, context 7446.
32. Form uncertain, Dect 12, F1.5. SFB F7337, context 7338.
33. T13, F1.1. SFB F7337, context 7338.
34. Form uncertain, Dect 6, F1.2. SF 571, SFB F7698, context 7699.
35. T1 variant, F4.1. Pit F7345, context 7347.
36. T14, F1.2. Pit 7345, context 7372.
37. T10, F1.2. Pit 7404, context 7344.
38. T13, F1.4. SFB F7403, context 7348.
39. T5, F1.4. Post-hole F7479, context 7480.
40. T5, F1.2. Drainage ditch F7319, context 7320.
41. T13, F1.1. Drainage ditch F7319, context 7320.
42. T5, F3.1. Ditch F7353, context 7831.
43. T18, Dect 14, F5.5. Ditch 7525, context 7526.
44. Form uncertain, Dect 1, 3 and 5, F1.6. Unstratified.

Discussion

Several of the forms only occur in one fabric type (Table 11), and most are in Group 1, organic fabrics, which is merely a reflection of the dominance of the fabric group in the assemblage as a whole. Jar forms (1–7) seem to be in a slightly wider range of fabrics than bowls, occurring in eight, although this again is probably only a reflection of the ratio of jars to bowls identified (Table 12).

The distribution of vessel form by feature type (Table 12) might be significant, though once more a *caveat* must be given with regard to the quantity of material in each feature and the inevitable dominance of SFB F7339. Nevertheless, the buildings on the east side of the site (SFB F7339 and SFB F7445) do appear to contain a much wider variety of forms than the other features, including the large pits. The two buildings contain all types of vessel, excluding the enigmatic amphora or lamp base, type 18. The pits, and the remaining features, only contain six types, with form 5 occurring in six out of the eight features which produced diagnostic sherds. Whether this distribution can be said to reflect a domestic function for the easterly buildings is debatable, and an alternative explanation might be that there is a chronological difference between the two areas and features. Such a chronological distinction is not, however, borne out by the distribution of fabrics (above). But to add weight to it, the decorated material, which is almost all from SFB F7339, seems to date to the 6th century, whereas the pits on the west have produced later metalwork and worked bone (Davies and Riddler this volume). The occurrence of a single sherd of calcite-gritted fabric in SFB

Table 11. Abbots Worthy (W79). Correlation of vessel form and fabric.
(* occurrence, – no occurrence)

Form	Probable Jars							Probable Bowls							Bases/Misc			
	1	2	3	4	5	6	7	8	9	10	11	12	13	14	15	16	17	18
Fabric																		
Group 1: Organic Inclusion																		
1.1	★	–	★	–	★	–	–	–	–	–	–	–	★	–	★	–	–	–
1.2	★	–	–	–	★	–	–	–	★	★	★	–	★	★	–	–	–	–
1.3	★	★	–	★	–	–	–	–	–	–	–	–	–	–	–	–	–	–
1.4	–	–	–	–	★	★	–	–	–	–	–	–	★	★	–	–	–	–
1.5	★	–	–	–	–	–	★	★	–	–	–	–	–	–	–	–	–	–
1.6	–	★	–	–	–	–	–	–	–	–	–	–	–	–	–	–	–	–
1.7	–	–	–	–	–	–	–	–	–	–	–	–	–	–	–	–	–	–
1.8	–	–	–	–	–	–	–	–	–	–	–	–	–	–	–	–	–	–
1.9	–	–	–	–	–	–	–	–	–	–	–	–	–	–	–	–	★	–
Group 2: Sandy																		
2.1	–	–	–	–	–	–	–	–	–	–	–	–	–	–	–	–	–	
2.2	–	–	–	–	–	–	–	–	–	–	–	–	–	–	–	–	–	–
2.3	–	–	–	–	–	–	–	–	–	–	★	–	–	–	–	★	–	–
2.4	–	–	–	–	–	–	–	–	–	–	–	–	–	–	–	–	–	–
2.5	–	–	–	–	–	–	–	–	–	–	–	–	–	–	–	–	–	–
2.6	–	–	–	–	–	–	–	–	–	–	–	–	–	–	–	–	–	–
Group 3: Flint																		
3.1	–	–	–	–	★	–	–	–	–	–	–	–	–	–	–	–	–	–
Group 4: Limestone or Chalk																		
4.1	–	–	–	–	★	–	–	–	–	–	–	–	–	–	–	–	–	–
4.2	–	–	–	–	–	–	–	–	–	–	–	–	–	–	–	–	–	–
4.3	–	–	–	–	–	–	–	–	–	–	–	–	–	–	–	–	–	–
Group 5: Miscellaneous																		
5.1	–	–	–	–	–	–	–	–	–	–	–	–	–	–	–	–	–
5.2	–	–	–	–	–	–	–	–	–	–	–	–	–	–	–	–	–
5.3	–	–	–	–	–	–	–	–	–	–	–	–	–	–	–	–	–
5.4	–	–	–	–	–	–	–	–	–	–	–	–	–	–	–	–	–
5.5	–	–	–	–	–	–	–	–	–	–	–	–	–	–	–	★	–	–

F7339, which has been postulated elsewhere to be of Middle Saxon date (Newing 1987), does not necessarily preclude an early date for the feature at Abbots Worthy.

The Environmental Evidence

The Animal Bones, by J P Coy

The bones described here were given an urgent first appraisal by Mrs Jennifer Bourdillon in 1985 (Bourdillon nd) in which it was recommended that the material should be recorded in detail. A more detailed contextual analysis was possible after full stratigraphic details and the results of sieving were available (Coy nd 1). This account is based on these two earlier ones. The methods used were the normal ones of the Faunal Remains Unit based on the Ancient Monuments Laboratory's computer coding system.

The bones were recorded by layer and studied according to the features in which they were found. Detailed results for all sunken-feature buildings (SFBs) and the six most productive pits are tabled in the archive according to species and anatomical element. There is also a record of all measurements in archive and a bone by bone record which includes butchery and taphonomic data.

The data archive is housed at the Faunal Remains Unit and at the Trust for Wessex Archaeology. The bones are stored in the Hampshire County Museum, Chilcomb House, Winchester.

Results

Table 14 shows the overall animal bone finds. A full list of species abbreviations used both in the text

Table 12. Abbots Worthy (W79). Occurrence of vessel form by feature type.

| Form | Probable Jars | | | | | | | | Probable Bowls | | | | | | Bases/Misc | | | | |
	1	2	3	4	5	6	7	8	9	10	11	12	13	14	15	16	17	18	?
SFB																			
F7339	5	2	5	3	10	3	2	2	1	1	2	5	6	3	4	1	1	–	–
F7445	1	–	–	–	1	2	1	–	–	–	–	–	2	–	–	–	–	–	1
F7337	–	–	–	–	–	–	–	–	–	–	–	–	1	–	–	–	–	1	–
F7698	–	–	–	–	–	–	–	–	–	–	–	–	–	–	–	–	–	–	1
PIT																			
F7345	3	–	–	–	1	–	–	–	–	–	–	–	–	1	–	–	–	–	–
F7404	–	–	–	–	1	–	–	–	–	1	–	–	1	–	–	–	–	–	–
F7483	–	–	–	–	1	–	–	–	–	–	–	–	–	–	–	–	–	–	–
OTHER																			
F7353	–	–	–	–	1	–	–	–	–	–	–	–	–	–	–	–	–	–	–
F7319	–	–	–	–	1	–	–	–	–	–	–	–	1	–	–	–	–	–	–
F7858	–	–	–	–	–	–	–	–	–	1	–	–	–	–	–	–	–	–	–
F7479	–	–	–	–	1	–	–	–	–	–	–	–	–	–	–	–	–	–	–
F7525	–	–	–	–	–	–	–	–	–	–	–	–	–	–	–	–	–	–	1
TOTALS	9	2	5	3	17	5	3	2	1	3	2	5	11	4	4	1	1	1	3

82
(17 Roman)

and in archive is given in Table 13. Tables 15 and 16 give the collated values for all five SFBs and for all pit results, respectively.

Domestic ungulates – relative importance

Most of the bones are either specific to domestic cattle and sheep or small fragments probably derived from them (LAR and SAR categories), with a much lower proportion of pig. Ovicaprid remains were recorded as 'sheep or goat' except where distinctive specific anatomical criteria were present. Bourdillon recognised probable goat fragments but the bones on the site are overwhelmingly sheep and the code for sheep has therefore been used in all the tables in this report to include all the ovicaprids. The results for the whole site in Table 14 give roughly equal quantities between large and small ungulate remains. Table 17 gives the specific percentages for the whole site, the two major types of feature and the eight individual features with the largest samples. It finally shows the percentage of ungulate fragments which could be identified to the cattle, ovicaprid, and pig categories rather than left as 'large or small ungulate'. A sample size of 100 ungulate fragments was taken as the arbitrary lower limit.

There are minor differences observable in the distribution of the species and in fragmentation, but these are difficult to pin down and variations in sample size may account for some of them. There seems to be more cattle in SFB deposits and more sheep and pig in pits (Tables 15, 16 and 17). There is a slightly higher level of identifiability in pit than in SFB material. A more detailed analysis of fragment size and the products of individual layers might show the extent to which this is a depositional phenomenon. Perhaps material arising from the hut depress-

Table 13. Abbots Worthy (W79). Abbreviations used in animal bone Tables 14–18.

HOR	domestic horse
COW	domestic cattle
SHE	domestic sheep or identified to 'ovicaprid'
PIG	domestic pig
LAR	large ungulate
SAR	small ungulate
RED	*Cervus elaphus*, red deer
RAB	*Oryctolagus cuniculus*, rabbit
DOG	domestic dog
CAT	domestic cat
SMM	small mammal
MAM	unidentified mammal fragment (probably mostly LAR/SAR)
FOW	domestic fowl
GOO	domestic goose
BIR	unidentified bird fragment (probably mostly FOW)
AMP	amphibian
FIS	unidentified fish fragment
HC	horn core
LB	long bone
SCA	scapula
HUM	humerus
RAD	radius
TIB	tibia
MC	metacarpus
MT	metatarsus

Table 14. Abbots Worthy (W79). Distribution of animal bone fragments.

	hor	cow	she	pig	lar	sar	red	rab	dog	cat	smm	mam	fow	goo	bir	amp	fis	TOTAL
antler/hc	–	3	7	–	–	–	19	–	–	–	–	–	–	–	–	–	–	26
skull	–	60	34	12	35	4	–	–	–	–	–	1	2	–	–	–	1	149
hyoid	–	6	1	–	–	–	–	–	–	–	–	–	–	–	–	–	–	7
maxilla	3	7	2	4	–	–	–	–	–	–	–	–	–	–	–	–	–	16
mandible	–	60	65	12	3	–	–	–	–	–	2	–	–	–	–	–	–	142
vertebra	1	47	19	5	26	16	–	–	–	–	3	–	3	4	–	7	20	151
rib	–	49	13	2	107	250	–	–	–	–	–	–	–	3	5	–	–	429
sternum	–	–	1	–	–	–	–	–	–	–	–	–	1	3	–	–	–	5
coracoid	–	–	–	–	–	–	–	–	–	–	–	–	3	1	1	–	–	5
scapula	1	32	17	10	11	3	–	1	–	–	–	–	4	1	–	4	–	84
humerus	1	17	21	6	6	2	–	–	–	1	1	–	6	3	–	9	–	73
radius	–	15	30	5	2	3	–	–	1	3	–	–	8	–	–	–	–	67
ulna	1	13	9	4	–	–	–	–	–	–	–	–	7	–	–	–	–	34
pelvis	–	20	9	1	5	2	–	–	–	1	1	–	1	–	–	11	–	51
femur	–	16	8	2	3	13	–	–	–	–	2	–	5	–	–	11	–	60
patella	–	–	–	–	–	–	–	–	–	–	–	–	–	–	–	–	–	1
tibia	2	28	54	5	7	2	–	–	–	1	–	–	10	1	–	11	–	121
fibula	–	–	–	8	–	–	–	–	–	1	–	–	1	1	–	–	–	11
carpal/tarsal	1	24	3	–	–	–	–	–	–	–	1	–	4	–	–	–	–	33
metapodial	–	47	59	9	–	–	–	–	–	–	–	–	15	–	–	–	–	130
phalanx	1	17	9	3	–	–	–	–	1	–	1	–	–	–	–	–	–	32
loose teeth	8	43	82	20	–	–	–	–	–	–	8	–	–	–	–	–	–	161
l.b. fragment	–	–	–	–	360	429	–	–	–	–	–	–	–	–	3	46	–	838
fragment	–	–	–	–	128	43	–	–	–	–	–	231	–	–	–	–	–	402
TOTALS	19	502	443	108	693	767	19	1	2	7	19	232	70	17	9	99	21	3028

Table 15. Abbots Worthy (W79). Distribution of animal bone fragments in sunken-featured buildings.

	hor	cow	she	pig	lar	sar	red	dog	cat	smm	mam	fow	goo	bir	amp	TOTAL
antler/hc	–	1	4	–	–	–	16	–	–	–	–	–	–	–	–	21
skull	–	42	20	2	14	3	–	–	–	–	–	1	–	–	–	82
hyoid	–	3	1	–	–	–	–	–	–	–	–	–	–	–	–	4
maxilla	–	7	–	1	–	–	–	–	–	–	–	–	–	–	–	8
mandible	–	41	30	4	–	–	–	–	–	2	–	–	–	–	–	77
vertebra	–	23	10	1	13	10	–	–	–	1	–	2	–	–	1	61
rib	–	36	7	–	81	170	–	–	–	–	–	–	–	–	–	294
sternum	–	–	–	–	–	–	–	–	–	–	–	1	2	–	–	3
scapula	–	18	14	4	5	2	–	–	–	–	–	4	–	–	–	47
humerus	1	3	6	1	2	1	–	–	–	1	–	3	1	–	1	20
radius	–	8	17	3	2	2	–	1	1	–	–	8	–	–	–	42
ulna	1	8	1	1	–	–	–	–	–	–	–	1	–	–	–	12
pelvis	–	10	4	–	1	–	–	–	–	–	–	1	–	–	1	17
femur	–	7	1	1	1	10	–	–	–	2	–	5	–	–	–	27
tibia	1	11	25	2	2	2	–	–	–	–	–	9	–	–	–	52
fibula	–	–	–	5	–	–	–	–	1	–	–	–	–	–	–	6
carpal/tarsal	–	10	–	–	–	–	–	–	–	–	–	4	–	–	–	14
metapodial	–	19	28	7	–	–	–	–	–	–	–	7	–	–	–	61
phalanx	–	8	2	2	–	–	–	–	–	–	–	–	–	–	–	12
loose teeth	–	23	26	2	–	–	–	–	–	–	–	–	–	–	–	51
l.b. fragment	–	–	–	–	169	251	–	–	–	–	–	–	–	1	–	421
fragment	–	–	–	–	78	40	–	–	–	–	230	–	–	–	–	348
TOTALS	3	278	196	36	368	491	16	1	2	6	230	46	3	1	3	1680

Table 16. Abbots Worthy (W79). Distribution of animal bone fragments in all pits.

	hor	cow	she	pig	lar	sar	red	rab	dog	cat	smm	mam	fow	goo	bir	amp	fis	TOTAL
antler/hc	–	2	3	–	–	–	1	–	–	–	–	–	–	–	–	–	–	6
skull	–	8	14	10	20	1	–	–	–	–	–	1	–	–	–	–	1	55
hyoid	–	2	–	–	–	–	–	–	–	–	–	–	–	–	–	–	–	2
maxilla	3	–	2	3	–	–	–	–	–	–	–	–	–	–	–	–	–	8
mandible	–	17	34	8	3	–	–	–	–	–	–	–	–	–	–	–	–	62
vertebra	1	22	9	4	13	6	–	–	–	–	2	–	1	4	–	6	20	88
rib	–	12	6	2	23	72	–	–	–	–	–	–	–	3	4	–	–	122
sternum	–	–	1	–	–	–	–	–	–	–	–	–	–	1	–	–	–	2
coracoid	–	–	–	–	–	–	–	–	–	–	–	–	3	1	1	–	–	5
scapula	1	14	3	5	6	1	–	1	–	–	–	–	–	1	–	4	–	36
humerus	–	14	14	5	4	1	–	–	–	1	–	–	2	2	–	8	–	51
radius	–	7	13	2	–	1	–	–	–	2	–	–	–	–	–	–	–	25
ulna	–	5	7	2	–	–	–	–	–	–	–	–	5	–	–	–	–	19
pelvis	–	10	5	1	4	2	–	–	–	1	1	–	–	–	–	10	–	34
femur	–	9	7	1	2	3	–	–	–	–	–	–	–	–	–	11	–	33
patella	–	1	–	–	–	–	–	–	–	–	–	–	–	–	–	–	–	1
tibia	1	17	29	3	4	–	–	–	–	1	–	–	1	1	–	11	–	68
fibula	–	–	–	2	–	–	–	–	–	–	–	–	1	1	–	–	–	4
carpal/tarsal	1	13	3	–	–	–	–	–	–	–	1	–	–	–	–	–	–	18
metapodial	–	27	31	2	–	–	–	–	–	–	–	–	7	–	–	–	–	67
phalanx	1	9	7	1	–	–	–	–	1	–	1	–	–	–	–	–	–	20
loose teeth	8	18	55	17	–	–	–	–	–	–	8	–	–	–	–	–	–	106
l.b. fragment	–	–	–	–	186	173	–	–	–	–	–	–	–	–	2	46	–	407
fragment	–	–	–	–	48	2	–	–	–	–	–	1	–	–	–	–	–	51
TOTALS	16	207	243	68	313	262	1	1	1	5	13	2	20	14	7	96	21	1290

Table 17. Abbots Worthy (W79). Specific percentages for common ungulates.

	identified to species				grouped only			% id
	Cattle	sheep	pig	n	LAR	SAR	n	to species
All	48	42	10	1053	47	53	1460	42
SFBs	55	38	7	510	43	57	859	37
Pits	40	47	13	518	54	46	575	47
SFB F7339	57	38	5	387	39	61	602	39
SFB F7445	60	34	6	70	58	42	183	28
F7341	41	56	3	78	48	52	66	54
F7345	42	44	14	57	54	46	52	52
F7483	45	33	22	89	71	29	123	42
F7623	31	54	15	71	59	41	96	43
F7627	38	42	20	60	57	43	65	48
F7809	27	68	5	60	49	51	83	42

ions was either more heavily exploited, or at least some of it resulted from trampled material from nearby which came to rest in the depressions after they had ceased to be used. There is a high incidence of splinters as opposed to cylinders in the fragmentary animal bones, which suggests a degree of trampling.

The SFB results, with their suggestion of greater fragmentation of small ungulate material, are largely a reflection of the results from F7339, which had the largest bone sample of any feature on the site. But this feature alone cannot account for the suggestion of higher cattle results for SFBs, as the sample from F7445 has high results for cattle too and does not present a lot of small ungulate fragments. The results for individual features are discussed in more detail in the contextual section.

The overall low value for pig is comparable with values for nearby downland in Roman times and there is no doubt that these well-drained lands provided good grazing for cattle and sheep (Maltby 1985a). But it is difficult to pitch the proportion that pig would have represented the diet at Abbots Worthy, as pits provide a different story from SFB deposits. Pig bones show different patterns of fragmentation from those of cattle and sheep (Coy 1987) and a number of factors which influence pig percentages obtained from bones have been discussed elsewhere (Coy 1985). One of these, referred to as the 'King Index' after the work on Roman pigs by King (1978), is low at this site, that is, it has a high representation of long bones, showing that the pig results here are not unnaturally biassed downwards by preservation only of jaws.

There were only 19 bones of horse for the whole site and 16 of these came from pits. They are detailed in the contextual section.

Domestic ungulates – size

The individual measurements are in archive. Few cattle bones were measurable, but four metapodials gave withers height estimates of 1.18m (from the metacarpus) and 1.14, 1.17 and 1.35m (from metatarsi). The first three are around the mean for Middle Saxon *Hamwic*, and the fourth slightly above the current *Hamwic* maximum (Bourdillon in prep). The length of this metatarsus is high for a Saxon context, but individual breadth measurements are generally below the *Hamwic* means and those from Ramsbury (Coy 1980).

Sheep bone breadths are in every case below the *Hamwic* and Ramsbury means. There are no wither height estimates. A comparison of several sheep measurements (or in the case of tibia, sheep/goat measurements) in Table 18 suggests that the large sample size is not necessarily the only reason for the higher maxima at *Hamwic*, as reasonable sample sizes from Winchester Northern Suburb sites for the later Roman period also do not reach such high maxima as *Hamwic* (Maltby nd 3). The sample from Abbots Worthy is too small to make a great deal of these comparisons, but it suggests that sheep there were on the small side compared with those represented at *Hamwic* and yet not necessarily in line with the very small Iron Age sheep at nearby Winnall Down (Maltby 1985a). The recent figures obtained from later Roman deposits in the Winchester

Northern Suburb sites are a better match (Maltby nd 3), but such comparisons can only be tentative at this stage.

The limited amount of horse material matched large pony size, although no withers heights could be estimated.

Domestic ungulates – age

The cattle with toothwear evidence were either young with molars not fully erupted or quite old animals with well worn third molars. The prime meat group is largely absent. Although sheep ages are more varied, the jaws of young adults are again few. Loose teeth recorded basically confirm this pattern. Pig remains are few and ageing data scarce, but what there is represents immature animals.

Other domestic species

Other domestic animals represented are the dog, cat, fowl and goose. Dog produced only two fragments, from SFB F7337 and Pit F7345. Cat bones were from several widespread locations and could all be domestic, although one cat bone, a fibula in SFB F7339, could equally well have come from a wild individual. Some of the cat remains were immature. Fowl bones are from all areas of the settlement but not distributed in any particular pattern. All SFB deposits contained some fowl bones but even some of the quite rich pits did not. The fowl bones that can be sexed were all from hens but no trace of medullary bone was found in any of the femora suggesting that no laying hens had been eaten. There was no evidence of caponisation. Young fowl were also present.

Pit F7623 contained a high proportion of fowl and goose bones. Domestic goose was represented by a total of only 17 bones, and 13 of them came from this pit.

Wild species

There is, as usual on Saxon settlements in Hampshire, very little evidence of the exploitation of wild

Table 18. Abbots Worthy (W79). *Comparison of measurements of sheep bones from Abbots Worthy, Hamwic and Winnall Down.*

| | | AW Saxon | | | Early Hamwic | | | Winnall – MIA | | |
	meas	n	range	mean	n	range	mean	n	range	mean
SCA	GLP	3	24.2,28.9,31.4	–	20	28.9 – 33.7	31.6	3	25.5,26.6,30.2	–
SCA	LG	3	20,24,24.8	–	19	22.4 – 26.3	23.8	4	20.2 – 24.3	21.8
HUM	Bd	7	27.0 – 30.7	28.7	21	27.4 – 31.2	29.5	7	24.7 – 27.6	24.7
	BT	5	23.3 – 26.6	24.7	9	25.5 – 29.2	28.0	9	23.4 – 26.7	24.8
RAD	Bp	2	28.5, 29.5	–	13	26.8 – 33.8	29.7	7	23.2 – 27.7	25.5
MC	Bp	5	19.6 – 22.0	20.5	8	20.3 – 23.6	22.6	13	18.1 – 21.2	19.5
TIB	Bd	2	23.8, 24.4	–	21	23.7 – 29.0	25.9	14	21.1 – 23.7	22.3
MT	Bp	3	17.7,18.5,19.8	–	8	16.6 – 21.8	19.6	13	16.2 – 18.8	17.5

KEY : n = number of bones in sample
Measurements are those taken by Von den Driesch 1976.

species. The picture from Ramsbury, Wiltshire, was a little different (Coy 1980). Red deer antler was utilised at Abbots Worthy for working. Bones of *Microtus agrestis*, the short-tailed vole, were widespread on the site and have turned up wherever sieving has taken place. This is a common small mammal of grassland and would have been likely to fall into sunken features. It does not have a great leaping ability. The single bone of *Oryctolagus cuniculus*, the rabbit, in Pit F7341 is probably a later contaminant as this species does not normally seem to have been present in the Saxon period. The remains marked as unidentified mammals are virtually all from the sieving of features and are mostly small crumbs of bone from the ungulates.

Apart from a sparrow-sized immature passerine coracoid bone from Pit F7345, all the unidentified bird remains could be fragments of domestic birds. Amphibian remains were found wherever sieving took place and represent both frog, probably the common brown frog, *Rana temporaria*, and toad, probably the common toad, *Bufo bufo*. The frog, toad, and short-tailed vole remains were in some cases obviously from partial skeletons.

Fish bones represented in the material from wet-sieving of bulk samples are from the ubiquitous common eel, *Anguilla anguilla*, which could easily have been caught in or near the River Itchen nearby and was commonly eaten on Saxon settlements in Wessex. A more extensive sieving programme might have shown up evidence of freshwater cyprinid fish as it did at *Hamwic* (Bourdillon and Coy 1980; Coy in prep) and Wraysbury (Coy 1984b).

Although four of the bulk samples examined were from the large SFB feature F7339, only three separate toad bones were produced. SFB F7445 produced, in addition, a partial skeleton of short-tailed vole from layer 7487. No fish remains came from SFB material.

Contextual account

The layers involved in each feature discussed are given in the archive. The overall SFB and pit results are in Tables 15 and 16. Detailed results of the eleven major features discussed below are in archive tables. These features are discussed in number order below. Some preliminary analysis of the distribution of species detected no apparent pattern compared with the position of the feature in the settlement.

In addition, there were no traces of specialised treatment or disposal of ungulate carcasses or bones; occupational, butchery and bone-working evidence was widely dispersed. This is fairly typical of Middle Saxon occupation in Hampshire.

Sunken-feature buildings (SFBs)

Only twelve fragments were retrieved from SFB F7337 and these merely show the presence of cattle, sheep, dog and domestic fowl. Half the fragments are long bone splinters.

SFB F7339 provides a useful sample from this type of structure, but only a preliminary attempt has been made to sort out the different layers. The layers with most bone were 7417, 7497, 7498, 7512, 7522 and 7544. Most of the bones identified to species are from cattle, sheep and pig, with cattle forming the major species and pig representing only 5% (Tables 15 and 17). There were three horse bones in layer 7498 which, judging by the butchery details discussed below, represent food remains. Large and small ungulate unidentifiable fragments were heavily weighted towards the small ungulates. Cat, fowl and goose are also represented and there is a little amphibian bone from the wet-sieving of bulk samples.

Indicators of occupation, such as butchery and burning, were present throughout the layers. The butchery is widespread and on all the domestic species and all anatomical areas, showing that all parts of the body were utilised. A number of skulls and long bones have been split open and there is evidence for the utilisation of horns of cattle and sheep.

The types of butchery are quite varied, with knife cuts being used, occasionally for disjointing – as with the horse humerus in layer 7498. Both the eating of horse and this type of butchery are more usually seen in the Iron Age than the Saxon period. There is also evidence for a great deal of chopping with a heavier implement that seems to leave no marks of its blade. This often goes right through even the largest bones and includes longitudinal splitting of some metapodials. This type of butchery is quite common at Middle Saxon *Hamwic*. Occasionally there are cut surfaces with blademarks of what seems to have been a very sharp knife. There are such examples in SFB F7339 – in layers 7498 (cattle zygomatic), 7511 (cattle rib) and 7514 (cattle pelvis and sheep scapula). This is referred to by Bourdillon in her report as 'clean' or 'neat' cuts and it is possible that what she refers to as sawing might be a similar knife butchery.

There are two examples of paramedian butchery, with blademarks on vertebrae, both in layer 7522 (cattle lumbar vertebra and sheep thoracic vertebra). This method of halving the carcase is described in detail for Late Saxon deposits at Winchester (Coy nd 3) and is overtaken in the Medieval period by accurate halving down the centre of the neural canal. In SFB F7339 there are two possible occurrences of such medial splitting in a cattle atlas in layer 7512 and a later cervical vertebra in layer 7511.

A high proportion of the bones here are either dog-chewed (23%), ivoried (24%), or both. Some of the chewing has destroyed the surface or occasionally even the identity of the bones. In some ways, the association of these two conditions is strange, as the dog-chewing suggests the bones had been lying around the settlement, whereas the 'ivoried' condition is usually considered to be the result of swift burial. But Sarah Colley's discussions on Saxon rubbish disposal may be relevant here (Colley in prep), and it is suggested that the rubbish may have been lying around, giving access to dogs, for only a short time and was then tipped into relative inaccessibility. Only 17 bones, less than 2%, showed evidence of burning. Presumably this type of disposal took place after the SFB phase of this structure. More evidence could be gained by comparing the bones in detail with some of those from the sunken features at West Stow where an attempt was made to distinguish deposition which occurred during and after occupation of the buildings (P Crabtree pers comm).

There were several examples of bone working in this feature, especially shavings from the working of red deer antler.

In addition to several cases of crowding of cheek teeth in sheep/goat jaws, and periodontal disease in one old animal, there are two interesting occurrences of deformity of the lower jaw condyle (both from left jaws) in this feature, one in layer 7522, the other in layer 7498. There is also a sheep horn core with very marked thumbprint-like depressions often thought to represent an uneven nutritional history (Bourdillon and Coy 1980, 92; Bourdillon 1983, 146). There was a regular scattering of the remains of calf and immature cattle, of lamb, and of immature domestic fowl throughout this feature. Most pig remains were from skeletally immature animals, as would be expected. For most species where bones could be sexed both sexes were represented, but all fowl tarso-metatarsi represented hens.

SFB F7403 produced only 24 fragments from one layer, all from the common domestic ungulates. On the other hand, SFB F7445 ranked second amongst such features for bone production, with 493 fragments, although only 253 of these fragments were from ungulates; the total is swelled by the inclusion of 230 unidentifiable mammalian fragments in the bone bags, which probably came from dry sieving. The remaining bones show a similar species distribution to SFB F7339, although unidentifiable ungulate fragments are more likely to have been from cattle (Table 17). In addition there are remains of domestic fowl. Even excluding the small mammal bones and small crumbs of larger animals, this feature gives lower values than SFB F7339 for dog-chewing (13%), and ivoried fragments (13%). The value for charred bones is about the same. There is a small amount of butchery, again of various types, recorded. One cervical vertebra of cattle in layer 7488 shows paramedian butchery, and a small ungulate rib is blademarked by sharp knife butchery. Again there is evidence of immature cattle and sheep.

SFB F7698 produced only 94 fragments from one layer. These represent cattle, sheep and pig in roughly equal proportions, twice as many small ungulate as large ungulate unidentifiable fragments and a single bone of domestic fowl. The proportion of bones which show dog-chewing (22%), ivoried condition (23%) and charring (1%) compares with F7339. Both knife cuts and chopping butchery were found; there was also a worked pig fibula.

Pits

The pits generally represent deeper features than

the SFB depressions and the types of bones deposited may therefore be expected to be different. Some discussion of this has already occurred in the 'Domestic ungulate' section.

Pit F7341 produced 189 bones which included 39 of amphibians and fish from sieving, and a rabbit scapula in layer 7376 that was probably intrusive. Cattle, sheep, pig, cat and kitten are represented, but no trace of the domestic birds (Table 17). This pit, like many of the others, shows a higher number of sheep bones than cattle bones. If the fish and amphibian fragments from sieving are excluded, the pit gives values for dog-chewing similar to some SFBs (22%) but much lower values for ivoried bone (3%), and higher ones for burnt and calcined bone (8%). Blademarked butchery appears on a cattle scapula, there is a fragment of a sheep skull which had been split axially, and a split cattle metapodial. Layers 7377, 7390, and 7391 in particular, produced frog and toad remains from wet-sieving and layers 7377 and 7388 included eel remains.

Pit 7345 showed some similarities to Pit 7341 and the two were near one another, near SFB F7403. Of the 162 bones recorded, 45 are from frog, toad and eel from wet-sieving (Table 17). The other bones are from horse (a single maxillary fragment with all molars in wear), cattle, sheep, pig, dog and fowl, with a shaped piece of red deer antler tine in layer 7349. Identified fragments of cattle and sheep are in equal numbers and small and large ungulates are evenly balanced too. This is not the same as most other pits. The value for pig, like that in the previous pit, is very low indeed, lower than in the SFB deposits and nowhere near as high as the rest of the pits. The percentage of bones dog-chewed is 28%, ivoried 7%, and charred less than 2%. Very little butchery was noted on these bones.

Pit 7483, with 223 bones, provided the largest pit sample (Table 17). It was the only pit which produced more identified cattle bones than sheep bones. Unidentifiable ungulate fragments are also heavily weighted towards large ungulate (71%) with some of the cattle bones looking rather large. At 22%, pig is better represented here than anywhere else on site, although two pits discussed below come near. The seven horse fragments are all teeth or jaw fragments except for one piece of scapula. One of the teeth represents an animal of about 9 years. Cat and fowl are also represented. Of the 223 bones, 27% are canid chewed, 5% ivoried, and only one charred. Blademark butchery is present on a cattle pelvis fragment in layer 7507, which also produced a longitudinally split metapodial. In addition, there are a few occurrences of both knife cut and chopping butchery. There is a large ungulate bone splinter with possible wear through use.

Pit 7623, very close to Pit 7483, produced the second largest ungulate sample for a pit, with identified sheep outnumbering cattle, as is more usual in the pits here. The large cattle metatarsus mentioned in the ungulate section came from here. Pig results, as for the last pit and the next one, are unusually high at 15% of identifiable ungulates (Table 17), but large ungulate unidentifiable fragments exceed small ungulate. With such small samples and such a wide variety of anatomical elements represented, these shifts are highly likely. Fowl and goose are well-represented in this pit.

Pit 7627 was an isolated feature which produced 129 fragments (Table 17). Cattle and sheep are equally represented, but the value for pig, at 20%, is the second highest for the site. Canid chewing is on 28% of bones, only one fragment is ivoried, and none charred. There is a blademark cut on a cattle femur and a small ungulate rib.

The only other pit which produced any quantity of bone was another isolated one, F7809, which produced the lowest value for cattle and the highest for sheep of any of the eleven features discussed here (Table 17). This is interesting to look at in more detail as it has some preservational similarities to SFB deposits, with a high value for ivoried bone (16%). Canid gnawing occurs on 23% and there is no charred bone. There is also a high proportion of immature sheep and lamb bones compared with other pits and at least one individual was a newborn or foetal animal. One fragment shows blademark butchery and a sheep metapodial is longitudinally split.

Pit 7680 only produced 49 bones but included four bones of horse; two teeth have very heavy wear suggesting a senile horse. Cattle, as in F7483, seemed a little larger than elsewhere.

Pit 7404 with 39 fragments is of interest as it contained a butchered cervical vertebra of horse and evidence of a 16–18 year old horse in the same layer, 7398.

Other features

A handful of bone fragments came from ditch, gulley and post-hole features and none of these collections is worthy of comment.

Conclusions

In terms of fragment numbers, cattle and sheep are the most commonly represented species but their proportions vary according to fragmentation and deposition, as Table 17 shows. The cattle were of a good size and would have provided most of the meat. There is some suggestion, though, that they were not generally quite as stocky as those found in Middle Saxon *Hamwic*, although one individual was as tall as the *Hamwic* maximum.

Sheep (there is no definite evidence for goat) bone breadths are consistently smaller than the *Hamwic* means and may be more consistent with other rural Saxon material from Hampshire studied by Bourdillon (1983; nd) and with Late Roman material from Winchester (Maltby nd 3).

It is too early to provide a detailed survey of animal size changes in Hampshire from Iron Age to Saxon, especially as most large samples for both Roman and Saxon periods have come from towns. More samples from Roman villa and other rural sites will need to be studied before we can know whether the good sizes of the animals of the Roman period 'dipped' prior to the sizes shown at *Hamwic* and whether urban/rural factors complicate the issue.

Like the measurements, the butchery from Abbots Worthy produces a mosaic of results. Some results, such as the evidence for eating of horse and the small knife cuts on some bones, are similar to Iron Age butchery. The incidence of smooth, blade-marked butchery, and a trace of paramedian splitting, is not typical of Middle Saxon *Hamwic*, but has been seen at Late Saxon Winchester.

Should time permit further study, there are a number of archaeological questions relating to site formation processes which it would be interesting to address using this sample, for example, those discussed below.

The deposit from the deepest SFB, F7339, may be a good representation of what was happening in terms of waste disposal during one period of occupation of this site. The type of deposition compares closely with what occurs in a *Hamwic* pit and this deposit might repay further study. There is slight evidence from Abbots Worthy, however, that deposition into SFBs, if these were used for disposal of rubbish, differed slightly from that in the pits. Despite its much smaller size and bone sample, SFB F7445 shows this as well as SFB F7339 (Table 17). The amount of ivoried bone in pits was much lower, showing that bone in them may not have been excluded from the action of the atmosphere so rapidly as those deposited in the SFBs F7339 and F7698, and yet the identifiability of SFB bones is low (37%) compared with that in pits (47%). There are many factors which might influence this, not least the percentage of loose teeth involved and the incidence of splinters, which could be quantified from the archive. The figures do suggest that the material deposited in the SFB deposits has been more heavily utilised, and further analysis of the factors would be interesting.

On the whole, the bones were well preserved and very few bones were recorded as eroded in the computer archive. In future work, erosion rates could, however, be calculated from this archive, where three levels of erosion have been recorded. Another aspect which might shed light on the formation processes involved in the different types of feature, and the depositional picture on the different areas of the settlement, is the density of bone deposition (number of fragments per cubic metre of soil) as calculated for some Iron Age settlements (*eg* Maltby 1985a). Some pits seem slightly different from others, for example F7483 and F7680 are suggested as containing larger cattle material. This might suggest that they are from a different phase of occupation.

The Plant Remains, by Wendy Carruthers

Samples were received by the author as unsorted flots. These had been obtained by manually floating

8–10 litres of soil and pouring off the flot through a 250μ meshed sieve.

Some of the flots were found to contain mineralised plant remains. These remains possessed the semi-translucent amber colouring typical of calcium phosphate replaced material. As the majority of mineralised remains are too dense to be recovered by flotation it was considered neccessary to process a selection of the remaining unsieved samples specifically for the recovery of this material. Where samples were available, 1 litre of soil was sieved down to 600μ in a stack of sieves, with the flot first

being poured off through a 250μ mesh sieve. The residues and flots were slowly air-dried before being sorted under a binocular microscope.

Results

The carbonised, mineralised and silicified plant remains recovered from the flots and residues are summarised in Table 19. A total of 180 samples was examined, 26 of which contained no plant remains other than charcoal. Of the 111 contexts represented by the remaining samples, a third contained min-

Table 19. Abbots Worthy (W79). The plant remains: taxa by feature type.
Abbreviations at end of Table.

TAXA	HABITAT	sunken-featured huts	large pits	?cess pits	other pits	post/stake-holes	ditches
GRAMINEAE							
Triticum aestivocompactum (bread/club wheat) caryopses		6	2	1	4	6	
Triticum aestivocompactum rachis frag.				1			
Triticum spelta L. (spelt) glume base			1				
Triticum spelta / dicoccum (spelt/emmer) caryopses		1	3	1	2	6	1
Hordeum vulgare L.emend. (hulled 6-row barley)		25	12	7	7	14	
Hordeum vulgare rachis frag.		4	3	1	5		
Hordeum sp. caryopses		3	2		1		
Avena fatua L (wild oat) floret base			1				
Avena sp. (oat)			10		1	1	
Avena sp. (oat) awn frag.		1	4				
Secale cereale L. (rye)			1				
Secale cereale rachis frag.					1		
Indeterminate cereals		159	90	28	52	115	2
Cereal bran			[64]	[81]			
Cereal culm nodes			19				
Cereal/grass internode frags			1470[273])146)	[>500]			
Cereal culm bases			8				
Grass culm bases			9				
Bromus sect. *Genea* (barren brome)			8[1]		1		
Bromus sect. *Bromus* (chess)			2	2			
Gen.et sp.indet. (grasses)		1[3]	41[5]	1[5]	8	1	
POLYPODIACEAE							
cf. *Pteridium aquilinum* (L.)Kuhn (bracken) frond frag.	EWa		[2]				
RANUNCULACEAE							
Ranunculus cf. *bulbosus* L. (bulbous buttercup)	Gd		10			1	
R. acris/bulbosus/repens (buttercup)	G	[3]	3	[4]			
R. sardous Crantz (hairy buttercup)	ADp		1				
Ranunculus subg. *Batrachium* (DC.) A.Gray.	P		1				
cf. *Thalictrum flavum* L. (common meadow rue)	BG		[1]				
PAPAVERACEAE							
Papaver dubium L./*hybridum* L. (long-headed poppy)	AD			[16]			
P. argemone L. (long prickly headed poppy)	ADl			[1]			
P. somniferum L. (opium poppy)				[2]			
Papaver sp. (poppy)				[17]	[2]		
FUMARIACEAE							
Fumaria sp. (fumitory)	ACD		1				
CRUCIFEREAE							
Brassica sp./*Sinapis* sp.	ACD	1[1]	4[22]	[141]	5[1]	1	
Indeterminate				[1]			
VIOLACEAE							
Viola sp. (violet)	ADG		1	[1]			
CARYOPHYLLACEAE							
Silene cf. *alba* (Mill.) E.H.L.Krause (white campion)	CDH			[17]			
S. cf. *vulgaris* (Moench) Garcke (bladder campion)	ADG		3				
Silene sp.			[1]	[12]	1		
Agrostemma githago L. (corn cockle)	A		4	[6]			
Stellaria media (L.) Vill. (chickweed)	AD	[2]	6				
S. graminea L. (lesser stitchwort)	EGWl		2				
Indeterminate			3				

Table 19, continued. Abbots Worthy (W79). The plant remains: taxa by feature type.

TAXA	HABITAT	sunken-featured huts	large pits	?cess pits	other pits	post/stake-holes	ditches
CHENOPODIACEAE							
Chenopodium album L. (fat hen)	CDn	8	15	1	1		
C. rubrum L. (red goosefoot)	CDn		2				
Atriplex hastata L./*patula* L. (orache)	CD		108				
Chenopodium sp./*Atriplex* sp.		[5]	7[1]	[9]	3	7[2]	
MALVACEAE							
Malva sylvestris L. (common mallow)	DR	[1]					
LINACEAE							
Linum usitatissimum L. (cultivated flax)		[2]					
L. catharticum L. (purging flax)	GEc	[8]					
LEGUMINOSAE							
Medicago lupulina L. (black medick)	GR		3				
Medicago sp./*Trifolium* sp.	G		1				
Trifolium sp. (clover)	G	1	1	2			
Vicia cf. *sepium* L. (bush vetch)	GHS		1				
V. cf.*sativa* L. (common vetch)	G	1	1				
V. faba var.*minor* (horse bean)			14				
Vicia sp./*Lathyrus* sp./*Pisum sativum*		6	9	4	21	2	
Pisum sativum L. (pea)					1		
Pisum sativum hilums				[55]			
Pisum sativum testa fragments				[101]			
Indeterminate hilum frag.			[3]				
ROSACEAE							
Filipendula ulmaria (L.)Maxim. (meadow-sweet)	BpGMW		5				
Rubus fruticosus agg. (blackberry)	ADW	1	[2]	[19]			
Potentilla sp. (cinquefoil)	DG		9				
Aphanes arvensis agg. (parsley piert)	AGdo		1				
Prunus spinosa L. (sloe)	HSW	1					
cf.*Prunus* sp.			[1]				
Malus sylvestris Mill. (apple)	HSW		[10]	[9]			
Malus sylvestris/*Pyrus communis* L. (apple/pear)	HSW		[6]				
UMBELLIFERAE							
Torilis japonica(Houtt.) DC. (upright hedge-parsley)	GH		1				
cf.*Torilis* sp.				[4]	[2]		
Conium maculatum L. (hemlock)	BpDW		1	[1]			
Apium graveolens L. (celery)	Bd			[1]			
A. nodiflorum (L.)Lag. (fool's watercress)	P		1				
cf.*Aethusa cynapium* L. (fool's parsley)	C			[1]			
Daucus carota L. (wild carrot)	cG	[5]	[3]	[2]			
Indeterminate		[1]		[2]			
POLYGONACEAE							
Polygonum aviculare agg. (knotgrass)	AD	[1]	36		1		
Polygonum sp.		1	1				
Bilderdykia convolvulus (L.)Dumort. (black bindweed)	AD	1	13				
Rumex acetosella agg. (sheep's sorrel)	CGEa	1	1	1	1		
R. cf.*crispus* L. (curled dock)	CDG		143	4	2		2
Rumex sp.			14	[4]			
URTICACEAE							
Urtica urens L. (small nettle)	CDl	1[1]	6				
U. dioica L. (stinging nettle)	DGHWn		5	1[14]	1[2]		
CORYLACEAE							
Corylus avellana L. (hazel)	HSW	2	4	1	2	2	3
PRIMULACEAE							
Indeterminate		1	1				
BORAGINACEAE							
Lithospermum arvense L. (corn gromwell)	Ab		[8](6)	[38]	[1]		
Myosotis sp. (forget-me-not)				[2]			
SOLANACEAE							
Hyoscyamus niger L. (henbane)	Dn	3	1	2[10]			
Solanum nigrum L. (black nightshade)	D	1	2				
SCROPHULARIACEAE							
Euphrasia sp./*Odontites verna* (Bell.)Dum.	CDEG	3	29				
LABIATAE							
Mentha sp. (mint)	DMR			1	2		
Lamium sp. (dead-nettle)	CDH	[1]					
PLANTAGINACEAE							
Plantago major L. (great plantain)	CGRo	[9]	[1]				
P. lanceolata L. (ribwort plantain)	G		2				
RUBIACEAE							
Galium cf. *cruciata*(L.)Scop. (crosswort)	GcHSW		2		1		
G. cf. *verum* L. (lady's bedstraw)	GH		2				
G. palustre L. (marsh bedstraw)	BM		11[2]	[1]			
G. aparine L. (cleavers)	DH		33	3	4	1	
Galium sp.			1	1			
VALERIANACEAE							
Valerianella sp.	AH				1		
CAPRIFOLIACEAE							
Sambucus nigra L. (elder)	ADRWn	[1]	38[9]	[53]		[3]	

Table 19, continued. Abbots Worthy (W79). The plant remains: taxa by feature type.

TAXA	HABITAT	sunken-featured huts	large pits	?cess pits	other pits	post/stake-holes	ditches
COMPOSITAE							
Anthemis cotula L. (stinking mayweed)	ADh		242	4	1		
Anthemis cotula-type			[3]		[1]		
Indeterminate				[1]			
JUNCACEAE							
Juncus sp. (rush)	pEGM		1				
IRIDACEAE							
Iris pseudacorus L. (yellow flag)	BMpW				2		
CYPERACEAE							
Eleocharis subg.*Palustres* (spike-rush)	M		29(27)	[3](1)	2		
Carex sp. (sedge)	GM	[1]	17[2](2)	[4]	[1]	1	
SPARGANIACEAE							
Sparganium erectum L. (bur-reed)	MP		5		1		
	TOTAL	278	1150	538	139	172	8
	Vol.sieved (litres) : flot sorted	190	340	160	200	310	43
	Vol. (litres) sieved : flot & residue	3.5	20	10	2	–	–

[ ] = mineralised ( ) = silicified

Habitat Preferences:

A=arable	E=heath	P=shallow water,	W=woodland	h=heavy soils	p=damp soils
B=bankside	G=grassland	ponds & ditches	a=acidic soils	l=light, sandy soils	
C=cultivated land	H=hedgerows	R=roadsides	c=calcareous soils	n=nitrogenous soils	
D=disturbed land	M=marsh	S=scrub	d=dry soils	o=open habitats	

eralised material. Where the residues were sorted, 29 out of 32 contexts contained mineralised material.

Table 20 presents the data according to habitat type and illustrates the differences in the nature of waste being deposited in the different types of feature. It should be noted, however, that where it was not possible to examine the residue from the samples, mineralised plant remains may have been lost. This would have affected the percentages of remains according to habitat groups, as certain taxa, for example fruit seeds, are more likely to have been preserved by mineralisation than by carbonisation.

The results of presence and dominance analyses for the cereals are shown in Table 21.

Cereal identification

Barley

Most of the barley recovered could be identified as hulled 6-row barley (*Hordeum vulgare* L.emend.), due to the presence of twisted caryopses and adhering fragments of lemma or impressions of

Table 20. Abbots Worthy (W79). The plant remains: percentage composition by feature type.

	Sunken-featured huts			Large pits				Cess pits			Other pits	Post/stake holes	Ditches
	7339	7445	7698 :	7345	7404	7341 :	7680	7485	7809 :	(9)	(29)	(3)
Total seed number ★	214	48	16	817	188	145	116	157	265	139	172	8
% mineralisation ★	20	0	0	1	28	16	84	90	87	16	+	0
Volume sieved (1)	130f	40f	20f	140f	100f	100f	40f	80f	40f	200f	310f	43f
(flot/residue sorted)	3.5fr	0fr	0fr	5.5fr	10fr	4.5fr	2fr	4fr	4fr	2fr	0fr	0fr
Seeds per litre ★	1.6	1.2	0.8	5.6	1.7	1.4	2.8	1.9	6.0	0.7	0.6	0.2
% grain	66	84	100	8	19	12	10	1	5	56	85	38
% chaff	2	0	0	3	0	0	0	0	+	2	1	0
% arable weeds	0	0	0	25	24	7	6	12	15	1	0	24
% wetland taxa	+	0	0	32	26	26	1	1	5	5	1	0
% grassland taxa	10	0	0	7	5	9	3	5	3	7	1	0
% nitrophilous weeds	4	10	0	2	0	8	2	8	5	1	0	0
% fruit and nuts ★	2	2	0	3	11	14	44	1	11	1	0	38
bran present				x	x	x		x				

f = flot

r = residue

★ = greatly influenced by processing method

+ = < 1%

For pits, post/stake holes and ditches () = number of features sampled and values given are averages.

Table 21. Abbots Worthy (W79). The plant remains: presence and dominance analysis.

PRESENCE ANALYSIS

% of total samples (154)

Triticum aestivocompactum	9	********
Triticum dicoccum/spelta	6.6	*******
Hordeum sp.	32	**************************
Avena sp.	6	***********
Secale cereale	0.6	*

DOMINANCE ANALYSIS

% of total samples (154)

Triticum aestivum s.l.	6	*****
Triticum dioccum/spelta	6.6	*******
Hordeum sp.	30	********************
Avena sp.	4	*****
Secale cereale	0	

lemma veins. The lemma base and rachis fragments recovered were too damaged to show whether they were from lax or erect barley. No naked barley was identified.

Wheat

Free-threshing hexaploid wheat was recorded as *Triticum aestivocompactum*, broadly defined to both bread wheat and club wheat. No intact rachis internodes were present to indicate the presence of club wheat, but two well preserved caryopses had length: breadth ratios which easily fell within the range given by van Zeist (1968) for carbonised club wheat (*Triticum compactum* Host.). It is likely that both species were present.

Caryopses of glume wheat were generally recorded as spelt/emmer, since identification using grain characters alone is unreliable. A few well preserved caryopses were tentatively recorded as *Triticum* cf.*spelta*. A glume base characteristic of spelt confirmed the presence of this species, but no such evidence was found to confirm the presence of emmer.

Oats

Only one floret base was recovered to enable the distinction between cultivated and wild oats to be made, and that was from a wild oat (*Avena fatua* L.).

Rye

A single grain of rye (*Secale cereale* L.) and one rachis fragment were recovered.

Discussion

The carbonised, mineralised and silicified plant remains recovered represent waste products from a number of activities occuring within the settlement. Taking into account differences in the processing of the samples, the features can be grouped according to the nature of waste deposited in them (see Table 20).

The sunken-featured buildings (SFBs)

Samples from three of the SFBs were processed, but it was only possible to examine the residues of samples from one, SFB F7339. Carbonised cereals were predominant in all of the samples, in particular barley (*Hordeum* sp.) which accounted for 83% of the grain recovered from the SFBs. Some free-threshing wheat (*Triticum aestivocompactum*) and a little spelt/emmer (*Triticum spelta diccocum*) were also present. Other plant groups occurred in relatively small percentages in comparison with results from other features. No arable weed seeds and only a little chaff was present. The composition of the samples suggests that most of the plant remains represent processed grain discarded or dropped in the preparation of food. The few grassland species present may have been brought into the hut amongst hay for bedding or kindling for the fire, or they may have been grown as arable weeds. There are notably few wet-grassland taxa present compared with the assemblage in the possible hay deposit in the large pit F7345.

A few mineralised remains and the seeds of several nitrophilous species were present, suggesting that some organic waste had been allowed to accumulate. Mineralised plant remains are frequently recovered from cess pits which contain high concentrations of minerals from faecal material and provide anaerobic conditions (Green 1979). However, this type of preservation may also occur in deposits which are rich in ash and other kinds of organic debris, as has been found in the Late Bronze Age midden at Potterne (Carruthers, forthcoming). The damp nature of some of the soils on this site and the proximity of the River Itchen suggest that some of the deposits may have been at least periodically waterlogged. This undoubtedly would have assisted the formation of mineralised plant remains where sufficient organic waste was present. However, most of the mineralised assemblages contained seeds of edible taxa such as fruit remains, peas or bran, indicating that the mineralisation was primarily due to the presence of faecal material.

Several mineralised seeds of purging flax (*Linum cartharticum* L.) were present in SFB F7339. This common chalk grassland species may have been brought into the hut with hay for bedding or tinder. Its restriction to samples from within the building and the fact that it was preserved by mineralisation could suggest that it had been collected and used as a purgative or emetic. Mineralised seeds of cultivated flax (*Linum usitatissimum* L.) recovered from SFB F7339 may represent the cultivation of this plant as a fibre crop or for the oil from its seed.

The large pits

A number of flots and residues were examined from samples from the large (>2.0m diameter) pits 7345, 7404 and 7341. These three deep, steep-sided pits were grouped together in one area of the site. They each possessed several layers which appeared to contain waste from a number of different activities.

Mineralised plant remains were present in a few layers of each pit. The presence of fruit pips and bran in these deposits indicated that they contained redeposited faecal waste. Mineralised rodent droppings were present in some of these layers. A sample of the mineralised concretions from pit F7404 were examined by Andrew Jones at the York Environmental Archaeology Unit for parasite ova, but none were found.

The pits had also been used for the deposition of industrial waste, as indicated by the presence of slag. Pit F7341 contained layers of ash and slag that produced silicified plant remains as well as carbonised remains. Silicification is most frequently found in ash from ovens or kilns, where high temperatures and oxidising conditions are present (Robinson and Straker 1991). Grass stems, spike-rush and sedge seeds had become silicified due to the presence of high quantities of silica in their tissues. These taxa probably represent only a small proportion of the species originally present, but the remains suggest that hay from damp grassland had been used to kindle the ovens or kilns or burnt as waste.

Most of the samples examined from these pits contained carbonised remains, although cereal grains were present in fairly low numbers. The cereal remains were more characteristic of domestic refuse than crop processing and drying waste, as only a small amount of chaff was recovered. Samples from the site as a whole produced very little crop processing waste. It seems likely that these activities were being performed elsewhere, possibly closer to the arable fields themselves. The chaff and straw may also have been used as fodder and as temper for ceramics and building materials. Arable weed seeds were more in evidence, suggesting that the later

stages in the processing, such as fine sieving and picking over by hand to remove weed seeds (Hillman 1981, stages 13 and 14), may have been carried out nearer to home. Several carbonised grass culm bases were present indicating the up-rooting of plants or the burning of turf.

All of the cereal types were present in small numbers in samples from the large pits, but there was a notably larger number of oat caryopses in pit F7345 than elsewhere on the site. It is likely that these represent arable weeds rather than a cereal crop, as a floret base of a wild oat (*Avena fatua*) was recovered from this pit.

Several samples from these pits contained carbonised grass culm fragments and seeds of both wet and dry grassland species. Context 7378 in pit F7345 contained particularly large numbers of these remains, indicating the presence of burnt hay. The hay may have been used for bedding, fodder, litter or kindling. This material is discussed in more detail below.

Horse beans (*Vicia faba* var.*minor*) were also recovered from context 7378 but from none other. Nine of the fourteen beans present had diagonal slits in their testas (Fig 41). Leguminous seeds possess particularly tough seed coats and one explanation for the slits may be that they had been 'nicked' to facilitate germination. This is common gardening practice for sweet-pea seeds today and implies that the beans were being cultivated on a garden scale only. The testa may also split if the seed is subjected to water stress during ripening, and on germination of the seed. However, no elongated radicles were observed to indicate that germination had taken place.

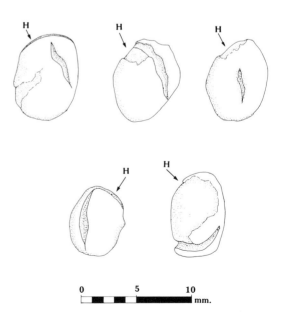

Fig 41.   Abbots Worthy (W79). Horse bean, *vicia faba* var, *minor*, with diagonal slits in the testas. H shows the position of the Hilum.

Fig 42. Abbots Worthy (W79). Hilums and fragments of testa of peas, *Pisum sativum*. Scale in millimetres. Photo: M Brookes.

Possible cess pits

Samples from a number of smaller pits were examined. Of the samples where both flots and residues were available, the results from three pits stood out as containing high percentages of mineralised plant remains. Pits F7680, F7485 and F7809 were larger (*c* 1.3–2.0m diameter), deeper and more steep-sided than most of the other pits. All of the layers within them contained some mineralisation, although some layers contained larger quantities of mineralised material than others. The presence of high percentages of fruit remains, such as apple pips (*Malus sylvestris* Mill.), blackberry/raspberry seeds (*Rubus fruticosus/idaeus*), and bran, indicates that faecal material was present in these deposits. It is, therefore, suggested that the pits were used primarily as cess pits. A few carbonised cereals and arable weed seeds were also recovered from these pits, demonstrating that they may have also been used for the deposition of small amounts of waste from other sources.

As further evidence of the presence of faecal material, pit F7809 contained a large number of pea (*Pisum sativum* L.) hilums and fragments of testa (Fig 42) such as may be produced by chewing or mashing peas. Peas have not previously been recovered in large numbers from Saxon sites in Wessex (Monk 1977, Green 1981) but may be under-represented in the archaeological plant record. Carbonisation is less likely to occur with peas than with cereals which were often oven-dried as part of the processing. Peas may have sometimes been oven-dried prior to storage, but when carbonised, features

essential for the identification of peas, such as the hilum, are frequently damaged or lost. Only one carbonised pea was identified from these samples, although many fragments of large leguminous seeds that may have been peas were recovered. Mineralisation of these tough coated seeds is more likely to occur when the testa is broken, such as when ground to make a soup or flour, or when chewed. Some poorly preserved mineralised hilums which appeared to be from peas have been recovered from the Saxon site at Meonstoke, Hampshire (F Green, pers comm).

The reasons for the recovery of pea remains from only one pit are difficult to determine. The pit may have been in use for a period when peas were in season, although peas would, no doubt, also have been dried and stored for consumption out of season. It may indicate that the use of the pit was limited to one family only, thus demonstrating differences in diet between households. Alternatively, it may be that conditions suitable for the preservation of these remains existed for this deposit only. Fruit seeds and bran were more widely distributed around the site.

The mineralised remains in flots from some of the other pits suggested that they may have also been used as cess pits, particularly pit F7483. However, the residues were not available for sorting.

Other pits

Samples from nine other pits were examined. For two of the samples the residues were sorted. Taking into account the differences in processing methods, these pits generally contained less mineralisation and more carbonised cereals than the possible cess pits. They appear to have been used primarily for the deposition of general household waste.

Post-holes and stake-holes

No residues were sorted from these features but a few mineralised remains in the flots demonstrated that organic waste had been widely distributed around the site. Few seeds were recovered from the samples. Carbonised grain occured most frequently, but this was usually in a poor state of preservation and often could not be identified even to the level of genus.

The economic plants

The results of presence and dominance analysis for the cereals in samples from the site are presented in Table 21. It can be seen that barley produced by far the highest percentages in both analyses. It was particularly numerous in samples from the SFBs. Free-threshing wheat occurred a little more frequently in the samples than glume wheat. Oats had quite a high presence value but were recovered mainly from the large pit F7345 and may have been present only as a crop contaminant. The single grain and rachis fragment of rye may also have been weeds. It is evident that rye was not an important crop plant on this site.

This order of importance of cereals is comparable to the results from *Hamwic* (Monk 1977) and a similar pattern has been observed by Green (1991) for rural sites in Hampshire. The sites have been shown to have a predominance of barley over wheat, with few oats, and rye being of importance only on one site, at Romsey. The wheat was almost exclusively a bread-wheat type and the small amount of evidence recovered for spelt was of uncertain origin.

The origin of the spelt in samples examined from this site is also open to question. Four out of the ten features that contained glume wheat also contained redeposited Roman pottery indicating that these plant remains may be residual. However, the number of Roman sherds recovered was small and it is unlikely that residuality has affected the results of the botanical analysis as a whole to any great extent.

The local calcareous soils would have been suitable for the cultivation of barley, which prefers a well-drained soil. The wheat may have been grown on the richer, heavier colluvial soils of the valley bottom.

The presence of a small number of carbonised horse beans (*Vicia faba* var. *minor*) in one deposit is not unusual for a site of this date. As they were recovered from what appears to have been waste hay and from no other deposits, they may have, in this instance, been used as animal fodder.

Cess deposits can provide direct evidence of human diet, if the limitations of preservation are taken into account. Cereal remains, for example, were represented in the samples only as a relatively small number of bran fragments, although cereals were undoubtedly of major importance in the diet. Peas and beans would have provided useful sources of protein and helped to improve poor soils if grown in rotation or as a mixed crop with cereals. Fruits such as apples, blackberries, sloes and elderberries were represented, along with hazelnuts, but it is not possible to say whether these fruits were cultivated. There is no direct evidence to demonstrate the cultivation of fruit in Britain prior to the Norman Conquest (Roach 1985), but monastic records show that orchard cultivation had developed by the Early Medieval period (Green 1984). No imported fruits, such as grapes, were recovered. These appear to have been available mainly in the wealthier towns such as Southampton (Monk 1977) in the Saxon period. Mineralised seeds of carrot (*Daucus carota* L.), celery (*Apium graveolens* L.) and cabbage/turnip/mustard (*Brassica* sp./*Sinapis* sp.) may represent the use of these plants for food, although those plants consumed as vegetables are less likely to have been recovered as seeds in faecal deposits.

Grassland and riverside taxa

A number of samples contained seeds of both damp and dry grasslands. One layer in the big pit F7345 also contained a large number of carbonised grass stem fragments, indicating that burnt hay waste had been deposited in the pit. Within this deposit taxa considered to be characteristic of both meadows and pastures were present. Meadow-sweet (*Filipendula ulmaria* (L.) Maxim.) is said to suffer under continuous grazing, according to Baker's (1937) comparison between meadows and pastures by the Thames at Oxford. However, Walters (1949) observed it growing with yellow flag (*Iris pseudacorus* L.), rushes, sedges, spike-rush (*Eleocharis* subg-.*Palustres*) and creeping buttercup (*Ranunculus repens*) on rough-grazed pasture at Hagley pool in Berkshire. All of these taxa were present in samples from this site. Spike-rush is said to occur more frequently in pastures, as it is unable to compete with tall growing grasses and herbs in meadows (Robinson 1979). It is likely that the lush grasslands bordering the River Itchen provided both hay and pasture for livestock. Such valley bottom grasslands were developed during the Saxon period to provide hay and pasture for plough oxen and other livestock. These lush meadows would have been particularly important to a settlement surrounded by well-drained chalk soils. Tubbs (1978) suggests that clearance of the biologically rich Itchen flood-plain may have begun as early as the Iron Age, and that the valley was systematically drained for meadow by or before the eighth century AD. The meadows may have been managed in a similar way to the 'Lammas Lands' (Sheail and Wells 1969), being cultivated for hay during the spring and summer and used for grazing during the autumn and winter. If this was the case, some taxa of both meadows and pastures may have been able to survive the alternating unfavourable regimes.

Hay is more usually recovered from waterlogged deposits, such as wells, and carbonised evidence for the cultivation of hay is rare (Grieg 1984, 221). Knörzer (1979) examined the remains of carbonised hay from a Roman stable in Germany. From the mixture of meadow and pasture species recovered, he deduced that the hay had been cut from a field which was used in the latter part of the year for pasture. This practice would appear to have been adopted for meadows in the Itchen valley.

A few seeds of grassland species prefering drier, and in some cases calcareous, soils were recovered (*eg* purging flax and wild carrot), suggesting that hay may also have been cut from the well-drained chalk soils of the valley sides.

The seeds of riverside and aquatic plants may have been gathered with hay cut right up to the water's edge. These include plants like fool's watercress (*Apium nodiflorum*(L.)Lag.), mint (*Mentha* sp.) and bur-reed (*Sparganium erectum* L.).

Summary

Samples from this site produced a wide range of species and a large number of carbonised and mineralised plant remains, the nature of which is comparable only to one other Saxon site, Meonstoke (Green forthcoming). They also provided evidence for the cultivation of peas and the use of hay, examples of which are scarce from sites of any period.

Analysis of the carbonised, mineralised and silicified plant remains provide some indication as to the different uses to which the pits were put. They suggest a simple diet of cereals, hedgerow fruits and nuts, and peas and beans.

Of the cereals, barley was the most important. This would have suited the surrounding well-drained, calcareous soils. Wheat, free-threshing and possibly hulled, was grown in a lesser quantity. There was little evidence to demonstrate the culti-

vation of oats or rye, although these cereals may have been grown on a small scale for specific uses.

Evidence for hay-making suggests that the lush grasslands of the valley bottom were used to provide both hay and pasture for livestock.

Calcium Phosphate-replaced Remains, by M Robinson

Mineralised anthropod remains were identified from some of the pits (Table 22). They comprise a limited range of taxa which are quite frequently preserved by calcium phosphate replacement in Saxon and Medieval cess pits. The Sphaeroceridae include sewage flies of the genus *Leptocera* and *Fannia scalaris*, which is the latrine fly. The larvae of these flies feed on liquid sewage, and the remains identified presumably represent individuals which lived and pupated in the pits. Diplopoda (millepedes) are unlikely to have found suitable living conditions in these deposits, but the presence of calcium carbonate in their exoskeletons greatly facilitates their preservation by calcium phosphate mineralisation, thus leading to a bias in their preservation amongst the anthropods which fell into the pits.

Some Considerations, by P J Fasham

The Anglo-Saxon settlement at Abbots Worthy comprises sunken-featured buildings, pits, postholes and a ditch. The site was buried under colluvial soils, but the circumstances of its discovery precluded a sophisticated archaeological response and the machine clearance may have removed some of the slighter features.

A careful scrutiny of the exposed surface during and after machining ensured that few, if any, features were not recorded. The excavation was completed under considerable duress in the midst of the motorway construction and this will have had some effects on the excavation and sampling process.

Table 22. Mineralised arthropod remains from Abbots Worthy

Pit	Context	Sample	Sphaeroceridae – puparia	*Fannia* cf *scalaris* – puparia	Diplopoda – frags
F7341B	7373	831	5	–	1
F7341B	7373	832	4	–	2
F7345	7376	932	–	–	15
F7345	7485	933	–	–	8
F7404	7396	927 928	–	–	2
F7404	7398	915	1	–	12
F7419	7420	943	–	–	14
F7483	7484	1167	3	–	–
F7499	7515	1158 1159	4	–	–
F7625	7626	1004	–	12	–
F7680	7700	1102 1103	–	–	2
F7827	7828	1163	–	–	2

The sunken-featured buildings (SFBs)

The SFBs were of two-post types and generally of small dimensions. Measuring from the centre of the end posts, the long axes were 2.5m in SFB F7339, 2.65 in SFB F7445 and between 2.75m and 3.4m in SFB F7698; no measurements are available for SFB F7403. These compare with the two-post Type A structures from West Stow, where comparable dimensions are from 2.1m to 4.9m with 42% between 3.4m and 4m long, with a peak at 3.8m (West 1985). The Abbots Worthy examples all have different characteristics although they are on the same general east-west alignment. In the case of SFB F7403, the east end had been cut away by a later pit, but at the west end a post-hole stood on the central axis but about 0.75m outside the sunken element. SFB F7445 was shallow, like SFB F7403, but one of its gable post-holes was also outside the sunken element. There were replaced posts in SFB F7698, and again one of these posts was outside the sunken area. The best preserved of these buildings was SFB F7339 with replaced posts in the sunken area and an arrangement of peripheral posts on the surface. It is impossible to determine whether the greater depth of SFB F7339 was a factor of function or a consequence of less damaging clearance. A similar arrangement may have occurred with the adjacent damaged example, SFB F7337. The occurrence of gable posts outside the buildings and the posts around SFB F7339 clearly indicate the likelihood that floors were suspended above the cellar components as West (1985) has suggested was the case for examples at West Stow. It has not been possible at Abbots Worthy to separate two distinct phases of filling for the features, one when in use and the other a phase of post-abandonment infill, but the extent of domestic rubbish in SFB F7339 must indicate a post-abandonment period of rubbish disposal. The assumption of a superstructure around SFB F7339 would provide a building measuring 3.5m by 3.5m, thus almost doubling the floor area from 6.25m^2 in the bottom of the cellar to 12.25m^2 on the surface.

Explanations for the absence of post-holes along the sides of the other SFBs could include their inadvertent removal in the machine clearance (unlikely), the use of sill beams having no trace on the ground to support vertical posts, or the use of posts simply resting directly on the ground.

At Abbots Worthy there are examples of SFBs where one and sometimes two of the gable posts were outside the sunken area and there are two examples which seem to have gable posts within the sunken zone but incorporate an exterior superstructure represented by post-holes.

The SFBs at Old Down Farm, Andover, which ranged in length from 2.2m to 3.3m, all had internal posts (Davies 1980), as did the generally larger structures, about 3.75m long, at Portchester where 52 had a wide entrance straight off a Roman street (Cunliffe 1976). The single SFB at Cowdery's Down had external posts placed 3.5m apart (Millett and James 1983).

It is unusual to find pits on rural Anglo-Saxon sites. There are none at Cowdery's Down, Old Down Farm or Chalton, but plenty in the more enclosed conditions at Portchester Castle and Hamwic. Rubbish from rural sites would normally be spread on the fields as manure: it is curious that it was being 'wasted' at Abbots Worthy.

The pits

Simple shape analysis indicates that three types or groupings of pits may be distinguished among those excavated at Abbots Worthy. The first group, comprising F7470, F7532, F7499 and F7541, was shallow, sub-circular with irregular bases. These features could be more aptly described as scoops, if they were not natural features, eg F7470 and F7532.

The second group, comprising pits F7680, F7627, F7623, F7345, F7809, F7483, and F7885, was generally sub-square or oval, and had steeply sloping sides down to a flattish base. These pits may have been initially for storage, but the environmental data indicates at least a final use for cess.

The third group, comprising pits F7341, F7345 and F7404, was related as much by location as by shape and by size. These three pits, clustered on the west side of the motorway, were much larger than any others, and had overhanging sides. Although the evidence was not very strong, they may have been used for some industrial process involving large quantities of water, such as the finishing of textiles. There was no obvious water supply for the three pits but it is feasible, if unlikely, that a leat could have been constructed to take water from the course of the Roman aqueduct, if it still flowed. A more mundane solution may be that they were silage clamps, as suggested by traces of hay in F7345.

Samples were taken from deposits in the pits which might have yielded technological information. The majority of the samples were of fuel ash slag, which is formed in hot fires. However, there was no evidence that these fires were connected with any technological activity. The only other significant samples contained iron smithing slag, almost certainly from a blacksmith's hearth (Wilthew 1986).

The discovery of apple pips, blackberry seeds and bran has led to the suggestion that pits F7680, F7485, F7809 and possibly F7483, were all cess pits.

In the absence of detailed analysis of their contents, it is a matter of speculation whether all the other small pits in the western group were used for cess. At Portchester there is a suggestion of clustering of such pits (Cunliffe 1976). The evidence from the SFBs, particularly F7339, suggests that the plant remains were of processed grain dropped or discarded during food preparation. From the larger pits came evidence for hay, making use of both the wet and dry zones of pasture land available. The suggestion of garden scale cultivation of horse beans is an interesting one. The function of the three larger pits is not clear.

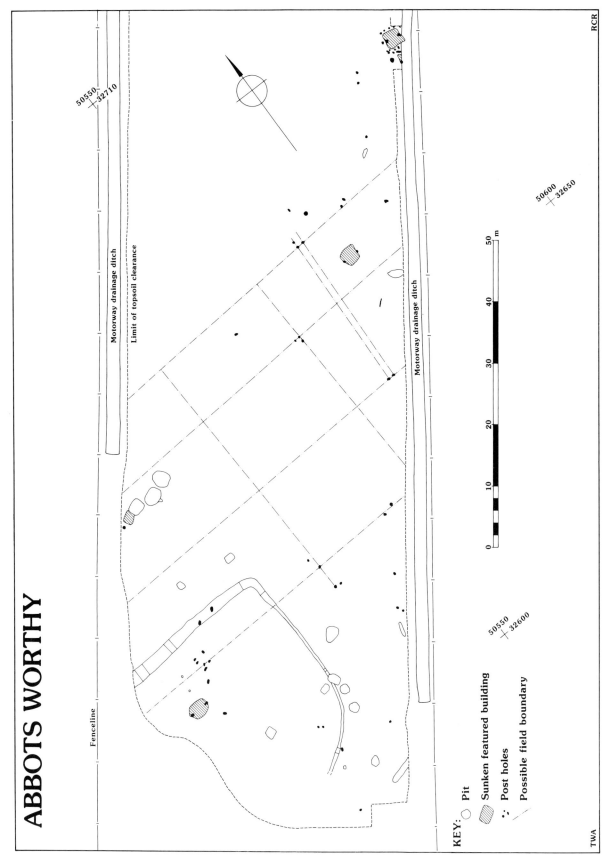

Fig 43. Abbots Worthy (W79). Reconstruction of possible field boundaries around the Anglo-Saxon settlement.

The post-holes

At first glance, the post-holes seem to be rather scattered about. They did not form part of ground-level 'hall-style' timber buildings and do seem to have been isolated features. A more detailed consideration suggests that they are not quite so isolated and scattered as they first seem (Fig 43). The ditch runs north–south and east–west, there are natural gravel bands running east–west and the SFBs are aligned east–west. The River Itchen is also flowing from east to west. There is thus a general trend on the site to an east–west axis. This hypothesis assumes that most of the isolated, paired or triple post-holes were field markers, in which case a series of rectangular fields can be postulated, which generally separate the feature groups. For example, the cess pits can be seen to lie along the edge of the river while the three big pits are on one edge of the suggested field system. It is accepted that this interpretation has severe limitations and is proposed as an hypothesis in an area where so little is known. The 'garden scale' cultivation of horse beans may be related to the use of small fields.

Chronology

The site seems to have been in use from the sixth to the eighth or ninth centuries AD and it is possible that the eastern group of features, which includes SFB F7399, was earlier than those to the west. No attempts were made to obtain radiocarbon dates, as most of the suitable material came from one feature and the general duration of settlement makes it unlikely that a chronology could be refined adequately.

Elements of the site must have been contemporary with the cemetery in Worthy Park and three of the pottery stamps occur on both sites. The stamps are not rare and it cannot be suggested from them alone that the people who lived at Abbots Worthy were burying their dead in Worthy Park. However, the extreme proximity of the two sites (Figs 20 and 64) makes any other course of events seem unlikely.

Settlement patterns

The settlement site at Abbots Worthy represents a sprawl of activities on the banks of the River Itchen. The activities include possible bone working, smithing, animal and cereal farming and perhaps a small-scale garden-type of agriculture. It seems reasonable to assume that the focus and different functional elements of the settlement changed location through time. The village at West Stow was not static (West 1985) and shows various movements around the site. Catholme seems to be a more nucleated site showing continuous internal development from the fifth to the ninth centuries AD (Losco-Bradley 1974, Losco-Bradley and Wheeler 1984). In many ways the site excavated at New Wintles Farm, Eynsham, in Oxfordshire, has similarities with Abbots Worthy (Hawkes and Gray 1969). New Wintles Farm was occupied at about the

same time, from the sixth to the eight centuries AD, and spread over three hectares – the full extent of Abbots Worthy is not fully known. The occupation and activity areas were scattered but there were rectangular post-built structures in addition to eleven SFBs. The SFBs range in size from 3.5m by 2.5m to 5.5m by 4m. It was suggested that two of them, 5 and 123, were used for weaving. It is the scattered nature of the settlement that is reminiscent of Abbots Worthy.

It is not necessary to evoke suggestions of a catastrophic decline of Roman rule leading to a migration from Winchester to the countryside to account for the settlement at Abbots Worthy, indeed some continuing presence was probably maintained in Winchester (Biddle 1976). The Itchen Valley had been intensively settled and farmed for the best part of 2,500 years before the coming of the Anglo-Saxons. Only one kilometre to the north was a large Iron Age enclosure of 3.25 hectares, which was replaced by a Roman settlement with streets extending over nine hectares (Fasham 1980a). This is just one of a series of sites which occur at one kilometre intervals along the north side of the valley, set back about one kilometre from the river. Subsequent Saxon settlement on these sites can neither be proved nor disproved. There are suggestions that, from the fifth or sixth centuries through to the eight or ninth centuries AD, Anglo Saxon settlement was in the valley bottom. The Worthy Park cemetery, the Abbots Worthy settlement, the Easton pottery – a surface collection of organic-tempered sherds kindly reported by Mr Mark Brisbane – and the newly discovered fifth century cemetery at Itchen Abbas, are all spread along 3.25 kilometres of the river bank.

It has long been suspected that the string of villages along the upper Itchen valley – Headbourne Worthy, Kings Worthy, Abbots Worthy, Martyr Worthy, Itchen Abbas, Itchen Stoke – are the river-side successors of a series of farms, villages and perhaps even a small town (Fasham 1980a, 37) which occupied the south-facing slopes of the upper Itchen valley during the Iron Age and Romano-Britsh periods. The river-bank location of the Anglo-Saxon village at Abbots Worthy demonstrates just such a shift in settlement location, and partially fills the long gap between the end of the Roman administration in the early fifth century, and the Domesday survey, by which time all the present villages seem to have been in existence. Abbots Worthy is the only excavated river-side rural settlement of the Middle Saxon period in Hampshire, and adds a new element to the settlement pattern of the post-Roman period in the county.

The well-preserved and probably extensive nature of the Abbots Worthy settlement demands full-scale evaluation to enable recommendations to be proposed for the eventual protection of the remainder of the site as a scheduled monument. The surviving elements of the site would be exceedingly vulnerable to any proposals for widening the M3.

Chapter 3

M3 Archaeology 1972–88: Reflections
by P J Fasham

Introduction

Archaeological investigation along the line of the M3 motorway and the subsequent analysis and writing up of the discoveries has spanned the best part of two decades from 1972 to 1988. The sites investigated are shown on Fig 44 and listed in Table 23. When the history is written of field archaeology in the twentieth century it is possible that the 1970's will be seen as the golden decade of rescue archaeology, at least in terms of increased availability of funding from central government and the number of excavations actually in the field. In retrospect it created a millstone of unpublished work around the necks of many individuals and excavating bodies, a burden which created severe restrictions on the availibility of funds for new fieldwork in the 1980's. The 1970's was also the decade when the approaches of theoretical archaeology were taking a hold, although in many instances in British archaeology, practical applications were not to be seen in or on the ground until the end of the decade when various sampling strategies for both survey and excavation programmes were designed and implemented. Although archaeological work on the M3 must be seen in the light of what then were the emerging trends of 'new archaeology', it must be stated that the investigation of the route of the M3 was always considered by both the Department of the Environment and the M3 Archaeological Rescue Committee to be first and foremost a rescue archaeology project.

Once the need for a trunk road has been determined, the selection of a motorway route is governed, amongst other things, by the necessity of linking two places as expediently as possible in engineering terms and with minimal disturbance to existing settlements. The choice of route is dictated not by the niceties of archaeological concepts but by the harder requirements of civil engineering, although the preservation option is now pursued with more vigour, or at least is more fully considered, than was likely to be the case sixteen years ago. The route of the M3 is therefore not a sample in any probabilistic sense of the archaeological heritage of central Hampshire, nor should it ever be considered as such. From an archaeological view, the motorway was a haphazard slice across the country-side which happened to contain archaeological sites of varying nature and differing dates. The threat to the archaeology of this thin slice of the Hampshire countryside emerged at a time when there were reasonable resources available to deal comprehensively with the discovery, survey, excavation and analysis of the threatened sites. Archaeological awareness of the likely levels of destruction caused by road construction had been raised by the work along the M5 (Fowler 1972, Fowler and Bennet 1973, Fowler and Walthew 1971) and M40 (Rowley and Davies 1973). The M3 was to provide an opportunity for a less frantic response to the threat than had been possible before. Indeed the published starting date for construction kept receding as Public Inquiry followed Public Inquiry and the immediate threat faded to such an extent that all of the known sites where access could be negotiated had been excavated and the archaeological unit wound-up with all the major reports completed, even if not published, almost two years before construction started. Even as this text is written, in late 1987, a Public Inquiry is still hearing evidence for the southernmost element of the route which had formed part of the original project.

Developing the archaeological response

The formulation of the archaeological response to the M3 was a reflection, in microcosm, of archaeological developments from the late 1960's almost to the present day – indeed, with parts of the road still not built, one should perhaps say into the future. The response went from a primary, amateur initiative which was chaired and supported by professionals, to a threat-specific professional unit which attempted to incorporate the needs of the amateur, and ended a decade later with an exclusively professional collaboration between a large regional unit and a District Council on both an excavation with a clear sampling design and the watching brief during construction. At all stages the work was supported financially by the Directorate of Ancient Monuments and Historic Buildings of the Department of Environment or its successor, the Historic Buildings and Monuments Commission for England, more popularly known as English Heritage. The Royal

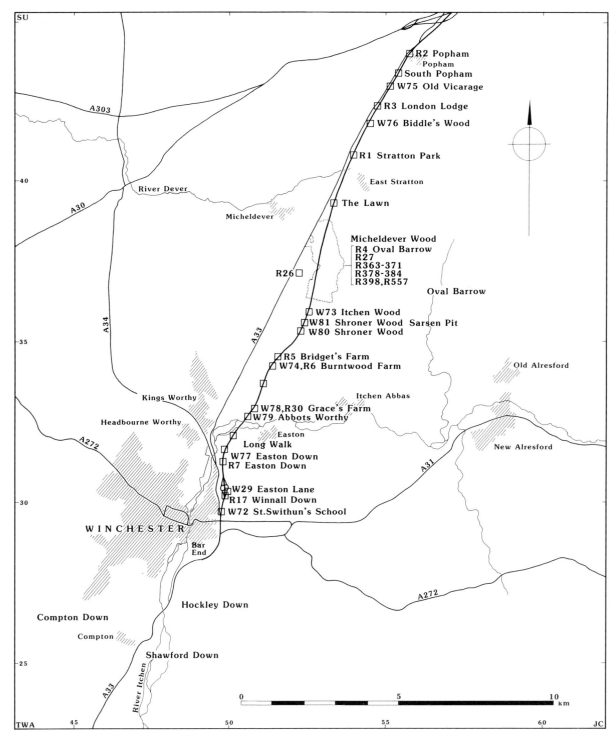

Fig 44.   Location of all archaeological investigations on the line of the M3.

Commission on Historical Monuments lent its moral and practical support to the project. A summary of the development of the archaeological response provides a useful background to the archaeological tactics and methods.

A decade after the first 72 miles (115 kilometres) of Britain's first motorway, the M1, were opened to traffic, Peter Fowler's missionary zeal from his west country work on the M5 and, to a lesser extent the M4, created a focus of concern about the M3 which

was picked up in Winchester by Victor Emery. The M3 Archaeological Rescue Committee was formed with Martin Biddle as chairman and Victor Emery as secretary at a meeting convened by the Hampshire Standing Conference for Local History and Archaeology on Tuesday 1st Febuary 1972 in Winchester. The meeting resolved to undertake a preliminary survey of the route, to plan for rescue excavation of selected sites, to form local groups for inspection of road works and subsequent limited excavations and

Table 23. The sites excavated as part of the M3 project. The prefix R before site numbers was introduced at the start as a specific identifier for M3 sites and the prefix W relates to investigations done from 1982 onwards under the aegis of the Trust for Wessex Archaeology.

Site No	Site Name	Period	Type	Advance Excavation	Watching Brief	References
R1	Stratton Park	Roman & Saxon	Road & Activity	Yes Yes	Yes —	Fasham 1981
R2	Popham	Medieval	Settlement	Yes	Yes	Fasham 1987a
R3	London Lodge	Iron Age Roman	Activity Road	Yes Yes	— —	Fasham 1981
R4	Mich Wood	Bronze Age	Oval Barrow	Yes	—	Fasham 1979 Fasham and Ross 1978
R5	Bridget's Farm	Prehistoric Roman	Activity Road	Yes Yes	— —	Fasham 1980
R6	Burntwood Farm	Prehistoric Roman	Activity Road	Yes Yes	— Yes	Fasham 1980
R7	Easton Down	Bronze Age	Ring-ditch	Yes	—	Fasham 1982
R17	Winnall Down	Multi-period	Settlement	Yes	—	Monk and Fasham 1980 Fasham 1982 Fasham 1985
R27	Mich Wood	Iron Age	Settlement	Yes	—	Monk and Fasham 1980 Fasham 1987b
R30	Grace's Farm	?Bronze Age	Ring-ditch	Yes	—	Fasham 1982
R363	Mich Wood	?Bronze Age	Ring-ditch	Yes	—	Fasham 1983
R364	Mich Wood	Roman	Field boundary	Yes	—	Fasham 1983
R365	Mich Wood	Roman	Field Boundary	Yes	—	Fasham 1983
R366	Mich Wood	Roman	Hollow-way	Yes	—	Fasham 1983
R367	Mich Wood	Roman	Hollow-way	Yes	—	Fasham 1983
R368	Mich Wood	Roman ?Saxon	Field boundary Linear ditch	Yes Yes	— —	Fasham 1983
R369	Mich Wood	Roman	Field boundary	Yes	—	Fasham 1983
R370	Mich Wood	Roman	Field boundary	Yes	—	Fasham 1983
R371	Mich Wood	Roman	Hollow-way	Yes	—	Fasham 1983
R378	Mich Wood	Roman	Field boundary	Yes	—	Fasham 1983
R379	Mich Wood	Roman	Field boundary	Yes	—	Fasham 1983
R380	Mich Wood	Roman	Bank & ditch	Yes	—	Fasham 1983
R381	Mich Wood	Iron Age	Hollow-way	Yes	—	Fasham 1983
R382	Mich Wood	Roman	Bank & ditch	Yes	—	Fasham 1983
R383	Mich Wood	Roman	Bank & ditch	Yes	—	Fasham 1983
R384	Mich Wood	Uncertain	Bank & ditch	Yes	—	Fasham 1983
R398	Mich Wood	—	Trial pits	Yes	—	Fasham 1983
W29	Easton Lane	Multi-period	Settlement	Yes	Yes	Fasham 1989
W72	St Swithun's	Bronze Age	Ring-ditch	—	Yes	This volume
W72	St Swithun's	Uncertain	Ditch	—	Yes	This volume
W73	Itchen Wood	Multi-period	Earthworks	—	Yes	This volume
W74	Burntwood Farm	?Roman	Ditch	—	Yes	This volume
W75	Old Vicarage	?Prehistoric	Ditch	—	Yes	This Volume
W76	Biddles Wood	Roman	Road, part or R1	—	Yes	This volume
W77	Easton Down	Prehistoric	Lynchets	—	Yes	This volume
W77	Easton Down	Prehistoric	Ditches	—	Yes	This volume
W78	Grace's Farm	Roman	Aqueduct	—	Yes	This volume
W79	Abbots Worthy	Saxon	Settlement	—	Yes	This volume
W80	Shroner Wood	Uncertain	Ditch	—	Yes	This volume
W81	Shroner Wood	Geological	Sarsen pit	—	Yes	This volume
—	Long Walk	Prehistoric	Ditches etc.	—	Yes	This volume
—	Shroner Wood	Uncertain	Earthworks	—	Yes	This volume
—	The Lawn	?Roman	Pits	—	Yes	This volume
—	Stratton Park	?Modern	Ditch	—	Yes	This volume
—	South Popham	Uncertain	Ditch	—	Yes	This volume
R26	West of Mich Wood	Roman	Ditches	Yes	—	Fasham 1982
R557	Mich Wood	Medieval or later	Bank	Yes	—	Fasham 1982

Sites R26 and R557 lay off the line of the motorway and are not included in any of the counts relating to the various totals for the scheme.

to prepare 'a paper for submission to the Department of Environment and Hampshire County Council in October 1972, with a view to obtaining the services of a professional archaeologist as Director'. At the meeting, a representative of the South Eastern Road Construction Unit of the Department of Transport indicated that construction would probably start in 1974/75. The Royal Commission on Historic Monuments had already arranged a series of aerial photographs of the route. The proposed paper became a costed project design which was formally published in the spring of 1973 (Biddle and Emery 1973).

In the course of 1972 and early in 1973 a variety of activities took place which reflected the strong tradition of amateur involvement in Hampshire archaeology. These were funded by £250 from Department of the Environment and £25 from Hampshire County Council. Five groups surveyed and fieldwalked, where possible, a 300m wide corridor along the 19.6 kilometre length of the route. From north to south, the groups came from the Basingstoke Archaeological Society, the Farnborough District Archaeological Society (now the Northeast Hampshire Archaeological Group), the Itchen Valley Archaeological and Historical Society (now defunct), Winchester City Museums and the now disbanded South Hampshire Archaeological Rescue Group. Archaeology students in the Department of History at King Alfred's College did archival research of the area along the route and produced a list of sites, possible sites and place-name information gleaned from Tithe Maps, Ordnance Survey Antiquity Cards, Victoria County History and various local publications including the *Proceedings of the Hampshire Field Club*. This was all done in those long ago days before there was a centralised Sites and Monuments Record for Hampshire.

The project design prepared by Martin Biddle and Vic Emery included a logical sequence of tasks from survey through excavation and watching brief to report-writing over a six year period intended to start

in June 1973 and end in March 1979, for a grand total of £73,043 at 1972 (pre-freeze) prices. The actual cost of the archaeological work on the 17 kilometres so far built has been £392,177 as expended, with no adjustments to equivalents of either 1972 or 1988 values. The estimated programme of work and expenditure is compared with the actual results in Table 24, which shows only the expenditure of the M3 Archaeological Rescue Committee. In 1980, the responsibility for overseeing the completion of the existing post-excavation programme was transferred, with the author, to the Trust for Wessex Archaeology, and expenditure from 1980–81 is shown in Table 25. From 1980 all fieldwork was a collaboration between the Trust and the Archaeology section of Winchester City Council.

In the autumn and winter of 1973/4, work involved observing and recording all ground disturbances during the geological site investigations along the route, preliminary fieldwork especially in the woodland, arranging with the Ancient Monuments Laboratory a geophysical survey of the route, establishing recording systems for all eventualities and locating and renting suitable office, hostel and storage facilities in or near Winchester. From April 1974 to March 1976 continous excavation took place, six days a week. Eight sites were excavated and the survey of earthworks in Micheldever Wood was started. In the spring of 1976 the excavation of those earthworks commenced but the major piece of work that year was the first stage of the excavation of Winnall Down. A ring-ditch was excavated in the autumn of 1976 and the archaeological investigation of Micheldever Wood was completed in spring 1977. The rest of 1977 was occupied primarily with the second stage of the excavation of Winnall Down. In December of that year and in the spring of 1978 fieldwork concentrated on the entrance of the 'banjo' enclosure and another ring-ditch on the west side of Micheldever Wood.

In 1974 it became obvious that the volume of fieldwork and the likely schedules for both fieldwork

Table 24. Estimated and actual expenditure of the M3 Archaeological Rescue Committee. All income was from the Department of the Environment apart from a £50 grant from Winchester City Council in 1973/4. Administrative expenses do not include office rental. The estimated costs are those published in the project design (Biddle and Emery 1973).

	1973/1974		1974/1975		1975/1976		1976/1977		1977/1978		1978/1979		1979/1980		1980/1981	
	Est	Act	Est	Act	Est	Act	Est	Act	Est	Act	Est	Act	Est	Act	Est	Act
Permanent Staff	1820	1456	5502	7607	5720	11966	5930	11785	4430	16246	4570	17108	–	20660	–	4825
Temporary Staff	1018	502	13232	9606	13232	11217	5216	11767	1304	4475	1304	–	–	–	–	–
Transport	550	1226	300	1679	300	2483	300	3444	150	3604	150	990	–	*6202	–	86
Admin expenses	–	614	–	1448	–	2385	–	3819	–	2892	–	2037	–	2693	–	1619
Plant Hire	–	–	2000	1864	500	1521	300	791	–	2194	–	49	–	–	–	–
Other	1250	365	1710	2896	775	4881	640	9391	460	10484	480	6587	–	**10306	–	2036
	4088	4163	22744	25100	20527	34453	12386	40997	6344	39895	6504	26771	–	39861		8566

*inc new vehicle
**inc data input

Table 25. Expenditure on M3 projects under the aegis of the Trust for Wessex Archaeology.

Project	1980/81	1981/82	1982/3	1983/4	1984/5	1985/6	1986/7	1987/8
Marc 3 Post Ex	517	15456	7960	7739	7370	–	–	–
Easton Lane	–	–	37899★	5705	16800	13214	20324	–
M3 Watching Brief	–	–	5317	14762	12424	10438	11391	9085

Income

★English Heritage	£31649
Winchester City Council	£4000
Hampshire County Council	£2250

and report preparation were going to be greater and tighter than originally anticipated. In order to ease what could have become an overwhelming problem of post-excavation, the decision was taken to appoint a Report Preparation Assistant that autumn. It was perhaps one of the earliest Department of Environment-funded posts specifically intended to deal with the problems of post-excavation. In 1975 a computerised recording system was implemented for all aspects of the excavation programme based on the mainframe of Hampshire County Council. Post-excavation work was seen as an integral part of the overall continuous programme, whereas in the Biddle and Emery project design report writing came after the fieldwork phase. The responsibility for that programme remained with the M3 Archaeological Rescue Committee until May 1980, when the few remaining responsibilities for post-excavation for fieldwork completed up to that date were transferred to the Trust for Wessex Archaeology (then the Wessex Archaeological Committee).

In 1981 a revised timetable for construction of the northern section of the route as far south as Bar End was understood to involve a start date of spring 1983. Consequently, a proposal was submitted for the sample excavation of the one last major area to merit advance investigation. The excavations at Easton Lane lasted from July 1982 to the end of March 1983, with a mid-winter break. This was a jointly arranged programme with the Winchester District Archaeologist (acting for the Archaeology section of Winchester City Council), and as the excavation developed, funding was received from Hampshire County Council and Winchester City Council, in addition to the original allocation of recources in kind from the former and grants from English Heritage. The watching brief during the construction stage in the spring and summer of 1983 was a combined Trust and City Council project during which the discovery of the Abbots Worthy Anglo-Saxon settlement led to a revision of the construction programme in accordance with various annexes and arrangements contained in the relevant Department of Transport manuals.

Since 1983 attention has been paid to the completion of the post-excavation programme of which this summary should form the ultimate statement. The expression 'post-excavation programme' was deliberately used in preference to publication, as the actual publication of the results has often lagged behind the completion of the reports. Happily that position is improving. This brief summary hopefully sets a background for the rest of this review. The early days of the project were set against the background of the frenetic pace of the rescue boom, though with consideration for the attendant post-excavation, and the end of the project was firmly set in the era of project funding and the incipient days of contract archaeology and competitive tendering.

Survey Methodology

The principle aim of all the survey work, including the observation of the Geological Site Survey, was to discover archaeological sites. This objective was supported by the concept of setting the sites and monuments within their contemporary landscapes, and a desire to be able to correlate the results of both the survey and the advance excavation work with the known sites as recorded during construction. From the outset it was felt that the landscape was the main element under examination, and that the notion of the simple site was out of date, as each site needed to be considered in conjunction with its fields, approach ways and ancillary features within the overall landscape. Ironically, the only way to work towards a non-site specific landscape study was through the excavation of sites which could be funded because of their imminent destruction. There were several heady discussions in 1973, at meetings of the M3 Archaeological Rescue Committee, of being able to obtain advance entry onto land and removing, under archaeological control, the topsoil over several miles to record the totality of the archaeological record preserved in the chalk. Inevitably such a programme never came to fruition and the fieldwork was completed in a more prosaic manner. Sites were discovered and some were related to each other and to the landscape. This paper investigates, *inter-alia*, the pre-construction results with the observations from the watching brief.

Each of the main approaches to the discovery of new sites is described separately.

By the end of the 1980's nearly every county in England had a Sites and Monuments Record (SMR), and it is perhaps now difficult to appreciate that one of the main problems for the survey phase was the lack of a county SMR for Hampshire on which to base any form of intelligence and forward planning. It is worth just wondering if a county SMR had been in existence whether there would have been any justification for the formation of an archaeological unit whose sole purpose was to mitigate the archaeological problems of a single, relatively short, piece of motorway. A sites and monuments record for the area around the route was established along the lines of the Oxfordshire example, but without the ability for complex retrieval of information (Benson 1973). Based on cards and 1:10,560 maps it was the first specifically archaeological record in Hampshire and ended with over 500 sites on its records. Fig 45 reproduces a distribution map (Fasham 1974, 3) which presented these records and summarised the extent of the available information. The whole record has been copied and incorporated within the Sites and Monuments Records held by both Winchester City and Hampshire County Councils.

The first indication of the quantative increase in the recorded archaeology held in the M3 Sites and Monuments Record was published in 1974 (Fasham 1974, Fig 1; this volume Fig 45) and is here reproduced as a reminder of the primitive nature of the presentation of such records in comparison to modern computer-generated data bases and maps.

Geological site survey

The objective of an engineering geological survey is to ensure the compatability of the road design with the existing geological formations, particularly with regard to the stability of earthworks, cuttings and bridge foundations. To obtain the relevant information various bore-holes and pits are dug. For the M3 a total of 142 bore-holes were sunk, usually 150mm diameter and up to 30m deep, but only nine were visited as the ground disturbance was minimal. Similarly, only five of the 31 Special Test Holes, 100–150mm diameter and up to 25m deep, were visited. Complementing the bore-holes, 75 test pits were dug to permit geological mapping of the substrata and for the engineers to see at first hand the nature of the materials to be used in the embankments. Visits to 69 of the test pits led to the discovery of eleven possible sites or findspots, including the first view of an oval barrow still extant as an earthwork in Micheldever Wood (Fasham 1979), and, also in the Wood, the first hint of the 'banjo' enclosure (Fasham 1987b) and under colluvium at the foot of St Catherine's Hill a Middle Iron Age ditch containing saucepan pottery. Soakaway pits were dug to various sizes and shapes to assess the rate of water absorption, and of the twenty excavated, it was possible to visit seventeen and discover one new site or findspot.

The survey included various test pits and bore-holes in the bottom of the Itchen Valley. Peat from these disturbances and from specific samples was examined by Dr K Barber of Southampton University, who found that, due to unfavourable conditions at the time of deposition and subsequent variations in the water table, the peat was unfossiliferous and contained virtually no pollen and few worthwhile plant remains. Fortunately Dr P V Waton eventually found some suitable deposits a few hundred metres downstream (Waton 1982).

Fieldwalking

The development of the now highly refined technique and art of surface collection is an example of diffusion of ideas. In part, the early stimulus may well have come from motorway archaeology (Fowler 1972), where it formed part of the programme of field-checking. During the early 1970's fieldwalking was being applied to non-threatened areas to investigate the landscape and context of threatened sites within those areas (Woodward 1978). By the middle of the decade some projects were covering large areas of downland where agricultural activities were the only threat (Richards 1978). On the M3 route, a basic system was used which related to the fields affected along the line. All collection units, whether rectangular or linear, were related to the field boundaries; the basic technique has been described on several occasions (Fasham et al 1980b, Fasham 1986a). The main fieldwalking programme was done by amateurs in 1972/1973, with a limited amount of additional systematic work in the winter of 1973/1974. From then on the pressure of continous excavation meant that no further fieldwalking exercises could be contemplated until the winter of 1977/78, when it was planned to cover a 90m wide corridor. It was anticipated that a length of about ten kilometres would be suitable and available. This was an exercise to try to establish the maximum number of sites and findspots along the route, at a time when the immediate threat of construction had receded, to enable future programmes of work to be established. It was an aspect of the work that could only be carried out with the assistance of the local groups. Unfortunely, the response was poor and the scheme had to be abandoned and replaced by a programme that concentrated on a few selected fields, mainly those west of Micheldever Wood (Fasham 1983). A local group had fieldwalked part of the parish of Micheldever but the results have never been properly assimilated.

Geophysical survey

The first fluxgate gradiometers to be extensively used in archaeology were made by the Plessey Company, not far away from the M3 in Havant. This type of magnetic prospecting instrument has advantages over the well-known proton magnetometer: continuous output, lightness and mobility. The first archaeological version was commissioned by the

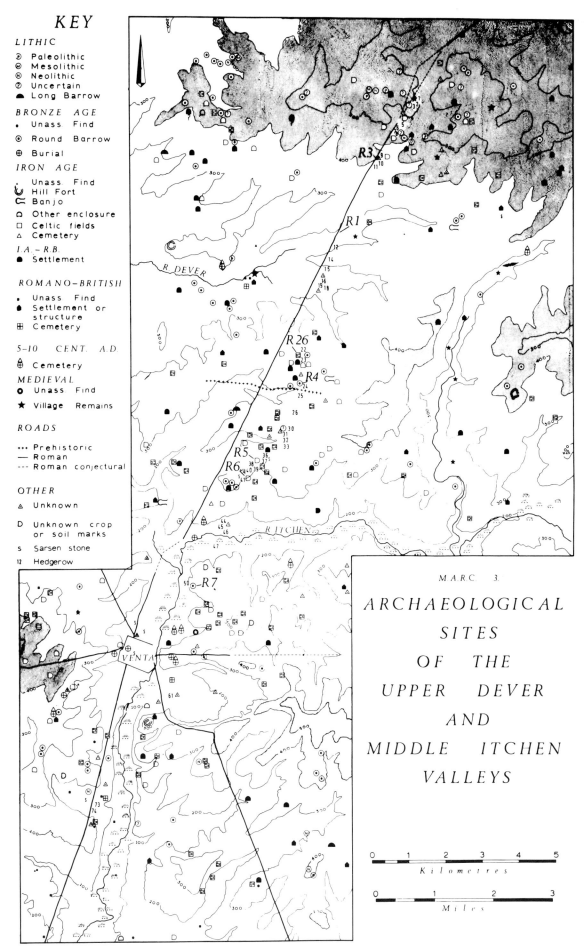

M.A.R.C. 3.

ARCHAEOLOGICAL
SITES
OF THE
UPPER DEVER
AND
MIDDLE ITCHEN
VALLEYS

Fig 45.   The distribution of archaeological sites as known and published in 1974 (Fasham 1974 Fig 1) in the
valleys of the rivers Itchen and Dever.

Geophysics Section of the Ancient Monuments Laboratory who undertook the M3 survey, primarily for detailed site survey in combination with an automatic plotting system, but also as an effective tool for rapid free scanning of large areas in which archaeological signals were interpreted directly from the instrument dial by the operator.

The M3 project was the first in which magnetic scanning was applied on a large scale, scanning more than just known sites. Its use was necessary to help ensure that no significant archaeological sites were missed in the strip of countryside that was to be affected by the road. It was specially effective as a complement to air photography and fieldwalking in areas where those techniques were of limited value, such as in woodland or permanent pasture. For such a survey to be possible, there must be a clear contrast in magnetic susceptibility between subsoil or bedrock and topsoil, so that the silted archaeological features are readily detectable. The chalk in central Hampshire, overlain by topsoil enhanced magnetically by an element of Clay-with-Flints, provided these conditions, although natural pockets and spreads of the Clay-with-Flints sometimes caused misleading indications.

The process used on the M3 was extremely simple. The survey was tackled field by field by two people, one operating the instrument, the other doing auger tests and plotting. Three longitudinal scans were made, two just within the sides of the potential route and the third along the centre line; and also two diagonal lines to provide an extra check and slightly closer coverage. It seemed reasonable to assume that no archaeological sites of any substance, especially those including ditches, would be missed by this density of coverage of a swathe of countryside averaging 60m in width. Magnetic anomalies of archaeological type were marked with flagged canes. The survey was intensified around these in order to define the plan of the site, and futher flags inserted. If these formed linear or circular patterns a human origin was assumed, but discrete anomalies were examined with a coring auger, as they were sometimes due to natural pockets of Clay-with-Flints. It was possible to cover about a mile of the route a day, including the plotting of the features discovered. In one case (London Lodge), the scan was followed by an intensive survey because of the difficulty of distinguishing features of some complexity and subtlety from the magnetic 'noise' due to Clay-with-Flints.

Among the new sites discovered were the pit and ditch complex at London Lodge (Fasham 1981) and the initial prospection was of major importance in establishing the nature of the 'banjo' enclosure in Micheldever Wood by confirming that a ditch, which had been recorded in a geological survey test pit, was part of an enclosure. The element recorded by the fluxgate gradiometer was a flattened part of the enclosure in fairly wide-spaced beech stands adjacent to the impenetrable stands of Giant Arborvitae into which earthworks disappeared. The fluxgate survey confirmed the existence of an enclosure, thereby enabling a programme to be developed

leading to the investigation of all parts of the enclosure which were subsequently destroyed (Fasham 1987b). A linear ditch adjacent to a ring-ditch known from air photgraphs near St Swithun's School was recorded, but interestingly, when the topsoil was cleared during the watching brief, the ditch was not visible in the chalk, although another slight ditch was recorded in a nearby location. Another discovery was of a double-ditched trackway coming down to the River Itchen from the west, south of Winchester near Compton on part of the motorway that has still not been built. The nature of this feature has not been examined by excavation.

The pre-excavation knowledge of the ring-ditch on Easton Down was enhanced by the fluxgate gradiometer prospection, with a strong anomaly being interpreted as a possible Anglo-Saxon inhumation in the earlier barrow. Excavation proved the anomaly to be a rubbish or latrine pit filled with enamelled buckets and other iron debris relating to the military camps established in that area both during the First World War and also prior to D-Day in 1944. The results of the watching brief demonstrated that, with the exception of the extensive but very slight, shallow and weakly magnetic features at Easton Lane and the settlement remains at Abbots Worthy buried beneath colluvium, the geophysical survey identified all major features in those plots of land where access was permitted.

Aerial photography

Various aerial sorties were flown and there was a considerable volume of data from aerial photographs (an example is shown on Fig 46). Local efforts started with reconnaissance flights by the Army Air Corps at Middle Wallop, and flights were also arranged by the Farnborough District Archaeological Society. At times the service provided by Army Air Corps was quite outstanding, with slides and photographs being taken and delivered back to the site by helicopter within forty-eight hours.

The major work from the air was done by the Aerial Photographic Section of the National Monuments Record who flew the line of the route on several occasions and produced detailed plots of several complexes on or adjacent to the route (Hampton 1974). The route was first flown by the NMR in 1968, and in 1971 a plot of all known marks was produced on paper at a scale of 1:10,560. Unfortunately, only a single copy of this plot was made and it has not survived to be placed into the archive. The interest in the route was created in the Salisbury office of the Royal Commission on Historical Monuments by Collin Bowen on the basis that, at that time, the next county to be surveyed was Hampshire. The Commission continued to fly the route until construction started in 1983.

Phosphates

Experiments with phosphate analysis had been carried out over several years in different parts of

Fig 46.　Aerial view of the site at Winnall Down (R17). Note that, although the ditched enclosure of the Early Iron Age settlement is clearly visible to the top right of the photograph, the open settments of both Bronze Age and later Iron Age date are not identifiable. See Fasham *et al* 1989 Figs 64, 66 and 67 for the extent of settlements as excavated. Photo: National Monuments Record, reproduced by permission of the Royal Commission on Historial Monuments England. Crown copyright reserved.

Europe. Arrhenius (1963) had tried area surveys of sites and Dauncey (1952) had demonstrated the existence of the expected accumulations of phosphates over occupation sites in Nottinghamshire. Although the use of phosphates was being included in text books in the early 1970's (Limbrey 1975) the interpretation of phosphate values as indicators of human settlement or activity areas was a matter of considerable debate.

In terms of the discovery of new sites, the analysis of phosphates did not, at that time and under the local conditions which were generally favourable to other prospecting techniques, seem to have any advantages over other survey techniques. Phosphate analysis was not perceived as a cost-effective tool of discovery and was not used as such. As with the extensive surveys of Grimes Graves (Sieveking *et al* 1973) and elsewhere in East Anglia (Craddock *et al* 1985), the benefits of the technique were seen to their best advantage in site enhancement surveys. In

Micheldever Wood one of the 'banjo' enclosures was surveyed in detail (Fasham 1983) and the data recorded have provided useful comparative material with that of the excavated 'banjo' enclosures in Micheldever Wood (Fasham 1987b) and at Bramdean (Perry 1972, 1982). Clark has used phosphates in association with geophysics on a 'banjo' type enclosure at Tadworth in Surrey (Clark 1977, 1983). At Popham the phosphate values of a single medieval building were recorded (Fasham 1987a) and spot samples were taken from the topsoil at Winnall Down immediately before the topsoil was stripped (Fasham 1985).

Very limited field experiments were done on the fields belonging to the Roman estate in Micheldever Wood. It was hoped that the analysis of soil phosphates would demonstate a difference between permanent or even temporary pasture and land that had primarily been used as arable. The tentative results were encouraging but could not be pursued (Fisher 1977).

Earthwork survey

Two areas of earthworks were known to exist on the line of the M3 north of Bar End and these were surveyed as part of the project. Earthworks south of the Bar End junction were not recorded, but include the important and rare examples of major medieval hollow-ways, known locally as the Dongas, the complex remains of prehistoric and Roman date on both Twyford and Hockley Downs (Birkbeck and Stuart 1936, Fasham 1980b), and the earthworks of uncertain date on Shawford Down at Compton. These three groups at the south end of the route were not surveyed, as uncertainty grew about the line and timing of the southern part of the road. The final route was not decided until 1990.

The earthworks in the northern sector were at Popham and in Micheldever and Itchen Woods. The remains of the medieval village of Popham presented no substantial surveying problems once access had been agreed and the thoroughbred racehorses had stopped eating the tapes and the surveyors. The earthworks at Popham lie to the east and west of the extant village; those to the west were continuations of cottage boundaries and were not recorded as they were not under threat, but those to the west, representing an expansion of the village, were threatened and therefore recorded (Fasham 1987a).

There were only five sites known in Micheldever Wood in the summer of 1973. Three years later 21 sites or features of interest and 41 linear features extending for 7.1 kilometres had been surveyed (Fig 47). The survey work was done in very close collaboration with the Royal Commission on Historic Monuments for England and evolved into a four-stage operation of field survey, excluding the excavation and post-excavation stages. In the spring of 1974, the route was walked and earthworks were sketched onto 1:10,560 Ordnance Survey maps as a means of establishing the nature and scale of the problems. These included lack of clear sight lines, an abundance of undergrowth, the physical impossibility of entering certain stands where closely sown Giant Arbor-vitae presented a solid wall of foliage, and the volume of leaf debris and trash left lying on the ground after thinning. It was possible to take action over undergrowth, leaf debris and trash, and a pilot scheme saw the total ground clearance of the central part of a Roman villa with the removal of undergrowth and trash and the raking of leaves to provide a fairly clear surface on which considerable detail was visible. However, this was very labour intensive and soul destroying. Thus it was decided to reduce the clearance element to a minimum, relating to the junction of features and crucial parts of sites that were obscured. Having experimented with the relatively well-defined remains of a villa some distance from the line of the motorway, the third stage was the survey of a 300m wide corridor based on the centre line of the motorway and thus 56 hectares were recorded. It was decided to work in a reasonably wide swathe to enable the earthworks to be better understood. The benefit of this approach can be seen when comparing the results obtained from Micheldever Wood (Fasham 1983) with those from Itchen Wood (this volume), where the dense nature of the stands on the route meant that advance survey was not possible. It was agreed with the Department of the Environment that it was prudent to enter a fourth stage of survey and to record everything that could be discovered in Micheldever Wood. It was impossible to examine about 90 hectares, but the remaining 170 hectares of the Wood were examined and earthworks recorded extending over 130 hectares.

The ground cover on the easement in Itchen Wood was too dense to allow survey work until construction started, but on the east side of the Wood a new and well-preserved 'banjo' enclosure was surveyed (Fasham 1983).

Hedgerows

In the summer of 1974, Dr Max Hooper examined all the 75 hedgerows affected by the motorway. The purpose was to establish a broad set of dates for the hedges, based on the number of species present in any 30m length of hedge. The assumption Hooper had arrived at, following extensive fieldwork, was that apparently one new species colonised a hedge every hundred years or so (Hooper 1971). There are, of course, problems with the Hooper hedgerow hypothesis, not least that of mixed planting of hedges (Pollard et al 1974). There does, however, seem to be some level of agreement about the basic principle that an older hedge will contain more species (Johnson 1978) but that allowance must be made for regional variations and mixed planting regimes. The detailed analysis of 595 hedgerows on the Weld estate in Dorset suggests that some variation in the rate of colonisation may be related to geological variables but that the basic assumption of one species every hundred years provides only a rough indication of date (Archer-Thomson 1987).

Only a brief summary account of the results of the hedgerow counts on the line of the M3 has been published (Hooper 1974) but the full field records are housed at the Hampshire County Museum Service. Fifty-three of the hedges were potentially datable by species and or shrub counts. Eighteen contained numbers of species to suggest they were of medieval or Tudor date and documentary evidence supports the case for fourteen of them, while two seem to contradict the documents and the other two have no documentary evidence. The other 35 hedges seem to be of post-Tudor date; around East Stratton they can be related to various estate maps. However, around Easton, a group of late eighteenth or early nineteenth century hedges, not recorded on any documents that have been examined, suggest a land management scheme was introduced at that time.

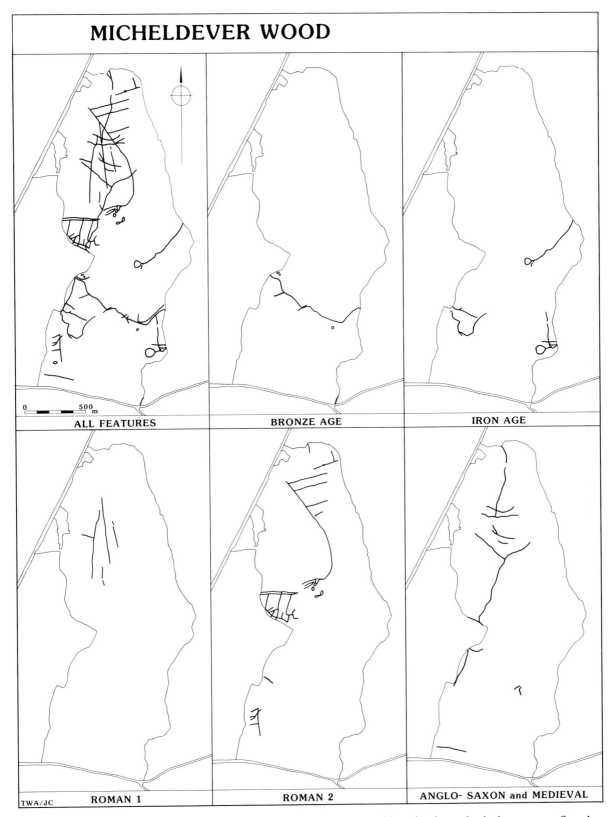

MICHELDEVER WOOD

ALL FEATURES

BRONZE AGE

IRON AGE

ROMAN 1

ROMAN 2

ANGLO- SAXON and MEDIEVAL

TWA/JC

0   500 m

Fig 47.   The earthworks surveyed in Micheldever Wood, presented here in chronological sequence. See also
Fasham (ed) 1978, 3–7 and Fasham 1983, 5–45.

Approaches to Excavation

Excavation strategies

In the original project design it was stated 'that only 1974 will be available for large-scale excavations of selected sites before the commencement of contract works' (Biddle and Emery 1973, 11). The only criteria for the selection of sites for controlled excavation in the one year then believed to be available was that 'the sites chosen should be few in number and selected on the basis of a general understanding of the total archaeological potential of the route, period by period. These selected sites should thus provide the basis for a secure interpretation of the temporal and spatial patterns resulting from study of the total of sites and finds' (Biddle and Emery 1973, 17). Apart from archaeological and academic criteria, a major factor in establishing the excavation programme was the ability to gain access to the land. It is only when a road construction scheme has gone into the Department of Transport's firm programme and is definitely going to be built that the Department is able to arrange advance entry onto the land for archaeological investigations. This involves early purchase of the land and may require two compensation payments for loss of crop, depending on how far in advance the purchase takes place, and the farming cycle. Prior to this all access has to be negotiated between the archaeologist and the landowner, agent and tenant. Nearly all of the owners were very helpful, even if there was understandable reluctance to let anyone onto the land who was associated, however remotely, with the road scheme that was going to alter the farm or estate. The Inspectorate of Ancient Monuments did agree that it was a legitimate archaeological expense, in exceptional circumstances, to pay loss of crop compensation. This was paid once and in another case a payment was made for undersowing a cereal crop with grass. In view of the archaeological importance of Micheldever Wood, agreement was reached with Treasury to enable an arrangement to be reached between the Departments of Environment and Transport and the Forestry Commission to allow advance entry and felling of sections of the Wood.

The basic criteria for selection of a site for excavation were agreed in December 1973. Any site which was to be destroyed was to be considered, but the requirement for total excavation needed to satisfy two points: that excavation would add measurably to our knowledge of that type of site or of its period, and that it could provide data about earlier land-use. The precise function and the extent of preservation into the subsoil of soil and crop marks was accepted as an area of interest. All earthwork sites were given a high priority for their environmental potential. In fact most of the earthworks were located on Clay-with-Flints and produced minimal environmental evidence. Multi-period sites were also considered a main priority, as were small parts of larger sites or features related to larger complexes where the core of the site was off the line of the road. It was perceived that there might be four different types of excavation:

1. Selected excavation of earthworks and buried soils.
2. Small excavations to deal with specific problems such as soil marks.
3. Trial excavation by machine.
4. Large scale stripping of non-earthwork sites and intervening areas, thus creating a long section through the countryside which could be examined by soil scientists and other ecological specialists.

There proved to be no trial excavation by machine and there was no large scale strip of areas between sites, but otherwise the excavations did relate to the criteria and types proposed in December 1973. They were not necessarily done in the order in which they were planned because of the difficulties of access.

In 1974 the excavation programme opened, appropriately, with the investigations of the Roman road from Winchester to Silchester, which were of the first type of suggested works. The preserved length of the Roman road was also surveyed, but it was not possible to expose a length of the surface. Where this has been done, the exposure can be a very evocative symbol to people today of a direct contact with the past, as for example with the recently excavated *Via Domitia* at Ambrussum near Villetelle (Hérault) in France (Fiches and Roux 1982 and references in Fiches 1986).

The next site to be excavated was the oval barrow at the south of Micheldever Wood, a careful manual excavation, and this was followed in the late summer of 1974 by the stripping and investigation of the ring-ditch on Easton Down. The winter of 1974 was spent in the excavation of three large-scale sites, all machine cleared, which related to the development of the landscape and were ancillary to other sites. At Burntwood and Bridget's Farms were soil and cropmark sites which were also surveyed with the fluxgate gradiometer, while the site at London Lodge had been discovered by the geophysical survey.

In establishing the programme for 1975/6 there was considerable pressure from the Department of the Environment to tackle settlements. The M3 Archaeological Rescue Committee was also very keen to investigate occupation sites, as these would provide the fixed points around which so much else could be constructed. Parts of the medieval village at Popham were the first to be excavated and further work was done on the Roman road, but most of the year was concerned with the excavation of the 'banjo' enclosure in Micheldever Wood. Excavation had been continuous for two years, but by the winter of 1975/6 it was quite apparent that the construction date for the motorway was slipping to a time several years away. A new approach to the fieldwork programme was needed.

The fieldwork programme was revised to a format of shorter excavation campaigns rather than the previous style of continuous excavation in all seasons. In 1976 a selective programme was established of small-scale trenching of the threatened earthworks in Micheldever Wood, to be followed by excavations at Winnall Down. On Friday 23rd July 1976 the farmer was approached about an autumn excavation at Winnall Down and made the site immediately available until September 20th. Machine clearance started on 26th July and the manual cleaning and excavation on Sunday August 1st; work continued until the September deadline but necessitated the curtailing of the programme in Micheldever Wood. Winnall Down was extensive and could not be totally excavated within such a tight time-scale and it was therefore agreed to pay compensation for loss of crop in order to have access to the site for another twelve months. In the autumn of 1976 a small ring-ditch was dug on Grace's Farm and by early 1977 the programme of small-scale investigations in Micheldever Wood was largely completed. The summer of 1977 was spent finishing Winnall Down and in the winter of 1977/8 a Job Creation Scheme from the Manpower Services Commission examined the entrance, outside the easement, of the 'banjo' enclosure in Micheldever Wood and started the excavation of another ring-ditch which lay half in and half out of the Wood. This piece of work was completed in the summer of 1978.

This was the last excavation of the M3 Archaeological Rescue Committee, which was wound up in June 1980 with most of the post-excavation work completed. Some of the staff were successfully boarded for posts with the then Wessex Archaeological Committee.

The final set-piece excavation was started in the summmer of 1982 with the sampling programme at Easton Lane which developed into a major project and ran until March 1983, to be followed in the spring of 1983 by the watching brief. These latter two projects were organised jointly by the Trust for Wessex Archaeology and Winchester City Council.

Excavation tactics

Within the overall recording system, which developed considerably during the lifetime of the scheme and was supported from April 1975 by a computer based recording and analysis system, the archaeological requirements of each site were individually considered.

Linear features like the Roman road were sectioned, sometimes by machine and then by a parallel hand dug trench. The earthworks in Micheldever Wood were all investigated by hand, either by simple section or by more complex arrangements of trenches at junctions or other areas of special interest. The oval barrow was excavated by hand and the flint debitage recorded in one metre squares (Fasham 1979, Fasham and Ross 1978). Within the 'banjo' enclosure two exploratory trenches revealed a lack of preserved occupation deposits and so it was possible to clear the interior by machine while leaving a safety zone adjacent to the extant earthworks. The entrance of the enclosure was examined within the Wood but

outside the line of the easement, and the details of the approaches to the entrance were recorded in the adjacent arable field (Fasham 1987b). Ploughing had been cutting into the surface of the chalk for several years and so the ploughsoil was removed carefully to the surface of the chalk. The exposed features were cleaned and recorded but not excavated, and thus a complex of ditches and features was elucidated. The sub-surface archaeology was not damaged, although it is acknowledged that finds suspended in the ploughsoil will have been moved considerably from their original position. Whether this will seriously affect future research is a moot point as it seems unlikely at the present time that anybody will return to do further fieldwork in the area.

In the same field, small-scale excavations investigated the nature and the depth to which some soil marks survived in the chalk bedrock (Bowen 1975, Fasham 1983). In places the only sub-surface evidence of the features was very slight depressions, and the basic soil-mark seemed to be suspended in the plough soil (Taylor 1979).

At the medieval site at Popham the finds were recorded in two metre squares in the first excavation (Fasham 1987a). In terms of national priorities for medieval village studies, Popham was not ranked highly and resources were not made available for the complete excavation of the threatened part of the site. The 1975 programme of work made it quite clear that because of the nature of the Clay-with-Flints and the slightness of the archaeological remains, a watching brief during construction would not be very rewarding. As construction started, the worst fears about the speed of destruction were confirmed and so, with sufficient time existing within the contractors earth-moving programme, an archaeologically controlled machine clearance was implemented. This controlled watching brief seems to have been a reasonable and relatively cheap compromise between the low national status of the site and the basic archaeological desire to record as much as possible before destruction.

The sites at Burntwood Farm, Bridget's Farm (Fasham 1980b) and London Lodge (Fasham 1981) were cleared using a box-scraper in order to obtain the largest possible plan. Winnall Down was stripped at very short notice with a Cat DC9; in the first season the area of the enclosure was stripped and the spoil dumped around the edge. In the second season, when excavation of the interior was complete, the area under spoil heaps was excavated, allowing a strip outside the enclosure to be examined. The need to examine the areas outside enclosures has often been suggested and the results from Winnall Down completely justified the approach.

The sampling excavation at Easton Lane was the culmination of the set piece archaeology of the entire motorway project. It was a rare chance, within the confines of rescue archaeology, to conduct a large-scale experiment. The archaeological problem to be addressed was whether there was any trace of past human activity in the fifteen hectares of what was to become Junction 9. The only feature known was a single linear ditch running north–south. Although it had been possible to arrange for the excavation of Winnall Down, it proved impossible to gain entry for detailed surface collection after 1973 and for detailed geophysical survey after spring 1974. The area of the proposed interchange was surrounded by archaeological sites and it was hard to accept the apparent absence of archaeological features within it. The location seemed suitable for a Saxon settlement when compared with the topographic situations of both Chalton (Addyman and Leigh 1973) and Cowdery's Down (Millett and James 1983) which were both on chalk ridges. However, not even that simple topographic model worked, as quite unexpectedly, a large array of Late Neolithic and Bronze Age features and structures came to light. A 10% sample was achieved by parallel, but randomly selected, transects. The first four transects contained only the linear ditch that was already known from aerial photographs and nerves were beginning to get frayed at the prospect of initiating the archaeological white elephant of the year. The rational argument had always been that the sampling exercise was to see if anything existed and there had always been a 'gut feeling' that something would be found, but the early stages of the sampling were disconcerting with money, machines and manpower all arranged but no significant archaeology. Fortunately there proved to be plenty of archaeology and blushes were spared.

The Watching Brief

In a town where there has been a long tradition of archaeological research and formal excavation, the watching brief can be a useful tool in the archaeologist's kit. Similarly, the observation of a major construction scheme in the countryside will only be of real value if sufficient effort has been put into earlier reconnaissance in the form of excavation, or field survey, or the basic study of aerial photographs. Know your enemy may not be quite the right description but it is certainly the correct sentiment. A watching brief is no substitute for a proper archaeological record even if it does throw up some surprising sites like the odd aqueduct or Saxon settlement.

At Winnall Down/Easton Lane a watching brief could never have been engineered to produce adequate time for more than a most cursory prospection, which might have been misleading. If it had been recorded during a watching brief it is conceivable that the abundance of saucepan type pottery could have led to the suggestion that the Winnall Down enclosure was of Middle Iron Age date rather than of the Early Iron Age. Certainly the slight post-holes of the Bronze Age structures may well not have been visible, or if they were, they might have been removed within minutes. The archaeological record might have consisted of a Middle Iron Age enclosure, a group of unenclosed pits of Iron Age date, linear ditches and traces of a Roman field system – so very far from the truth of the complex

and shifting patterns of settlement and activity extending over three millenia that were recorded.

Civil engineering, in its construction phase, tends to see big as beautiful, especially when there is a lot of material to be moved. The nature of road construction is no different, and topsoil is stripped by machine, usually large box-scrapers pushed by monstrous D8 bulldozers. The exposed surface is not very amenable to archaeological research. The archaeological features are relatively well-defined on chalk, with the dark infill looking quite clear. But even on chalk it is hard to observe features after heavy machinery has been at work. There are no optimum conditions; when it is dry it is too dusty for features to emerge from the covering of chalk dust and when it is wet it becomes a sea of white mud. The only reasonable conditions occur when the stripping is in progress: a noisy and time consuming affair, but the best way to see a freshly stripped surface when features can be noted for further work once the plant has moved. This, of course, assumes that there is adequate man-power to watch the machines and to investigate the exposed features. As much as possible of the M3 was watched at the stage of machine stripping of the topsoil. Two separate contracts were awarded for the construction of the motorway, but fortunately the topsoil strips were more or less consecutive rather than simultaneous, a situation which would have been intolerable.

Drainage ditches down the sides of the carriageways are often dug at an early stage in the contract and their inspection provides an easy way of detecting possible archaeological features. Subjectively, there seemed to be fewer side-ditches on the M3 than on the M40 (Rowley and Davies 1973). The Saxon settlement at Abbots Worthy was discovered in side ditches which sliced through sunken-featured buildings.

Once the topsoil is removed, the cut and fill operation for embankments and cuttings starts and here the bedrock is removed from a series of vertical faces which, where necessary, are graded, but not in horizontal bands, by box-scrapers. At this stage the archaeological interest is over. If it was hard to see archaeological traces on the chalk, it was impossible on the Clay-with-Flints which was baked hard in the sun. There was no visible trace of the 'banjo' enclosure in Micheldever Wood after the topsoil strip. It is salutary to think that without the advance survey and set-piece excavations, a major archaeological site would have disappeared without trace. The unanswerable question is, how many sites were never discovered despite all the advance efforts? With twelve new sites from the watching brief it would be naive to suggest that the totality of the archaeological record was recovered.

A considerable area of land is used in excess of the easement line for borrow pits, surplus or waste soil dumps, for temporary topsoil dumps, site offices, contractors' compounds for plant and concrete manufacture, and the temporary caravan cities for the workforce. The Resident Engineer has power over the works directly related to the road and the provision of their office compound, but all the other ancillary works are the responsibility of the contractor who negotiates separate arrangements with each landowner.

To complete the recording of Easton Lane it was necessary to secure a difficult arrangement for the office compound. The office compound is the first thing to be built and is always wanted as a matter of urgency. It was necessary to agree a programme whereby the contractor stripped the site and then made it available for two to three weeks for archaeological research in a phased way so that there was minimal delay to the construction. Caravan city was the next part of the Easton Lane site to be stripped, and so even before the main earthmoving contract had started recording was taking place on 4.75 hectares. The advanced archaeological programme at Easton Lane provided the necessary data to promote a proven case for archaeological work on the contractors' areas and the existing archaeological presence ensured that a satisfactory compromise was achieved between the interests of the archaeologists and those of the contractors. The archaeological record was not jeopardised by this arrangement. A 1–2% evaluation of the area would have stood a good chance of returning a negative result. The requirement for assessments to produce first class archaeological data is of paramount importance as the profession moves into the decade of consultancies, contracts and competitive tendering.

The two small pits at The Lawn were in the area of a surplus soil dump. Most of these dumps, including temporary topsoil dumps, involve the removal of the topsoil in the area concerned, and so there is bound to be some archaeological damage. It is within the power of the local authorities to impose conditions or seek legal agreements for most of the dump or borrow sites either at District level or frequently at County level, since the latter are, or can be, regarded as mineral extraction and thus are subject to planning control. In 1987 during construction of the Warminster By-Pass it was realised that extra material was needed for embankments. The only suitable and available material was under an archaeological site. Planning permission was needed and an archaeological agreement was reached whereby the contractor commissioned and paid the Trust for Wessex Archaeology to do all necessary works including preparation of the report for publication (Farwell in prep). The estimate included provision for the actual publication costs.

At all times on the M3 the relationships were good between the Department of Transport's consulting engineers, Mott, Hay and Anderson, the main and the earthmoving contractors, and the archaeologists. No reasonable request for time or help with machines was denied. Although the archaeological background to the route was well known to the main personnel on the construction side who where therefore expecting an archaeological response, it is correct to believe that the professional attitudes from the archaeological side struck a sympathetic chord. There is no doubt that archaeologists are not always the most popular people on construction projects where, even in the late 1980's, it was still possible to encounter the traditional image of an archaeologist as an elderly, slightly eccentric, white-haired man or woman behaving in an amateurish way without any understanding of the cost implication of a delay to a construction programme which might be spending more than a hundred thousand pounds every week. As the increasingly expanding free-market economy affects archaeological work, such an antiquated perception of the archaeologist has, however, more or less disappeared.

The Department of Transport has various manuals covering most eventualities that might occur when a road is being built. In Annex 4 of Manual TRU 504, which was valid in 1983, there is provision for rearrangement of construction work in the event of an archaeological site being discovered. It goes without saying that the site must be of national importance and deemed to be so by the Department of the Environment, presumably now by English Heritage. An agreement was readily reached by all concerned when the Saxon site at Abbots Worthy came to light. The existence of provisions in the manual undoubtedly helped, as did the professionalism from the archaeological side and the enthusiasm of the Resident Engineer. It could not be argued that any other site discovered during the watching brief merited such attention.

The main problems encountered during the watching brief were not of working with and amid the construction teams, but were purely archaeological, relating to the difficulties of recognising archaeological features.

Approaches to the Environment

'The aim of the MARC 3 Committee is to reconstruct the landscape as formed by man's activities over some 5,000 years. . . .'

'The value of the excavation campaign is directly comparable with the volume of environmental work that is undertaken. Without the detailed environmental and ecological studies the worth of any archaeological assessment of settlement and cultivation patterns is reduced by perhaps a margin of 50%.'

These quotes are from a paper outlining the environmental requirements for the M3 which was prepared in Febuary 1974. The first sentiment indicates that the theoretical aims of the whole project wished to move on to a plane somewhat higher than the initial aims of discovering and recording archaeological sites. The second extract is an unequivocal statement of the importance that was beginning to be attached to environmental work in most areas of archaeology in the early 1970's, and of its perceived relevance to the likely programme of fieldwork on the M3. Although the environmental work could never be co-ordinated and integrated as much as had been hoped, its importance is demonstrated by the contributions from Coy and Maltby, Evans and Williams, and Monk in this volume.

In the first half of the 1970's Dr Jane Renfrew was supervising a series of post-graduate students at the University of Southampton in the arts of studying seed and plant remains from archaeological sites. The timing could not have been more propitious, with students wanting material and an excavator having samples in abundance. At the same time, the Department of the Environment established the Faunal Remains Project at Southampton University and there was very close collaboration in the retrieval of animal bones from the the main settlement excavations. Dr Evans had also completed a major set of work and was prepared to supervise a programme of molluscan analysis. Charcoal was the province of the Ancient Monuments Laboratory and yet another Southampton University student was able to find some pollen in the peats of the Itchen Valley. Sadly none of the ancient soils buried under earthworks contained pollen.

A combined flotation and wet-sieving machine was developed which was able to make use of an available supply of compressed air and thus generate a high level of froth agitation (Lapinskas 1974). The excavation of the settlement sites was particularly geared to programmes of environmental recovery, with the Micheldever Wood 'banjo' enclosure perhaps being more rigorously sampled than Winnall Down. Easton Lane was not sampled to the same level as the two earlier excavations. Various tests were run on the validity of the sampling strategy and on the mechanical qualities of the flotation machine itself (Fasham and Monk 1978, Monk and Fasham 1980).

One advantage of the continuing delay in construction was the oppurtunity to leave open some of the pits excavated within the 'banjo' enclosure in Micheldever Wood. These were re-excavated after a three-year interval and the study of the infill process was extremely instructive, enabling clear recognition – with hindsight – of the natural processes of collapse and infill in the Iron Age in comparison with the artificial midden component of the abandoned pit.

As in 1974, the same importance is still attached to the environmental work and thus the major participants in the programme have contributed to this volume with their own thoughts, sometimes with new and further levels of analysis, about the work they were involved with on the M3 project.

Attitudes towards Post-excavation

In the 1973 project design (Biddle and Emery 1973), the preparation and publication of excavation reports was referred to on several occasions but surprisingly the likely real scale of the work was not stressed. The complexity of urban excavation, and the resulting post-excavation problems, were well known; for example the amount of effort needed to produce a chronological sequence based on stratigraphy was being examined by Harris who published two years later (Harris 1975). Gravel extraction had led to some big excavation and salvage operations in the Thames valley in the 1960's (Case *et al* 1965) and

Pryor had started his major series of excavations at Fengate (Pryor 1974). Dr Wainwright, with work at sites such as Marden (1971), Durrington Walls (Wainwright and Longworth 1971) and Tollard Royal (1968), and Professor Cunliffe at Fishbourne (Cunliffe 1971), had demonstrated the value of large scale excavation in the countryside. They had also published the results with great speed and clarity and made the process seem effortless, so that it is perhaps understandable that the full post-excavation requirements of large rural excavations were not fully considered in the 1973 project design. It was a time when the problems of report writing and non-publication were just beginning to be aired in archaeological debate, but the forward planning of post-excavation work was not regarded as an essential element of archaeological work. Post-excavation research designs were a long way off in the future.

In 1974 Tye Brisbane was appointed as Finds Assistant and was keen to develop a machine-aided finds processing system. In discussion with Hampshire County Council it was agreed to establish a suite of programmes to enable all aspects of the archaeological work to be stored and manipulated on the Council's mainframe. The programme started to be used in April 1975 and once the 1974 data had been entered it proved to be of considerable value in post-excavation work. The system was hierarchical and commenced at the site level, although the full details of the site were in practice never entered, and descended through feature, layer, recorded find, sample and unrecorded find (*eg* bulk finds of pottery). The unrecorded finds categories, particularly the pottery, could be enhanced by recording the fabric, form, decoration and all the other important attributes a single sherd of pottery might contain. The data were entered in batches on simple input forms and each record could hold up to forty attributes. Standard interrogation packages were provided for basic listing and the system was designed to enable specific *ad hoc* interrogations accessed through the County's existing programmes. The programme was designed by staff of Hampshire County Council Treasurer's Department to cover most of the likely archaeological needs that could be anticipated by archaeologists in 1974, when this level of machine utilisation was almost unknown and there were no easily available models to work with. It was never an easy system to use, with the need to codify data, with batch entry, and the fact that neither the hardware nor the software were under the immediate control of archaeologists. It was designed to enable the M3 Archaeological Rescue Committee to prepare reports for publication and to maintain an archive. The data are still held by the Hampshire County Council and can be interrogated, in the same way as the original users were able to, through the County Museums Service. It was never intended that an external user would wish to copy the tapes for use on other machines with all the associated problems (Rodgers 1987, Fasham and Hawkes 1987). The staff of the Treasurer's Department developed a system which, it is estimated, holds 30,000,000 characters relating to about 2,000,000 retrievable and manipulatative data. The value of the system has been discussed before (Fasham and Hawkes 1980). It was calculated that the average annual cost for the years 1975–1980 was £2500, which realised a substantial benefit in that results were being produced in one year which would have taken four man-years to achieve with a manual system. The increased efficiency of available man-days was one of the important advantages of the system. The most satisfying application was in the production of listings and plots which made possible the tentative steps to spatial analysis in the Winnall Down report.

The introduction of the computer system was reflected in all the operational aspects of the project. The site recording system was forced to become more logical, as was the process of excavation. The computer did not dictate the approach to the archaeological record but it certainly ensured a more rigorous approach. Unlike Pryor's early experiences (Pryor 1980), we did not find that the division between excavation and post-excavation disappeared. On a philosophical basis, certainly, the whole process of digging and writing was seen as a single entity, but on a practical level there was compartmentalisation, with field records created on site and data being prepared for input in one office and taken to the machine in another building three miles away.

As the computer system was developed in 1974 it became obvious that a large amount of paper and data were going to be generated and that it would need to be arranged and maintained sensibly as it could not all be published. This not very conscious strand was brought into sharp focus by the Frere report (DOE 1975) with its four levels of record and the positive use of archive.

In March 1974, before excavation had started, the need for a draughtsman and report preparation assistant had been outlined. These posts were additional to the staff levels recommended in the original 1973 project design. Within six months of starting a continuous programme of fieldwork, it was decided that a volunteer should help with preparation of work for publication. That decision was taken in October 1974 and was considerably improved upon when, in January 1975, the post was formalised and a Report Assistant was appointed. The need to prepare the way for archive preparation and report writing was recognised and the means of following the task through were being made available.

The last paragraph referred to the use of a 'volunteer', the improvement in employment standards since the inception of the M3 project has been one of the most important developments within archaeology, buttressed by the formation in 1982 of the Institute of Field Archaeologists, an organisation designed to promote professional standards.

The Results

Earlier sections of this review summarised the main approaches employed on the scheme and sketched, very briefly, some of the trends and constraints of the time. This section will summarise the results of the survey and the set-piece excavations in straight number terms and compare the numbers with the results from the watching brief.

The number game

The initial survey discovered 81 sites within a broad corridor. Only four were on the precise route, although on the basis of other motorways it was anticipated that, on average, there would be a site every half mile (Fowler and Walthew 1971, Fowler 1973, Rowley and Davies 1973). In considering the results, it is only right to refer to the 17 kilometres of motorway that was built in 1982/3. By the time the intensive survey and set-piece excavations were completed, 34 sites or features were known on the route. The figure of 34 includes the individual components of the earthworks that were excavated in Micheldever Wood; they have been counted in this way on the basis that, had the ditches been found in a ploughed field, each would have been credited with the term 'site'. Itchen Wood is immediately south of Micheldever Wood and also contains earthworks, but as it was impossible to survey them in advance, they are counted as a single site. Counting on the same basis, there were 28 excavations before construction started. Four of the outstanding sites were excavated as part of the watching brief and there was no archaeological evidence for the other two possible sites. Thirteen new sites were recorded during the watching brief, but although these were mainly isolated pits or ditches, the Anglo-Saxon site at Abbots Worthy and the Roman aqueduct were important additions from the construction stage.

There were thus 45 sites recorded on the line of the M3. The sites are listed in Table 23. Winnall Down and Easton Lane have been counted as separate sites as they have always been administratively discrete. Taking those two as separate, there were three prehistoric settlements, one Saxon settlement and one Saxon activity area, with one Medieval settlement. One barrow and five ring-ditches were excavated, as well as three sites relating to roads and communications in the Roman period; the remaining sites were pits, banks, ditches and other features.

The 45 sites along 17 kilometres of motorway occurred on average every 378m (413 yards) or, put another way, there were almost 2.7 sites per kilometre (4.3 per mile).

The last few paragraphs demonstrate the absurdity of thinking in terms of sites. The Winnall Down/Easton Lane complex extended for 0.8 kilometre along the route and occupied an area of 11 hectares (28 acres) within which had occurred a range of different human activites for 5,000 years from the middle of the fourth millenium BC – the ring-ditch (Fasham 1982) – through to the end of the first millenium AD with the Late Saxon ditched enclosure. These were not two sites but a part of the ever-changing landscape which man exploited differently at various times, right up to the destructive use of the topography by a motorway inter-change.

Micheldever Wood and, to a lesser extent, Itchen Wood are classic examples of the nonsense of the concept of site, with their preserved landscapes, although that in the latter has not yet been properly deciphered. The trees of Micheldever Wood stand on what are broadly three landscapes (Fig 47): a relict and incomplete later prehistoric one with traces from the Bronze Age; an extensive Roman estate of two phases; and a post-Roman, probably Medieval, system of coppices and woodland manage-ment remains. The level of preservation of the Roman landscape is remarkable with the field boundaries being slight spread banks which would leave no evidence in an arable field. It is debatable whether the hollow-ways would leave any trace visible to the aerial archaeologist and, thus, if that site had been not preserved by woodland, the only evidence of that landscape would have been the main building itself and one or two of the ditches. It would

have been represented as two or three separate sites, just dots on the distribution map.

A larger theoretical and practical framework than was available was required to come to terms with intra-site spatial relationships and the full diachronic development of the landscape, but some elements not often excavated were investigated. One was the rural Roman track on Bridget's and Burntwood Farms, where the detail of the wear pattern of traffic was clearly exposed in the hollow-way, with the six burials in very large graves alongside a slight linear ditch. That road and its flanking diches were carved across a countryside which had been evolving with assistance from man for two thousand years in much the same way as, two thousand years later, the motorway itself marched across the landscape. The molluscan evidence for landscape change in this area north of the River Itchen is dramatic.

The real answer to the question of how many sites were dug in the course of the M3 project is that there were 45 investigations but only one site.

Chapter 4

The Animal Bone Analyses on the M3 Project – A Review
by J M Maltby and J P Coy

Introduction

Animal bones from all of the excavations of this project were examined at the Faunal Remains Unit, Department of Archaelogy, University of Southampton, by various members of the Unit's staff. Identification lists, archives and reports are housed at the Unit. Most sites produced only a handful of bones and therefore no detailed analyses could be carried out. Two excavations, however, produced samples of sufficient size for more substantial studies to be undertaken and it is the results from these which will now be discussed.

The first of these samples was obtained from the excavations of the 'banjo' enclosure on the west side of Micheldever Wood (R27). About 8,000 fragments were recorded from normal retrieval methods and a further 264 fragments from sieving. About two-thirds of the fragments were obtained from Middle Iron Age deposits (Phase 2); most of the remainder were found in Late Iron Age–Early Romano-British contexts (Phase 3). The results of the detailed analysis of this material can be found in a report by Griffith (nd) and in the excavation report (Coy 1987).

The second set of material worthy of consideration was obtained from excavations at Winnall Down (R17). Faunal samples from three of the phases were of sufficient size to allow detailed analysis to be carried out. Early Iron Age (Phase 3) contexts produced over 3,000 fragments and Middle Iron Age deposits provided over 7,000 fragments (including articulated bones) for analysis. Early Romano-British contexts (Phase 6) contributed a further 3,000 fragments. Results from the detailed analysis of this material can be found in the site report (Maltby 1985a). Additional analysis of the ageing data has also been published (Maltby 1981, Maltby 1982, Cribb 1985). Aspects of the intra-site variability of the faunal remains at Winnall Down have also been discussed by Maltby (1981, 1985b). The subsequent excavations of the area adjacent to the settlement at Winnall Down at the Easton Lane Interchange (W29) produced further data that can be added to the information obtained from the Winnall

Down excavations. About 1,700 fragments of Iron Age to Early Romano-British date were collected during the excavation at Easton Lane and another 1,000 fragments were retrieved from wet-sieving (Maltby 1989a).

Methodological Approaches to the Faunal Analyses

The samples of animal bones from Micheldever Wood and Winnall Down/Easton Lane were not particularly large. Other sites in Hampshire have produced much larger collections. The assemblages from the Iron Age hill fort at Danebury (Grant 1984a) and the Middle Iron Age–Late Romano-British farmstead at Owslebury (Maltby nd 1) both provided over 100,000 fragments. Nevertheless, the samples from Micheldever Wood and Winnall Down are still two of the larger Iron Age assemblages from Britain to have been studied to date (Maltby nd 2), and the main value of their analyses lies in the methods employed rather than in mere sample size.

When the analysis of the assemblage from Micheldever Wood was carried out in 1976–1977, very little work had been done on the examination of the processes that created faunal assemblages on sites such as these. At the time the word 'taphonomy' (the study of change in organic remains after death) was rarely encountered in British archaeozoological circles, although the results of such work in America and Africa were beginning to be heeded.

In Britain, problems of differential preservation of faunal assemblages were only just beginning to be tackled seriously. Similarly, although there was an increasing awareness that assemblages could vary substantially within a site because of differential carcase processing activities, little work of that nature had at that stage been carried out on rural assemblages. The problems of differential retrieval rates through the lack of sieving had received greater recognition (eg Payne 1975, Barker 1975), but once again few experiments had been carried out in Britain to test for the possible degree of bias. It was still common for archaeozoologists to assume that their samples were always typical of the bones originally deposited and, by inference, that they directly reflected the pastoral economy of the inhabitants of the settlement under study. The strategy for sampling and analysis of the faunal remains at Micheldever Wood was designed in conjunction with the excavators to investigate such intra-site variability in detail.

Niall Griffith's painstaking analysis of the bones from the excavations involved the study of many of the possible mechanisms that could have resulted in differential deposition and preservation. It was soon realised that there would be no simple answer. In collaboration with Tim Holt of the Department of Social Statistics, University of Southampton, analysis of the relationships of a number of variables (*eg* fragment size, species, anatomical element, deposit type) was carried out using multivariate contingency testing. The results were able to pinpoint various trends and interactions amongst the variables, and some of the conclusions will be discussed below. Unfortunately, the sample size restricted the analysis but the results nevertheless clearly demonstrated the amount of variability that could be encountered even on a comparatively simple Iron Age site.

The analysis of the Iron Age and Romano-British samples from Winnall Down followed the lead of the work carried out at Micheldever Wood. Although some of the methods were different (analysis relied, for example, on fragment counts as opposed to 'whole bone equivalents' and multivariate contingency testing was not employed), the approach was essentially the same. The first priority was to understand what processes had created the faunal assemblage and how much variability there was. Only then could more general statements be made about animal husbandry and exploitation. In the light of earlier work both at Micheldever Wood and elsewhere, more detailed records of the faunal data were made. This was facilitated by the use of computer-recording methods employing the Ancient Monuments Laboratory system of coding.

Sieving Programmes

The results from sieving experiments were unspectacular. At Micheldever Wood, it was shown that knowledge that a deposit was going to be sieved had an adverse affect on normal retrieval rates. In total, the partial sieving of the fills of twelve features through a 3mm mesh produced 51 bones identifiable to species, of which only nine belonged to amphibians or small mammals. During the Easton Lane excavations results from wet-sieving of samples from over 100 Iron Age and Romano-British contexts through a 1mm mesh produced much larger quantities of such bones. Out of a total of 1,266 fragments obtained from sieved samples, 705 were identifiable, of which 668 belonged to small mammals, birds and fish. The results showed that freshwater fish were

occasionally exploited at the settlement during the Iron Age.

Amongst the major food species, sieving produced a greater proportion of sheep and pig bones in comparison with cattle and horse. Throughout this paper 'sheep' will also include all elements originally assigned to the 'sheep/goat' category, since bones specifically identified as goat were extremely rare. The same pattern is reflected amongst the unidentifiable material. The majority of such fragments belonged to sheep-sized mammal (sheep, goat, pig, roe deer or dog). It can therefore be inferred that normal retrieval, to some extent, biased the samples in favour of the large mammals. The degree of bias has not been clearly established, since the numbers of identifiable bones of the major species were limited, but it may have been quite low. A rough guide to retrieval rates can often be established by comparing the relative numbers of first and second phalanges in the samples of cattle and sheep. Calculations on the Winnall Down samples indicate that retrieval rates were amongst the best of the 31 samples from Britain and Europe that were compared (Maltby 1985b, 37–40).

Results of sieving experiments on these and other chalkland sites in Wessex have shown that wet-sieving of 5-litre soil samples through a 1mm mesh provides evidence for which species of small mammals, birds, amphibians and fish were present. In addition, it may be worthwhile to experiment on a future excavation of a site of this sort with a much more extensive sieving programme. This would involve the wet or dry sieving (depending on soil conditions) of a much larger proportion of the soil through a larger mesh size. This programme would be designed to trap a greater proportion of the bones of the major species and would provide a sample of sufficent size to establish more clearly what the effects of any retrieval bias upon the samples of the major species are on Iron Age and Romano-British sites of this nature. Such a programme would bridge the gap between the results obtained from samples collected by trowelling large amounts of the archaeological deposits and those obtained from the intensive study of small amounts of material from soil samples.

Density Analysis

One of the most successful methods of analysis of the faunal remains from both sites consisted of the calculation of fragment (and whole bone equivalent) densities per cubic metre of deposit excavated. Using such figures it was possible to trace the pattern of intensity of bone deposition across the sites. At Micheldever Wood, for example, pits near the centre of the Phase 2 banjo enclosure tended to produce greater bone densities. Similarly, at Winnall Down, there was a tendency for bone densities to decrease in pits as they got further away from the hut circles and nearer to the periphery of the Middle Iron Age settlement. In the Early Iron Age phase of the same site, fragment densities in the enclosure ditch tended to be greater in sections near the entrance, whereas low densities were encountered in sections of the ditch on the other side of the enclosure. This would suggest that there was a greater amount of activity involving animal carcases in the former area.

At both sites bone densities tended to be higher in pits than in ditches. Whether this was due to behavioural factors or to differential preservation was not clear. The answer probably lies in a combination of the two. One of the merits of density studies is that the volume of earth excavated acts as an independent variable against which various attributes of faunal assemblages can be assessed. In most faunal analyses calculations have to rely on the relative abundance of particular attributes (*eg* the relative numbers of fragments of the different species, or the percentages of the different skeletal elements represented). Such calculations can be biased by unusual concentrations of a particular species or element. By using volume as an independent variable, such biases can be spotted more easily. It is hoped that more excavators will be encouraged to provide detailed information about the volumes of archaeological deposits excavated to enable further studies of this sort to be carried out.

Analysis of Bone Preservation

The systematic recording of preservation evidence on the bones was an important component of the faunal analyses. Quantification of gnawing marks, surface erosion, ivoried and burnt bones was carried out at both sites. Such information, coupled with detailed recording of fragmentation data, can assist greatly in the understanding of how assemblages were created and modified taphonomically.

The results of such analyses revealed some interesting patterns. At Micheldever Wood, ivoried and burnt fragments were found almost exclusively in pits. The very presence of such bones may be indicative of domestic rubbish disposal. For example, animal bones are most likely to be burnt during cooking or in house or rubbish fires. At the time of excavation there was speculation about the possible function of 'banjo' enclosures. Some had suggested that they may have been cattle corrals. However, the excavations and the subsequent work on the faunal and plant remains clearly showed that Micheldever Wood was an occupation site of people involved in a mixed farming economy.

As at Micheldever Wood, most of the ivoried bones from Winnall Down belonged to sheep-sized mammals, although small fragments of all the major domestic species were sometimes affected. The process by which bones get an ivoried texture has still not been satisfactorily explained and experiments designed to test the origin of this texture are long overdue. It was thought that roasting may have been the cause (Coy 1975) but such an explanation cannot account for all occurrences of ivoried fragments. Analysis of the Iron Age pits at Easton Lane and other Iron Age samples has shown that ivoried fragments were more common in the lower fills of such features and it seems possible that the speed and depth of burial may have some bearing on the matter.

Evidence for gnawing on animal bone fragments is commonly encountered in settlements such as Micheldever Wood and Winnall Down. Scavenging by dogs in particular is likely to have moved and modified or destroyed many of the bones originally discarded. However, it is only in recent years that attempts have been made to quantify both the proportions of gnawed fragments present and the possible destructive effects scavenging had on the assemblages. Canid gnawing tends to destroy more of the parts of the skeleton that have a high cancellous bone content, such as the vertebrae and the ends of longbones. Analysis of the samples from these sites also indicated that the bones of sheep and pig were more likely to be modified or destroyed than those of cattle and horse. At Winnall Down, for example, consistently fewer articular surfaces of sheep limb bones survived in comparison with the cattle sample throughout the deposits. The analysis revealed that most of the deposits contained bones that had suffered from scavenging. In some cases it is possible that animal gnawing may have taken place in the exact locations where the bones were recovered. However, gnawed bones in the lower layers of the deepest pits are more likely to have been modified prior to final disposal. Indeed, it seems possible that most bones were only deposited into the pits and ditches after they had been accessible to dogs. Only when such features became disused were animal bones sometimes thrown in, along with other rubbish.

At Winnall Down, many of the bones had been damaged by surface erosion. This was especially severe in shallow features such as quarries and hut gullies. This, together with gnawing, may have destroyed much of the assemblage originally deposited. The effects can clearly be seen in the relative frequency of the skeletal elements that were recovered. Dense elements, particularly loose teeth, survived in much greater numbers than fragile elements. The percentage of loose teeth showed strong positive correlations with the shallowness of the deposit and the amounts of surface erosion observed on the surviving bones (Maltby 1985b, 42–44). The results showed not only that there was increasing bias towards the survival of the denser elements but also that there was differential preservation between species. The cattle and horse assemblages contained fewer loose teeth and, although they were also increasingly biased towards denser elements in poorly preserved and shallow contexts, different parts of the skeleton were more evenly represented. The poorer survival of sheep and pig bones was made worse by the fact that more of their carcases belonged to immature animals, whose more fragile skeletons were more likely to be destroyed. Estimates of bone loss at Micheldever Wood also suggested that a large proportion of the bones of all species had not survived, although variations between species were not as clear as at Winnall Down.

In addition to variability caused by differential preservation of bones in context types of different depths, it seems likely that assemblages within each context type will also vary according to depth. This factor was not tested during the initial analyses at Micheldever Wood and Winnall Down, but work at other Iron Age sites has demonstrated that it should be taken into account (Wilson 1985, Maltby nd 1). Further studies of depth-dependent variability amongst faunal material at Winnall Down are included in current research (P Rodgers pers comm).

The analysis of various preservation criteria has therefore assisted greatly in the understanding of how the assemblages were created. In many respects, the analyses of these samples and others in the past ten years can be seen as pioneering work. Various methods of quantification have been attempted and these undoubtedly will have to be refined once further studies and experimental work have been completed. Nevertheless these initial studies have shown that a lot of useful information can be obtained that is of interest to archaeologists attempting to interpret site formation processes as well as to archaeozoologists themselves. Without a clear understanding of taphonomic processes, accurate assessments of animal exploitation cannot be achieved.

Analysis of Intra-Site Variability

A comparison of faunal samples from different deposit types was high amongst the priorities of the analyses at Micheldever Wood and Winnall Down. In general, ditch deposits contained a higher proportion of bones of large mammals than pits at both settlements. Multivariate contingency testing at Micheldever Wood further suggested that relatively more pig bones were found in the enclosure ditch. Similar contrasts have been observed between pit and ditch contents at several Iron Age and Early Romano-British sites (Maltby nd 2). Sheep bones were consistently better represented in pits. It has already been shown that variability between context types may partly be dependent upon their depth. For example, bones have been shown to preserve quite poorly in most shallow gulley and quarry features. This will tend to bias these samples towards cattle and horse.

However, studies at these sites have shown that not all the variability can be explained by taphonomic factors alone. Preservation in some of the deeper ditches and most of the pits was not that dissimilar. In addition, cross-tabulation analysis on the Early Iron Age assemblages at Winnall Down showed that the density distribution of most cattle elements did not have significant positive correlations with sheep or sheep-sized elements, whereas they were usually positively correlated with most other cattle and horse bones. Conversely, the sheep

and sheep-sized elements tended to have significant correlations only with each other, irrespective of deposit type. In other words, it seems that cattle and horse bones tended to be deposited together more often than sheep and cattle bones were.

One likely explanation for this is that the processing of carcases varied according to species size and sometimes took place in different parts of the settlement. The carcases of large mammals may more often have been butchered near the periphery of the settlement. Carcase segmentation and filleting of meat from the bone may have resulted in fewer of their bones being incorporated in the cooking process. More of the segmentation and filleting of the smaller sheep and pig carcases may have been performed during or after cooking (Halstead et al 1978). Such processing variability may be reflected amongst subsequent rubbish disposal patterns. Although such an explanation may appear to be oversimplistic, the results from both these sites and others (eg Wilson 1985) fit broadly into such a pattern. In support of this, intra-site variability in species representation can also be seen within context types. It is perhaps significant that the two Middle Iron Age pits (6595 and 4006) at Winnall Down which had the greatest concentrations of cattle bones were not amongst the main pit groups. In addition, contemporary pits from the Easton Lane excavations, which were in an area seemingly peripheral to the main focus of the settlement at that time, contained relatively more fragments of cattle and horse than the majority of the pits excavated at Winnall Down.

Most of the animal bones examined at these sites had probably been subjected to secondary deposition. In other words, they had originally been discarded elsewhere and had only subsequently been dumped in the various subterranean features, when these became disused. This would account for much of the fragmentation and modification of the original assemblage, since various destructive agents such as scavengers, trampling and weathering, are likely to have severely disturbed any bones lying on the ground surface for any length of time.

Examples of the primary disposal of large numbers of bones were comparatively rare. Indeed, such cases usually produced assemblages of a quite different nature to the rest of the deposits. Certain features (usually pits) contained complete or partial skeletons. At Winnall Down such groups could be subdivided into three main categories. The first consisted of articulated burials of complete or substantially complete carcases with no evidence for butchering or skinning; the second included bones of neonatal or foetal skeletons; the third consisted of smaller sets of bones dumped after skinning and dismemberment. Occasionally this third category included gnawed bones, but most of the articulated groups seem to have been the subject of primary deposition. Grant (1984a, 1984c) attributed 'special' significance to most of the skeletons found in pits at Danebury. At Winnall Down, most of the articulated groups may simply have been dumped as part of the largely functional process of disposing of carcases down a convenient hole. There may have been exceptions, such as pit 6595 at Winnall Down, where burials of a dog and pig associated with a concentration of bones consisting mainly of cattle and horse were found sealed by a layer of compressed, rammed chalk (Maltby 1985a, 25). This and the faunal contents of several other Middle and Early Iron Age pits were notable for the lack of gnawing marks associated with quite large assemblages of butchery waste. Such dumping may have occurred when unusually large numbers of carcases were processed at the same time, creating suffcient waste to induce immediate deposition and burial. Such processing events are likely to have provided more meat than could be consumed immediately by the inhabitants of the settlement. This would imply either that much of the meat was preserved, possibly by salting, or that such processing was associated with some sort of redistribution of meat, possibly by means of feasting.

Intra-site variability can also be seen in other aspects of the faunal data. The age distribution of sheep mandibles varied significantly between the pits and enclosure ditch in the Early Iron Age phase at Winnall Down. The pits contained a much higher proportion of juvenile animals (Maltby 1982). This was again probably the result of a combination of differential preservation conditions and disposal practices. At Micheldever Wood, the pits contained higher proportions of juvenile and old sheep mandibles than the enclosure ditch. Eleven of the fourteen specimens from the ditch belonged to immature animals; only nineteen of the 48 mandibles from pits were assigned to the same stage. Similar contrasts were encountered at Owslebury (Maltby nd 1).

The intra-site analyses demonstrated how variable samples can be from different context types and from different areas of a settlement. Such contrasts obviously have serious implications for any interpretations of the pastoral economy of a site. The results showed that overall species percentages can depend largely on the relative proportion of different context types sampled. For example, the increase in the percentage of sheep bones in the Middle Iron Age phase at Winnall Down is largely a reflection of the fact that a much greater proportion of the sample was derived from pits located towards the centre of the settlement than in the Early Iron Age deposits. Comparisons of pit contents alone suggest that there was comparatively little change in species representation between the two phases. Similarly, the mortality profiles also appear to be subject to significant intra-site variability. Interpretations of exploitation patterns therefore must take such variations into account.

Sampling strategies on excavations of similar chalkland sites must be carefully considered in the light of this evidence. Although the best preserved and most abundant faunal material is likely to be found in fills of pits, concentration on the acquisition of samples from these at the expense of other features may well result in a very biased and atypical sample. In retrospect, it would have been better to

have sampled a higher proportion of the ditches at Micheldever Wood and Winnall Down for animal bones in order to obtain statistically viable samples to compare with the pits. Nevertheless it is hoped that these analyses have made a valuable contribution towards the investigation of site formation processes.

Interpretations of Animal Exploitation

Having established how much variability in faunal assemblages can be caused by factors other than changes in the dietary preferences of the inhabitants of a settlement or in their exploitation of their domestic stock, it follows that we have to be cautious in how we use the evidence to interpret possible developments in animal husbandry. It is, in fact, very difficult to give precise answers to seemingly simple questions about the relative importance of the different species in the meat diet and for which products the species were most valued. The problems are compounded by the fact that we cannot assume that settlements such as Micheldever Wood and Winnall Down existed in isolation. It is conceivable that there were substantial regional variations in animal husbandry resulting from different management strategies or localised environmental conditions. It is also possible that stock management in some cases may have been organised on some sort of regional basis. Grant (1984b), for example, has argued that cattle in Iron Age Wessex could have calved on upland settlements, such as Danebury, but were then grazed on lower pastures associated with valley settlements until they were of an age when they could be used as draught or breeding animals. Stock movements and redistribution of both livestock and carcases are likely to have been common activities. Consequently, it cannot be assumed that all the bones deposited at a settlement only represent animals that were bred, exploited and subsequently culled by its inhabitants. Archaeozoologists have to interpret their evidence within the framework of regional exploitation patterns and redistributive networks. Unfortunately, the general regional picture has not been obtained. Existing faunal samples in Wessex are heavily biased towards upland, chalkland settlements, whether they are hill forts or smaller settlements. Samples from settlements in valley bottoms are rare, as they are from sites on the Hampshire coast and the New Forest. This may be a very difficult problem to solve, since many possible valley settlements may be protected by colluvial cover from most threats of destruction and will not need to be excavated. Faunal samples from the New Forest and some of the coastal areas are unlikely to survive because of the high acidity of the soil.

Accordingly, even in circumstances where excavators have produced adequate samples that take possible intra-site variability into account, the sample must not necessarily be regarded as being representative of any regional exploitation patterns. It is with these points in mind that we shall briefly compare the results from Micheldever Wood and Winnall Down with those from other Iron Age and Romano-British sites in the area.

Species Representation

Adequate samples were obtained from Micheldever Wood and Winnall Down/Easton Lane to establish that cattle and sheep were the most commonly represented species. The former would have provided by far the most meat and the latter were probably exploited in the greatest numbers. It is perhaps premature to give estimates of what the exact ratios of the two species were, since the problems of differential preservation, retrieval, and disposal strategies are particularly acute in the comparison of these two species. Calculations carried out on some of the larger and more robust skeletal elements of the two species at Winnall Down would indicate that approximately twice as many sheep as cattle were represented in the successive Iron Age and Early Romano-British deposits at the settlement. No dramatic chronological changes were detected. The results are consistent with several other chalkland settlements in Hampshire (Maltby nd 2).

Pig bones were relatively poorly represented, although there is some evidence that the species may have become more important at Micheldever Wood in the later phases. In the various periods, the percentage of pig to sheep fragments was higher at Micheldever Wood (22–30%) than at Winnall Down (14–17%). The differences may lie in the nature of the samples. Pig bones were significantly better represented in the ditch deposits at Micheldever Wood. However, the ratios at Micheldever Wood are similar to those at Owslebury, where the proportion of pig fragments also rose between the Late Iron Age and Early Romano-British periods and it is possible that pig exploitation may have become more important on some sites at that time. The low levels of pig at Winnall Down contrast with some of the Early Roman samples from the towns of Winchester and Silchester, where the percentage of pig to sheep bones often rises to over 40% (Maltby nd 1). This may result from variations in dietary preference and meat redistribution practices. Very high percentages of pig were also recorded in the more wooded valley location of the Iron Age settlement at Groundwell Farm in Wiltshire (Coy 1982a), demonstrating that the full range of regional variability in species representation during this period may not have been encountered in the samples examined to date.

Horse bones were found more frequently than pig bones at Winnall Down, whereas they provided a much smaller component of the assemblage at Micheldever Wood, particularly in the Middle–Late Iron Age deposits. Their carcases may have been more intensively exploited at Winnall Down, where the frequency of butchery marks on horse bones seems to have been more common. On neither site, however, were their bones as fragmented as those of cattle, and their meat value is unlikely to have been the principal reason for their exploitation. The high percentages of horse fragments on these and other Iron Age and rural Romano-British sites contrasts markedly with Roman urban samples, where numbers of horse bones are generally very low, since they did not play a significant role in the large scale meat redistribution activities that took place in towns such as Winchester.

The most consistent evidence for the presence of dogs at the sites comes from the numbers of gnawed bones. Their bones, however, were also encountered in the deposits and there is evidence from both sites that their carcases were at least occasionally skinned and/or butchered. Their bones were, however, more often found in associated or articulated groups than any of the other major domestic species, and this suggests that many of their bodies were not processed. The presence of the bones of foetal or newborn puppies in some deposits at Winnall Down confirms that a breeding population of dogs was kept by the inhabitants. These may have been required for a variety of uses.

Other domestic and wild species seem to have only been rarely exploited. Only two goat horn cores were found at Micheldever Wood and only four fragments (including three horn cores) were identified as goat in the Iron Age deposits at Winnall Down. A partial skeleton of a goat was recovered from an Early Middle Iron Age pit during the Easton Lane excavations. Although more goat bones may be represented amongst the category originally assigned to the 'sheep/goat' category, the vast majority of these probably belonged to sheep. Goat horns (as well as red deer antlers) may have been used occasionally in tool or ornament manufacture at these sites. The flesh of these species, however, was rarely eaten.

Two domestic fowl bones were recovered from Middle Iron Age deposits (Phase 2) at Micheldever Wood. They were not found in any Early or Middle Iron Age deposit at Winnall Down, where they only occur in small numbers in the Early Romano-British levels. The appearance of this species only in the Late Iron Age is typical of other Wessex sites (Maltby 1981, Coy 1984a). Other possible food species include hare and mallard (at both sites), woodcock (Micheldever Wood), other indeterminate species of goose and duck, grey heron, conger eel and indeterminate freshwater species of fish (at Winnall Down/Easton Lane). None of these would have been more than a very occasional resource. In particular, the exploitation of wild animals appears to have been minimal and this is typical of other Iron Age sites in Wessex (Coy 1982b, Grant 1981).

Exploitation of the Major Species

This discussion has repeatedly emphasised the problems of interpreting exploitation strategies from potentially biased samples. Consequently, the results from Micheldever Wood and Winnall Down must be treated with caution until further samples from such sites are analysed.

The results of the ageing analysis of sheep mandibles at Winnall Down are typical of several other Early and Middle Iron Age samples from chalkland sites in Wessex (Maltby 1981, Maltby nd 2, Grant 1984a, Grant 1984b). These samples contain a high proportion of mandibles of neonatal and juvenile lambs under a year old. The neonatal mortalities probably reflect natural deaths amongst flocks lambing in or near the settlement. Relatively few sheep culled at the optimum age and size for meat production (c 18–36 months) were represented. Most of the remaining jaws therefore belonged to adult animals that could have been breeding stock and sources of milk, wool and manure. At Micheldever Wood there was a higher proportion of immature animals. This might imply that meat production was more important at Micheldever Wood and there is a tendency for Late Iron Age samples to produce higher proportions of sheep of this age (Maltby nd 2). We have already seen, however, how much the age profiles of sheep varied in different parts of the sites at both Micheldever Wood and at Winnall Down.

Consequently, the interpretation of the mortality profiles of sheep at these sites is not straightforward. Statements about the relative importance of meat, milk and wool production depend on whether the samples reflect typical mortality rates of the sheep population. It is not clear whether these samples do this. Consequently, although mortality profiles like those from Winnall Down and Danebury may well reflect that both milk and wool production were more important than meat (Grant 1984b, Cribb 1985), further analyses are required to establish whether these samples provide a representative picture.

In addition, discussions of the relative productivity of sheep management systems in the Iron Age must take into account the evidence of metrical data, which demonstrate that the animals were of a small, slender type, which would have produced much less meat, milk and wool per animal than modern commercial breeds. It should also be pointed out that Iron Age sheep management strategies (like any other) would have had to balance the demands for their various products against cost restraints. High first year sheep mortalities (excluding neonatal mortalities) may, for example, reflect that suitable pastures or fodder were restricted and herd sizes had to be controlled. Any greater emphasis on meat and, particularly, wool production, would have resulted in greater investment in the care of the flocks, as a higher proportion of them would need to have been kept alive longer. Consequently, Iron Age mortality profiles may reflect an exploitation strategy designed to maintain stock numbers at the least cost, rather than any conscious concentration on the acquisition of a particular product.

The sample of cattle from Micheldever Wood was too small for detailed ageing analysis. The Winnall Down mandibles were dominated by those from adult animals. Here, and at most other contemporary Iron Age sites in the Wessex chalklands, there was no emphasis on the culling of immature cattle for meat. It is likely that the culling of cattle would only have been done sparingly in order to maintain breeding stocks and to provide transport and draught animals. The value of cattle was such that kill-off strategies may well have been conservative, in order to guard against unexpected stock losses due to disease or rustling.

Clear patterns for the exploitation of cattle in Wessex during the Iron Age and Romano-British periods have yet to be established. Variations in mortality profiles do exist (Grant 1984b, Maltby nd 2), but a more representative sample of sites is required.

Cattle represented at Micheldever Wood and Winnall Down were typical of the small horned type found in Iron Age sites in the area. Some larger cattle were, however, found in the early Romano-British deposits at Winnall Down, suggesting either that new stock had been introduced or that some improvements in the existing stock had been made (assuming of course that the larger cattle belonged to the inhabitants' herds). Butchery styles and carcase utilisation appear to have continued largely along the lines common in the Iron Age periods. Although more bones produced marks made with cleavers in comparison to the Iron Age samples, knife cuts were still more commonly observed. This evidence contrasts markedly with the situation in Winchester, where cattle carcases were much more heavily butchered with cleavers and occasionally saws (Maltby 1985c, 1989b).

Discussions about the exploitation of pigs and horses at these sites are again limited by sample size, particularly at Micheldever Wood. There was no evidence to refute Harcourt's (1979) suggestion that horses were not bred on Iron Age settlements but captured from wild herds and trained. No neonatal or juvenile horses were represented in the deposits. Nearly all were adult animals valued no doubt for their transport qualities and possibly their prestige value. This did not preclude their carcases often being butchered for meat when they died or were killed. Metrical data suggested that the horses were of small stature. Most of the pigs at both Micheldever Wood and Winnall Down were immature. At Winnall Down the most common age for culling appears to have been between 18 and 24 months, an age when free-ranging pigs may have been fattened to a suitable size for slaughter.

Conclusions

Archaeozoologists commonly complain about the small size of their samples, whether they are discussing the evidence from a particular excavation or from a broader regional or diachronic survey. Despite the fact that Hampshire has produced a large number of faunal assemblages in recent years, this is still the case. The samples from Micheldever Wood and Winnall Down/Easton Lane, despite the quality of sampling and retrieval, can only provide a limited understanding of husbandry practices in the Iron Age and Romano-British periods. However, to dwell on this would detract from the many positive achievements of the M3 studies.

The setting up of the Faunal Remains Unit coincided with the impetus provided by the M3 project. The samples from these sites were important because they were the testbeds for pioneering work that investigated how faunal assemblages were created. Such work has clearly demonstrated that interpretations of animal husbandry and exploitation depend on this type of detailed analysis. The results have led to significant modifications in the methods of study and have helped to make the study of animal bones in this country more relevant to archaeological questions, rather than being simply a zoological appendix.

Attempts to strip off the taphonomic overprint in the faunal assemblages from these sites have raised questions about the validity of some traditional views of Iron Age animal husbandry, at least as far as Hampshire is concerned. Sheep, for example, did not necessarily become more important during the Iron Age. Nor was wool production necessarily the principal reason for keeping sheep. Exploitation of wild animals was minimal. The studies, in particular, demonstrated vividly that variability in faunal remains was much greater than had been suspected. The discovery of this variability and the attempts to come to terms with it have occupied much of the subsequent time of the members of the Faunal Remains Unit, and the approach has been extended to cover sites of all periods in Wessex (Coy and Maltby 1987). Apart from providing valuable information about individual sites, such studies will eventually enable us to make general statements about the pastoral economy that are more securely based than those made in the past.

Chapter 5

The Archaeobotanical Work carried out for the M3 Project – A Retrospective View
by M A Monk

Historical Perspective and Background

The mass flotation recovery programme undertaken using the M3 machine (Lapinskas 1974, 16–18), with advice from Pete Lapinskas and Peter Murphy, was one of the initiators in the wider large-scale application of such machines on archaeological sites in southern Britain in the middle 1970's. As it happened, many of the sites where this development occurred, in common with the M3 sites, were Iron Age in date and excavated in advance of destruction; other sites included Gussage All Saints in Dorset, Balksbury, Old Down Farm and Portway in Hampshire and Ashville Trading Estate, Abingdon, in Oxfordshire. The mass of material recovered from these sites using flotation machines offered the prospect of completely revolutionising the understanding of crop husbandry in later prehistoric Wessex. As Jones (1981) has implied in a discussion based in part on the analysis of this material, it has probably also accentuated a bias in plant remains evidence towards this region that has existed since the formative studies of Jessen and Helbaek (1944) and Helbaek (1952). The publication of this work has, nevertheless, been useful in its own right in uncovering important questions and some tantalising enigmas that would not have arisen if it had not been for such work. Amongst them, the detailed M3 studies, particularly those on Micheldever Wood and Winnall Down (also Easton Lane), represent a significant contribution to our knowledge of general agrarian practices, on-site activities and context related studies of plant remains from non-hillfort sites of Middle and Late Iron Age Wessex. The work in Wessex relates mainly to these periods and thereby highlights the absence of detailed evidence for the preceding Early Iron Age and Bronze Age and the succeeding Roman period in this area.

Since the work on the archaeobotanical remains from these sites, particularly the non-charcoal material, was concluded (1979–80 for Micheldever Wood and Winnall Down), important comparanda and three relevant syntheses (Green 1981; Jones 1981,

1984a) have also been completed and published. The latter have sought to put the evidence into a wider perspective. Jones' research in particular has contributed in this respect and boldly pointed to the prospects for future work (1984a, 1985). It is against this background, and with a belief that new insights can be forthcoming from looking back at previously recovered evidence in the light of new material and methodological developments, that the following retrospective review has been undertaken.

Context Complexes, their Interpretation and Archaeobotanical Remains – Possibilities and Limitations

Although sampling for charred macroscopic plant remains was undertaken on all the M3 sites, the two most significant sites in terms of results were the 'banjo' enclosure in Micheldever Wood and the unenclosed Middle Iron Age settlement and Late Iron Age enclosure at Winnall Down, the subject of a 1980 paper (Monk and Fasham 1980), which in particular sought to explore the possibilities of functional interpretation of the contexts from which the plant remains were obtained. In the main, this study concentrated on those contexts that produced not only the most samples but the most productive samples (even though the average density of remains per unit volume of soil was quite low: 2.30 fragments per 1000ml soil for Winnall Down).

In terms of the context range sampled, Winnall Down produced material from the widest range of context types. In addition to pit fills, from which the majority of samples came, samples were also taken from the enclosure ditch, a quarry area, house gulleys and post-holes. The pits were the most productive in terms of remains, which was also true for Micheldever Wood, and all the other context types produced a markedly low incidence of remains per unit volume of deposit processed. The content of these samples, possibly symptomatic of the low frequency, were variable and inconsistent, for instance the samples from the enclosure ditch at Winnall Down produced either a low incidence of seeds of arable weeds or indeterminate cereal grain with eroded surfaces. The appearance of the grain, its low incidence and indetermination has also been noted from ditch fills on other sites of Iron Age date, for example at Poundbury, Dorset. In other types of contexts that contained mixed deposits, like the quarry area at Winnall Down, an equal mixture of damaged grain of several species and seeds of weeds was produced. The few house gulleys were a little more consistent in the remains they produced, usually of charred cereal. This was more evident in a larger number of similar house gulley samples from Poundbury, Dorset, but in all cases the frequency of remains was low. The mechanisms that may lead to the accumulation of such material in former structural features are discussed in Monk (1991; Engelmark 1981, Van Vilsteren 1983) but it can be said that, unless a house structure is burnt down, the areas of such buildings that produce interpretable quantities of remains are most usually in the vicinity of hearths, although not necessarily in the hearth areas themselves.

In contrast to Micheldever Wood, the sampling strategy for pits at Winnall Down was extensive rather than intensive due to time constraints, which meant that, with some exceptions, samples were not taken from every layer. However, where complete sampling did occur and in situations where layer by layer comparisons were possible (pit 5789, layers 5827 and 5828, pit 5597 and pit 7372), it was possible to study the relative abundance of grain against weed seeds and the chaff element from each layer. This study revealed a high frequency of grain against weed seeds in the primary fills of pits 5789, 5597 and 7372, unlike the upper fills of these pits which produced a much higher incidence of seeds of arable weed plants; on this basis it was suggested that what was represented were the charred residues of a semi-cleaned storage product, the chaff produced in Hillman's stage 23/24 while redrying the grain for bulk storage, stage 26 in the Near Eastern ethnographic model for hulled cereals (Hillman 1984); this may have been charred while sterilising a pit for storage (Reynolds 1981). The supporting evidence for this interpretation rested with the high incidence, probably *in situ*, of charred deposits in the primary fills of these pits; similar deposits were also noted in two further Iron Age pits studied by the author in the Poundbury Iron Age extramural settlement (Monk 1987a).

The storage of grain in Iron Age type pits, while demonstrated by experiment and suggested by the literary sources (Pliny, Columella, Varro), had not been studied from the archaeobotanical angle until the M3 work, although independently Jones has published (1984b) the results of a micro-excavation of a large basal deposit of charred material in one of the Danebury pits and has demonstrated more positively, via the increased incidence of 'chitted' grain towards the base and sides of the deposit, the likelihood of storage of grain in Iron Age pits in southern Britain.

It is important to note that opportunities for detailed functional studies of particular context types – as at Danebury and to an extent Winnall Down and Poundbury – only present themselves relatively rarely and need, as demonstrated by Jones, to be targeted for micro-excavation and combined archaeological and specialist attention, using rigorous data recording methodologies (Schofield 1980, MacLeod *et al* 1988, Spence 1990). The usual situation is more complex and leads to interpretative problems where several possibilities need to be considered in the absence of independent data that may account for the mechanisms of deposition. This was the case for many of the samples from the Winnall Down, Micheldever Wood, Easton Lane and Poundbury pits, where the layers produced a predominance of crop processing waste, particularly seeds of arable weeds but also chaff remains of spelt wheat (glume bases and spikelet forks) and barley rachis. Good examples of high incidences of crop processing wastes occurred in the Winnall Down and Easton Lane pits 4928 and 4983, and in the primary fills of pits 1631, 7257, 4475 at Winnall Down. In hindsight, four alternative possibilities offer themselves: either, as Pliny's difficult reference suggests, the charred residue of chaff flooring for storage pits is the explanation; or the remains represent the residue of the chaff which, on the basis of recent ethnographic evidence from central Europe (Fenton 1983), made up part of the pit's seal; or we could be dealing with the charred residues of crop processing waste used as tinder to light domestic fires, as suggested by Hillman for the similarly composed waste product from stage 34 and 35 of his ethnographic model (Hillman 1984); or, as seems very probable, with the remains of chaff used to ignite the sterilising fires hypothesised by Reynolds (1981) to cleanse the fermented residue in the pits before reuse. This charred waste could then remain in the base of the pit if it was not in fact used again and hence remain as primary refuse or could be dumped into a nearby pit that had already gone out of use. Any one of these four alternatives could explain the pattern of charred debris in the Winnall Down and Micheldever Wood pits, as well as the two studied by Carruthers at Easton Lane.

It is also important to note that, as in Jones' Danebury pits and the Iron Age pits at Poundbury and the M3 sites, the upper fills of several of the pits had a very different complement of remains, mainly a low incidence of mixed remains. Although this could not be clearly demonstrated in all cases, these deposits are often very much later in date than the primary fills (*eg* Micheldever Wood layer 303 in pit 298, layer 294 in pit 293 and the upper layers of pit 8). In the body of the pits both at Winnall Down and Micheldever, there was some consistency in the complement of remains within individual pits, as suggested by Jones (1984b) for the Danebury pits he studied in detail. For example at Micheldever Wood, pit 298 and, to a lesser extent, pit 293 consistently produced remains with a high wheat chaff and to a lesser extent grain content, with a medium to high frequency of large-seeded weeds (the *Galium, Bromus, Rumex* groups). In the case of the Winnall Down pits, the more predominant complement of remains included a dominance of barley grain amongst the cereals in the samples, but in many cases the absolute number of weed seeds, including arable weeds with smaller seeds (*Medicago/ Trifolium*), exceeded the cereals, a complement that Jones interprets as crop processing waste used for animal fodder. However, as inferred above from the evidence in pit 293, in some cases the complement of remains in adjacent layers was by no means consistent. In this case, although some layers produced remains with a high wheat chaff content similar to pit 298, two adjacent deposits, 412 and 413, produced a dominance of barley grain, although wheat chaff and weed seeds had a high frequency in both.

A pit and its fills cannot be treated as one entity in time or function as was wrongly implied in the 1980 paper (Monk and Fasham 1980). A pit will have a primary fill (possibly containing archaeobotanical or other evidence of its primary function) and immediate post-function infills such as rubbish either of mixed origin, and/or including residue resulting from its original function. If these secondary infills include organic rubbish, there is likely to be subsidence as such deposits collapse with decay. It is highly likely that such collapse will cause inter-deposit mixing, as indeed may result from rodent action. What is especially important to note is that, if the pits are completely infilled with secondary organic refuse over a short time, subsidence will in time result in depressions at the surface. These depressions may be progressively infilled during the course of the occupation or may occur much later than the activities that gave rise to the original pits, depending on the breakdown of organic material in the pits. Some of these depressions, 'pit holes', may be purposely infilled with whatever topsoil is available by later occupants of the site or, if the site is abandoned, may be subject to a gradual infill of plant debris and leaf-mould and worm-cast material. As Jones (1984b) appreciated in his Danebury report, the charred remains, if any, in these upper fills, as well as deriving perhaps from many sources, will have suffered more 'decay', *ie* surface attrition, wetting and drying activity, by comparison with the earlier deposits in the pits.

To appreciate these various possibilities, it is necessary to take a context-by-context approach not only to the analysis of the archaeobotanical plant remains from samples but also to the sampling strategy adopted to recover them in the first place. It is perhaps apposite to clarify what is meant by a context approach in this sense, because although it ideally attempts to ascertain a functional interpretation for each context and context complex (*ie* reasons for its being), it is only rarely possible to make a clear interpretation, although every excavation may, in fact, present some possibilities. The rarity of attaining a clear-cut interpretation for contexts and the complexity caused by secondary and tertiary deposition or reuse of particular complexes has led to

suggestions (Jones 1985) that studies of discrete areas of contexts and context complexes on sites offer better possibilities in terms of overall interpretation of site activities, particularly in regard to crop processing and domestic use of plants, and changes in these by area through time, than do context-by-context studies. Certainly such a higher order of interpretation, even to the extent of inter-site and regional comparisons based on sites sampled uniformly, needs highlighting but it is fundamental that the quality of the data is assessed by a careful consideration of both the material basis of the remains themselves, sample representation and problems of differential preservation through charring and subsequent deposit or exposure, and the composite nature of the archaeological record based on a context approach. In such a situation, it is essential that the results of archaeobotanical study be integrated with the context-by-context analysis. The term context as it is used here strictly means the lowest individual definable/describable archaeological entity (stratigraphic unit) on the site (Schofield 1980, Monk 1990, Macleaod *et al* 1988, Spence 1990). By taking such an approach, it is impossible to avoid the reality that the archaeological record is a composite structure, amongst other things of post activity accumulations; it is a truism that these deposits only hold indirect evidence of on site activities and past economies, and generalisations made on this basis are inevitably several stages removed from the original source of the evidence.

The context approach is also fundamental, not just to appreciate the interpretative limitations, but also the possibilities of archaeobotanical remains and to see them on a par with other artefactual or ecofactual inclusions in deposits, none of which can be properly interpreted at any higher level unless first fully integrated with the structural archaeological record and its sequence. Only by so doing is it possible to consider the conditions on the data caused by inter-deposit contamination and residuality. Each context in a context-based approach should be analysed in its own right for any patterns, whether those patterns have a human behavioural, functional and/or symbolic meaning or not (for recent theoretical arguments for a contextual approach in archaeology see Butzer 1982 and Hodder 1986). Some deposits representing separate contexts may, in some cases, relate directly to past activities, particularly where sudden events like fires have fossilised them in time without post-depositional disturbance. These deposits may not be common, but when suspected should be targeted for detailed work, as at Micheldever Wood for pits 293 and 298 and the micro-excavation of deposits in pit 1078 at Danebury.

For the most part then, a pit is a context complex, made up of several different contexts, not least its separate fills which may equate with the model of primary, secondary and tertiary deposits outlined above. Although all go to form the pit as a context complex, some considerable lapse of time may separate the original cutting of the pit and its original use from its final filling. A context approach removes the need to treat the pit as a single closed unit and allows for a context by context assessment in the creation of the archaeological record. It is not until such an approach is undertaken that we can possibly have a sound basis for the spatial studies desired by Clarke (1972) and recently argued for archaeobotanical material by Jones (1985). The desirability of a higher level approach is without question but the detailed analysis of single contexts, many of which may not lead in that direction, is the only way to create a sound basis for such speculation. The study of the bioarchaeological remains from the M3 sites represented an early attempt at such an integrated context-orientated approach.

The Crop Plants recovered from the M3 Sites

Although in the case of both the Micheldever Wood and Winnall Down samples most of the remains represent crop processing waste, probably from stages 34 and 35 in Hillman's model (1984), so that deductions about the relative importance of the crops grown are difficult (Dennell 1974), there is sufficient evidence to suggest, qualitatively, the most usual crops grown on these sites. At Micheldever Wood, for example, both six-rowed hulled barley and wheat, much of it probably spelt, are present, but in dominance the latter is most significant both in terms of grain and the chaff element. The same cereals are most clearly evident at Winnall Down, but in terms of general presence and dominance barley is more frequent. These sites produced an unequal number of samples per definable archaeological phase. The majority of samples from Winnall Down and Easton Lane were 'datable' to the Middle Iron Age phase of activity, while at Micheldever Wood the spread of samples included a considerable number that represented a Later Iron Age occupation as well as some that were contemporary with those at Winnall Down. The temporal difference is just one of the variables that have to be considered when making inter-site comparisons between sites that have produced plant remains in this area.

Apart from the cultural influence on the choice of crops grown (Monk 1987b), one important variable that has had attention drawn to it by Dennell (1977) and Jones (1981, 1984a) is soil type in the catchment areas of the sites and their change in fertility through time. The influence of absolute soil type, whether deep, moist, relatively fine-textured loams, or dry, friable, chalkland rendzinas, on choice of crop type has probably been overstated. It has been argued on this basis that wheats prefer the fine-textured, moist clay loams, whereas barley is better suited than wheat to the dry upland soils of the chalk downs. As Jones (1981) has pointed out, this is quite likely to be a generalisation. While barley will not grow where the drainage is poor, it can grow on either heavy or light soils. In the case of wheats, there is indeed a preference of some species, particularly bread wheat (*Triticum aestivum*), for deeper, moist silt/clay soils;

emmer and spelt grow equally well on lighter, dry soils. Spelt, according to Percival (1974, 326), replaces bread wheat on lighter, dry soils and indeed has grown very successfully over a number of years at Butser Ancient Farm (Reynolds 1979, pers comm) on the Middle/Upper Chalk rendzinas. Winnall Down, Easton Lane and Micheldever Wood are all on the Upper Chalk, although within their catchment areas there are deeper loam or clay soils (the Itchen valley in the case of Winnall Down and Easton Lane). The Micheldever Wood site is near the Dever valley, but is located on an expanse of Clay-with-Flints. Whether, in either case, the relative presence in the samples of the two main cultivars, spelt wheat and six-rowed hulled barley, reflects which soils in the catchment areas were being exploited is at least debatable and arguably cannot be ascertained from the relative presence of the cereals themselves, not least for their broad tolerances and the difficulty in using modern soil type as an index for soil status in the past. Bell has indicated from his work that the soils in some areas of the chalkland may have been quite different in early prehistoric times than they are at present. As Jones (1984a) and Carruthers (1989) indicated, the possibility of making such deductions lies in the difficult assessment of the weed flora from charred remains.

In the region as a whole, the other Iron Age sites that have produced plant remains present some important comparanda. At Danebury, Jones (1984b) notes that the most abundant cereal taxa present is *Triticum spelta*, but also present is six-rowed hulled barley, bread/club wheat and emmer, and he also notes that spelt is dominant throughout the occupation at Danebury. By contrast Owlesbury, in a not dissimilar location to Micheldever Wood but to the southeast of Winchester, produced a dominance of barley, although a similar range of wheats to those found at Danebury were also recovered from the Iron Age samples (Murphy 1977). Indeed, on the basis of both the % presence and % dominance assessment that Murphy carried out, barley increases in importance at Owlesbury.

Apart from cereals, the evidence for other crop plants is meagre, not only at Winnall Down, Easton Lane and Micheldever Wood but on the other Iron Age sites referred to earlier. Beans, *Vicia faba*, were identified in samples from Owlesbury as well as individual instances at Winnall Down and Easton Lane, while possible pea fragments, *Pisum sativum*, were identified at both Micheldever Wood and Winnall Down and can be paralleled at Owlesbury. It has been noted previously by Dennell (1972) and Green (1981) that the low incidence of pulses in charred deposits is probably not a true reflection of their importance as a dietary component in the past.

Two further non-hillfort, downland Iron Age occupation sites in Hampshire have been intensively sampled for plant remains – Old Down Farm and Portway. In his study of the remains from these sites, Murphy notes a representation of cereal remains similar to that from Winnall Down and Micheldever Wood. At both sites, the wheats, particularly spelt, dominate the samples and this is particularly so for those of the Middle Iron Age phase at Portway (Murphy 1977). In the late occupation phase at Micheldever Wood (Late Iron Age/Early Roman), although the wheats predominate, the significance of barley increases. In both cases, however, the sample size is much smaller, so it is difficult to make any confident interpretation from this.

Implications of the Weed Flora

Attention has been drawn both in the M3 work (Monk and Fasham 1980, Carruthers 1989) and in Martin Jones' work on Danebury and the Upper Thames Valley (Jones 1978, 1984a) to the potential information that the weed flora can provide about cultivation practices, and more significantly perhaps, for indicating which parts of the catchment area of the sites were being exploited and the changing fertility in those areas. In terms of indicator species for those areas being exploited, Carruthers has suggested the presence of *Anthemis cotula* (Kay 1971) as indicating that areas of heavier clay loams were being exploited from the Winnall Down/Easton Lane site, although the very low frequency of that species, if frequency data can be used in this way, would suggest that these areas were only peripherally exploited. Independent evidence for the cultivation of these soils anywhere in the region at this time is, however, minimal. Carruthers further suggests that *Anthemis* occurs in those pits at Winnall Down that have a higher incidence of wheat than barley, highlighting, as discussed earlier, the possible preference of that species for the deeper, moister loam soils. By contrast, Carruthers points out that *Tripleurospermum maritimum* ssp *inodorum* (which occurs at a far higher incidence in the samples as a whole) occurs more predominantly in samples with a barley dominance, this species along with barley preferring disturbed, dryer, friable soil. There are several instances recorded at Winnall Down where Scentless Mayweed occurs at reasonably high frequency in samples with a high incidence of wheat; this can be paralleled at Danebury in at least one case where a high incidence of wheat and Scentless Mayweed occur together. One of three possibilities may account for this: the mixing in the deposit of crop processing refuse deriving from different crops; that some variations in ecological preferences exist in a humanly amended environment; or that spelt was simply being grown on the dryer, chalkland soils.

Jones makes some further relevant points about the implications of the occurrence of certain weeds in samples from Iron Age contexts in southern Britain (Jones 1981, 1984a, 1984b). He has argued that the presence of some particular species in the samples suggest an expansion of arable land into less well-endowed areas for cereal cultivation, or those less easily cultivated with the then available technology. The incidence of *Chrysanthemum segetum*, a plant that occurs primarily on soils with an acidic ten-

dency, may, at Micheldever Wood and Danebury, indicate the exploitation of such soils in their catchment areas, possibly the Clay-with-Flints in the case of Micheldever Wood. Jones argued that the presence of spike rush *Eleocharis* ssp *palustris* and the sedges in samples from Danebury suggested arable agricultural infringement of marshy areas with the expansion of land exploited for cereals. The occurrence of sedges at all three M3 Iron Age sites and spike rush at Easton Lane, as well as the Buttercup group in some samples, may argue for a similar interpretation, although the numbers of occurrences in each instance are relatively low per sample, except in pit 4978 at Easton Lane. Some areas of heavy soils and others with more acid soils were probably being cultivated, but the extent to which this was occurring cannot be securely estimated.

The presence of areas of grassland within the vicinity of the arable fields, plants from which may have been colonising the fields to a considerable extent, is indicated both by the high incidence of seeds of the grasses themselves in the samples from the M3 sites (particularly Winnall Down) and also by the presence of *Chrysanthemum leucanthemum*, a species common to grassland on good soils (Clapham *et al* 1962). Amongst the grasses, the most distinctive genus present was the Brome group, particularly *Bromus secalinus*. Hubbard (1975) argues that *Bromus secalinus* could have been utilised in the Iron Age as a food source. While this is possible, equally it could have been a weed of spelt wheat (Murphy 1977) and, because of its similar size range to cereal grain, may have been retained in cereal crops following processing, perhaps even tolerated because of its food value. The important implication of this interpreted tolerance of Brome grains is that it opens up a debate on the categorisation of this and other edible wild plants as 'weeds' and may highlight the warping caused by translating contemporary attitudes to our view of crop cleaning efficiency in the past. The models by which archaeobotanists interpret crop processing evidence must always be treated carefully so as not to make interpretations too inflexible.

The association of *Bromus secalinus* with wheat is not as clearly defined for the Winnall Down samples, where it occurs at a high incidence in samples with a greater dominance of barley. Clapham *et al* (1962) refer to chess, *Bromus secalinus*, as once being a significant weed of winter sown wheat. Whether such an association would hold true for the Iron Age is difficult to say. Jones (1981, 1984a) has argued, on the basis of observation at Butser Ancient Farm, that the occurrence of *Galium aparine* may also be related to a winter sowing regime and that this might fit in with the widespread cultivation of spelt as a winter sown crop, barley being more inclined to spring sowing. Seeds of the *Galium* group, including *Galium aparine*, have, like *Bromus* sp, been found in some numbers from the M3 sites although there is no clear association between a high incidence of these species with wheat dominant samples. Indeed, in some instances, as at Winnall Down, the converse is true (pits 4475, 5548, 555 and 5597), although at least in the case of 4475, the remains may represent mixed wheat and barley crop processing waste. For pit 4928 on the Easton Lane site, however, the association does hold true: the waste in this instance being clearly from a spelt crop. The sowing regime of particular crops and the associated weed flora is, however, perhaps not as easily interpretable as might be suggested from the recent experimental and ecological studies made so far. Hillman has also made similar cautionary remarks (Hillman 1981).

Overall, the numbers of weed seeds and their size range at Winnall Down is greater than at Micheldever Wood, including many small-seeded plants. This could be partly accounted for by selective preservation, better conditions generally at Winnall Down, but equally may reflect the nature of the crop processing waste and its subsequent history, including either mixed storage of fine and coarse waste or mixed disposal of the charred material in the pits (Hillman 1981, 1984).

A further point of relevance that may have some general implications, as Jones (1984a) has also argued, is the presence of members of the Leguminosae family in significant numbers. The agricultural importance of legumes lies in their nitrogen fixing capacity and, therefore, their independence from the surrounding soil, unlike other plants, for their nitrogen (Gill and Vear 1980, 139–40). Their increased incidence in samples through time at Old Down Farm, Gussage All Saints and Ashville in the Thames Valley, as well as at Winnall Down, may, as Jones argues, relate to a decreasing soil nutrient status, giving such nitrogen fixing plants a selective advantage over other species. At Winnall Down, the Leguminous species, in particular the *Medicago* (particularly Black Medick, *Medicago lupina*), have an overall dominance over the cereals in the samples. The economic value of these plants in terms of both their nitrogen fixing capacity and their resultant potential as green fertiliser, as well as their value as a fodder crop, may not have been fully appreciated at the time. As a component in the flora of chalk grassland, it is likely that *Medicago lupina* was, however, extensively grazed by the domestic animals belonging to the occupants of Winnall Down and more than tolerated for that reason alone; as to its purposeful propagation, there is no independent evidence. The arable fields, surrounded as they probably were by grassland verges if not fallow fields, would, however, have been readily colonised by such plants, as the nitrogen of these areas, perhaps along with other essential nutrients, decreased. Various other grassland species and field margin plants are likely to have similarly colonised the fields, as suggested by the number and range of such species in the samples. This perhaps progressive colonisation from the field boundaries may have been very significant in the Iron Age, given the relatively small size of the fields: per unit area there would have been a high proportion of field boundaries from which colonisation by field margin weeds of arable fields could take place. On the other hand, it could be argued that, with the level of technology

available in the Iron Age, such small fields could be more easily cultivated and crop managed, including weed removal. However, a decline in soil fertility may have selectively encouraged more robust, less nutrient demanding weeds, as against cereals, leading to less growth development of the latter and lower yields.

The possibly decreasing soil fertility of chalkland, indicated by the plant evidence, should also perhaps be seen against the evidence in southern Britain for not only increased alluviation in river valleys but, perhaps more importantly for the chalkland areas, colluviation from the Bronze Age onwards (Shotton 1978, Limbrey 1978, Bell 1981, Bell 1983) causing considerable changes to the chalkland soils, that may have originally been more of a brown earth type (Allen 1988, 83). The long term problems in some areas, caused by progressive colluviation hand in hand with decreasing soil fertility and consequent effects on cereal yields and weed infestation, may have caused the expansion of arable land into areas that, up to that time, were considered marginal, either because they actually were or because the level of Iron Age technology available at the time had not developed sufficiently to cope with such areas, although from his work at Butser Reynolds (pers comm) would doubt the latter explanation. The high incidence of small legumes in the samples, relative to other plants, if not an artefact of the level of crop processing to which the remains relate, may be both an indication of decreasing soil fertility and an indication of the tolerance of such plants for redressing the balance.

The persuasive hypothesis Jones presented in his 1984a paper, based on detailed studies in the Wessex region, of which the M3 sites form an important part, and the Upper Thames Valley, has much to commend it. Whether the deterioration in the soil fertility was simply caused by continuous, progressive use of the chalkland and soil erosion, with a minimal manuring strategy, or by intensification necessitated by demand, population increase or hierarchical development, cannot be fully ascertained.

It is important, however, to draw back from the realms of hypothesis and end on a note of caution. Even though there is some very good evidence from the area of central Hampshire as a result of intensive sampling programmes in the 1970's, it is important to point out, as Jones argues (1984a and b), that the sampling strategies from the various sites cited are not compatible, and that the material basis of the remains from each site varies not only as a consequence of varying depositional factors and context influences but also as a result of crop processing factors. To what extent these influences are mediated at the general level cannot be easily appreciated without further methodological study. The work in Wessex in the early 70's, the M3 studies included, provide, however, an important basis, which had not existed up to that time, for further studies in-depth of specifically targeted sites and contexts in the area; therein lies the importance of this work historically in the development of archaeobotany in southern Britain.

Chapter 6

Charcoal Identifications – A Review
by Carole Keepax

Note: this paper was written in 1980 and was the first summary paper for the M3 project.

Sampling

A total of 901 samples from thirteen of the M3 sites were submitted for identification, of which 849 contained identifiable charcoal. The majority of the samples (815) came from the Micheldever Wood 'banjo' enclosure with 41 from Winnall Down. The remaining sites each produced a few samples only (R4, R5, R6, R7, R364, R366, R367, R368 and R369 – see Fig 44 for locations, and Table 23 for site list).

The charcoal was scattered within pit and ditch deposits and fragments were collected individually during excavation. Most of the samples were therefore small, originating from a few fragments or a single fragment only. Two sets of samples obtained by water flotation were also included: 31 from a single pit in the 'banjo' enclosure and 41 from Winnall Down.

Identification

All of the fragments in the hand collected samples were identified. Flotation material which had passed through the 1mm sieve was not examined, as identification difficulties may arise which produce biased results (Keepax, unpublished data). Twenty fragments were picked out from each of the remaining flotation samples and the number from each taxon recorded. Further fragments were then identified until most of the sample had been examined or it was felt that a representative amount had been processed: usually 50, 100 or 150 fragments per sample.

Identifications were carried out by examination of fractured tangential surfaces under reflected light at 10–30× magnifications. When necessary, features were checked at higher magnifications (up to 250×), by examination of longitudinal surfaces and by comparison with modern reference material. Hazel, alder and hornbeam, for example, may only be separated satisfactorily by examination of longitudinal surfaces; this was checked in most cases.

Results

The nineteen taxa identified are listed in Table 26 in approximate order of frequency occurrence. It is not usually possible to identify tree types to species level by wood anatomical features. Specific names are therefore given only if there is a single native species. *Salix* and *Populus* spp. may be difficult to separate, but it seems likely that both were present on the M3 sites.

Discussion

As would be expected, the sites with the largest number of samples produced the most taxa: fourteen from the 'banjo' enclosure and thirteen from Winnall Down. None of the remaining sites yielded more than seven taxa from the few samples examined.

Therefore, only Winnall Down and the Micheldever 'banjo' enclosure produced sufficient material to allow comparisons to be made. The five most common taxa on these sites were, however, the most common generally. Only five of the eleven smaller sites (ranging in date from Neolithic to Medieval) contained a few fragments from taxa other than these most common types. There is therefore no evidence for any major variations in charcoal composition on the M3 sites. Similarly, there were no significant differences between the Early and Middle Iron Age samples at Winnall Down (Keepax 1979, 1985). The results for Winnall Down and the Micheldever Wood 'banjo' enclosure were also very similar (Fig 48). The more spiky histogram for the latter is probably related to the smaller sample sizes on that site (Keepax, unpublished data).

This pattern is repeated on many sites of all periods within lowland Britain (Keepax 1977a). *Quercus* sp., Pomoideae, *Corylus* sp., *Prunus* sp. and *Fraxinus* sp. are often the most common charcoal types. This may be due to both environmental and human factors. These taxa provide good firewood and are also common on many soil types.

Interpretation is complicated by the fact that most of the M3 charcoal was scattered in pits and ditches and removed from its original context. Some of the

Table 26. Charcoal identification review: occurrence of charcoal taxa from different sites. Detailed results are in the site archives. See Table 23 for explanation of site codes.

Taxon	Sites present
Quercus sp.	All except R7, R367, R369.
Corylus avellana L. (Hazel)	All except R364, R367, R368, R369.
Rosaceae, subfamily Pomoideae (eg Hawthorn)	All except R364, R368, R369.
Fraxinus excelsior L. (Ash)	R2, R7, R17, R27.
Prunus sp. (e.g. Blackthorn)	R2, R4, R5, R17, R27.
Acer sp. (Maple)	R7, R17, R27.
Sambucus nigra L. (Elder)	R17, R27.
Rhamnus catharticus L. (Buckthorn)	R17, R27.
Alnus glutinosa (L.) Gaertn. (Alder)	R17, R27.
Fagus sylvatica L. (Beech)	R4, R17.
Ulmus sp. (Elm)	R4, R6, R17?
Larix/Picea sp. (Larch/Pine)	R4, R5, R369.
Betula sp.	R17.
Ilex aquifolium L. (Holly)	R27.
Salix sp. (Willow)	R27.
Populus sp. (*eg* Aspen)	R27.
Taxus baccata L. (Yew)	R17.
Carpinus betulus L. (Hornbeam)	R27.
Rosa sp. (Rose)	R27?

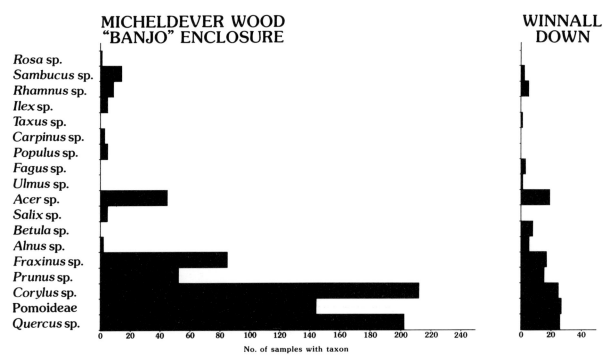

Fig 48.   Charcoal identification review: comparison of results for the Micheldever Wood 'banjo' enclosure (R27) and Winnall Down (R17).

charcoal could have been derived from earlier deposits, which would blur any temporal variations.

There is no evidence for importation of wood to the sites. The tree types are largely those that would be expected on the local chalky soils. The few fragments of *Larix/Picea* sp. are an exception: these are probably modern contaminants.

The presence of a few fragments of Fagus sp. is of interest. Although it is known to have been present in Hampshire since Atlantic times (Pennington 1969), its charcoal is rarely found until the Iron Age (Keepax, unpublished data). The good representation of *Fraxinus* sp., *Betula* sp. and *Acer* sp., which all increased environmentally with forest clearance from the Neolithic onwards, is in keeping with the largely open environment indicated by molluscan evidence (Keepax, unpublished data).

Chapter 7

Land Mollusca from the M3 Archaeological Sites – A Review
by J G Evans and Diane Williams

Introduction

The molluscan assemblages from seven of the M3 sites, ranging from the Neolithic to the present, are discussed. The sites are Stratton Park (R1), London Lodge (R3), Bridget's Farm (R5), Burntwood Farm (R6), Easton Down (R7), Winnall Down (R17) and Grace's Farm (R30). They span a distance of 13.5 kilometres, and are in three downland areas (Fig 49) separated from each other by the Itchen flood-plain in the south and an area of non-calcareous drift in the north. Most contexts are the infillings of sub-surface features, there being no well-developed buried soils from beneath monuments.

Samples were taken by the excavators and analysed in Cardiff. Sample weights were usually 1kg and depth spans about 100mm. Molluscan assemblages are referred to by their site and sample numbers. Nomenclature follows Kerney (1976a). Interim reports have been published (Fasham 1980a, 1981, 1982, 1985). Here we discuss the data as a whole, particularly its numerical analysis. Details of archaeology, contexts and ^{14}C dates are published (references under individual sites) and are in the excavation archive (see also Table 41 this volume). Additional ^{14}C dates are in Hedges *et al* (1989).

Stages of Analysis

The data were dealt with in the following stages (A–E), although these are not sequential:

A. The assemblages were characterised by relative abundances of species and ecological groups, diversity indexes, cluster analysis and a combination of these methods. Chronology was not a factor at this stage.

B. Site molluscan zones (SMZs) were established. These were based on the characteristics of the assemblages as detailed in stage A and their place in time. No environmental interpretations were made at this stage.

C. The environment of the assemblages (not the SMZs) was proposed, especially of the groups identified in the cluster analysis. This was done irrespective of chronology.

D. The SMZs were translated into environments and sequences established for each site.

E. The site environments and sequences were considered in terms of the total area and time spanned by the sites as a whole. This was the most tenuous part of the analysis because molluscs represent the site rather than the local or regional environment.

Conventional Presentation of the Results

The data (Tables 29–40) are presented as histograms, with each species or ecological group as a percentage of the total assemblage (excluding *Cecilioides*, a burrowing species, and the limacid slugs which were not always extracted). Percentages are used because they counter the effects of varying shell input which are more a function of the rate of deposition and the amount of coarse debris than of frequency changes in life. In the case of London Lodge (R3) and Winnall Down (R17) where numbers were often low, the histograms are based on counts.

There are three broad ecological groups: woodland, intermediate and open-country. Woodland species occur in damp, shaded places where there is a minimum of disturbance. Woodland provides the best conditions, but practically all the species can occur in open-country habitats, although not in the driest ones. Open-country species are those which most commonly occur in unshaded, dry habitats, although some can occur in woodland, most notably *Vallonia costata*. On the whole, the open-country species are more tightly confined to open-country than are the woodland species to woodland. The intermediate species occur in a wide range of habitats, especially when considered over a long period of time or a wide area.

The composition of the three groups is as follows:

Woodland species: *Carychium tridentatum, Azeca goodalli, Columella edentula, Vertigo pusilla, Lauria*

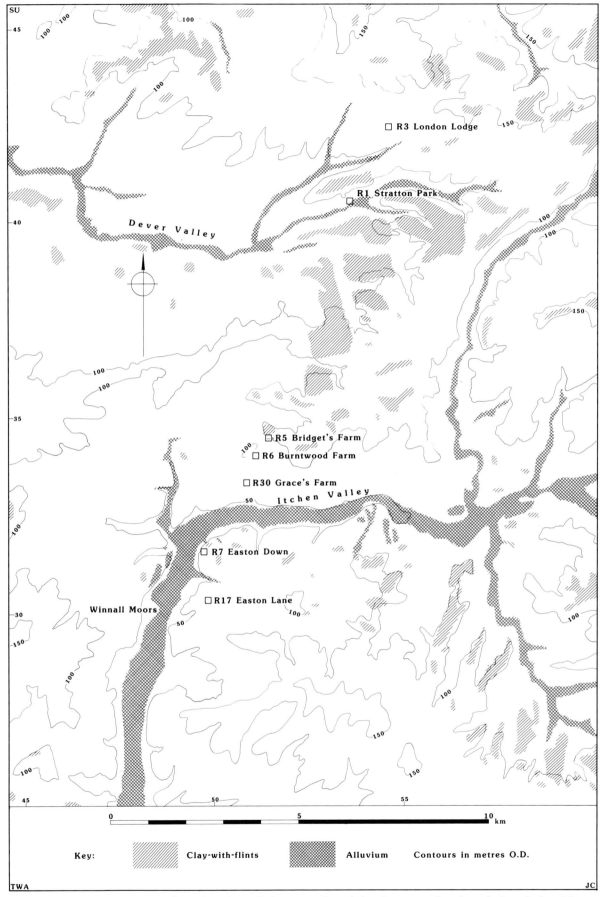

Fig 49.   Land Mollusca review: location of sites mentioned in the text, showing their relationship to topography and drift geology.

cylindracea, Acanthinula aculeata, Ena montana, Ena obscura, Discus rotundatus, Vitrea crystallina agg., *Aegopinella pura, Aegopinella nitidula, Oxychilus cellarius, Oxychilus alliarius, Cochlodina laminata, Clausilia bidentata, Balea perversa, Helicigona lapicida. Vitrea, Aegopinella* and *Oxychilus* are in the family Zonitidae.

Intermediate species: *Pomatias elegans, Cochlicopa lubrica, Cochlicopa lubricella, Punctum pygmaeum, Vitrina pellucida, Nesovitrea hammonis,* Limacidae, *Euconulus fulvus, Trichia striolata, Trichia hispida, Arianta arbustorum, Cepaea nemoralis, Cepaea hortensis, Helix aspersa.*

Open-country species: *Truncatellina cylindrica, Vertigo pygmaea, Pupilla muscorum, Vallonia costata, Vallonia pulchella, Vallonia excentrica, Candidula intersecta, Candidula gigaxii, Cernuella virgata, Helicella itala.*

Assemblage Structure

Assemblages can be characterised by structure as represented by species-abundance relationships and expressed as a diversity index. The main reason for this approach is that a species can reflect a variety of habitats depending on the circumstances. So before discussing diversity indexes, areas of uncertainty in using named species and ecological groups, and justifications for using assemblage structure, are outlined.

First of all, many species, although narrow in their habitat preferences in individual localities, have a wide range of habitats when viewed regionally. Likewise through time, a species may live in a succession of different habitats in a single locality. This phenomenon may be related to spatial and temporal variation in climate and factors such as long-term human disturbance and pollution. For example, *Pomatias elegans* in oceanic western Britain occurs in open places, but in the more continental southeast is confined to shaded habitats. Correspondingly through time, *Pomatias elegans* may vary from being an open-country to a shade-demanding species according to climate and location (Kerney 1968).

Second, molluscan communities may have taken time to adjust to the creation of new habitats on the country-wide scale. This applies to grasslands, and especially to those that were grazed by domesticated herbivores. Such habitats were largely absent from Britain in the earlier part of the Holocene.

A third point is that it is difficult to use the species composition of present-day open-country communities as a guide to the situation in prehistory because they often contain species not present until about 2,000 years ago.

Fourthly, species vary in their rates of migration and their ability to become established, so that where environments were transient, as often in archaeological contexts, the full possible complement of species may not have been established before the environment changed. Environments identical in all aspects but age may therefore have had different faunas. With a knowledge of the time span of a sequence and the rate of migration of its species, the distance and size of source habitats might be deduced, although such an ideal is a long way off. However, the diversity of an assemblage is an indicator of the surrounding environmental diversity, whatever its species composition, and such a concept is applicable when sequences from similar contexts are compared.

Finally, the physiological needs of Mollusca are not always easy to translate into environment because different environments may offer the same conditions. This is the case not only with the differences of climate and habitat-development mentioned above, but also at a local scale. Moisture and food, important factors in land molluscan ecology, are provided at similar levels and quality in a variety of habitats. This is seen particularly in the recognition of assemblages indicative of woodland, for which the proportion of 'woodland' species as an undifferentiated group is not precise enough. Faunas from rock rubble and the early stages in the colonisation of ditches often consist of woodland species and yet come from quite open environments (Evans and Jones 1973). One way of distinguishing such assemblages is to identify recurring suites of species, *eg Vitrea* and *Vallonia costata* in ditch bottoms, and to reconsider the traditional groups. Another is to examine the structure of the assemblage, its diversity or species-abundance relationships, on the assumption that this reflects habitat diversity.

Rank-order

One way of considering assemblage structure is by rank-order, in which the percentages of all species in an assemblage are plotted in order of abundance. A rank-order curve thus presents two pieces of information: the number of species and the way in which numbers of individuals are distributed among these species. Four assemblages illustrate the problems and benefits of this approach (Fig 50). The meaning of H' in these figures is explained in the next section. Extremes of woodland and open-country are brought out clearly. Bridget's Farm sample 152 (R5.152), a rich woodland assemblage, has a large number of species, none of which is especially abundant. The difference in the abundance of adjacent species is never large, and the curve is uniform. Burntwood Farm sample 13 (R6.13), an extremely impoverished open-country assemblage, has few species, and two of these occur in much greater abundance than the others. The curve is L-shaped.

Even without knowing the ecology of the species, general environmental conclusions can be drawn. R5.152 is from a rich, diverse environment. R6.13 is from a more specialised habitat. More detailed interpretation can be made against a background of the general contemporary environment, which in the case of the M3 project assemblages was dry, calcareous land in a temperate climate. Thus assem-

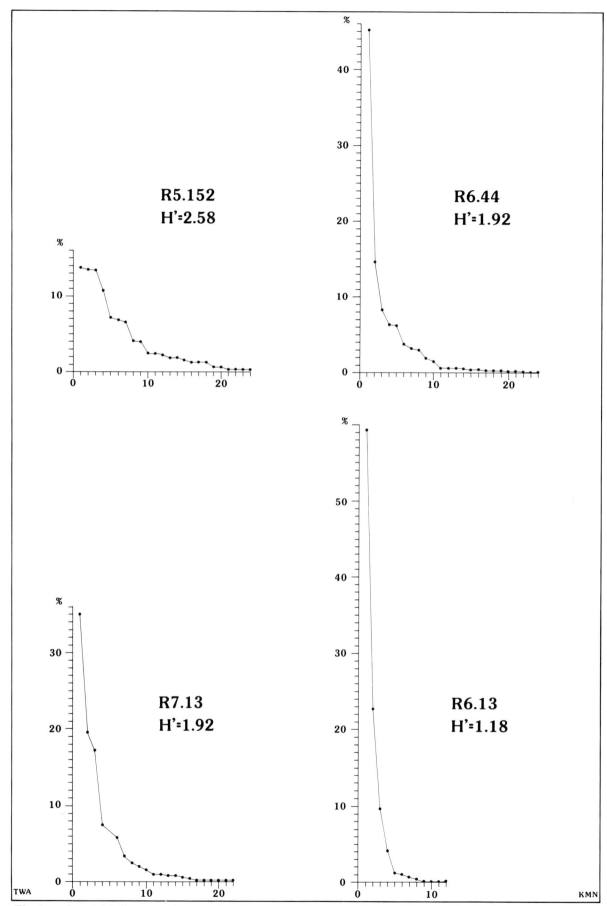

Fig 50.   Land Mollusca review: rank-order curves for selected assemblages. The horizontal axis of each curve is species in order of rank. For an explanation of H', see p 117.

blages of the kind illustrated by R5.152 are likely to be from deciduous woodland, while those such as R6.13 are likely to be from short grassland or arable.

The two examples discussed, however, are extremes. Two other assemblages, again one of woodland (R6.44) and one of open-country (R7.13) as interpreted conventionally, have similar rank-order curves (Fig 50), and are not distinguished by this approach.

Diversity Indexes

Species-abundance data can be presented as a 'diversity index', the value of which in archaeological work is twofold. First, data from many assemblages can be presented concisely and clearly as a single plot in a way that would be impossible with individual rank-order curves. Second, the display of a general impression of faunal change is important to the non-specialist, unfamiliar with molluscan ecology.

Five diversity indexes, the Shannon-Wiener index, the Brill-ouin index, the Simpson-Yule index, the Berger-Parker index and Fisher's Alpha, were calculated for 76 assemblages and plotted next to each other in the same order. All five plots showed the same trends and appeared to be influenced by the same underlying distribution, presumably the logarithmic series. The relative merits of the indexes are discussed in Southwood (1971), Poole (1974) and Pielou (1975). It is pertinent to remember that despite the theoretical difficulties of applying these indexes to biological material (eg Goodman 1975, Hurlbert 1971), they are here being used as descriptions of archaeological assemblages. They are an additional commentary on the data, not an exclusive alternative to other methods. As will be evident, they are useful in some instances but not in others.

The Shannon-Wiener index (H') was chosen because it takes into account the number of species and the distribution (or evenness) of individuals amongst the species. Total numbers of individuals are not incorporated. The index is thus applicable to samples (eg all the shells in a soil sample) as opposed to total collections (eg all the molluscs living at one time in a pit) and, as such, is relevant to archaeology. It is quoted with a standard error.

$$H' = -\sum_{i=1}^{s} (p_i) (\ln . p_i)$$

where H' = index of diversity
s = number of species
p_i = proportion of total belonging to the ith species
ln = log to the base e.

$$\sigma H' = \sqrt{\frac{\sum p_i \ln^2 p_i - (\sum p_i \ln . p_i)^2}{n}}$$

where   p = proportion of total belonging to the ith species
n = number of individuals
ln = log to the base e
σH' = standard error on the index of diversity.

Cluster Analysis

Groups of assemblages in terms of patterns of species abundance were suggested from a visual inspection of the data, and the aim of the cluster analysis was to define these more clearly. We might expect the samples to be different from each other by the same degree, or to seriate, but there are good

ecological and environmental reasons why these alternatives should not occur. Cluster analysis brings together a large number of pieces of information and sorts them into groups such that the degree of association is high between members of the same group and low between members of different groups. The information comprises the number of individuals in each species in each sample. One hundred and thirty-seven assemblages were selected (Figs 52 and 53), characterised by a predominance of either open-country or woodland species, the two groups being analysed separately. Assemblages in which intermediate species predominated or in which there were more or less equal proportions of woodland and open-country species were excluded, partly on the grounds that such assemblages were more likely to be allochthonous, and partly to simplify the procedure. Selection was based on various criteria (exceptions being part of a sequence or having particular assemblage or contextual characteristics).

For the open-country assemblages (total, 89) these were: (a) shell numbers per assemblage greater than 100, although in 17 assemblages they were less (lowest, 60); (b) assemblages from single samples in all cases except three, where two or three samples were amalgamated; (c) assemblages which contained less than 15% woodland species, although in six it was higher. For the woodland assemblages (total, 48) similar criteria were used. Only one assemblage had less than 100 shells and all but one were from single samples. The percentage of open-country species (excluding *Vallonia costata*) was generally less than 15%, being greater in only nine assemblages.

The CLUSTAN package (Wishart 1978, Everitt 1980) was used, with free-format, non-standardised percentage data, in the first instance with Ward's Method and then with 'average linkage' cluster analysis. Both perform hierarchical agglomerative clustering but Ward's Method is more robust (Wishart 1978). The results of both were essentially the same. To ensure the validity and stability of the groups we used the RELOCATE option from both a random restart and a specified classification array. These produced identical results and indicated that a few assemblages could be re-assigned. In deciding on the number of groups to use (cf Everitt 1980), we followed Gower (1975). The classification criterion (in this case Euclidean squared distance) was plotted against the number of groups. A sharp step in the plot indicated the number of groups to be used, and it is these groups that are hereafter referred to as 'CLUSTAN groups'.

The main way of characterising the CLUSTAN groups is by the frequency-density of the species, either using abundance terms such as 'high', 'moderate', 'low' or 'absence', or mathematically. On the whole we have used the former, but in the case of the open-country groups we have expressed frequency-density of the main species mathematically (Table 27, Fig 51). Each species occurs at a particular level of abundance in each group, and because this approximates to a normal distribution,

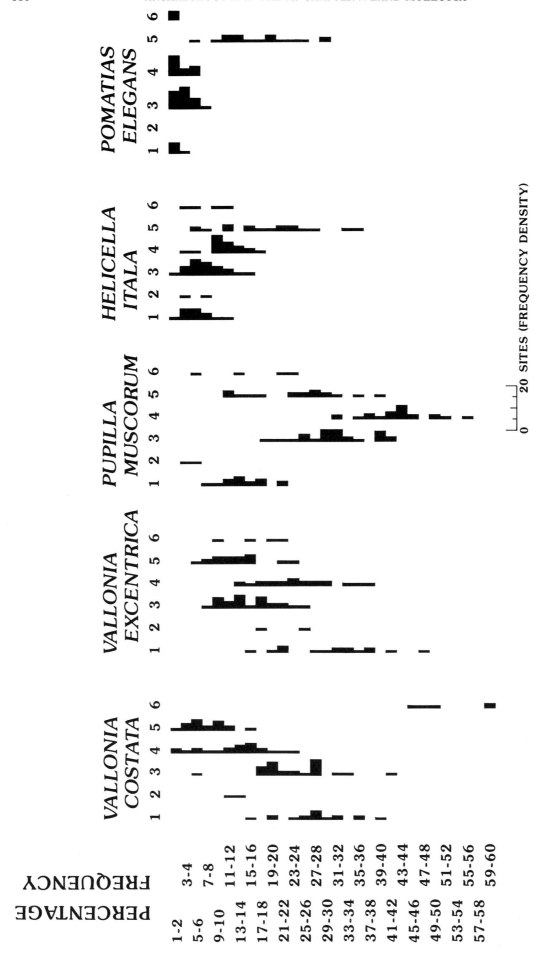

Fig 51.   Land Mollusca review: frequency-density histograms for selected species, separated into open-country CLUSTAN groups 1–6. See also Table 27.

Table 27. Land Mollusca review: abundance data for selected species in the open-country CLUSTAN groups. x̄ = mean; σ = standard deviation.

	Group	1	2	3	4	5	6
Vallonia costata	Range	22.5	1.8	35.4	23.2	14.1	13.6
	x̄	27.6	13.3	23.0	12.5	7.0	52.5
	σ	6.0	1.3	6.7	6.3	3.6	6.4
Vallonia excentrica	Range	16.6	7.2	18.3	24.9	16.5	21.4
	x̄	30.2	21.7	14.9	23.8	12.9	13.2
	σ	8.9	5.1	4.9	6.7	4.7	8.6
Pupilla muscorum	Range	14.3	0.9	23.6	24.9	29.1	22.9
	x̄	14.5	4.4	30.8	42.5	23.9	12.7
	σ	3.9	0.6	6.5	5.9	8.5	10.1
Helicella itala	Range	10.5	3.3	13.7	16.6	31.4	11.9
	x̄	5.8	4.9	7.3	10.8	18.4	5.9
	σ	2.8	2.3	3.4	3.5	9.0	4.6
Pomatias elegans	Range	2.0	0.0	6.6	5.9	23.9	1.7
	x̄	0.6	0.0	2.9	2.0	17.1	0.9
	σ	0.9	0.0	1.9	2.1	6.5	0.6

it can be described by the mean and standard deviation. In each CLUSTAN group there are many assemblages in which a species is in moderate abundance and fewer in which it is very abundant or rare. This is visually clear for *Vallonia costata* in groups 4 and 5, *Vallonia excentrica* in group 3, *Pupilla muscorum* in groups 1 and 4 and *Helicella itala* in groups 1 and 3. A chi-squared test on group 3 indicates that all the main species except *Pomatias elegans* are normally distributed.

Pomatias elegans needs further explanation. In groups 1, 3, 4 and 6, it occurs in low abundance in many assemblages and is common in the same number or fewer. Only in group 5 does the distribution approximate to the normal. The explanation is that in groups 1, 3, 4 and 6, the shells are largely residual, small apices that have accumulated in the deposits because of their resistance to destruction. Only in group 5 are most of the specimens adults and unweathered young, contemporary with the rest of the assemblage.

Further characterisation of the CLUSTAN groups was done using the Shannon-Wiener index, H'. The calculation of weighted means of H' for each CLUS-TAN group (Table 28) may be invalid because of the different ways in which H' and the CLUSTAN groups are derived. H' is based on presences only and is related to species-abundance data and species numbers, but not to named species. The CLUSTAN groups are based on similarities and differences between assemblages as defined by the presence, abundance and absence of named species. Nevertheless, the data show some groupings (Figs 52 and 53).

CLUSTAN Groups

Six open-country groups, 1 to 6, were identified (Table 27, Fig 52). Eighty-two of the 89 open-

Table 28. Land Mollusca review: H' values of the CLUSTAN groups, expressed as weighted means (x̄ H') and standard deviations (σ H'); n = number of assemblages in the group.

CLUSTAN group	x̄ H'	σ H'	n
1	1.61	0.02	16
2	1.36	0.06	2
3	1.78	0.01	27
4	1.50	0.01	21
5	1.94	0.02	18
6	1.26	0.02	5
7	2.28	0.03	7
8	2.38	0.01	10
9	2.44	0.02	9
10	2.10	0.01	22

country assemblages fall into four main groups of similar size, 1, 3, 4 and 5. The remaining seven fall into two subsidiary groups, 2 and 6. Their characteristics, site and age distributions and environmental interpretations are now described.

Group 1

Molluscan assemblages: *Vallonia costata* and *Vallonia excentrica* are the main species. *Pupilla muscorum* and *Helicella itala* are at their lowest for the main groups. Woodland and intermediate species, including *Cochlicopa*, are consistently present in abundances that are average for the open-country assemblages. *Pomatias elegans* is virtually absent.

Site and age distribution: with one exception, the assemblages are divided between two sites, Grace's Farm (R30), of probable prehistoric age, and Stratton Park (R1), dating from Roman times onwards. A difference not brought out in the CLUSTAN

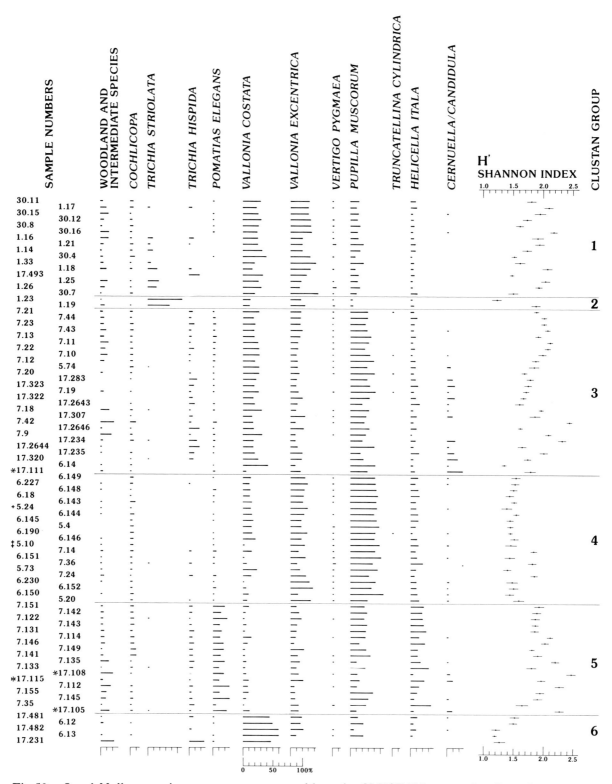

Fig 52.   Land Mollusca review: open-country assemblages by CLUSTAN group. ★ = R17, feature 1972;
+ = R5, 24+25; ‡ = R5, 10+11+12.

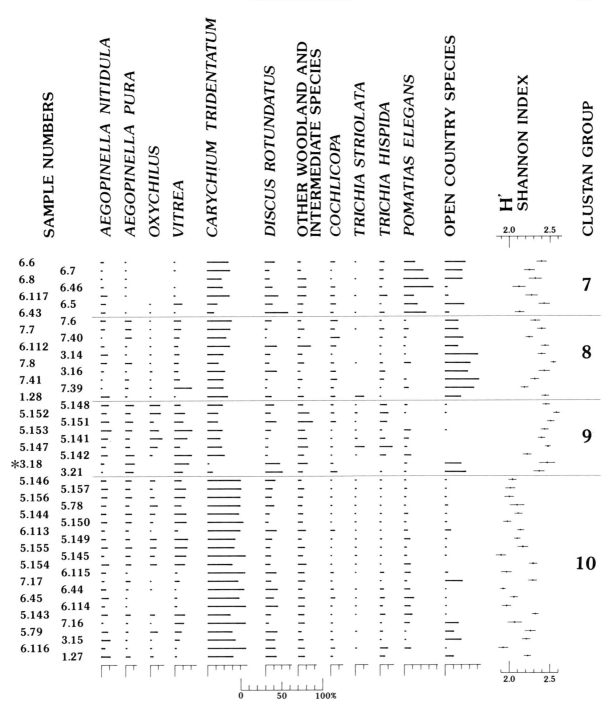

Fig 53.   Land Mollusca review: woodland assemblages by CLUSTAN group. ★ = R3, 18 +19+20.

analysis but which is probably significant is the presence of *Trichia striolata* at R1 and its absence at R30. This is probably a feature of the historic age of R1 (*cf* Kerney 1966), and the same comments apply to group 2.

Environmental interpretation: grassland, lightly grazed or not grazed at all (both species of *Vallonia*); little or no bare ground (low *Pupilla*); tall herbaceous vegetation and possibly some scrub (low *Helicella itala*, presence of woodland and intermediate species).

Group 2

Molluscan assemblages: *Trichia striolata* abundant.

Site and age distribution: the assemblages are from Saxon/Medieval colluvium at Stratton Park (R1).

Environmental interpretation: as for group 1, possibly with more tall herbaceous vegetation and scrub.

Group 3

Molluscan assemblages: *Pupilla muscorum* is the main species, with *Vallonia costata*, *Vallonia excentrica* and *Helicella itala* in descending order of abundance. *Trichia hispida* is characteristic; *Cernuella/ Candidula* are present in about half the assemblages; *Pomatias elegans* is low. The contrasting ratios of *Pupilla muscorum* and *Vallonia excentrica* separate group 3 from 1.

Site and age distribution: the assemblages are characteristic of the Winnall Down/Easton Down area, although also sporadic at Bridget's Farm/ Burntwood Farm. They are Iron Age or Early Roman.

Environmental interpretation: dry grassland with broken ground (*Pupilla*); grazing by large mammals low (*Vallonia costata*). Some scrub (woodland and intermediate species), but on the whole the environment was probably drier and more open than that of group 1 assemblages (higher *Pupilla*, lower *Vallonia excentrica*).

Group 4

Molluscan assemblages: *Pupilla muscorum* is the main species, as in group 3, but in greater abundance. *Vallonia excentrica* exceeds *Vallonia costata*. Woodland and intermediate species, excepting *Cochlicopa*, are virtually absent, as is *Trichia hispida*. Diversity is the lowest of the four main groups.

Site and age distribution: group 4 assemblages occur almost exclusively in the Bridget's Farm/ Burntwood Farm sites (R5, R6), although sporadic at Easton Down (R7). They are late in the M3 project sequence, being probably entirely Roman.

Environmental interpretation: dry, low diversity grassland (low values for H'), much broken ground (*Pupilla*). Comparison with groups 1 and 3 raises problems with this interpretation. By contrast with group 1, group 3 shows an increase in *Pupilla* and a decrease in *Vallonia excentrica*, but a further increase in *Pupilla* in group 4 is not matched by a further decrease in *Vallonia excentrica*. The high *Pupilla* suggests short grassland, broken ground, and south-facing slopes, factors giving optimum dryness and warmth. *Vallonia excentrica*, on the other hand, is a grass sward species. It often occurs in undiversified grassland and can withstand grazing by large mammals. It is thus possible that in group 4, *Pupilla* is indicative not of broken ground but of a closed sward, although of lower diversity than that of the group 2 grassland. The alternative, that *Vallonia excentrica* was occurring in broken ground, is unlikely because the species is more tightly confined to grass swards than *Pupilla* is to broken ground. So there is a contrast between groups 1 and 3 on the one hand which indicate grassland, lightly grazed (if at all), and with varying amounts of scrub and broken ground; and group 4 on the other which indicates heavily grazed grassland with no scrub.

Group 5

Molluscan assemblages: the main features are the high abundance of *Pomatias elegans* and *Helicella itala*. *Vallonia costata* is at its lowest. Woodland and intermediate species, including *Cochlicopa* and *Trichia hispida*, are consistently present. Diversity is high.

Site and age distribution: the assemblages occur at Easton Down (R7) and Winnall Down (R17) feature 1972, in the same area of downland (Fig 49).

Environmental interpretation: rich grassland and other herbaceous vegetation with some areas of short sward (*Helicella itala*); loose surface in part (*Pomatias elegans*) and some scrub; grazing by large mammals probably absent. The association of high *Helicella itala* and *Pomatias elegans* is unusual today in the chalklands, the two species occupying different habitats. However, they are associated and common, on steep south-facing sparsely vegetated slopes, especially on coasts where there is little or no grazing, so it is possible that the group 5 assemblages are a response to particular environmental features of the Easton Down/Winnall Down area. Note, for example, that the group 5 assemblages from Easton Down are all from contexts that are shallow pits (pre- and post-barrow), whereas the open-country assemblages from the ring-ditch itself are group 3. Additionally (or alternatively), the features of group 5 may be connected with the age of the assemblages. Most of the assemblages are early in the M3 project sequence, whereas later assemblages from Easton Down and Winnall Down belong to different CLUS-TAN groups, reflecting the general decline of *Pomatias elegans* and *Helicella itala* since later pre-history.

Group 6

Molluscan assemblages: *Vallonia costata* predominates and all other species are in moderate to low abundance. Diversity is low.

Site and age distribution: the assemblages are from Iron Age deposits at Winnall Down (R17) and Burntwood Farm (R6).

Environmental interpretation: open grassland, not grazed (*Vallonia costata*); perhaps much bare ground (low diversity). The low number of assemblages and their low diversity suggests an unusual environment. Experience from other sites indicates that *Vallonia costata* is able to spread into and rapidly colonise new habitats such as those formed by the digging of a ditch, and this would certainly apply to assemblages R6.12, R6.13 and R17.231.

Four woodland groups, 7 to 10, were isolated (Fig 53).

Group 7

Molluscan assemblages: distinctive features are the abundance of *Pomatias elegans* and the paucity of the Zonitidae (except *Aegopinella nitidula*). Open-country species reach over 20% in four of the seven samples.

Environmental interpretation: youthful and/or unstable environments of scrub and tall herbaceous vegetation; not woodland. Broken ground surface and loose soil.

Group 8

Molluscan assemblages: slightly better representation of Zonitidae (except *Oxychilus*) than in group 7 and sparser *Pomatias elegans*. Open-country species well represented.

Environmental interpretation: more mature and stable environment than group 7, such as open woodland or scrub; some open country. Ground surface intact, with little or no bare ground.

Group 9, except R3.18 and R3.21

Molluscan assemblages: all Zonitidae generally abundant; *Pomatias elegans* very low; open-country species virtually absent. Diversity higher than in other groups.

Environmental interpretation: established woodland; diverse ground surface. No open country.

Group 9, 3.18 and 3.21

Molluscan assemblages: the assemblages stand out from the others in group 9 by their high open-country levels and low numbers, or complete absence, of many woodland species, *eg Aegopinella nitidula*, *Oxychilus*, *Carychium* and *Trichia striolata*.

Environmental interpretation: similar to group 8.

Group 10

Molluscan assemblages: high values for *Carychium*. Zonitidae are well represented, although *Oxychilus* is often low or absent. Open-country species are low.

Environmental interpretation: woodland, but with less diverse ground environment than in group 9; probably deep leaf litter.

One of the main problems with the woodland assemblages is in the interpretation of the open-country component. There are three possibilities. First, the assemblages are a true reflection of living communities. This is likely with groups 7 and 8 especially, where Zonitidae are poorly represented and open-country species consistently present, so that we can suggest an environment of mixed scrub and/or woodland and open-country. A second possibility, and one that is likely in an archaeological context, is that the area of deposition was close to a boundary, between woodland and grassland for example, and that the snails from each moved from one to the other for a short distance during life. The problem, therefore, is to distinguish between habitat boundaries and mixed habitats, although these are just two points in a general continuum of environments from a bush in open-country, to a small clearing in woodland. A third possibility is that the assemblages are allochthonous.

The Sites

Stratton Park (R1, SU 537405)

The area is gently sloping ground, south-facing, at around 87m OD, at the source of the Dever Brook. The site is a cutting across the Roman road from Winchester to Silchester (Fasham 1981, Figs 2 and 3, cutting B). It incorporated a ditch of the seventeenth century AD which was a part of the western boundary of Stratton Park. Earlier contexts were mainly Medieval and Saxon land surfaces and colluvium.

Assemblages used in the histograms are listed below in chronological order from latest to earliest (Fasham 1981, Fig 3).

Feature	Context	Sample
18th century AD colluvium	54	31
17th century AD ditch fill	55	30
	–	29
	56	28
	91	27
	92	32
	93	26
	95	25
Medieval/Saxon colluvium	58	19
Saxon colluvium	217	18
Saxon buried soil	57	17
Saxon/Roman colluvium	214	16

Sample 25 is considered on stratigraphical and faunal grounds here to belong to the seventeenth century ditch fill rather than, as by Fasham, to the Roman road.

Additional open-country assemblages used in the CLUSTAN analysis are:

Feature	Context	Sample
Medieval colluvium	51	14
	64	23
Saxon/Roman colluvium	214	21
	207	33

The molluscan assemblages (Table 29, Fig 54) are rich in open-country and woodland species, although there is a paucity of 'other woodland species'. *Trichia hispida* is present in only the earlier part of the sequence. On the other hand, *Trichia striolata* is characteristic throughout and often abundant, an almost unique feature of the M3 project assemblages (except Bridget's Farm, R5). *Pomatias elegans* is absent.

Three SMZs are recognised:

SP.1. Low woodland species; moderate to high *Trichia striolata*; *Vallonia costata* and *Vallonia excentrica* in more or less equal abundance; open-country species generally high. CLUSTAN group 1, except sample 19 which is group 2 (high *Trichia striolata*). H' around 2.0.

SP.2. High woodland species; moderate *Trichia striolata*; low open-country species. CLUSTAN groups 8 and 10. H' high, between 2.2 and 2.5.

SP.3. Woodland species moderate to low; open-country species high; *Vallonia costata* greatly exceeded by *Vallonia excentrica*; *Candidula* and *Cernuella* present. H' falls from 2.45 to 1.7.

From the time of the Saxon/Roman colluvium to an early stage in the infilling of the seventeenth century ditch, the area was open country, probably of rich grassland and other herbaceous vegetation (SP.1). There was some scrub or woodland, and there were periods of surface instability as shown by the colluvium. During the infilling of the seventeenth century ditch, woodland became established (SP.2). There was some open country, and the woodland was not of the richest kind, features which probably relate to the local nature of the woodland (was it perhaps confined to the park boundary?), and to the fact that it lasted little more than a century. The final environment (SP.3) was grassland and arable.

London Lodge (R3, SU 547424)

The area is more or less level ground at around 124m OD, 2.1 kilometres northeast of Stratton Park (R1). The archaeology comprised small ditches spanning the Late Iron Age and Early Roman periods (Fasham 1981, Figs 2 and 11).

Table 29. Land Mollusca review: Stratton Park (R1).
A number of assemblages not used in the CLUSTAN analysis or in the histograms have been excluded. The Cepaea banding patterns are: C. nemoralis, 00300; C. hortensis, all 5-banded.

Sample	33	21	23	14	16	17	18	19	25	26	32	27	28	29	30	31
Carychium tridentatum	1	2	1	1	14	4	4	3	5	7	48	220	107	35	18	1
Cochlicopa lubrica	–	–	–	–	–	–	–	–	–	2	1	5	9	4	7	–
Cochlicopa lubricella	–	–	–	–	1	2	–	–	–	–	–	–	2	–	1	–
Cochlicopa spp.	1	7	–	4	7	6	4	4	1	3	10	14	13	15	13	2
Vertigo pygmaea	–	7	1	–	2	4	2	5	3	15	7	3	9	12	26	6
Pupilla muscorum	25	28	6	16	38	18	11	9	15	38	19	17	6	11	12	7
Vallonia costata	24	34	22	32	72	37	23	23	34	72	45	29	20	16	43	3
Vallonia pulchella	1	–	–	1	–	–	–	2	3	–	–	–	–	–	–	–
Vallonia excentrica	50	27	28	19	57	48	48	47	23	35	45	25	44	58	109	24
Acanthinula aculeata	–	–	–	–	1	–	1	1	–	–	1	6	1	–	1	–
Ena obscura	–	–	–	–	–	–	–	–	–	–	1	–	1	–	–	–
Punctum pygmaeum	3	1	–	–	5	2	2	2	2	2	5	21	17	5	5	–
Discus rotundatus	1	–	–	–	1	2	4	5	1	1	11	100	31	36	13	1
Vitrina pellucida	–	–	–	–	–	–	1	–	–	1	–	–	1	–	–	–
Vitrea crystallina agg.	1	1	1	–	1	–	1	–	–	–	3	18	5	–	2	–
Nesovitrea hammonis	–	–	–	–	2	–	–	–	–	–	–	–	–	–	–	–
Aegopinella pura	–	1	–	–	1	–	–	1	1	–	14	40	11	2	1	–
Aegopinella nitidula	–	–	–	–	10	4	2	1	5	6	19	84	43	10	15	–
Oxychilus cellarius	–	–	–	1	–	–	–	–	–	1	4	38	10	6	2	1
Limacidae	1	–	–	5	5	2	6	1	5	5	7	2	5	7	2	–
Cecilioides acicula	50	74	85	34	63	55	74	145	71	45	49	28	49	52	19	2
Cochlodina laminata	–	–	–	–	–	2	–	–	–	–	–	4	1	1	3	–
Clausilia bidentata	–	–	–	–	–	–	1	1	1	–	1	9	6	8	3	–
Candidula intersecta	–	–	–	–	–	–	–	–	–	–	–	–	–	–	1	–
Candidula gigaxii	–	–	–	–	–	–	–	–	–	–	–	–	–	–	–	1
Helicella itala	6	10	5	8	16	16	6	12	5	7	8	3	2	–	7	4
Trichia striolata	6	5	91	9	22	6	23	69	24	37	36	52	45	17	7	–
Trichia hispida	–	2	–	–	22	8	7	–	–	–	–	–	3	–	–	–
Helicigona lapicida	–	–	–	–	–	–	–	–	–	–	–	–	–	2	1	–
Cepaea nemoralis	–	–	–	–	–	–	–	–	–	–	–	–	–	1	–	–
Cepaea hortensis	–	–	–	–	–	–	–	–	–	–	–	3	–	–	–	–
Arianta/Cepaea spp.	–	1	–	–	2	3	–	1	–	–	–	9	2	1	–	–
Helix aspersa	–	–	–	–	1	–	–	–	–	–	1	5	16	8	5	–

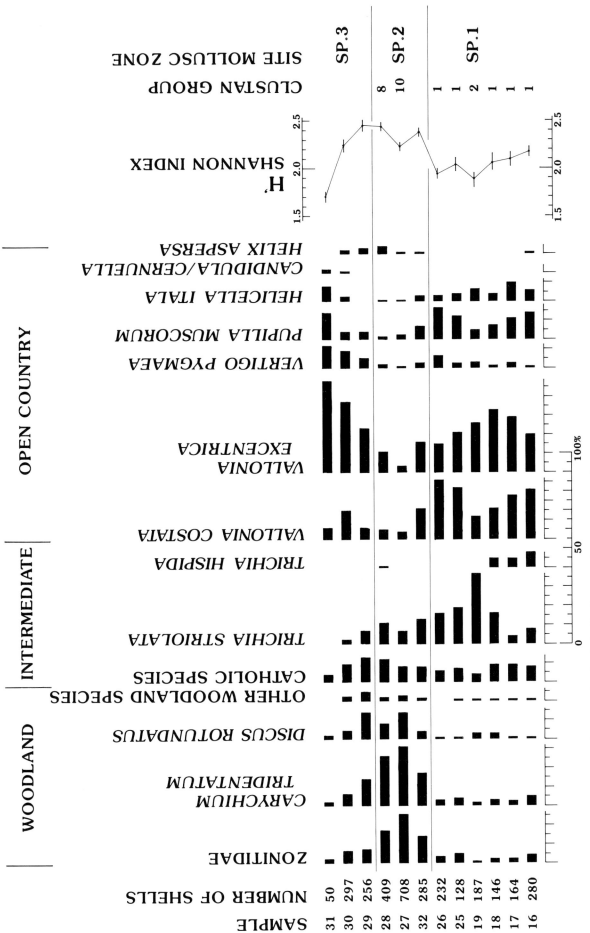

Fig 54. Land Mollusca review: Stratton Park (RI). Molluscan histogram, relative abundance.

There are three sequences of contiguous samples, listed in chronological order from the base upwards (Fasham 1981, Fig 13):

Feature	Context	Sample sequence
Late Iron Age ditch	120	18–23
Late Iron Age/Early Roman ditch (a re-cut of 120)	2G	13–16
Early Roman ditch	4F	5–7

The assemblages (Table 30, Fig 55) range from open-country to 70% woodland, the latter being similar to those of R1 with a paucity of 'other woodland species'. In the open-country assemblages, *Pupilla* and *Vallonia* are the main components. Differences from Stratton Park (R1) are the sporadic presence of *Pomatias elegans*, including some adult shells, and the absence of *Trichia striolata*.

Three SMZs are recognised:

LL.1. Low numbers of shells. *Vitrea* is important in the woodland group, reflecting unstable conditions in the earliest stages of ditch infilling (cf Winnall Down, R17, feature 5AA). Woodland species are present but there is an open-country component as well. H' ranges from 2.3–2.6. The CLUSTAN group is 9. Towards the top of the zone, woodland species become rare (R3.22–13).

LL.2. Increase in shell numbers. Woodland species reach almost 70% but open-country species persist. H' remains high. The CLUSTAN groups are 8 and 10, the latter with high *Carychium* which suggests dense leaf litter in the ditch.

LL.3. Reduction in shell numbers, and absence of woodland species, *Trichia hispida* and *Pomatias elegans*. H' is low at 1.45.

Late Iron Age ditch 120 was constructed in open country, and the environment remained open throughout its infilling (LL.1). The woodland species probably reflect baulks of uncultivated or ungrazed land at the edges of fields rather than woodland. The Late Iron Age/Early Roman ditch (2G) was constructed in open country, as is to be expected since it was a re-cut of ditch 120. But woodland or scrub (?planted) quickly spread into the ditch (LL.2), with open country on either side. In contrast, the Early Roman ditch (4F) was dug and became infilled in open country (LL.3), so there was clearance of woodland in early Roman times.

Bridget's Farm (R5, SU 514345)

The area is gently sloping ground, south-facing, at 100–104m OD. Three groups of features were investigated: Roman road ditches, Roman land-boundary ditches, and pits and/or natural hollows (Fasham 1980a). The two groups of ditches are part of the same system, converging at a complex junction, and avoiding, perhaps by design, the group of pits/hollows (Fasham 1980a, Fig 8). The nature of the pits/hollows is uncertain. Three radiocarbon dates from separate pits span a millennium of the

Table 30. Land Mollusca review: London Lodge (R3).

Feature	120						2G				4F		
Sample	18	19	20	21	22	23	13	14	15	16	5	6	7
Pomatias elegans	–	–	3	2	2	–	–	3	1	–	–	–	–
Carychium tridentatum	–	–	2	9	2	1	–	70	205	26	–	–	–
Cochlicopa lubrica	–	–	–	–	–	–	–	–	–	1	–	–	–
Cochlicopa lubricella	–	–	–	1	–	–	1	1	–	–	–	–	–
Cochlicopa spp.	–	–	3	10	2	–	1	3	22	7	–	–	–
Vertigo pygmaea	–	–	–	–	1	1	–	2	2	2	1	–	–
Pupilla muscorum	–	–	1	–	–	3	9	50	20	3	10	11	2
Vallonia costata	–	–	2	17	2	5	11	59	66	11	10	6	4
Vallonia excentrica	–	2	3	12	9	9	13	32	31	6	13	8	2
Acanthinula aculeata	–	–	1	2	2	1	–	1	1	–	–	–	–
Ena obscura	–	1	–	1	1	–	2	5	8	4	–	–	–
Punctum pygmaeum	–	–	1	1	2	1	1	7	19	1	1	–	–
Discus rotundatus	–	5	10	31	5	–	1	26	73	17	–	–	–
Vitrina pellucida	1	–	2	3	1	1	–	2	1	–	–	–	–
Vitrea contracta	4	8	3	13	3	1	5	25	37	7	–	–	–
Nesovitrea hammonis	–	–	–	–	–	1	–	–	–	–	–	–	–
Aegopinella pura	–	–	10	14	–	–	2	2	3	1	–	–	–
Aegopinella nitidula	–	1	2	3	2	3	–	33	68	4	–	–	–
Oxychilus cellarius	–	–	–	–	–	–	1	11	10	5	–	–	–
Limacidae	–	2	3	6	2	2	–	1	–	1	–	–	–
Cecilioides acicula	11	8	61	55	46	45	9	77	65	–	–	9	–
Cochlodina laminata	–	1	–	–	–	–	–	–	–	–	–	–	–
Clausilia bidentata	–	–	3	2	2	3	3	6	5	–	–	–	–
Candidula intersecta	–	–	–	–	–	1	–	–	3	2	–	–	–
Helicella itala	–	3	5	7	5	3	7	7	3	7	1	8	2
Trichia hispida	–	–	–	3	6	3	–	8	14	8	–	–	–
Arianta/Cepaea spp.	–	–	–	–	–	3	–	1	4	–	–	–	–

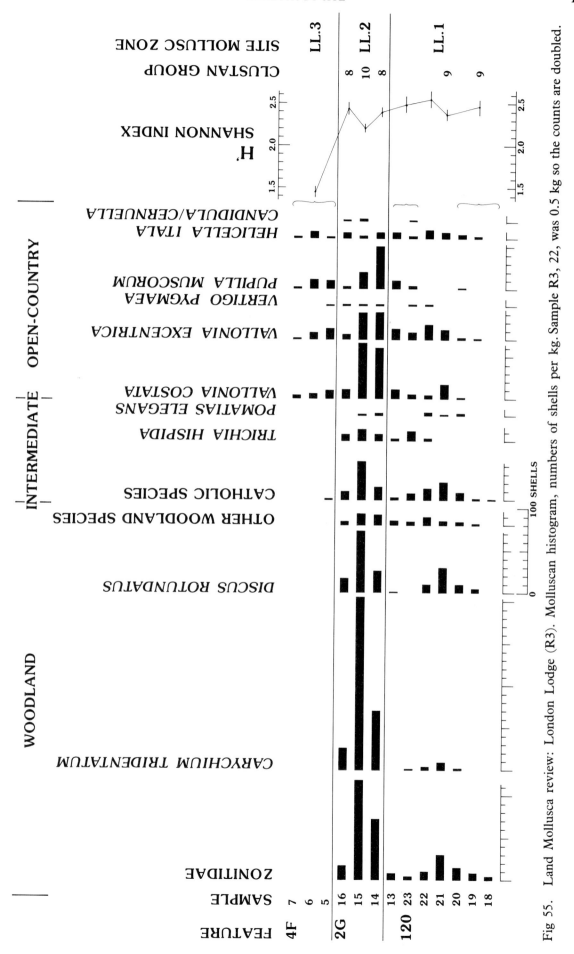

Fig 55. Land Mollusca review: London Lodge (R3). Molluscan histogram, numbers of shells per kg. Sample R3, 22, was 0.5 kg so the counts are doubled.

Bronze Age (HAR 1695, 3790±70; OxA 1410, 3420±100; and HAR 2745, 2800±80 BP uncalibrated for features 10, 28 and 27 respectively), but there is no datable archaeological material. Some of the features are probably tree-throw pits and the group probably represents a copse which may have persisted from the Neolithic period into Roman times.

The samples (see Fasham 1980a, Figs 9 and 16) are listed from the base of each sequence:

Feature	Context	Sample sequence
Pits/hollows	22	147, 141–146
	26	148–150
	28	151–157
	10	78, 79
Roman road ditches	1E	10–14
	2C/D	23–26
	7L/M	19–20
Roman land-boundary ditches	1A	1, 2, 4, 3
	1A/Y	73–75

Because of their closeness, the results of R5 and R6 (Tables 31, 32, 33 and 34; Figs 56 and 57) are considered together, below.

Burntwood Farm (R6, SU 511341)

The area is sloping ground, facing south/southeast, at 94–98m OD and about 450m from R5 (Fig 49). There were four groups of features: a circular hollow of uncertain age and origin, Late Neolithic pits, an Early/Middle Iron Age gully, and Roman ditches alongside a road belonging to the same complex as those in R5 (Fasham 1980a). A clearance horizon (layer 2) in pit 104 is dated to 4750±140 BP uncalibrated (OxA 1384).

The samples (see Fasham 1980a, Figs 4, 5, 10 and 14) are listed from the base of each sequence:

Feature	Context	Sample sequence
Hollow of uncertain origin	77	4–9
Late Neolithic pits	76	42–47
	104	111–120
Early/Middle Iron Age gully	6	10–14
Roman ditches	2H	15–18
	2K	145, 146, 148, 149, 143, 144
	84E	192–190
	85B	227–229
	87B	230–232

The earliest features are two Neolithic pits, 76 and 104, at R6. R6 feature 77 is included because its sequence is similar to that of features 76 and 104. The assemblages are woodland ones, but the Zonitidae are impoverished, with only *Aegopinella nitidula* common, and there is a low percentage of *Vallonia costata* and other open-country species. None is in the richest woodland CLUSTAN group, 9. The vegetation was dry woodland with the floor sparsely covered with leaf-litter and some open areas.

Within the sequences there is a distinctive pattern of change, with three SMZs (Fig 56):

BF.1a. *Vitrea*, *Vallonia costata* and 'other open-country species' abundant; *Pomatias elegans* low. Diversity high.

BF.1b. Eclipse of open-country species; *Vitrea* falls; *Pomatias elegans* increases; *Carychium* high. Diversity falls.

BF.1c. Open-country species return; *Vitrea* eclipsed; *Carychium* and *Discus* relatively low. Diversity high.

Some of these changes, especially the antipathetic behaviour of *Vitrea* and *Pomatias*, reflect the changing environment during pit infilling; others, such as the fluctuating open-country element, may be of wider significance. The pits were dug in an environment of woodland that had been subjected to some interference (BF.1a) and which subsequently regenerated (BF.1b). The later clearance zone (BF.1c) is Neolithic, this being the horizon from which the ^{14}C date OxA 1384 came.

The assemblages of the three deep pits of R5, features 22, 26 and 28, are woodland ones, characterised by an abundance and diversity of Zonitidae and an absence of open-country species.

Three SMZs are proposed (Fig 57), assigned to BF.2 because they are later than the pits of R6:

BF.2a. Low *Carychium* and *Pomatias*; high intermediate species and *Trichia*. H' is high at 2.4–2.5; CLUSTAN group 9.

BF.2b. Increasing *Carychium*; peak of *Pomatias*; decreasing *Trichia*. H' falling to 2.2; CLUSTAN groups 9 and 10.

BF.2c. High *Carychium*; low *Pomatias* and *Trichia*. H' low at 1.9–2.1; CLUSTAN group 10.

The similarity of the sequences (Table 31) suggests that the zones were synchronous and the proximity of the features also suggests a similar age, although only pit 22 is dated. The environment was deep woodland, probably with more leaf litter and less disturbed than that of the earlier R6 pits. The changes within the pits on which the SMZs are based are of site significance, a response to a reduction of bare soil and chalk and a deepening of litter as the pits filled up. The assemblages from the fourth pit in the group, R5 pit 10, are similar, but have a small proportion of open-country species.

The sequence from the Iron Age gully, R6 feature 6, is divided into two SMZs:

BF.3a (samples R6.10 and 11). Woodland (36–40%) and open country (44–54%) species.

BF.3b (samples R6.12–14). Open country, with

Table 31. Land Mollusca review: Bridget's Farm (R5), pits and hollows.
The Cepaea *banding patterns are:* C. nemoralis *in 141 and 144, unbanded;* C. hortensis *in 147, (12)(34)5, three shells; in 152, (1234)5; in 153 (12)(34)5.*

Feature	22							26			28							10	
Sample	147	141	142	143	144	145	146	148	149	150	151	152	153	154	155	156	157	78	79
Pomatias elegans	19	32	19	62	23	13	14	19	44	14	–	7	28	38	16	4	11	2	3
Carychium tridentatum	96	74	51	187	185	252	222	80	199	229	24	49	62	140	130	156	164	80	61
Cochlicopa lubrica	3	3	2	2	3	2	4	5	2	–	3	6	1	2	–	–	–	1	2
Cochlicopa lubricella	2	–	–	–	–	–	–	1	2	–	1	5	1	1	2	1	1	1	–
Cochlicopa spp.	9	7	3	7	4	6	5	9	8	9	8	8	3	9	4	10	2	–	2
Vertigo pusilla	–	–	–	–	–	–	–	1	–	–	–	–	–	–	–	–	–	–	–
Vertigo pygmaea	–	–	–	–	–	–	–	–	–	–	–	–	–	–	1	–	–	–	–
Pupilla muscorum	–	–	–	–	–	–	–	–	–	2	–	2	–	–	–	–	–	2	3
Lauria cylindracea	–	–	–	1	–	–	1	1	–	–	–	–	–	–	1	–	–	–	–
Vallonia costata	–	–	–	–	–	–	–	2	–	–	–	2	–	–	–	–	1	1	–
Vallonia pulchella	–	–	–	–	–	–	–	–	–	–	–	–	–	–	–	–	–	1	–
Vallonia excentrica	–	–	–	2	1	–	1	2	1	1	–	–	2	–	1	2	–	3	13
Acanthinula aculeata	7	4	6	11	7	12	8	–	7	16	8	14	10	11	13	12	9	2	2
Ena montana	–	–	–	1	1	1	–	–	1	1	1	–	1	1	1	–	–	–	–
Ena obscura	–	–	–	7	2	–	–	–	1	–	–	–	–	5	5	–	1	–	–
Punctum pygmaeum	9	31	10	25	17	16	10	13	18	19	4	7	8	15	9	9	14	5	–
Discus rotundatus	22	17	8	43	28	35	67	50	54	23	25	22	23	28	22	31	33	23	30
Vitrina pellucida	9	1	–	2	–	–	–	1	–	–	8	9	–	–	–	–	–	–	–
Vitrea crystallina agg.	38	67	50	93	69	82	47	36	98	78	21	47	47	58	59	53	59	18	21
Nesovitrea hammonis	1	–	1	2	3	4	2	–	2	1	–	–	–	3	–	3	3	1	2
Aegopinella pura	38	26	28	44	40	33	42	48	32	40	18	25	28	30	34	28	25	9	9
Aegopinella nitidula	32	33	20	48	32	21	37	45	34	39	19	23	42	46	33	28	29	14	17
Oxychilus cellarius	53	68	7	42	34	31	40	56	50	25	9	48	36	40	30	21	17	18	20
Oxychilus alliarius	–	–	–	1	–	–	–	2	–	1	–	1	2	–	–	–	–	1	–
Limacidae	–	–	–	–	–	–	–	–	–	–	–	–	–	–	–	–	–	1	4
Euconulus fulvus	9	1	–	1	1	4	2	–	–	1	6	5	–	2	–	–	1	1	–
Cecilioides acicula	26	29	26	107	74	91	112	36	97	108	31	78	207	71	72	79	119	203	107
Cochlodina laminata	1	2	–	2	1	3	2	1	1	–	–	2	–	4	–	–	1	–	2
Clausilia bidentata	3	3	1	1	–	–	2	2	2	–	2	5	2	2	1	–	–	–	–
Balea perversa	1	1	–	1	3	–	2	1	–	–	–	–	–	1	–	1	1	1	–
Candidula intersecta	–	–	–	–	–	–	–	–	–	–	–	–	–	–	–	–	1	–	–
Helicella itala	–	–	–	–	2	2	–	1	–	2	–	–	2	–	–	–	–	5	5
Trichia striolata	62	14	3	8	4	9	13	12	8	8	2	14	7	1	6	5	4	1	1
Trichia hispida	84	31	19	44	12	9	14	39	16	11	15	38	9	11	7	7	10	3	7
Arianta arbustorum	14	3	–	–	1	–	–	–	–	–	–	1	–	–	–	–	–	–	–
Helicigona lapicida	1	–	–	3	1	–	–	1	–	–	–	1	2	1	1	–	1	–	–
Cepaea nemoralis	–	2	–	–	1	–	–	–	–	–	–	–	–	–	–	–	–	–	–
Cepaea hortensis	4	–	–	–	–	–	–	–	–	–	–	1	1	–	–	–	–	–	–
Arianta/Cepaea spp.	10	4	1	2	–	–	1	1	–	–	5	9	3	5	1	2	–	1	3

Vallonia costata as the main species. CLUSTAN groups 6 and 3.

The Roman assemblages from R5 and R6 are placed in a single SMZ:

BF.4. Open country, the main species being *Pupilla* and *Vallonia excentrica*. Only in three samples does *Vallonia costata* exceed *Vallonia excentrica*. Of the intermediate species, only *Cochlicopa* is consistently present. Virtually all belong in CLUSTAN group 4.

Of these later features, the Iron Age gully (R6 feature 6) was dug in open woodland or scrub (BF.3a) which was later cleared (BF.3b). The Roman ditches were dug in an open landscape (BF.4).

Easton Down (R7, SU 495313)

The site, a Bronze Age ring ditch of the later second millennium BC, was on sloping ground facing southwest at 67m OD. There are six groups of contexts, ranging from pre-barrow later Neolithic pits, to post-barrow Iron Age and Roman features (Fasham 1982). The features were mostly fairly shallow pits whose infilling was only slightly younger than their excavation. The exception is the ring ditch in which the upper part of the infilling was of Iron Age date. 14C dates for a clearance horizon in the ring ditch are: segment 2/3, layer 3, 2980±90 (OxA 1413); and segment 2/4, layer 3, 3220±120 BP uncalibrated (OxA 1385).

The features shown on page 131 below Table 34 were analysed (see Fasham 1982, Figs 7, 9 and microfiche), columns of samples from the ring-ditch segments being listed from the base.

The assemblages (Tables 35 and 36; Fig 58) can be fitted into a sequence of five SMZs:

ED.1 (pre-barrow features; Bronze Age burials;

Table 32. Land Mollusca review: Bridget's Farm (R5), Roman ditches.
+ = *non-apical fragments only; ? = possible specimens included with* Helicella itala.

Feature	1AY			1A				7L/M		2C/D				1E				
Sample	73	74	75	1	2	4	3	19	20	23	24	25	26	10	11	12	13	14
Pomatias elegans	–	1	1	–	–	+	–	–	1	1	–	–	–	1	–	+	+	–
Carychium tridentatum	–	–	–	–	–	–	–	–	–	1	–	–	–	–	–	–	–	–
Cochlicopa lubricella	3	4	1	2	3	6	–	1	1	–	1	1	–	1	–	–	–	–
Cochlicopa spp.	2	2	4	4	3	8	5	4	3	–	–	–	–	2	1	1	1	–
Vertigo pygmaea	1	3	–	3	2	7	1	–	1	–	–	–	–	1	–	1	1	–
Pupilla muscorum	64	24	3	29	36	105	30	9	28	7	24	15	10	21	17	11	12	8
Vallonia costata	34	23	4	15	12	32	12	2	7	1	6	6	3	1	1	1	–	–
Vallonia pulchella	–	–	–	–	–	–	–	–	–	–	–	–	–	–	–	–	–	1
Vallonia excentrica	23	11	7	5	9	39	19	6	33	6	15	11	13	8	8	8	15	3
Punctum pygmaeum	–	–	1	–	–	–	–	–	–	–	–	–	–	–	–	–	–	–
Discus rotundatus	–	–	–	–	–	–	–	–	–	2	–	1	–	–	–	–	–	–
Vitrina pellucida	–	–	–	–	–	–	–	–	–	2	–	–	–	–	–	–	–	–
Aegopinella nitidula	–	–	1	–	–	–	–	–	–	–	–	–	–	–	–	–	–	–
Oxychilus spp.	1	–	2	–	–	–	–	–	–	–	–	–	–	–	1	–	–	–
Limacidae	1	–	1	–	–	–	–	–	6	–	–	–	–	–	–	–	–	–
Cecilioides acicula	37	74	49	24	47	37	109	48	95	47	59	76	75	85	52	91	126	40
Cochlodina laminata	–	–	–	–	–	–	–	–	–	1	–	–	–	–	–	–	–	–
Candidula intersecta	?	4	4	–	–	–	–	2	–	–	–	1	–	1	1	–	1	–
Candidula gigaxii	–	–	–	–	–	–	–	–	2	–	–	–	–	–	–	–	–	–
Cernuella virgata	–	1	1	–	?	?	–	–	–	–	–	–	–	–	–	–	–	–
Helicella itala	12	7	10	2	10	19	12	4	14	5	6	2	–	5	4	4	6	4
Trichia striolata	–	2	–	–	–	–	–	–	–	–	–	–	–	–	–	–	–	–
Trichia hispida	–	–	2	–	–	–	–	–	1	–	–	–	–	–	–	–	1	–

Table 33. Land Mollusca review: Burntwood Farm (R6), hollow of uncertain age and Neolithic pits.
The three specimens of Cepaea hortensis *are 5-banded.*

Feature	77						76						104									
Sample	4	5	6	7	8	9	42	43	44	45	46	47	111	112	113	114	115	116	117	118	119	120
Pomatias elegans	1	20	31	59	48	16	8	90	79	62	73	23	–	9	46	60	32	52	23	5	3	7
Carychium tridentatum	5	16	58	69	30	3	15	28	432	203	40	15	20	140	379	341	155	268	49	9	3	11
Azeca goodalli	–	–	–	–	–	–	–	–	–	1	–	–	–	–	–	–	–	–	–	–	–	–
Cochlicopa lubrica	–	–	–	–	–	–	–	–	2	–	–	–	–	–	–	–	–	–	–	–	–	–
Cochlicopa lubricella	1	5	2	–	1	–	–	2	3	2	1	–	1	7	7	2	1	3	1	–	–	–
Cochlicopa spp.	3	3	9	4	3	2	8	13	35	31	14	4	2	33	45	22	12	28	8	2	3	1
Truncatellina cylindrica	–	–	–	–	–	–	–	–	–	–	–	–	2	8	9	3	–	1	–	–	–	–
Vertigo pygmaea	–	–	1	1	–	–	1	–	–	–	–	1	1	1	–	–	2	2	–	3	–	–
Pupilla muscorum	2	19	14	12	8	5	7	10	3	2	1	6	16	18	3	3	2	1	2	4	4	6
Vallonia costata	–	2	14	13	7	4	3	5	6	2	1	1	4	56	53	6	7	4	1	2	6	13
Vallonia excentrica	–	1	9	15	15	7	–	–	–	1	2	9	–	–	–	3	2	1	2	1	3	12
Acanthinula aculeata	1	–	2	–	2	–	4	11	29	22	8	4	–	19	34	17	10	19	5	1	4	2
Ena montana	–	–	–	1	1	–	–	–	4	–	3	2	–	–	1	1	–	2	–	–	–	–
Ena obscura	–	–	–	1	–	–	–	–	–	1	1	–	–	10	3	5	–	1	–	–	–	–
Punctum pygmaeum	–	–	–	–	1	–	1	–	–	1	1	–	3	14	13	7	6	2	1	–	–	–
Discus rotundatus	2	12	27	15	10	–	13	93	139	57	21	4	4	76	135	117	48	76	31	10	1	5
Vitrina pellucida	–	–	–	–	–	–	1	–	–	–	–	–	–	2	1	–	–	1	–	–	–	–
Vitrea crystallina agg.	4	12	3	4	–	–	1	7	18	15	3	1	5	30	40	21	10	8	4	–	–	–
Nesovitrea hammonis	–	–	–	–	–	–	1	3	6	3	1	–	–	1	2	2	1	2	–	–	–	1
Aegopinella pura	4	–	2	3	1	–	4	6	31	7	5	–	–	10	30	16	4	4	3	–	–	3
Aegopinella nitidula	1	7	8	5	3	1	8	19	59	46	7	3	–	18	49	35	19	27	14	2	1	3
Oxychilus cellarius	–	2	–	1	–	–	–	2	4	–	–	1	5	1	2	–	–	3	–	–	2	1
Limacidae	–	–	–	–	–	–	–	–	9	7	3	–	–	–	–	–	–	–	–	–	–	–
Euconulus fulvus	–	–	–	–	–	–	–	–	–	–	–	–	1	1	1	1	–	–	–	–	–	–
Cecilioides acicula	–	64	80	155	120	83	–	6	–	7	11	26	–	7	16	11	14	15	14	53	78	116
Cochlodina laminata	–	4	4	5	7	1	–	6	6	9	6	7	1	24	19	8	1	3	5	–	–	1
Clausilia bidentata	–	1	1	2	3	2	–	–	2	4	3	–	–	8	12	9	1	8	1	–	–	–
Balea perversa	–	–	–	–	–	–	–	–	1	–	–	–	–	–	–	–	–	–	–	–	–	–
Candidula intersecta	–	–	3	1	1	–	?1	1	1	1	1	–	–	1	–	1	–	–	–	–	–	–
Cernuella virgata	–	2	–	–	–	–	–	–	–	–	–	–	–	–	–	–	–	–	–	–	–	–
Helicella itala	3	5	14	10	4	5	–	3	–	2	2	1	–	4	5	2	–	1	–	2	3	4
Trichia striolata	–	–	1	–	2	–	?1	3	14	1	–	–	–	–	1	3	2	1	1	–	–	–
Trichia hispida	1	3	11	13	7	3	3	21	60	40	8	2	1	2	20	30	21	53	18	1	1	–
Arianta arbustorum	–	–	–	–	–	–	–	–	–	–	–	–	–	–	1	–	–	–	–	–	–	–
Helicigona lapicida	–	2	–	–	–	–	–	–	3	–	–	1	–	2	2	3	1	–	–	–	–	–
Cepaea hortensis	–	–	–	–	–	–	–	–	–	–	–	–	–	–	1	–	–	2	–	–	–	–
Arianta/Cepaea spp.	–	1	3	6	6	1	1	1	5	4	1	1	1	7	2	11	7	6	7	–	1	–

Table 34. Land Mollusca review: Burntwood Farm (R6), Iron Age gully and Roman ditches.
+ = non-apical fragments only.

Feature	6					2H				2K						84E			85B			87B		
Sample	10	11	12	13	14	15	16	17	18	145	146	148	149	143	144	192	191	190	227	228	229	230	231	232
Pomatias elegans	4	5	3	15	12	–	1	3	4	2	+	7	3	3	2	–	–	1	–	–	–	1	1	–
Carychium tridentatum	15	3	3	6	5	–	–	1	–	–	–	–	–	–	–	2	–	–	–	–	–	1	–	–
Azeca goodalli	–	–	–	–	1	–	–	–	–	–	–	–	–	–	–	–	–	–	–	–	–	–	–	–
Cochlicopa lubrica	–	–	–	?	–	–	–	–	–	–	–	–	–	–	–	–	–	–	–	–	–	–	–	–
Cochlicopa lubricella	1	1	–	10	5	–	1	1	–	–	3	–	5	23	18	–	–	13	7	1	–	–	–	1
Cochlicopa spp.	1	3	3	17	17	1	–	–	3	4	2	2	3	16	9	1	3	14	–	1	1	4	–	2
Columella edentula	–	–	–	1	–	–	–	–	–	–	–	–	–	–	–	–	–	–	–	–	–	–	–	–
Truncatellina cylindrica	–	–	–	–	–	–	–	–	–	–	–	–	–	–	–	–	–	5	–	–	–	–	–	–
Vertigo pygmaea	–	2	–	2	–	1	–	–	1	–	1	1	1	3	5	–	1	7	3	–	–	2	–	1
Pupilla muscorum	10	13	69	316	357	24	16	26	67	52	38	59	58	192	153	3	35	191	65	2	1	38	26	22
Vallonia costata	21	25	53	817	362	2	4	7	17	23	21	17	20	69	68	1	12	80	19	–	–	1	3	4
Vallonia excentrica	5	9	48	133	65	7	2	9	32	23	18	31	35	94	98	1	14	131	42	1	1	29	17	24
Acanthinula aculeata	2	6	3	–	2	–	–	–	–	–	–	–	–	–	–	–	–	–	–	–	–	–	–	–
Ena obscura	1	–	–	–	–	–	–	–	–	–	–	–	–	–	–	–	–	–	–	–	–	–	–	–
Punctum pygmaeum	1	–	1	–	1	–	–	–	–	–	–	1	–	3	–	–	–	–	1	–	–	–	–	–
Discus rotundatus	7	12	4	2	5	–	–	–	–	–	–	–	–	–	–	–	–	–	–	–	–	–	1	–
Vitrina pellucida	–	1	1	–	–	–	–	–	–	–	–	–	–	1	–	–	–	–	–	–	–	–	–	–
Vitrea crystallina agg.	3	1	1	–	–	–	–	–	–	–	–	–	–	–	–	–	–	–	–	–	–	–	–	–
Nesovitrea hammonis	1	–	2	–	1	–	–	–	–	–	–	–	–	–	–	–	–	–	–	–	–	–	–	–
Aegopinella pura	1	6	1	–	1	–	–	–	–	–	–	–	–	–	–	–	–	–	–	–	–	–	–	–
Aegopinella nitidula	1	5	–	1	1	–	–	–	–	–	–	–	–	–	–	–	–	–	–	–	–	–	–	–
Oxychilus sp.	1	–	–	–	–	–	–	–	–	–	–	–	–	–	–	–	–	–	–	–	–	–	–	–
Limacidae	–	–	–	–	–	–	–	–	–	–	–	–	–	–	–	–	–	2	–	–	–	1	1	1
Cecilioides acicula	3	12	43	52	9	11	4	19	79	1	8	27	55	55	110	5	46	60	45	17	3	49	22	62
Cochlodina laminata	1	–	–	–	1	–	–	–	–	–	1	–	–	–	1	–	–	–	–	–	–	–	–	–
Clausilia bidentata	–	–	2	–	2	1	–	1	–	–	–	–	–	–	–	–	–	–	–	–	–	–	–	–
Candidula intersecta	–	–	–	–	–	–	–	4	–	–	–	–	1	–	–	–	2	–	2	–	–	4	–	–
Candidula gigaxii	–	–	–	–	1	–	–	–	–	–	–	–	–	–	–	–	1	–	–	–	–	–	–	–
Cernuella virgata	–	–	–	–	1	–	–	–	–	–	–	–	–	–	–	–	–	–	–	–	–	–	–	–
Helicella itala	2	7	14	58	31	4	8	11	22	15	11	18	17	38	47	–	5	15	13	7	1	9	3	8
Trichia hispida	3	–	–	–	–	–	–	–	–	–	–	–	–	–	–	–	–	–	1	–	–	–	–	–
Arianta/Cepaea spp.	–	–	–	–	1	–	–	–	–	–	–	–	–	1	–	–	–	–	–	–	–	–	–	–

Feature	Context	Sample
Pre-barrow	12	132
	33	135
	13	114
Bronze Age burials	255	112
	26	155
Ring-ditch segments	2/3	6–14
	4/5	38–44
	6/7	16–24
Bronze Age/Iron Age cremations	109	149
	102	122
Iron Age	113	146
	92	145
	112	143
	98	131
	57	133
	55	141
	22	142
	15	151
Iron Age/Roman	32	35, 36

and sample R7.38 of ditch segment 4/5). Variable proportions of woodland (8–43%) and open-country species; Pomatias elegans generally well represented; the main open-country species in more or less equal proportions. CLUSTAN group 5.

ED.2 (ring-ditch segment 2/3 samples 6–8; segment 4/5 samples 39–41; segment 6/7 samples 16 and 17). Mixed assemblages of woodland and open-country species. The woodland element is strong, around 60%. Excluding Vallonia costata which may be included with the woodland species in this context, the open-country component is around 10%. Shell numbers are high. CLUSTAN groups 8 and 10.

ED.3 (ring-ditch segment 2/3 samples 9–14; segment 4/5 samples 42–44; segment 6/7 samples 18–24). Open-country species, especially Pupilla, show a sudden and massive increase and there is an equally dramatic drop in the woodland component. These are not a function of the percentage calculations, they are absolute changes. CLUSTAN group 3. The base of the SMZ is dated to 3220±120 (OxA 1385) and 2980±90 BP uncalibrated (OxA 1413).

ED.4 (Bronze Age/Iron Age cremations; Iron Age features). Open-country species predominate, with Helicella itala and Pupilla most abundant. Pomatias elegans abundant. CLUSTAN group 5.

ED.5 (Iron Age/Roman features). Open-country assemblages, differing from ED.4 in low Pomatias elegans.

Before the construction of the barrow, the area

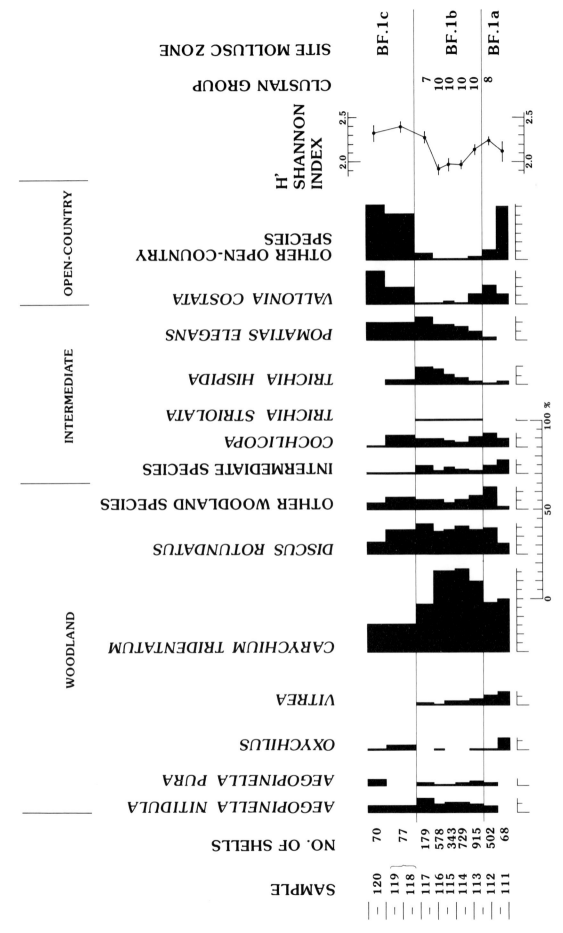

Fig 56. Land Mollusca review: Burntwood Farm (R6), pit 104. Molluscan histogram, relative abundance. Vertical scale is in 5- and 10-cm intervals.

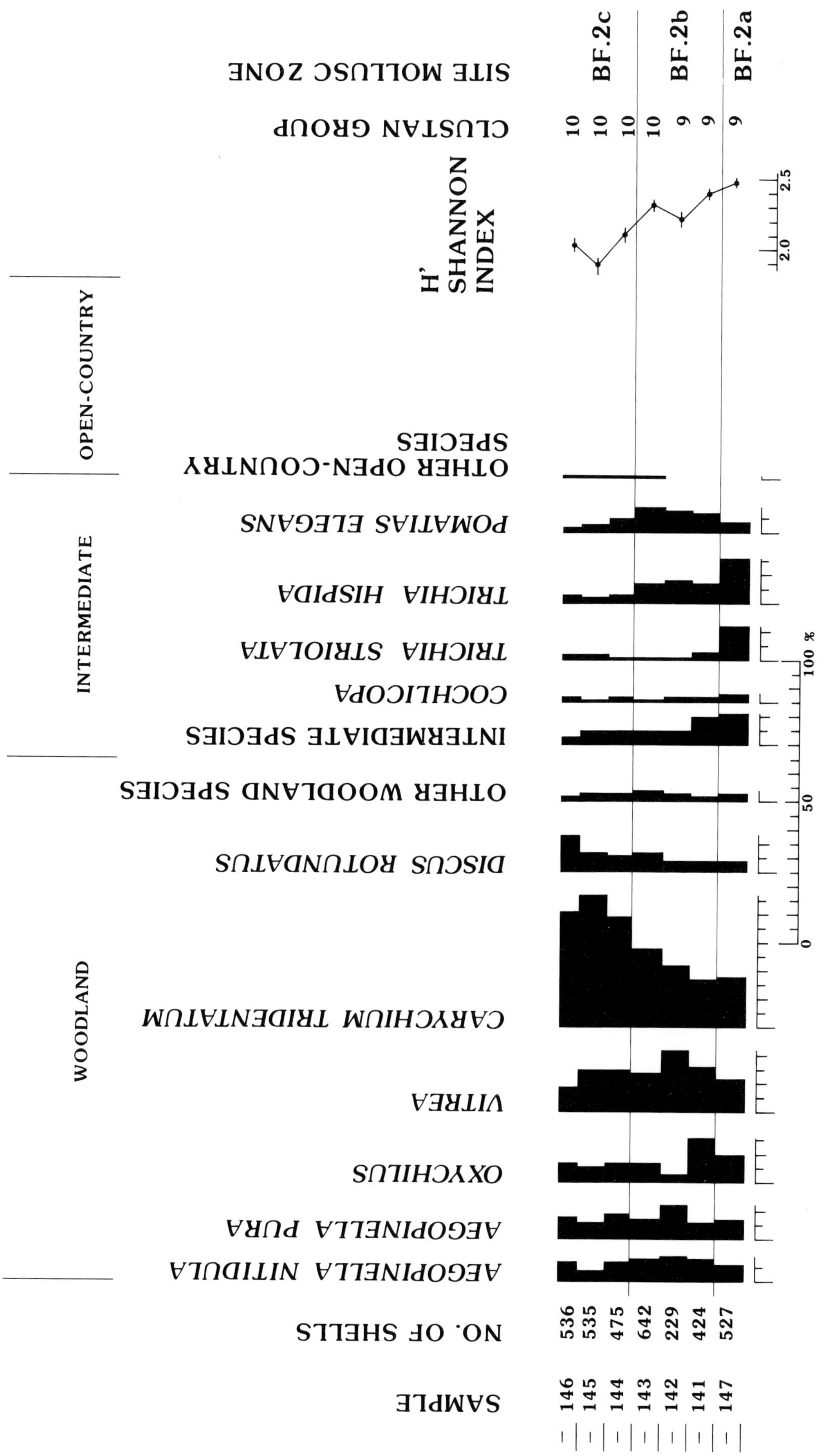

Fig 57. Land Mollusca review: Bridget's Farm (R5), feature 22. Molluscan histogram, relative abundance. Vertical scale is in 5- and 10-cm intervals.

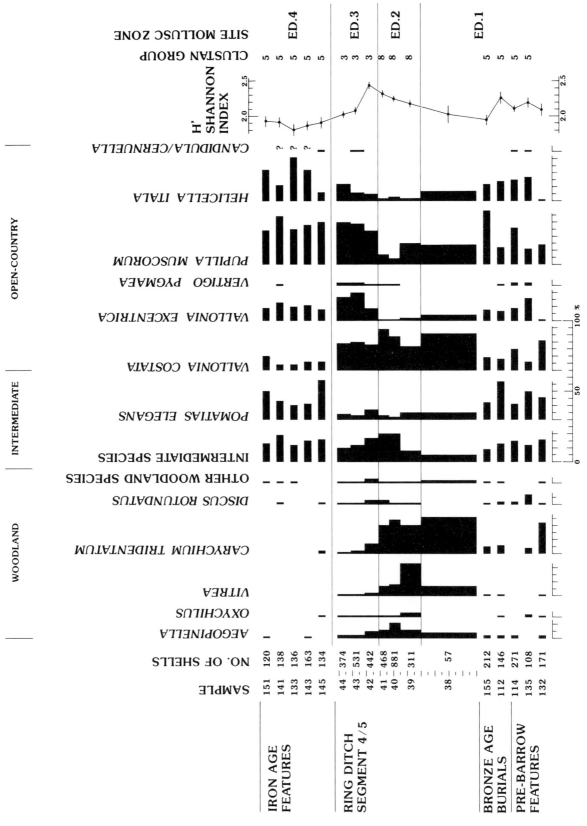

Fig 58.   Land Mollusca review: Easton Down (R7). Molluscan histogram, relative abundance. Vertical scale for ring-ditch segment 4/5 is
in 5- and 10-cm intervals.

Table 35. Land Mollusca review: Easton Down (R7), pre-ring-ditch features, Bronze Age burials, Bronze Age/Iron Age cremations, Iron Age features, Iron Age/Roman features.
? = possible specimens included with Helicella itala.

Sample	132	135	114	112	155	149	122	146	145	143	131	133	141	142	151	35	36
Pomatias elegans	27	22	29	40	26	23	31	15	37	18	18	13	18	13	23	3	6
Carychium tridentatum	38	4	–	8	10	–	–	1	2	–	–	–	–	–	–	–	–
Cochlicopa lubricella	2	–	9	1	–	5	2	–	1	4	1	3	4	2	5	–	3
Cochlicopa spp.	8	2	10	4	8	8	6	6	6	7	1	2	10	3	2	1	3
Vertigo pygmaea	–	2	4	1	–	–	2	–	–	–	–	–	1	–	–	1	8
Pupilla muscorum	24	12	69	17	81	34	32	13	40	46	33	33	47	27	29	17	66
Vallonia costata	36	6	41	12	19	5	4	7	8	10	4	5	6	5	12	1	11
Vallonia excentrica	2	17	24	10	17	29	22	5	11	18	13	14	18	13	11	9	31
Ena montana	–	–	–	–	–	–	–	–	–	–	–	1	–	–	–	–	–
Ena obscura	1	–	–	–	–	–	–	–	–	–	–	–	–	–	–	–	–
Punctum pygmaeum	1	–	4	–	–	–	–	–	–	–	–	–	–	–	–	–	1
Discus rotundatus	2	8	6	3	2	–	–	2	1	–	1	–	1	–	–	1	–
Vitrea crystallina agg.	1	–	–	1	1	–	–	–	–	–	–	–	–	–	–	–	–
Nesovitrea hammonis	1	–	–	1	–	–	–	–	–	–	–	1	–	–	–	–	–
Aegopinella pura	3	–	5	–	1	–	–	–	–	–	–	–	–	–	–	–	–
Aegopinella nitidula	1	–	–	3	3	–	–	–	–	1	–	–	–	–	1	–	–
Oxychilus cellarius	2	2	–	1	–	–	–	–	1	–	–	–	–	–	–	–	–
Oxychilus alliarius	–	–	–	1	–	–	–	–	–	–	–	–	–	–	–	–	–
Limacidae	5	3	10	7	8	1	3	3	5	10	5	10	5	4	1	3	2
Cecilioides acicula	54	48	78	62	21	142	70	55	57	42	81	96	55	56	70	35	65
Cochlodina laminata	–	–	–	–	–	–	1	–	–	–	–	–	–	–	–	–	–
Clausilia bidentata	–	–	–	2	1	–	–	–	–	–	2	1	1	4	1	–	2
Candidula gigaxii	–	1	1	–	–	?	–	?	1	–	?	?	?	–	–	–	–
Cernuella virgata	–	–	–	–	–	–	–	–	–	?	?	?	–	–	–	–	–
Helicella itala	2	18	40	21	25	15	28	20	7	36	33	42	15	18	26	22	35
Trichia striolata	–	–	–	–	–	–	1	–	–	–	–	1	–	–	–	–	1
Trichia hispida	7	10	17	8	8	7	2	7	6	8	10	10	8	5	6	6	8
Arianta/Cepaea spp.	8	1	2	5	2	1	4	3	8	5	4	–	4	1	3	–	1

was open country with diverse grassland, herbaceous vegetation and some scrub (CLUSTAN group 5, ED.1). After construction, this gave way to woodland with some open country (CLUSTAN groups 8 and 10, ED.2). There is no indication of how extensive this woodland was, and it may have been confined to the barrow, but the implications are that woodland was close by. Clearance took place in the Bronze Age (ED.3), and open country continued through the Iron Age into the Roman period.

Winnall Down (R17, SU 498303)

The area was on more or less level ground on a chalk spur at 67m OD, 30m above the valley floor of the River Itchen. The earliest feature was a ring-ditch, a penannular arrangement of eight hollows, dating to the first half of the third millennium BC (Fasham 1982), R17, feature 1972. None of the hollows was more than one metre deep. More extensive remains consisted of an Early Iron Age enclosure which continued in use into the Early Roman period. There was some medieval activity (Fasham 1985).

Four columns of samples were taken from the ring-ditch, each from a separate hollow, the samples being listed in ascending order for each hollow (Fasham 1982, Fig 3 and fiche):

Feature/Hollow	Sample column
1972B	112–115
1972E	103–104
1972F	106–108
1972H	109–111
4460	105

Feature 4460 was of Iron Age date, and the sample from it, 105, came from directly above 104. Otherwise the age of these deposits, apart from being Neolithic or later, is uncertain.

The following contexts from the enclosure were analysed, the samples in each column being listed from the base upwards (Fasham 1985, Figs 9, 28–30 and archive):

Feature	Context	Sample columns
Early Iron Age enclosure ditch	Section 5AA	225–236
	Section 5GG	294–307
Middle Iron Age pits	6038	473–482
	7372	308–323
Roman features	8581	493–496
	493C/1308F	280–283
	8817D/8818D/ 8082E	2641–2646

Table 36. Land Mollusca review. Easton Down (R7), ring-ditch segments.
? = possible specimens included with Vallonia excentrica. *The* Cepaea nemoralis *banding patterns are: in 42, unbanded (one specimen); in 17, 00300.*

Feature/Segment	2/3									4/5							6/7								
Sample	6	7	8	9	10	11	12	13	14	38	39	40	41	42	43	44	16	17	18	19	20	21	22	23	24
Pomatias elegans	11	24	72	27	18	27	18	29	20	3	15	21	15	29	18	15	6	24	30	7	11	22	20	13	16
Carychium tridentatum	105	128	111	46	12	12	4	8	–	15	61	213	92	30	13	3	108	259	66	7	4	4	8	5	2
Cochlicopa lubrica	2	3	8	2	–	–	–	–	–	–	1	11	–	–	–	–	2	–	–	–	–	–	–	–	–
Cochlicopa lubricella	4	4	5	13	5	13	12	10	9	–	–	5	2	16	16	6	–	2	13	5	5	11	11	8	2
Cochlicopa spp.	29	20	28	16	10	9	10	12	7	1	12	92	42	28	15	9	5	10	19	9	18	19	15	8	–
Columella edentula	–	1	1	–	–	–	–	–	–	–	–	–	–	–	–	–	–	–	1	–	–	–	–	–	–
Truncatellina cylindrica	–	–	–	–	1	–	–	–	–	–	–	–	–	–	–	–	–	–	–	1	3	6	–	–	–
Vertigo pygmaea	2	2	7	3	1	6	3	1	5	–	–	6	5	2	12	7	2	1	7	7	3	14	13	3	2
Pupilla muscorum	9	23	73	166	113	158	173	177	138	8	44	37	34	104	156	114	11	49	253	243	221	215	133	72	89
Vallonia costata	45	48	163	208	93	130	93	99	55	15	52	214	136	78	108	71	21	76	243	158	147	211	147	62	42
Vallonia pulchella	–	–	–	?	–	?	–	–	–	–	–	–	–	–	–	–	–	–	–	–	–	–	–	–	–
Vallonia excentrica	2	2	8	55	38	64	57	87	47	2	5	9	3	41	107	64	2	11	71	81	85	130	68	48	74
Acanthinula aculeata	1	21	30	9	–	5	–	–	–	1	1	3	3	8	2	1	7	19	1	–	–	2	–	–	–
Ena montana	–	1	–	–	1	–	–	–	–	–	–	–	–	–	–	–	–	–	–	–	–	–	–	–	–
Ena obscura	1	–	7	1	2	1	3	–	2	–	–	–	2	3	2	–	–	5	–	–	1	–	–	–	–
Punctum pygmaeum	8	12	17	6	2	3	1	1	1	–	2	10	5	6	3	2	3	16	1	8	1	3	2	–	–
Discus rotundatus	26	15	42	15	8	11	7	3	1	–	2	11	15	12	3	1	9	44	13	3	2	6	12	6	2
Vitrina pellucida	–	–	–	1	–	1	1	1	–	–	6	15	8	1	–	–	–	–	–	1	–	4	–	–	–
Vitrea crystallina agg.	29	41	44	13	4	7	1	1	–	4	71	61	31	9	5	2	27	44	13	–	1	–	1	–	–
Nesovitrea hammonis	4	3	3	2	–	3	2	4	–	–	–	4	7	3	4	2	1	5	1	1	1	1	3	–	–
Aegopinella pura	26	33	74	16	3	9	3	1	1	1	13	73	23	16	7	6	8	39	9	6	2	2	2	–	1
Aegopinella nitidula	19	22	54	13	2	6	2	–	1	1	4	21	7	4	1	3	4	27	8	4	3	–	5	3	1
Oxychilus cellarius	4	4	1	2	–	–	–	1	–	–	–	4	1	1	2	2	1	5	2	–	–	–	2	–	1
Oxychilus alliarius	1	–	1	–	–	–	–	–	–	–	?8	–	–	–	–	–	1	–	–	–	–	–	–	–	–
Limacidae	3	–	–	–	–	–	1	–	5	3	–	3	–	5	–	5	1	2	–	–	2	3	2	5	5
Cecilioides acicula	3	–	–	5	38	105	50	105	89	7	3	7	9	40	123	133	5	25	73	59	86	79	49	45	61
Cochlodina laminata	1	–	6	1	–	1	–	4	–	–	1	–	1	1	1	–	3	5	4	1	–	2	1	–	–
Clausilia bidentata	–	1	4	–	2	7	2	2	3	–	–	1	–	2	–	–	2	4	1	1	–	3	1	–	3
Candidula intersecta	–	–	–	–	1	–	–	–	–	–	–	–	–	–	–	–	–	1	–	–	–	–	–	–	–
Cernuella virgata	–	–	–	–	–	–	–	–	–	–	–	–	–	–	1	–	–	–	3	2	–	–	–	–	–
Helicella itala	2	1	11	8	10	19	36	38	31	4	7	30	11	23	32	43	4	15	22	27	26	47	38	20	17
Trichia striolata	–	1	1	–	–	–	–	–	–	–	–	–	–	–	–	–	–	1	–	–	–	–	–	–	–
Trichia hispida	11	28	29	11	8	10	10	17	14	–	3	32	21	15	20	16	2	13	13	19	15	43	42	26	20
Arianta arbustorum	–	–	–	–	–	1	–	–	–	–	–	–	–	–	–	–	–	–	–	–	–	–	–	–	–
Helicigona lapicida	–	1	–	–	–	1	–	–	–	–	–	–	–	–	–	–	2	5	–	–	–	–	–	–	–
Cepaea nemoralis	–	–	–	–	–	1	–	–	–	–	–	–	–	2	–	–	–	1	–	–	–	–	–	–	–
Arianta/Cepaea spp.	3	1	3	1	3	2	–	5	3	2	1	4	4	3	3	2	1	–	1	–	1	2	1	1	5

Infillings were of the same period as the respective features, with the exceptions of 5AA in which the deposits upwards of 230 (inclusive) were of the Middle Iron Age, 5GG in which 307 was Roman or later and pit 7372 in which the deposits upwards of 316 (inclusive) were Roman. Samples 294 – 306, 226, 227, 309 and 311 were rubbly and poor in shells; they are not listed in the tables.

Two SMZs are recognised (Tables 37, 38 and 39; Fig 59):

WD.1 (R17 feature 1972, all samples, including 105). Open-country assemblages; *Pomatias elegans* well-represented; woodland species, although sparse, in greater abundance than in WD.2. H' ranges from 1.8–2.5. CLUSTAN groups 5 (three assemblages) and 3 (one assemblage).

WD.2 (all assemblages from R17). Totally open country; *Pomatias elegans* sparse to absent; *Cochlicopa* low; *Trichia hispida* characteristic. With the exceptions mentioned below, no one open-country species is especially abundant. H' ranges from 1.3–2.2, but mostly is below 1.8. CLUSTAN groups

1 (one assemblage), 3 (ten assemblages) and 6 (three assemblages).

In segment 5AA of the Early Iron Age enclosure ditch, three subsidiary zones are recognised within WD.2 (Fig 59). These relate to the infilling of the ditch:

WD.2a (samples 225–229). Mollusca very sparse. Rapid infilling.

WD.2b (samples 230–233). Increase in shell numbers. Assemblage characterised by *Vitrea contracta* and *Vallonia costata*. H' very low. CLUSTAN group 6. This assemblage relates to the early stages of molluscan colonisation as the rate of infilling slowed. Unstable land surface with sparse vegetation.

WD.2c (samples 234–236). Further increase in shell numbers. An open-country assemblage, with the four main species in more or less equal abundance. H' above 2.0. CLUSTAN group 3. This reflects slow infilling and a substantial cover of herbaceous vegetation.

Practically all the sequences show increasing shell

Table 37. Land Mollusca review: Winnall Down (R17), feature 1972.

Feature	1972B				1972E		4460	1972F			1972H	
Sample	112	113	114	115	103	104	105	106	107	108	110	111
Pomatias elegans	–	3	7	10	3	4	21	–	10	19	1	3
Carychium tridentatum	–	–	–	–	–	–	–	–	5	6	–	–
Cochlicopa spp.	–	–	–	–	–	–	4	–	–	3	–	1
Vertigo pygmaea	–	–	–	–	–	–	–	–	–	1	–	–
Pupilla muscorum	–	1	1	14	–	–	9	–	–	14	–	20
Vallonia costata	–	1	1	9	–	4	10	–	–	7	–	4
Vallonia excentrica	–	–	1	19	–	–	12	–	2	15	1	12
Acanthinula aculeata	–	–	–	1	–	–	–	–	–	1	–	–
Ena obscura	–	–	–	–	–	–	–	–	–	1	–	–
Discus rotundatus	–	–	–	2	–	–	6	–	1	6	1	1
Vitrina pellucida	–	–	–	–	–	–	–	–	–	–	–	1
Vitrea crystallina agg.	–	–	–	–	–	–	1	–	–	–	–	–
Aegopinella pura	–	–	–	–	–	–	3	–	1	3	–	–
Aegopinella nitidula	–	–	–	–	–	–	–	–	–	1	–	–
Oxychilus cellarius	–	–	1	–	–	2	–	–	–	–	–	–
Limacidae	–	–	1	2	–	–	3	–	–	8	2	2
Cecilioides acicula	8	5	57	84	–	6	108	3	13	76	13	59
Cochlodina laminata	–	–	–	–	–	–	–	–	–	2	–	–
Candidula intersecta	–	–	2	1	–	–	–	–	3	–	2	–
Cernuella virgata	–	–	–	7	–	–	8	–	–	5	–	18
Helicella itala	–	–	4	20	–	–	4	–	4	7	3	5
Trichia striolata	–	–	–	–	–	–	1	–	–	–	–	–
Trichia hispida	–	–	2	1	–	4	3	–	1	4	1	–
Arianta/Cepaea spp.	–	–	–	1	–	–	3	–	–	3	–	1

numbers with time. In contrast to some other sites, for example Danebury (Cunliffe 1984), there are no peaks of abundance within the sequences and, with the exception of ditch segment 5AA, there are no peaks of woodland species. The implications are that the site and its surrounding were open and that vegetation was sparse.

Many of the Winnall Down (R17) assemblages contain *Cernuella virgata*, a species that did not enter Britain until later prehistoric or historic times (Kerney 1966). From their state of preservation, the shells appear contemporary with the assemblages. Note, however, that most are fairly high in the sequences, that they are not in well-sealed contexts, and that there was Medieval activity on the site, which could have been responsible for their introduction. See also Preece (1980) for a discussion of the history of *Cernuella virgata* in the Isle of Wight.

Grace's Farm (R30, SU 508335)

The area is a south-facing slope of a small dry valley at 80m OD. The site was a small ring-ditch possibly of the Middle Bronze Age (Fasham 1982). The age of the infilling was uncertain.

Four columns of samples were analysed (Fasham 1982, Fig 17 for details), the samples from each segment being listed from the base, upwards.

Ditch segment	Sample column
2B	1–4
2D	5–8
2F	9–12
2H	13–16

All the assemblages are of open-country type, characterised mainly by *Vallonia*. *Pomatias elegans* is present, and although in small numbers, there are some large shells, so it was probably contemporary. *Trichia hispida* is totally absent. All are in CLUSTAN group 1. An interesting local feature is that the assemblages from the western side of the site (11, 12, 15, 16) have a higher abundance of *Pomatias elegans* and woodland species and higher H' values than those from the eastern side (4, 7, 8).

Environmental Interpretation: the CLUSTAN Groups

In discussing the results in environmental terms we have used mainly the evidence of the woodland:open-country ratio and the CLUSTAN groups. Diversity and the abundance of individual species have been used to a lesser degree, although the latter is incorporated into the CLUSTAN group data. We have already discussed the interpretation of the woodland:open-country ratio and the way in which it can be enhanced by the Shannon-Wiener index and the recognition of distinctive species associations. Here, we go further into a discussion of the CLUSTAN groups.

First : 'Are the CLUSTAN groups real?', that is 'real' as discrete blocks of species in certain proportions (the assemblages), with differences between assemblages within groups being less than those between groups? The answer is 'yes'. The analysis was carried out in several rigorous stages with duplicate checks and the use of the RELOCATE

Table 38. Land Mollusca review: Winnall Down (R17), Iron Age ditches and pits.

Feature	5AA										5GG	6038									
Sample	225	228	229	230	231	232	233	234	235	236	307	473	474	475	476	477	478	479	480	481	482
Pomatias elegans	1	–	–	1	1	–	1	4	1	2	–	–	1	–	–	–	1	2	–	1	–
Cochlicopa lubrica	–	–	–	–	–	–	–	4	–	–	–	–	–	–	–	–	–	–	–	–	–
Cochlicopa lubricella	–	–	–	–	–	–	–	1	1	1	–	–	–	–	–	–	–	–	–	–	–
Cochlicopa spp.	1	–	–	1	–	2	2	2	3	–	1	–	–	–	–	–	1	1	–	–	–
Vertigo pygmaea	5	–	–	–	–	–	–	–	–	–	1	–	–	–	–	–	–	–	–	–	1
Pupilla muscorum	–	–	–	2	–	1	7	21	16	9	18	4	2	–	2	3	8	11	12	15	13
Vallonia costata	9	3	3	4	28	12	7	19	18	14	11	9	16	3	7	7	13	24	23	54	136
Vallonia excentrica	3	–	–	3	–	2	2	10	19	20	17	3	3	2	6	2	3	17	6	23	49
Discus rotundatus	–	–	–	–	1	1	–	–	–	–	–	–	–	–	–	–	–	–	–	–	–
Vitrina pellucida	–	–	–	–	–	–	–	–	1	–	–	–	–	–	–	–	–	–	–	–	–
Vitrea crystallina agg.	1	–	–	3	11	10	9	3	–	–	–	–	–	–	–	–	1	–	–	–	–
Aegopinella nitidula	–	–	–	–	–	–	–	1	–	–	–	–	–	–	–	–	–	–	–	–	–
Oxychilus cellarius	1	–	–	1	2	5	–	–	–	2	–	–	–	–	–	–	–	–	–	–	–
Limacidae	–	1	–	–	2	–	1	3	1	1	2	–	–	–	–	–	–	–	–	–	–
Cecilioides acicula	2	1	–	3	23	112	118	92	104	78	275	–	–	–	–	–	27	56	72	161	95
Clausilia bidentata	–	–	–	–	–	–	–	–	1	–	–	–	–	–	–	–	–	–	–	1	–
Candidula intersecta	–	–	–	–	–	–	–	–	–	–	1	–	–	–	–	–	–	–	–	–	–
Candidula gigaxii	–	–	–	–	–	–	–	–	1	–	–	–	–	–	–	–	–	1	–	–	–
Cernuella virgata	–	–	–	–	–	–	–	15	9	–	5	–	–	–	–	–	–	–	–	2	4
Helicella itala	4	–	2	3	–	–	3	8	13	8	7	–	–	1	–	2	7	6	3	14	20
Trichia hispida	6	–	–	6	15	1	6	15	8	5	4	4	7	7	1	–	2	4	2	8	6
Helix aspersa	–	–	–	–	–	–	–	–	–	–	1	–	–	–	–	–	–	–	–	–	–

Feature	7372													
Sample	308	310	312	313	314	315	316	317	318	319	320	321	322	323
Pomatias elegans	–	–	1	–	1	–	–	–	–	–	–	–	–	1
Cochlicopa lubrica	–	–	–	–	–	–	–	–	–	–	–	–	–	–
Cochlicopa lubricella	–	–	–	–	–	–	–	–	1	–	–	–	–	–
Cochlicopa spp.	–	–	–	–	–	–	–	–	–	–	1	–	–	–
Vertigo pygmaea	–	–	1	–	–	–	–	–	–	–	1	–	–	–
Pupilla muscorum	5	5	9	2	9	7	–	20	16	12	24	14	31	35
Vallonia costata	7	5	3	4	6	7	4	9	12	19	32	9	18	22
Vallonia excentrica	8	5	10	–	3	3	2	2	7	6	23	4	20	11
Discus rotundatus	–	–	–	–	–	–	–	–	–	–	–	–	–	–
Vitrina pellucida	–	–	–	–	–	–	–	1	–	–	–	–	–	–
Vitrea crystallina agg.	–	–	–	–	–	–	–	–	–	–	–	–	–	–
Aegopinella nitidula	–	–	1	–	–	–	–	–	–	–	–	–	–	–
Oxychilus cellarius	–	–	–	–	–	–	–	–	–	–	–	–	–	–
Limacidae	–	–	–	–	–	–	–	–	–	–	–	2	1	1
Cecilioides acicula	38	–	–	3	4	5	–	1	10	45	40	49	149	203
Clausilia bidentata	–	–	–	–	–	–	1	–	–	–	–	–	–	–
Candidula intersecta	–	–	–	–	–	–	–	–	–	–	–	–	–	1
Candidula gigaxii	–	–	–	–	–	–	–	–	–	–	–	–	–	–
Cernuella virgata	–	–	–	–	–	–	–	–	–	–	21	–	13	13
Helicella itala	4	1	–	–	6	4	–	4	5	4	6	6	9	13
Trichia hispida	5	–	–	–	8	11	6	7	3	4	9	4	6	10
Helix aspersa	–	–	–	–	–	–	–	–	–	–	–	–	–	–

option. The number of groups for further analysis was obtained by a standard method.

Second: 'Are the assemblages real associations of species, representative of formerly living communities?' Most are probably more or less autochthonous, coming from small ditches and pits rather than from colluvial deposits. But they are not as autochthonous as assemblages from the top of buried soils, and the large sample intervals and often low numbers of shells also imply assemblages that are not representative of life. On the other hand, the way in which, in many cases, the CLUSTAN groups equate with both chronological and spatial distributions is suggestive of life communities. Note, for example,

the occurrence of group 1 only at Stratton Park and Grace's Farm, and of group 4 only in Roman contexts. Another indication is that there are other areas where similar associations occur, for example, assemblages resembling group 1 are common in prehistoric grasslands in the Avebury area (Evans 1972). Also, not every possible combination of species occurs: for example, in the open-country groups there are no assemblages in which *Pupilla* and *Helicella itala* are the only main species, and this is in contrast to Danebury where *Pupilla* predominates to a much greater extent than in our group 4 in many of the assemblages (Cunliffe 1984).

The next question, then, is: 'To what are these

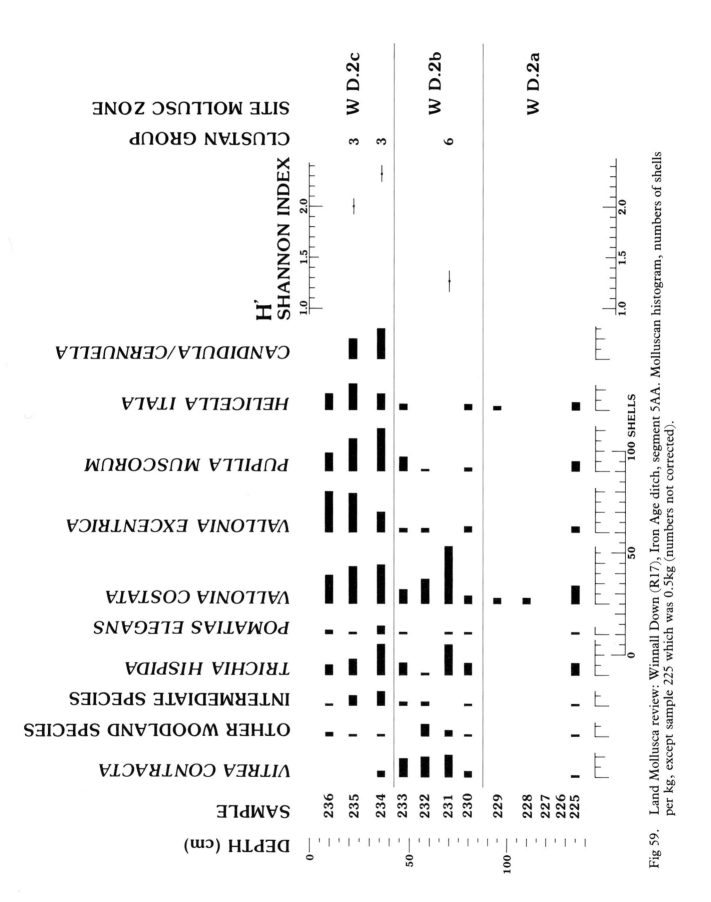

Fig 59.   Land Mollusca review: Winnall Down (R17), Iron Age ditch, segment 5AA. Molluscan histogram, numbers of shells per kg, except sample 225 which was 0.5kg (numbers not corrected).

Table 39. Land Mollusca review: Winnall Down (R17), Roman features.

Feature	8581				493C			1308F	8082E			8818D		8817D
Sample	493	494	495	496	280	281	282	283	2641	2642	2643	2644	2645	2646
Pomatias elegans	–	–	–	–	1	–	–	3	2	–	1	4	1	1
Succineidae	1	–	–	–	–	–	–	–	–	–	–	–	–	–
Cochlicopa lubricella	–	–	–	–	–	–	–	–	–	–	–	–	–	1
Cochlicopa spp.	–	–	–	–	–	–	–	1	–	1	1	–	1	–
Vertigo pygmaea	–	1	–	–	–	–	–	–	1	–	–	–	–	–
Pupilla muscorum	16	13	12	5	21	14	22	36	10	19	39	55	24	58
Vallonia costata	39	21	17	6	5	3	4	28	10	22	20	24	23	33
Vallonia excentrica	21	17	2	1	8	7	12	13	7	10	13	17	11	41
Limacidae	–	–	–	–	–	–	3	1	–	–	–	3	2	2
Cecilioides acicula	54	92	140	71	131	176	147	218	20	20	62	83	79	113
Clausilia bidentata	–	–	–	–	–	–	–	–	–	–	–	–	–	1
Candidula intersecta	–	–	–	–	1	–	–	–	–	–	–	–	–	–
Candidula gigaxii	–	–	–	–	3	–	2	–	–	–	–	–	–	–
Cernuella virgata	–	–	–	–	–	–	–	12	–	–	1	3	–	–
Helicella itala	7	3	1	–	15	5	19	11	2	2	15	7	11	17
Trichia hispida	20	11	2	–	7	4	6	18	9	5	10	27	9	33
Arianta/Cepaea spp.	–	–	–	–	–	–	1	–	–	–	–	2	–	–
Helix aspersa	–	–	–	–	1	–	–	–	–	–	–	–	–	–

Table 40. Land Mollusca review: Grace's Farm (R30).

Feature/Segment	2B				2D				2F				2H			
Sample	1	2	3	4	5	6	7	8	9	10	11	12	13	14	15	16
Pomatias elegans	–	–	–	2	–	–	–	1	–	–	4	4	–	–	1	3
Carychium tridentatum	–	–	–	–	–	–	1	–	–	6	2	–	–	–	2	3
Cochlicopa lubricella	–	–	–	14	1	–	1	2	–	3	1	5	–	–	1	1
Cochlicopa spp.	1	–	–	13	–	–	4	7	–	–	10	3	–	–	8	2
Vertigo pygmaea	–	–	–	7	1	–	1	4	–	–	3	6	–	1	–	1
Pupilla muscorum	–	–	3	30	3	–	10	28	5	19	28	26	1	–	15	15
Vallonia costata	4	–	11	125	8	–	18	44	4	13	54	62	2	1	27	28
Vallonia excentrica	1	1	11	108	20	5	44	57	12	16	56	69	2	8	31	43
Acanthinula aculeata	–	–	–	2	–	–	–	–	–	–	1	–	–	–	–	–
Ena obscura	–	–	–	–	–	–	–	–	–	–	–	–	–	–	2	1
Punctum pygmaeum	–	–	2	–	–	–	–	2	–	–	1	2	–	–	1	3
Discus rotundatus	–	–	–	1	1	–	–	–	–	–	1	2	–	–	2	4
Vitrina pellucida	–	–	1	–	–	–	1	–	–	–	–	–	–	–	–	–
Vitrea crystallina agg.	–	–	–	–	–	–	–	–	–	–	1	1	–	1	–	1
Nesovitrea hammonis	–	–	1	11	–	–	–	–	–	–	1	2	–	–	2	2
Aegopinella pura	–	–	–	–	–	–	–	–	–	–	1	–	–	–	–	–
Aegopinella nitidula	–	–	–	–	–	–	–	–	–	–	–	1	–	1	–	2
Limacidae	–	–	1	3	4	1	1	6	–	2	3	1	1	1	–	1
Cecilioides acicula	48	1	51	178	129	77	152	227	87	128	111	51	69	75	101	89
Cochlodina laminata	–	–	–	–	–	–	–	1	–	–	2	–	–	–	–	–
Clausilia bidentata	–	–	–	–	–	–	–	–	1	–	4	–	–	2	–	
Candidula gigaxii	–	–	–	–	1	–	–	1	–	–	–	–	–	1	–	
Cernuella virgata	–	–	–	–	–	–	–	–	–	–	–	–	–	–	1	
Helicella itala	–	–	4	6	–	9	11	9	1	7	15	9	1	–	3	4
Arianta/Cepaea spp.	–	–	–	–	–	–	–	1	–	–	–	–	–	–	3	–

different assemblages due? Why do we get different associations of species, or "communities" as ecologists call the living populations?' There are three main possibilities: small- and large-scale aggregations due to behaviour or the spread of founding communities; response to environmental segregation; and time.

Snails and slugs aggregate spatially at various scales – small groups of one species beneath a stone or log, larger groups on a woodland floor or in grassland. These are probably not registered in the CLUSTAN groups although they may be responsible for some of the differences between individual assemblages. Equally, there are small fluctuations through time, some of which may be unrelated to external environment, but the coarse-grained nature of the sampling probably does not pick them up. Larger associations, as are characteristic of particular areas in the M3 series, may reflect the composition of the founding community, its establishment, spread and persistence, rather than particular environmental factors. Barriers of non-calcareous land such as those presented by the Itchen floodplain or the area of Clay-with-Flints between the Bridget's Farm/Burntwood Farm/Grace's Farm and London Lodge/Stratton Park groups of sites (Fig 49) may have enhanced such effects.

Environmental segregation refers here to small- and medium-scale aspects, not to broad regional ones like climate. The main aspects are the distribution in time and space of vegetation and soil types at the sort of scale ranging from a few square metres to several hectares. At this scale, environment is a patchwork of discrete types, a series of quanta rather than a continuum, and, since the Neolithic period, largely created by man. It is the distribution of woodland, scrub, grassland, arable and hedgerows, and their nature – eg the sort of woodland and grassland, and the intensity of grazing – that are of most relevance to archaeology and that are probably the basis of the CLUSTAN groups. There are two main difficulties. First, in many cases we do not know what factors are responsible for the abundance of particular species. Second, the main species do not precisely co-vary.

To take the first point, the main factors, in general terms, are food and moisture. These can be translated into type of vegetation, degree of disturbance and nature of the ground surface and soil. For example, the distinction between CLUSTAN groups 9 and 10 probably reflects the woodland floor type, whether broken up into patches of bare soil, leaf-litter, fallen timber and so forth (group 9), or whether covered with a uniform and dense layer of litter (group 10). In open country, *Vallonia costata* shuns areas that are grazed by large mammals, so perhaps the differences between CLUSTAN groups 1 and 3 on the one hand and 4 and 5 on the other are a reflection of grazing pressure. Other factors such as food may be involved. Particular types of grassland may favour particular snail species because of what they eat. *Vallonia costata* prefers diverse calcareous grassland of the kind that becomes established as 'old downland', perhaps feeding on the needle-leaved, fibrous fescues, while *Vallonia excentrica* is more characteristic of pasture, there perhaps feeding on broader-leaved species. However, we do not know what *Vallonia* species eat, let alone whether they prefer different species of vegetation.

The second point concerns the absence of co-variation between certain species from one CLUSTAN group to another, discussed with regard to *Vallonia excentrica* and *Pupilla muscorum*. Response to change may vary according to the balance of the various parts of the environment, as with the different responses to climate. Alternatively, a given species might not necessarily respond on a one-to-one basis with environment, but instead might react as if it were a different species. Ecophenotypic

variation within a species might help. For example, there is a possibility that *Pupilla muscorum* shells from dry habitats are smaller and have more apertural denticles than those from damp habitats.

Lastly, some of the molluscan differences are related to age, that is age in years before present rather than age in relation to the development of individual habitats. These are a function of large-scale environmental change. Climate is probably the main factor, but long-term human interference, changes of land management, loss of soil fertility, decreasing size of habitats and introduction of new species are possibilities. The main molluscan changes have been a general decline in *Helicella itala*, *Pomatias elegans*, *Vallonia costata* and *Pupilla muscorum*; *Pomatias elegans* since the Bronze Age (Kerney 1968), the others from a later date. The main human introductions, most probably of later prehistoric or later date, are *Helix aspersa*, *Cernuella virgata*, *Candidula intersecta* and *C. gigaxii*. Additionally, new associations have developed. For example, an open-country association that is common today but completely absent from the M3 project assemblages is *Vallonia excentrica* + Limacidae + *Trichia hispida*.

From the above, it is apparent that single species are only useful in environmental reconstruction either when they are stenotypic, that is confined to a single set of environmental conditions, and have remained so through time, or when phenotypes can be likewise tied to a particular environment. There is only a very small number of species that behave in this way. Otherwise it is safer to use associations of species (CLUSTAN groups), assemblage structure (diversity indexes and rank-order curves) and the proportions of broad ecological groups (woodland:grassland ratios), and preferably, as we have done, in conjunction with each other.

Environmental Interpretation: Changes through Time and Space

Each assemblage refers with certainty only to the area and depth of the deposit from which it came. With increasing distance from the sample point, interpretation is less certain. The fact that snails in life move in and out of the area that is ultimately sampled and that only some of them die in it also allow that assemblages refer to a wider lateral area than the dimensions of the sample itself. But how much wider? This is the crucial question that is so often asked by archaeologists and that is so difficult to answer. The depth/time sequence is generally secure because there is usually a vertical series of contiguous samples. When there are trends through time which can be said to be ecologically meaningful (admittedly subjective), then it is valid to suppose that changes refer to an area beyond the horizontal bounds of the sample point as well. Duplicate or multiple sampling reinforces such observations, and this has been done for every site except London Lodge so that we can be fairly certain that at least the site molluscan zones are representative of the entire area of the site and that they can be translated into site environment zones. Admittedly some features of the assemblages represent microhabitats within features (*eg* the changing ratios of *Vitrea* and *Pomatias* in the Burntwood Farm (R6) pits), but others, such as the ratio of open-country to woodland species, are probably of general significance.

Beyond the individual sites, a broader pattern can hardly be discerned. No part of the molluscan data is equivalent to the regional component of pollen assemblages, even if certain trends are of country-wide significance. The environment is so diverse that enclaves or refugia of species can persist long after their general decline, and by the very nature of the archaeological contexts – copses, boundaries, barrows and pits in dead agricultural land – it is likely that such refugia are detected in the molluscan record. The molluscan record is of no more than site significance and the sites are an asymmetrical reflection of the landscape as a whole.

If woodland is assumed to have been present in the area in the mid Holocene, as Waton (1986) has proposed from his pollen studies at Winnall Moors in the Itchen valley (Fig 49), and as is thought to have been the case on the chalklands of southern England generally, then clearance had taken place by the Neolithic period at Burntwood Farm (R6) where two pits and a hollow of uncertain age were excavated in open country. Woodland persisted locally, for all three features became infilled in woodland, after which there was further Neolithic clearance (upper part of pit 104). At Bridget's Farm (R5), 450m to the northeast, there was a copse which was established by the Early Bronze Age and survived into the Roman period, when it was a focus for field boundaries. The richness of the molluscan assemblages suggests that this was a remnant of the primary woodland, and this is supported by the fact that it is close to a patch of Clay-with-Flints.

At Grace's Farm (R30), 750m to the southwest of Burntwood Farm (R6), there was open country, probably rich grassland, during the Bronze Age.

In another block of downland, about 3.5 kilometres to the southwest of the R5/R6/R30 group and separated from it by the Itchen valley and its flood-plain, are Easton Down and Winnall Down. At Easton Lane (SU 497303), very close to Winnall Down, a Late Neolithic pit was dug in woodland (M J Allen pers comm). On Winnall Down, on the other hand, a Late Neolithic ring-ditch (R17, feature 1972) was excavated in open country (although the dating of the deposits is uncertain). At Easton Down (R7), one kilometre to the northwest, primary woodland clearance had been achieved at the latest by the Early Bronze Age, with the round barrow site R7 being built in open country. Subsequently, a short period of woodland regeneration took place, to give way once more, still in the Bronze Age, to open country.

During the pre-Roman Iron Age there was essentially open country with episodes of scrub and woodland, probably short-lived and probably confined to the various boundary ditches. The evidence refers to the area of downland to the northwest of the Dever valley at London Lodge (R3) and to Winnall Down (R17), conditions at the latter being very open.

In the Roman period, represented at all three downland areas (R3, R5 and R17), the environment was open country throughout, and probably more open than previously. There was no woodland or scrub regeneration on any of the sites.

The post-Roman period is represented only at Stratton Park (R1) in the northwest of the area. Open country occurred throughout, with a short woodland interlude in the seventeenth century which was probably a plantation along the park boundary.

General conclusions

Numerical methods of analysing a large body of molluscan data have enabled distinct groups of assemblages to be identified, each characterised by its own species composition and proportions, diversity and broad ecological groups.

The assemblages illustrate the environments in terms of vegetation and human interference. They are of site significance only and cannot be used to establish a more general picture of environments and environmental change.

Chapter 8

Radiocarbon dates – A compilation
by P J Fasham

Introduction

A total of 49 samples produced ^{14}C determinations, of which 43 were selected to assist in the resolution of archaeological problems and six for environmental purposes. The 43 were processed at Harwell under the contract with the Ancient Monuments Laboratory and the six were accepted by Oxford University Radiocarbon Accelerator Unit as part of the revision programme by Dr Evans for the land molluscs. The results have now all been calibrated on the CALIB programme produced by the University of Washington Quaternary Isotope Laboratory utilising data by Pearson and Stuiver (1986), Pearson *et al* (1986) and Stuiver and Pearson (1986) and are displayed in calibrated chronological sequence in Fig 60 and are listed for each site in Table 41.

Results

Six of the ^{14}C determinations initially seemed to be at variance with dates reached by other means for the contexts: HAR 6122 from Easton Lane (W29), HAR 1039 from the Easton Down ring-ditch (R7), HAR 2795 and HAR 2800 from a pit in the Micheldever Wood 'banjo' enclosure (R27), HAR 2027 from Anglo-Saxon deposits in Stratton Park (R1) and HAR 2652 from Winnall Down (R17). The underlying question for these determinations is whether they are correct determinations but the material dated is not contemporary with what one believed to be associated artefacts, or whether the measurement is incorrect. Other determinations which seemed unacceptable could include the range of three determinations from Bridget's Farm (R5): HAR 1695, HAR 2745 and OxA 1410. In considering the problem determinations it seems that it can be argued that only two of the 49 dates from the M3 can be regarded as inaccurate and that explanations can be found for the other apparent problem dates.

HAR 6122 was obtained from the bone of an inhumation which was associated with an amber bead necklace at Easton Lane and produced a date some 300 years or so too recent for the occurrence of such jewellery. HAR 1039 produced an entirely anomalous determination of 32,460±1,110 BP and needs no further comment. Both HAR 1039 and

HAR 6122 would seem to be wrong determinations. The two Medieval dates, HAR 2795 and HAR 2800, from a Middle Iron Age pit in the Micheldever Wood 'banjo' enclosure cannot be explained satisfactorily. However, they are too consistent with each other to be simply dismissed. The pit must have been dug into during the Medieval period, although there was no obvious stratigraphical evidence for such disturbance. Similarly, the Roman determination provided by HAR 2652 from an apparent Early Iron Age pit at Winnall Down may well be a consequence of Roman activity that was not stratigraphically observed during excavation. This is a plausible occurrence at Winnall Down with the lengthy sequence of superimposed activities.

The three dates from the Anglo-Saxon deposits in Stratton Park, HAR 2027, HAR 1073 and HAR 2769, present some problems of intrepretation. All three could be perfectly valid measurements and be accounted for by the fact that the charcoal was of heartwood from a mature tree, or that buried soils – especially if ploughed – often contain charcoal of widely differing ages. HAR 2769 – the youngest date – is probably the best estimate of when the soil was buried.

The three results from Bridget's Farm are a field archaeologist's nightmare. The main purpose of the samples was to provide a broad and secure date for a small group of pits containing no artefacts diagnostic of date and which could not be reasonably associated with any nearby settlement. It seemed reasonable to assume that pits of such similarity and close physical proximity would be broadly contemporary. During excavation the pits were assumed to be of prehistoric origin and were thus rather inexplicable components of the landscape. Therefore, it was decided to establish a date by processing samples from two pits. HAR 1695 and HAR 2745 produced ^{14}C determinations separated by a millenium. These results did not assist in the understanding of the environmental sequence as gained from the land molluscs, and so a third sample was submitted to Oxford University. OxA 1410 falls in the millennia that separates the two Harwell dates. There was insufficient material for replicate dates for each feature and thus the features remain slightly enigmatic, except to say that the pit seemed to be of Bronze Age date.

Table 41. Calibrated radiocarbon determinations, listed in site order.

Lab Number	Uncalibrated years BP	Intercept method		Sample provenance
		one sigma	two sigma	

Stratton Park (R1), Roman road and Saxon activity

HAR 2027	1790±80	AD 123–338	AD 60–420	Charcoal from a buried soil, 57, with Anglo-Saxon artefacts
HAR 1703	1550±80	AD 415–601	AD 268–650	Charcoal from a buried soil, 57, with Anglo-Saxon artefacts
HAR 2769	1220±90	AD 677–894	AD 650–1000	Charcoal from a buried soil, 57, with Anglo-Saxon artefacts

London Lodge (R3), Iron Age activity and Roman road

OxA 1382	1970±90	96 BC–AD 118	190 BC–AD 230	Feature 2G, early Roman field ditch

Micheldever Wood (R4), oval barrow

HAR 1043	6900±170	5970–5630 BC	6090–5480 BC	Pit 104, sealed by barrow, possibly earlier than true date?
HAR 1042	3670±80	2192–1946 BC	2300–1828 BC	Layer 55, part of west mound material
HAR 1044	3370±90	1853–1528 BC	1900–1450 BC	Layer 28, secondary fill in ditch
HAR 1041	3100±90	1493–1266 BC	1591–1106 BC	Layer 13, in ditch sealing flint industry

Bridget's Farm (R5), prehistoric activity and Roman road

HAR 1695	3790±100	2455–2044 BC	2559–1950 BC	Feature 10, pit with no datable finds
OxA 1410	3420±100	1880–1620 BC	2020–1510 BC	Feature 28, pit with no datable finds
HAR 2745	2800±80	1045–847 BC	1253–810 BC	Feature 27, pit with no datable finds

Burntwood Farm (R6), prehistoric activity and Roman road

OxA 1384	4750±140	3700–3360 BC	3906–3100 BC	Neolithic pit 104, cut by lynchet of uncertain date
OxA 1383	2260±110	400–190 BC	760–50 BC	Pre-Roman feature 6A

Easton Down (R7), Bronze Age ring-ditch

HAR 1039	32460±1100	—	—	Trench 4, ring-ditch upper fill
OxA 1385	3220±120	1640–1410 BC	1854–1225 BC	Ring-ditch, above primary fill
HAR 3344	3160±70	1516–1400 BC	1608–1268 BC	Inhumation 26
HAR 1023	3130±70	1507–1321 BC	1530–1229 BC	Inhumation 24
HAR 3417	3080±80	1434–1263 BC	1520–1106 BC	Inhumation 43
HAR 1040	3070±120	1492–1165 BC	1620–1000 BC	Ring-ditch, ash and charcoal on top of primary fill
OxA 1413	2980±90	1389–1055 BC	1430–931 BC	Ring-ditch, above primary fill

Winnall Down (R17), multi-period settlement

HAR 2196	4800±80	3694–3387 BC	3779–3370 BC	Neolithic feature 1972
HAR 2202	4680±90	3620–3354 BC	3690–3108 BC	Neolithic feature 1972
HAR 2201	4650±110	3616–3200 BC	3690–3042 BC	Neolithic feature 1972
HAR 2653	2560±80	809–549 BC	893–410 BC	Enclosure ditch, layer 4749 sealing haematite coated pottery associated with shouldered jar
HAR 2251	2540±90	807–529 BC	893–400 BC	Hearth 574, immediately over primary silt in enclosure ditch, associated with tripartite jar and below haematite coated pottery
HAR 2651	2440±100	790–400 BC	810–370 BC	Enclosure ditch, associated with haematite coated pottery
HAR 2937	2250±90	399–196 BC	520–100 BC	Inhumation 629 in grave 10312
HAR 2591	2190±60	375–176 BC	390–100 BC	Pit 5789, from top of pit, mainly Middle Iron Age pottery, earlier than expected?
HAR 2194	2160±80	370–105 BC	400 BC–AD 0	Pit 3111, associated with Early Iron Age body sherds
HAR 2980	2150±80	366–100 BC	390 BC–AD 10	Inhumation 574 in grave 8630, associated with saucepan pots

Table 41, continued. Calibrated radiocarbon determinations.

Lab Number	Uncalibrated years BP	Intercept method		Sample provenance
		one sigma	two sigma	
HAR 2252	2140±80	362–96 BC	390 BC–AD 20	Pit 3738, top layer of pit, associated with wide-mouthed jar
HAR 2592	2100±80	340–35 BC	380 BC–AD 70	Pit 7399, charcoal from bottom of pit, filled with material derived from Early Iron Age midden
HAR 2195	2070±80	192 BC–AD 9	366 BC–AD 9	Inhumation 35 inserted into Early Iron Age enclosure ditch
HAR 2938	1990±70	96 BC–AD 77	180 BC–AD 130	Inhumation 500 from pit 8564, sealed by saucepan pots
HAR 2652	1830±70	AD 87–250	AD 20–373	Pit 1489, Early Iron Age

Micheldever Wood (R27), Iron Age settlement

Lab Number	Uncalibrated years BP	one sigma	two sigma	Sample provenance
HAR 2770	2150±70	362–105 BC	390–10 BC	Layer 354 in pit 14
HAR 2780	2070±90	196 BC–AD 15	370 BC–AD 110	Layer 75 in pit 14
HAR 2693	1930±70	2 BC–AD 129	100 BC–AD 230	Layer 103 in pit 14
HAR 2795	830±90	AD 1047–1270	AD 1010–1290	Layer 201 in pit 140
HAR 2800	750±80	AD 1221–1285	AD 1057–1392	Layer 206 in pit 140
HAR 2604	2290±110	408–200 BC	770–100 BC	Layer 500 in pit 415
HAR 2799	2290±70	402–257 BC	520–190 BC	Layer 575 in pit 415

Easton Lane (W29), multi-period settlement

Lab Number	Uncalibrated years BP	one sigma	two sigma	Sample provenance
HAR 8882	3800±70	2451–2140 BC	2470–2040 BC	Late Neolithic pit 5456, associated with Grooved ware sherds
HAR 6116	3240±120	1680–1420 BC	1872–1260 BC	Pit 4699, possible associated with Middle Bronze Age structure 2159
HAR 6121	3090±90	1445–1263 BC	1530–1100 BC	Late Neolithic circular structure 3918
HAR 6123	2960±80	1314–1043 BC	1420–931 BC	Early Bronze Age inhumation 595 Area F
HAR 6122	2740±70	986–823 BC	1050–800 BC	Early Bronze Age inhumation 3058 with amber beads
HAR 6120	2490±100	800–410 BC	830–390 BC	Late Neolithic circular structure 3918
HAR 6118	2220±100	400–170 BC	488–30 BC	Middle Bronze Age structure 2159, post-hole 965

All determinations calibrated on the radiocarbon calibration programme 1987 produced by the University of Washington Quaternary Isotope Laboratory utilising data by Pearson and Stuiver (1986).
NB Included in this table are four determinations not shown on Fig 60: Micheldever Wood (R4) HAR 1043, Easton Down (R7) HAR 1039 and Micheldever Wood (R27) HAR 2795 and HAR 2800.

It is perhaps worth considering the ^{14}C determinations on a site by site basis.

Four dates were collected in an attempt to unravel a chronology for features associated with the Roman road from Winchester to Silchester. The three from the Anglo-Saxon deposits in Stratton Park have been reviewed. The fourth date, OxA 1382 from London Lodge, straddles the centuries either side of the birth of Christ and can therefore be interpreted as confirming the perceived archaeological setting of a linear ditch being earlier than the Roman road.

Excluding HAR 1043, the three dates from the Micheldever Wood barrow present no problems of archaeological interpretation. HAR 1042, from mound material, was regarded as being too early for the Collared Urns of the primary cremations and was interpreted as being derived from earlier charcoal incorporated into the mound. This interpretation may not be correct, and HAR 1042 may well date the construction of the mound. HAR 1043 was from a feature sealed beneath the mound of the multi-

tumped oval barrow in Micheldever Wood where there was virtually no evidence for Mesolithic remains. The determination, however, seems to be valid and presumably is an indication of pre-barrow activity.

The three dates for Bridget's Farm have already been discussed as presenting one of the classic dilemmas facing a field archaeologist.

The two dates from Burntwood Farm confirm the broad dating from the excavation sequence, even if OxA 1384 is a little early. Assuming OxA 1384 to be valid, the arguments rehearsed in the report for later Neolithic standing stones being cleared and the site ploughed over in the Iron Age perhaps need reconsideration.

Six of the seven determinations from Easton Down have proved to be useful; the seventh, HAR 1039, is discussed above. Statistical tests on the three dates from the ditch fill, OxA 1385, OxA 1413 and HAR 1040, indicate that they most likely represent a single event, the filling of the ditch at 3067±62 BP.

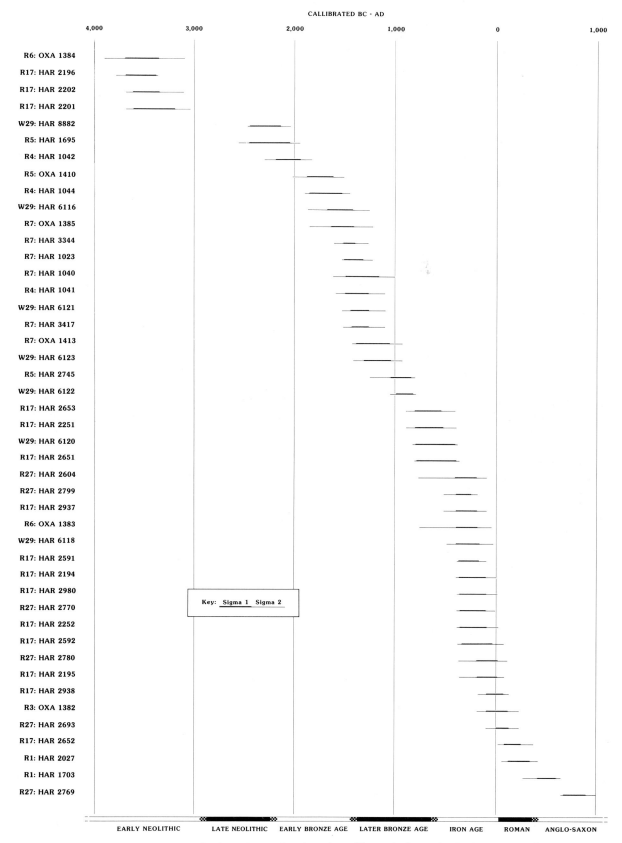

Fig 60.   Radiocarbon date compilation: determinations in calibrated chronological sequence from the M3 project. The determinations were calibrated according to the intercept method on the CALIB programme produced by the University of Washington Quaternary Isotope Laboratory utilising data by Pearson and Stuiver (1986). See also Table 41 for a complete listing by site, including four determinations not shown on this figure: Micheldever Wood (R4) HAR 1043, Easton Down (R7) HAR 1039 and Micheldever Wood (R27) HAR 2795 and HAR 2800.

The three dates from the inhumations, HAR 1023, HAR 3344 and HAR 3417, are contemporary in radio-carbon terms and also contemporary with the filling of the ditch.

Two of the dates from the 'banjo' enclosure in Micheldever Wood have already been discussed. The other five were taken in an attempt to provide a close dating sequence for the ceramics, but this was not particularly successful in a situation lacking the depth of stratigraphy which was so useful at Danebury (Cunliffe 1984). However they do come from two discrete pits with pooled dates of 2290±59 BP for pit 415 and 2047±43 BP for pit 14. These two dates may indicate, in general terms, the main period of activity on the site.

There are 22 determinations for Winnall Down and Easton Lane combined. HAR 2196, HAR 2201 and HAR 2202 provided a compact group, all from antler, for establishing a date in the middle of the fourth millenium BC for a rather enigmatic 'ring-ditch'. Almost as successful were the three determinations, two on bone and one on charcoal, for the Early Iron Age enclosure ditch, HAR 2251, HAR 2651 and HAR 2653. The range of the three dates, while broad, is acceptable. This is one of the more variable parts of the calibration curve. None of the other dates from Winnall Down present problems, but most of the Easton Lane dates reveal the dilemma created by the use of ^{14}C as a means of spot dating specific archaeological contexts, especially from a site with shallow or non-existent stratigraphy and which may have a lengthy history. Circular structure 3918, a circular hut with a sunken floor, contained within its infill Neolithic, Bronze Age and Medieval material. Despite careful excavation the true date of the feature could not be determined, although it is included in the Late Neolithic section of the report. The two ^{14}C determinations, both on animal bone, HAR 6120 and HAR 6121, did not assist in resolving the chronological dilemma. In the north of Easton Lane was a small cemetery which included an inhumation and two cremations, one of which was in a Collared Urn with a copper alloy awl. HAR 6123 was a sample from the inhumation which, unfortunately, provided a date two or three centuries later than the likely date of the Collared Urn. It seems unlikely that the three burials, occurring in close proximity, should be anything other than contemporary. The Middle Iron Age date from HAR 6118 did not accord with our predictions for the archaeological interpretation of circular feature 2159, which seems better placed in a Bronze Age rather than a Middle Iron Age landscape.

Conclusions

The programme of ^{14}C determinations was established on a site by site basis and, in retrospect, the number of dates for each site was probably inadequate. This ad hoc arrangement resulted in a relatively coarse set of dates which does not provide an integrated chronological sequence for the project. It might have been worth attempting to secure dates on comparable artefact assemblages from different sites, but usually the material was not present. The pre-Roman landscapes at Bridget's and Burntwood Farms have an uncertain chronological depth to them, an uncertainty which might have been clarified by a larger number of determinations. Most would have had to be counted on a small counter or accelerator and such facilities were not available to the project in 1975. The determinations from the M3 had to be argued for on a national basis with many other competing claims on the Ancient Monuments Laboratory's contract with Harwell.

Chapter 9

M3 Archaeology 1972–88: Considerations
by P J Fasham

Survey

There was plenty of motorway experience to build on for the processes of basic site discovery, and what might be called the standard procedures of field by field checking were implemented. There was an attempt to formalise the ways and means of field-walking, special plots of aerial photographic data were produced for the first time for a body other than the Royal Commission on Historic Monuments or a government department, the fluxgate survey was a first, and the importance of woodland as an archaeological preservative was realised. There was experimentation with phosphates, but there was no survey assessment by digging holes or even shovel testing.

Setting up a motorway project today, the fieldwalking and surface collection programme would be very different. Instead of looking for discrete sites and findspots with a view to their excavation before destruction, it would be reasonable to question the spatial variability and density of different artefact types, and classes within those types, to see whether it was possible to isolate areas of high and low occurrence and to attempt to understand and explain those variations in terms of past human activity and exploitation of the landscape. This could only be a sensible and satisfactory approach if the narrow linear element was part of, or incorporated into, a much bigger and wider-ranging project. By the time the main excavations were completed in 1977, archaeologists were wishing to probe the relationship of surface scatters with sub-surface features, where they survived. Soil marks were investigated in December 1974, to the west of Micheldever Wood, to examine their survival as features within the chalk, but the conceptual bridge and the hurdle of timetabling investigations of surface scatters, were never crossed.

Emerging out of the necessity of its early stumbling days, the techniques of surface collection have evolved into one of the great success stories of British archaeology in the 1980's. Shennan put the practice onto a rational level when he related it to sampling designs for large areas, both theoretical (Schadla-Hall and Shennan 1978), and practical in East Hampshire (Shennan 1985). Woodward's innovative paper in 1978 was a crucial element in the development, as he argued strongly for the collection not to be biased by the artificial nature of the fields of the modern landscape, but to base the survey on the national grid. There is now considerable literature on survey work incorporating surface collection both in Britain and Europe (Haselgrove et al 1985, Mac-Cready and Thompson 1985, Ferdière and Zadora-Rio 1986). The concept of densities and concentrations in the landscape was also explored with the vexing and seemingly unanswerable question of 'what is a site?'.

This is a problem which has been explored by the Stonehenge Environs Project, where some 752.5 hectares around Stonehenge have been walked in the period 1980–81 to 1983–84 and backed up by selective excavation of certain of the surface scatters (Richards 1985, forthcoming). Gravel extraction has always led archaeology by the nose but, at times, the opportunity has been taken to place the specific extraction threat into a landscape such as Heslerton (Powlesland 1986), or into a broader sub-regional framework as in the Kennet Valley (Lobb and Rose in prep), where the demand for development land for business parks and housing is leading to ever-increasing requirements for gravel extraction. There has also been considerable work in the area of the South Dorset Ridgeway, where separate sample zones were surveyed (Woodward forthcoming). Fieldwork around Dorchester and Maiden Castle has provided, in certain locations on the line of the Dorchester By-Pass, the only record of surface distributions and evidence in that particular form for previous human activity. An integrated landscape survey which included a large field-collection component was realised for the Maiden Castle Project (Wainwright and Cunliffe 1984). Although the full scale of work was tightly constrained by budget, the survey strategy was developed and extended to include the threatened area of the Southern Dorchester By-Pass, and provided a range of data which could place the By-Pass landscape section in a clear perspective. In this case the overlap of two projects, Maiden Castle and Dorchester By-Pass, has allowed the landscape to be treated as a single entity and the road as its section (Woodward and Smith 1987, forthcoming; Sharples 1985, 1986 interim notes), thus adding a considerable additional dimension to the archaeological record, a dimension which was never conceived of for the M3.

Today the detail of the survey work would be constructed differently and different resources would be used. In the early days there was great emphasis on the use of volunteers for fieldwalking, and soil phosphate analysis was done by a student on a part-time basis as he went through his university career. Pollen was tackled on a very *ad hoc* basis. There was professional assistance with aerial photographic work and geophysics. The diversity and disparate availability of the different resources led to considerable fragmentation. Today the archaeological team would all be salaried professionals, the basic surface collection and its subsequent analysis would be done by a small team of experienced workers and not on a part-time basis. The limitations on the scheme were related to cost and the fact that most of the resources had to be utilised on the basics of rescue excavation. A more integrated approach might have seen a multi-stage programme for the entire survey, working from the broader premise that the route should be exploited totally as a research tool to investigate the development of the landscape, rather than as a means of recording archaeological sites prior to destruction, and incidentally relating them to a landscape.

A multi-stage approach to the survey might have gone along the following lines.

The project design would need to be at two levels, the first level being a consideration of how best to incorporate the arbitrary line of a motorway into a major landscape framework either by survey of transects at right angles to the route or by selection of quadrats in a large area. The survey of East Hampshire (Shennan 1985) was based on transects designed to run across a range of topographic and geological variables. This would not have been particularly pertinent to the countryside around the M3. A sample based on stratified quadrats would perhaps be a more effective way of integrating a linear feature into a broader landscape. The quadrat survey would aim to establish from non-destructive survey techniques the totality of the occupation of the soil and any variations and changes through time of that human exploitation, to relate the background to the hard data provided by the more intensive work on the route. The sample would need to be stratified to be certain of including an element to examine peats in the valley of the River Itchen and to take into account the chalk and areas capped by Clay-with-Flints. A 10% random sample of one kilometre squares with one additional square for the Clay-with-Flints near Micheldever Wood and one in the Itchen Valley is shown in Fig 61. The quadrat survey should be designed to make a contribution to the complex field problem of background noise of artefact distribution and the definition of sites. There was an attempt to consider this problem using data from Micheldever Wood (Fasham 1983). Some experimentation has been done on the Greek islands of Kephallenia and Lefkas (Gallant 1986). The need

for a well-conceived sampling design and some suggestions for the sampling of areas with supposed unequal site density are discussed by Read (1986). The second level of design would be concerned with the detailed approach to the survey and the use of surface collection, test pit digging, aerial photographic work and perhaps geophysical and geochemical tests. A set of idealised relationships between aspects of the route work and the quadrat survey is shown in Fig 62.

Survey Methodologies

The quadrat survey would be established at a different level of intensity to the route survey but certain elements would be standard to both. Assuming the existence of an easily accessible Sites and Monuments Record, all known sites would need to be identified, and this information supported by basic place-name work and the plotting of all aerial photographic information. When this basic data had been gathered and assimilated, the fieldwork programme could be started. In the quadrat survey most of the fieldwork would be restricted to surface collection, geophysical scan and a regular amount of test pit digging.

Surface collection

The surface collection would need to be consistent between both parts of the survey. It has been demonstrated that a 10% sample of surface artefacts will produce useful archaeological data. This can be achieved by employing hectare squares within which eight 50m long transects spaced 25m apart are walked (Richards forthcoming). In south Dorset, a sample base approaching 20% was attempted with twenty 50m long transects spaced 10m apart in every hectare (Woodward forthcoming, Woodward *et al* 1987). This broad extensive approach could be supported on the route survey by more intensive collecting on a site specific basis when sites have been identified.

Within the quadrat areas, a set of long term experiments could be established to examine the effect of ploughing on both the artefacts themselves and their distribution. Perhaps of more value would be to monitor the dispersal of material from specially created artefact rich pits and ditches. The relative cheapness of recording damage and dispersal has been demonstrated from experiments in Calabria (Ammerman 1985). Suggestions for similar experiments have been put forward in the past (Reynolds and Schadla-Hall 1980) and one small trial was actually put into the field (Schadla-Hall 1978).

Test-pit digging

Test-pit digging would seem to have a limited role in the discovery of new sites, as the infinitesimal size of the sample provided makes it almost impossible to locate any features (Shott 1985). It must, however,

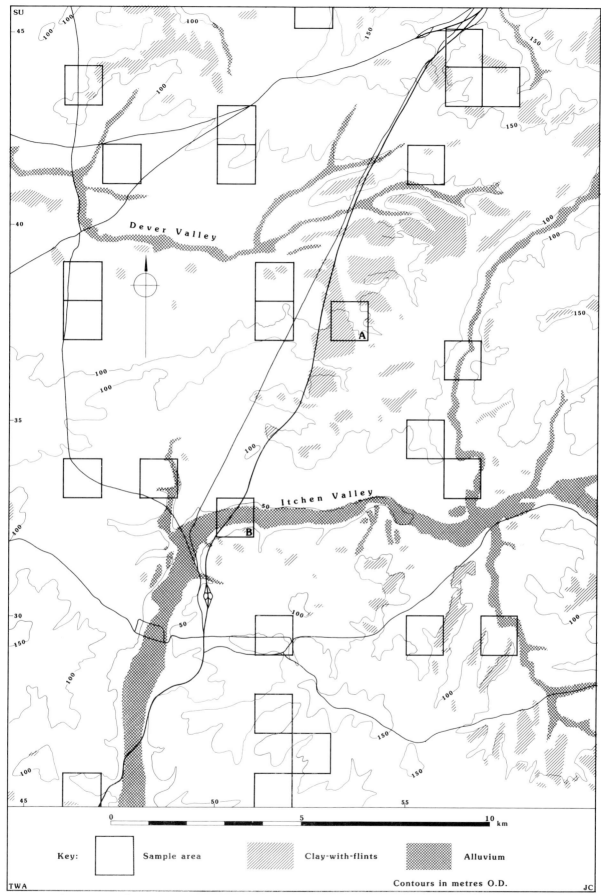

Fig 61. Structure of a possible 10% quadrat sample with the motorway running diagonally across the
survey area. Two additional squares have been selected to deal with the Clay-with-Flints (A) and
the Itchen valley (B).

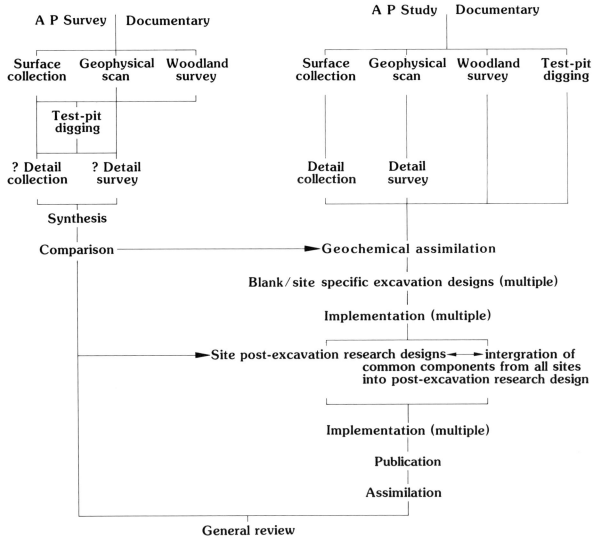

Fig 62.   A possible, but very simplified, scheme of works for a route survey and a complimentary area survey based on quadrats.

be considered as a technique to be used in woodland, but only if the sample fraction of the total surface area can be set at a reasonably large scale (Shennan 1985). As a means of assisting in the assessment of broad distributions of artefact types (Shott 1985), and assisting in the understanding of levels of background noise of material types in area surveys, a good case can be made for test-pit digging.

Geophysics

Geophysical surveys do locate new sites and must form part of the overall prospecting package. On the route, the scanning technique does seem to be valid and should be used, supported by a minimum 10% sample of detailed survey. It would be easier to organise if the sample were taken on a regular basis but a random selection may be more appropriate. The detailed sample would hopefully provide some

information on the blank areas. At this stage there would be no general requirement for detailed survey for enhancement of known sites. In the quadrat part of the survey it would not be cost-effective to survey all the sites known from aerial photography, but surveys of concentrations of artefacts from surface collection and some air photographic sites would be required to obtain some idea of site plan and morphology. Areas subsequently considered to be devoid of archaeological features, including woodland, should be sampled by intensive survey. A comparable 10% sample would be preferable, but the sheer size of the area involved and the amount to be surveyed would stretch the available geophysical resources in the country.

No other remote sensing techniques seem yet to be sufficiently cost-effective to use for the basic discovery of sites in the first stage of the survey. The detail of resolution from satellite photography which could be matched with images from an established data bank of archaeological features may lead, in the not too distant future, to new and exciting prospects for archaeological reconnaissance. The French have experimented with images from satellite SPOT in connection with the recently constructed Grenoble–Valence motorway, but it is too early to assess the results (Vicherd pers comm).

Phosphate survey

The cost and duration of even fast forms of analysis of soil phosphates preclude the use of the technique as an integral and efficient method of locating new sites. The best use for this form of analysis is as a site enhancement mechanism as suggested above. This is the clear conclusion reached by Craddock et al (1985) after ten years work dealing with twenty thousand samples. Field recording for magnetic susceptibility may be an equally fruitful approach to adopt.

Woodland survey

Woodland will almost certainly be present not only on the route but also in the quadrat areas. Ancient woodland and even fairly recent woodland may contain major archaeological remains in the form of earthworks and even if all above ground traces have disappeared there is every reason to anticipate the presence of buried archaeology. The main problem of woodland survey is the lack of opportunity for surface collection. One way of tackling the problem has been the use of test pits, but although there have been positive advocates (Krakker et al 1983) of this approach, it does not seem to be cost-effective on anything other than a very localised programme (Shennan 1985). Various evaluation investigations by the Trust for Wessex Archaeology have employed test pits in pasture or heathland zones. As part of the development of the Wytch Farm Oil Field, the Trust for Wessex Archaeology was commissioned by BP to undertake a variety of survey, excavation and watching brief work. One commission was on a flowline through pasture and $1m^2$ test-pits were dug for every $400m^2$ to be covered by the pipeline. From the 132 test pits there were finds in 25 and archaeological features in eight, including a previously unknown Medieval building and shell-midden. Very few of the pits, only 1–2%, were located on geophysical anomalies. Generally this was because, on the heathlands, the archaeological deposits equate with enhanced soil build-up which masks all but the most magnetically responsive features such as ash-filled ditches or kilns. It is worth noting that there were no traces of archaeology in the 52 test pits dug in a plantation (Cox and Farwell 1987). At the Norden roundabout, near Corfe Castle, a smaller sample of test pit excavation followed a geophysical survey, with some pits located to investigate specific anomalies. Ten pits were used to sample the rest of the area, maximum size 0.7 hectares, and none produced

archaeological results (Cox 1986). Although test pit digging may seem to be disappointing it is the only way of looking at or indeed under the surface in woodland and must be employed along with geophysical and earthwork surveys. The scale of woodland in southern Britain, apart from the New Forest, is such that total survey can be the only sensible approach and there can really be no justification for establishing a probabilistic survey in such circumstances (Alexander 1983).

Survey Integration

The suggested approaches to survey outlined above are really nothing more than an investigation of the topsoil in support of the archaeology of the plough zone, a term which conjurs up something much more than the 0.3–0.5m deep maximum covering of the chalk in southern England. There can be no doubt that, to maximize the archaeological record on sites that are to be totally destroyed, all possible survey techniques need to be used. They are complementary and not exclusive and should be used to produce some of the data on which the research design for any subsequent excavation should be based.

Excavation

Site specific

Although each excavation posed different problems, there were similar approaches adopted for certain types of site. Pressure of time and the necessity to maintain a viable year round programme within a tight budget sometimes meant that none of the topsoil investigations or the generalised ideas outlined above could be implemented. Linear features were usually sectioned, sometimes in several places, and for sites under arable management the topsoil was usually removed by machine. The tactics for each site varied after the topsoil was removed and different programmes of environmental work were established. In retrospect a more thorough examination of the topsoil, adopting many of the techniques outlined above, could have provided more archaeological data than was obtained. Rigorous excavation and research designs could have been developed for individual sites, perhaps with even greater emphasis on artefact retrieval as a means of examining spatial matters, and on the capture of environmental data. The Sutton Hoo project design is a good example built on initial survey and assessment work (Carver 1986). The strategy for each excavation was formulated before work started, but was not in the form of a written research design as was later used for the Easton Lane adventure (Fasham et al 1989, 1–6). In the 1970's, every archaeologist would have approached the excavation of each site differently and ten years on I, like everyone else, would not tackle those excavations in the same way.

Without any further data, particularly from the topsoil, it would be presumptuous to suggest how each excavation could have been treated differently, but now is the moment to make a couple of generalisations. The need for greater investigation of the topsoil evidence has already been suggested; it would probably also be useful to see lengths of linear features excavated – the Roman track at Burntwood Farm showed the value of this approach (Fasham 1980b), and the Winchester to Silchester Roman road and some of the features in Micheldever Wood would have made interesting subjects; finer recording of spatial attributes would allow for more rigorous testing of intra-site activities (Berry et al 1984).

Looking at the blanks

If it is not feasible to reconsider in detail the approach to specific sites, it is certainly possible to reconsider the attitude to the blank areas. The initial design by Biddle and Emery (1973) was quite clear on the need to arrive at the totality of archaeological activity on the route, by advance purchase and extensive stripping for archaeological purposes. In the end this target (? dream) was not attainable and the watching brief provided the only chance to make any assessment. The shortcomings of the watching brief for observing the total archaeological record have already been discussed, and that does not take into account the evidence that is preserved only in the topsoil.

On the assumption that the detailed and intensive survey reveals a few areas where there are no traces of past human activity, an investigative programme would need to be arranged. Policies adopted by County Councils and approved by the Secretary of State seek a clear statement about the archaeology of areas subject to planning applications, even where those areas contain little or no archaeological remains but are deemed to have potential, as for example with the Berkshire Environmental Policy EN26 (Royal County of Berkshire Planning Department 1989). Archaeological assessments or evaluations are now put out to tender and numerous organisations have been commissioned by developers to provide archaeological data which gives planning committees the opportunity for the fullest possible consideration of the treatment of the archaeological evidence. Sometimes evaluations have looked at areas considered to be of low archaeological potential, but in those cases usually no more than 1% has been sampled. These evaluation exercises have different aims to a motorway project but do highlight the necessity to comment on archaeological blanks.

Short of the complete removal of the topsoil under archaeological supervision after its thorough investigation, the only sensible approach is to sample. A sample fraction of say 1% as in some commercial evaluations for planning purposes is too small. The 10% sample of Easton Lane seems to have worked, at least it certainly found the archaeology, and a figure in the order of 10% would probably give an adequate reflection of any hidden remains. The nature of the archaeology recorded in the sample transects at Easton Lane was such that it was difficult to use the data to project total populations of different feature types by period. That would not matter, however, as any discovery in the sample framework would need to be further and fully investigated.

A quadrat sample for sites may be more effective than a transect, even if presenting slightly more problems of execution. The easement of a motorway line is in the order of 60–100m wide. A 10m by 10m square hole would be a convenient size to employ. The areas between known sites, concentrations of features, or however it can be defined, could be divided into 10m by 10m squares; those straddling the line of the easement would have to be examined as whole units, and the 10% sample randomly selected from the total population available. Within each square, ten 1m by 1m square units could be selected randomly for manual excavation to examine topsoil and the remaining 90 squares could then have the topsoil removed by machine. Thus one percent of the total blank areas would be investigated by hand. This is an awful lot of hand digging but is suggested, despite reservations expressed about test pit digging (Krakker et al 1983, Shott 1985).

Since the landscape contains archaeological features, both nucleated and dispersed, and areas without archaeology, the main problem for establishing the sample of the blank areas is the definition of the limit of the archaeological feature groups. The fundamental question still remains of what is a site and what are its limits, a problem which the presence of an enclosure ditch does not completely resolve, as has been seen at Gussage All Saints (Wainwright 1979) where it is suggested that the area immediately outside the entrance had a special role; or as at Easton Lane (Fasham et al 1989) where there was extensive settlement outside the enclosure, where indeed the settlement focus was highly mobile. The problem of archaeological inference and definition of a 'site' by surface collection has been discussed by Haselgrove (1985). Assuming that the limits of a concentration of archaeological data can be determined, then it might be worth considering a sample in excess of 10% in the immediate neighbourhood. Perhaps a sample of 20%, including 2% manual, in the first 100m linear of the route reducing to 10% for the remainder of the blank area might provide some insight into the possibilities of recovering data about fall-off distributions away from the main concentrations, or indeed about off-site activities.

Post-excavation

The diagram in Fig 62 touches briefly on post-excavation. The essential elements for rapid production of archaeological reports include a well-organised and clean field record, a research design which is rational and attainable within the likely available resources, the proper use of those resources, and an ability to concentrate on the project. This section on post-excavation is short because the process should be relatively straightforward and involves a series of logical steps, usually dependent on one another. Savings of scale can be made on a project where a number of excavations are going to occur in a relatively short space of time. The treatment of finds, especially pottery, and environmental data, can be done on a project wide base rather than on a site by site base, while each site will still need to have its archaeological account.

Suitable research designs for topics, supported where applicable from the beginning by relevant computer facilities, should enable report writing to be a speedy process. The publication of the results could be a problem. The fascicule concept can require considerable cross referencing and work by the reader to enable artefact types to be placed back into an understandable archaeological context. It may be possible to produce pottery and environmental reports for an entire rural project; certainly the pottery from the M3 was treated as though from a single project even if it was still published on a site specific basis. Assuming project wide topic reports can be suitably constructed, then the published, as opposed to the archive, material for each site could be limited and treated in a very selective way. The archaeological, as compared to the artefactual or environmental, element of a report is usually fairly restricted and perhaps equally tight constraints need to be imposed on all parts of a report.

All the basic reports from the M3 have been published by the Hampshire Field Club and Archaeological Society either in the *Proceedings* or in the monograph series, and only two more general articles have been published nationally (Fasham and Ross 1978, Monk and Fasham 1980). All the reports were reprinted in separate covers and numbered so that it has been possible to collect all the offprints in a single series, with the monographs as extra items. There was not much demand for the numbered series.

The whole business of post-excavation and publication would have been easier if the programme had been shorter; the fieldwork eventually continued for almost a decade, and the post-excavation could have therefore have been crisper. It is no one's fault that the project ran for so long. It is impossible to plan when construction dates are continually moving but not by a consistent amount. Initially, construction was about eighteen months to two years away and, although the start date kept slipping, there were times when it was only six months away, yet within a few months the start date would again be two years away. Forward planning in such circumstances is not easy. It is to the credit of the Department of the Environment that they wound up the programme in 1980 but made certain that the final work could be done when construction actually started in 1983. The final few kilometres of the route have still not been built and the reaction of English Heritage is awaited.

Against an uncertain background, it was almost impossible to plan for post-excavation. If all the fieldwork had been completed in two years then a very powerful post-excavation strategy could have been implemented.

Some Thoughts

The M3 project has undoubtedly enhanced understanding of the archaeology of central Hampshire. On a strictly site orientated basis, there have been the excavations of two prehistoric settlement complexes, part of the Medieval village of Popham, and the totally unexpected, albeit long-hoped for, Anglo-Saxon settlement at Abbots Worthy. One burial mound and four ring-ditches can be counted among the excavations and several tracks and roads, along with their preceeding, contemporary and succeeding landscapes have been investigated. There was an attempt to understand the archaeology of the countryside, with selected excavations to investigate the nature and means of representation of soil and cropmarks. Of concern to all involved in rural archaeology must be the investigation of soil marks west of Micheldever Wood where the archaeological features survived to varying depths in the chalk. In some places, they no longer survived as features in the subsoil and had somehow been fixed in the ploughsoil by a mechanism which is not understood. The rate of degradation of the chalk by ploughing is not known exactly, although various estimates have been made (eg Groube and Bowden 1982, 16–18). The awareness of the disappearing archaeology was a major item.

Interpretation of crop and soil marks was assisted by the excavations at Bridget's and Burntwood Farms where crucial elements of the landscape were investigated; elements described by Collin Bowen in frequent conversations as the grammar and syntax of rural and landscape archaeology. Broad linear spreads of soil were confirmed as the bottom of negative lynchets with traces of plough marks, and once again it must be accepted that some of these features were suspended in the ploughsoil. The correct understanding of other linear soil marks as tracks was established when the major soil mark at Bridget's and Burntwood Farms was found to be the infill of a sunken route, complete with rut marks, of a heavily-used track of Roman date. A notable bonus from a landscape viewpoint was the discovery, recording and selective investigation of the prehistoric and Roman landscapes fossilised under the trees of Micheldever, remains so slight they would not have survived a single ploughing.

The project was to benefit from contemporary developments in environmental archaeology in disciplines where archaeological value was being more fully realised. John Evans had already been involved on the Wessex chalklands, interpreting the environmental sequence through the study of land molluscs, and he welcomed the opportunity to supervise the wide-ranging programme of sampling for molluscs which the project offered. The study of faunal remains moved from the production of species lists to problems such as herd curation, animal specialisation and variations between contemporary rural and urban assemblages. As far as the M3 project was concerned, this work was pioneered at the Faunal Remains Unit which was sponsored by the Department of the Environment (now English Heritage) at the University of Southampton. The same institution was one of the few universities where palaeobotanical research was done in the 1970's. This work was organised firstly by Peter Murphy and then by Mick Monk, and its impact, especially where concerned with rigorous experimentation with flotation procedures, was felt by all involved with the M3.

Post-excavation analyses and the preparation of an archive was greatly assisted from 1974 onwards by the development of a computing facility that was made available to the project by Hampshire County Council. The preparation of the data base, which now seems quite long-winded and unnecessarily cumbersome, was a great improvement over manual systems of the time and provided a number of useful lessons for later projects.

The entire cost of the project was funded by public money but the amount of information that was readily available for the general public was not overwhelming. There were, of course, the usual lectures to as many local societies as were prepared to have the same speaker almost annually. Annual summary reports were produced with the intention of them being popular accounts of the work. In fact they were not even annual and were published for 1974 (Fasham 1974), 1975 (Fasham 1975) and jointly for 1976 and 1977 (Fasham 1977). A small booklet was produced about the Easton Lane excavations (Fasham and Whinney 1985), but this was not as successful as some other popular versions of excavations (Fasham and Hawkes 1983, 1986). There were two exhibitions in Winchester Museum and various accounts were broadcast on both local radio and TV. The BBC made part of a schools educational programme about the project. It was impossible to organise open days for two reasons. On the one hand, there was the reluctance of the landowners and tenants to have sites publicised, with large numbers of people visiting their property and perhaps trampling over sensitive crops. On the other hand, even if access was available, there was always the problem of where to park cars on an extremely busy and fast road or on the narrow lanes which would become blocked.

Most end of term reports have sentences suggesting that things could be better in certain subjects. This report is no exception. In the case of the M3 there are two very obvious areas where greater resources would have led to something better, apart from the intensification of research into the topsoil. The whole programme never really settled into a framework which would enable all the work, or at least most of it, to be seen in a broader perspective. There can be few counties, and certainly none of the other Wessex counties, where there have been more investigations into the Iron Age than in Hampshire,

with the Danebury project to the fore (Cunliffe 1984). And yet, as some reviewers have pointed out, there has been little integration of the many and diverse excavations of Iron Age sites in Hampshire over the last twenty years (Collis 1985, 1986; Haselgrove 1986). This was partly discussed a decade ago by some of the concerned participants (various contributions in Collis 1977).

Initially, it was felt that the valleys of the rivers Itchen and Dever formed suitable topographic entities to provide scope to compare and contrast settlement patterns in two areas (Fig 45), but in fact there is not sufficient distinction between these gentle valleys for valid comparison. The band of Clay-with-Flints that sweeps from the head of the Dever valley at Micheldever and eastwards through East Stratton to the head of the Candover stream may represent a valid division in the settlement pattern. There certainly seems to be a difference in the settlement pattern between the two geological entities. As work progressed, it seemed that archaeological sites north of the Itchen were related to a series of gentle ridges which run east-west from the Candover valley and dissipate in the Dever valley on the west. Micheldever Wood is on one such ridge and the main concentrations of archaeological features run along the top of the ridge or on the south facing slope. Very few sites were recorded on the north facing slopes of any ridge. The north side of the Itchen valley has an interchanging pattern of settlement from the Iron Age to the Late Saxon or even as far as the modern settlement pattern (Figs 63 and 64).

In the Iron Age, the west end of the valley immediately upstream from the right-angled bend in the river is dominated by an enclosure of 3.25 hectares defined by a ditch some seven metres wide at the ground surface. A little over one kilometre east are two 'banjo' enclosures, Bridget's Farm A and B, and another site is located almost one kilometre to the east. Two smaller, ?subsiduary or dependent, sites lie just to the northeast of the latter. Another extensive complex lies one kilometre to the east, but on the slopes overlooking the Candover valley, the probable Iron Age sites appear to be smaller than those overlooking the Itchen valley. This band of large sites is one to one and a half kilometres away from the River Itchen, towards the top of the gentle side of the valley, a distribution similar to that suggested for sites in the Danebury region (Cunliffe 1984). The next band of sites to the north are all sited on the next south-facing slopes.

The westernmost Iron Age site continued in use on a similar scale into the Roman period, but with a very different arrangement which included streets, buildings and enclosures – a large village. The sequence has been deduced from unpublished excavations. There does not seem to have been a Roman establishment near the site of the Bridget's Farm 'banjo' enclosures but there is a substantial Roman structure, complete with mosaic floors, a kilometre to the east (Collier 1878, 1879). A further possible Roman site occurs about the same distance again to

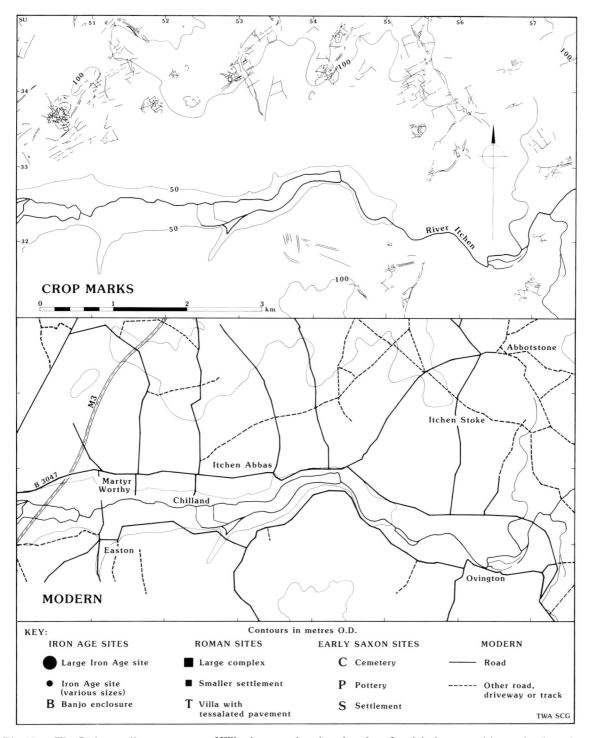

Fig 63.   The Itchen valley upstream of Winchester, showing the plot of aerial photographic marks (based on material supplied by Winchester Museums Service Archaeology Section) and the location of modern roads and villages before the motorway was built.

the east. These latter two sites both succeed Iron Age predecessors. There must be smaller components of the Roman rural scene within the air photographic evidence, but it is not possible to isolate them and portray them in the distribution map. It is most unlikely that there was no settlement in the Roman period on the land overlooking the confluence of the Candover Brook and the River Itchen.

If size is a valid indicator of influence, then the large site at the west of the valley must have played an important role in both the Iron Age and Romano-British periods. In the earlier period it may well have had a role as a social and commercial centre for the neighbourhood, standing as it does, almost equidistant from the hillforts of Norsebury and St Catherine's Hill, distances of six and a half and six

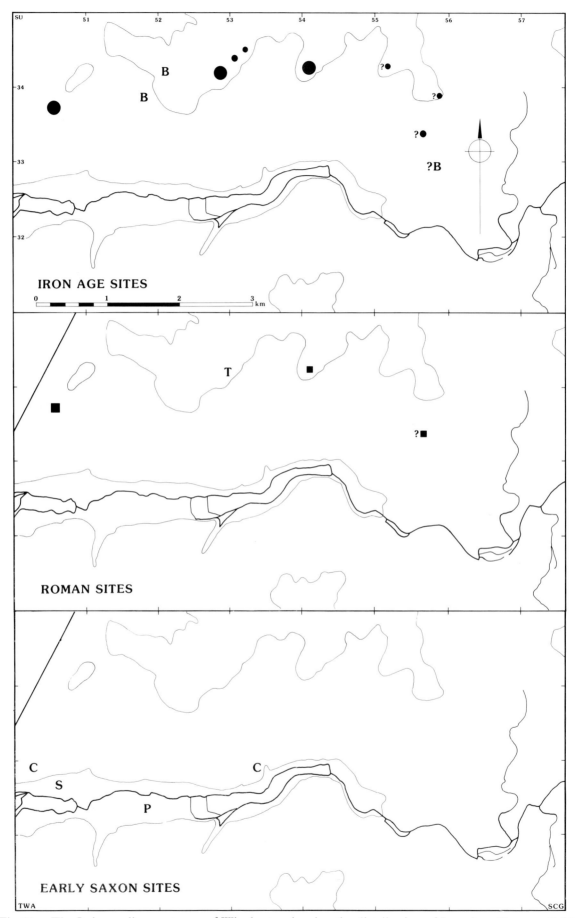

Fig 64.   The Itchen valley upstream of Winchester showing the distribution of Iron Age, Romano-British and Early Anglo-Saxon sites. For key see Fig 63.

kilometres respectively. In the Roman period, it is tempting to see the large complex as a rural clearing-house for produce before its transmission to markets in Winchester or further afield. The site is less than half a kilometre from the Roman road joining Winchester with Silchester. Perhaps grain was processed and packed here for export to Gaul or other parts of the Empire. A corn drying oven was uncovered in the unpublished excavations of 1971 and 1972. It takes no imagination to draw boundaries for the territories between the sites in these periods, to produce land holdings with riverside land and light arable chalklands with some heavier areas of Clay-with-Flints; several pockets of the latter superficial deposit are known but are too small to plot. Such territories are typical of the pattern expected from chalk valleys. In the Roman period, there seem to be fewer settlements, but this probably is a function of recognition, identification and interpretation of the evidence with the smaller outlying components of the Roman agricultural system proving to be elusive, although a larger-scale, more organised farming pattern may account for the apparent reduction in numbers.

It is not so easy to resolve the nature of the Anglo-Saxon settlement, as the occurrence of finds is limited and none of the sites recorded from air photographs can be interpreted as Anglo-Saxon. The evidence north of the Itchen consists of two cemeteries and one settlement, all much closer to the river than any of the earlier sites, while on the south there is a scatter of organic-tempered pottery from just east of Easton and a cemetery less than one kilometre to the southeast. The cemetery is located in an area where a series of earthworks south of the river have been regarded as of post-Roman date. The Saxon estate of Chilcomb may have emerged out of a Late Roman holding with some form of centralised control still operating out of Winchester (Biddle 1972). Such a development may not be too clear from the Early Anglo-Saxon evidence, but the Late Saxon settlement which includes Martyr Worthy, Chilland, Itchen Abbas and Itchen Stoke on the north bank, with Ovington and Easton on the south bank, may well reflect clear estate boundaries. The pattern of the modern nucleated settlement, as opposed to some of the ribbon development along the road on the north of the river, is very similar to the Late Saxon settlement.

The main differences between the periods are that in the Iron Age and Romano-British periods the settlements are set back from the river, and in the later period there seem to be fewer focal points. In the Saxon period, sites closer to the river seem to be preferred, although modern settlement and colluvial deposits may mask earlier sites. However they work, the boundaries of estates, perhaps represented by the modern roads running north from the river, may well have their origins in the Iron Age, if not earlier.

The archaeology of the Wessex Iron Age has long been a subject of considerable interest and not just at the level of the hillfort, although those mighty monuments have continued to be excavated and to

be a source of fascination, with relatively recent work at Winklebury (Smith 1977), Danebury (Cunliffe 1984), Balksbury (Wainwright 1969, Donaldson forthcoming) and Maiden Castle (Sharples 1985, 1986). Many of the smaller settlement sites have been investigated as part of a deliberate research policy, such as Gussage All Saints (Wainwright 1979), which followed up a research programme initiated thirty years earlier (Bersu 1940), and Owslebury (Collis 1968 and 1970); or, more prosaically, as a rescue excavation continuing in the tradition established in 1866 when gardening works revealed archaeological features which were assumed, rightly, to be later than the Stone Age but earlier than the Roman conquest (Stevens 1934), and coming right up to to the present day with work on the Dorchester By-Pass (Woodward and Smith 1987) and the 1987–8 excavations of a terraced settlement on the Western Link of the same road scheme (Chowne 1987). There has been a rapid increase in the number of excavations of the smaller, non-hillfort, sites over the last twenty years (Fig 65).

Iron Age Excavations in Wessex

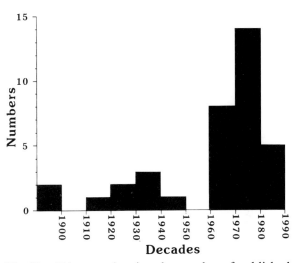

Fig 65. Diagram showing the number of published excavations of smaller (non-hillfort) Iron Age sites per decade in Wessex. Last decade not complete as figures were collected only until the end of 1987.

The smaller sites are very different and show variations in size, shape, being open or enclosed, with different sizes of ditches, apparent possession of buildings and so on. Some of these attributes are summarized in Fig 66, which portrays the approximate area of a site, whether it is open or enclosed, and the variations of those two elements through time. As Cunliffe (1978) has pointed out, there are elements which seem to be chronological indicators, as for example the early palisade ditches at Little Woodbury (Bersu 1940) and Meon Hill (Liddell 1933 and 1935) and the emergence of the medium-sized enclosures around the middle of the last millenium BC at sites such as Little Woodbury, Gussage All Saints, Highfield (Stevens 1934) and Little Som-

Fig 66.   Chart of published excavations of smaller (non-hillfort) Iron Age sites in Wessex up to 1984. Sites are depicted chronologically with a vertical indication of size and whether open or enclosed.

borne (Neal 1979). Possible regional differences may be seen in the proliferation of rectilinear enclosures from about the third century BC in the Basingstoke area, which, by the end of the first century BC, are markedly rectangular. This may be a reflection partly of an existing regional tradition and partly of contact with the Roman world. The sites in the Isle of Purbeck on the Ower peninsula (Sunter and Woodward 1987) and on Furzey Island (Cox 1985) display plans which must be accounted for by the special needs and purposes of these harbour-side sites. The most distinctive of all the enclosure types, and perhaps the only one which can really be classified as a type site, is the 'banjo' enclosure (Fasham 1987; Perry 1972, 1982), although it is possible to discern regional groups with the simple 'banjo' enclosures in central Hampshire and the multiple arrangements on the Hampshire and Dorset border in the Cranborne Chase area (Corney pers comm). There have been no excavations of the multiple examples and thus no positive confirmation that they are indeed contemporary with their simple, single counterparts to the east.

Most of the Iron Age sites that have been excavated and published (up to about 1984) are shown on Figs 67, 68 and 69, which reveal the variations in size and nature of the sites and in some cases the extent of the excavations. The data base for detailed comparative study of the Wessex sites is therefore not as secure as, perhaps, it has been perceived. The excavations have all been of different dates, different extents, different purposes and with exceedingly variable degrees of environmental work. The only sites where excavation has been anything like total are Gussage All Saints (Wainwright 1979), Winnall Down and Easton Lane (Fasham 1985, Fasham *et al* 1989), Old Down Farm, Andover (Davies 1981), and Portway (Champion and Champion in prep). Fairly complete plans have been obtained at Micheldever Wood (Fasham 1987), Viables Farm (Millett and Russell 1982, 1984) and Ructstall's Hill (Oliver and Applin 1978). Attempting to understand the nature and relationship of different occupation or activity sites from from aerial photographs has been explored in the Danebury area (Palmer 1984), and Cunliffe has suggested a variety of functions for different types of hillforts and lesser settlements (Cunliffe 1978, 1984). Unfortunately, there remains considerable gap between the theoretical study of settlement and functional patterns and the real data available from the excavated record to test the theories.

The tragedy is that, in Hampshire, the opportunity existed to take a single area and study Iron Age settlement complete with hillforts. Three main areas have seen extensive archaeological investigation, always of a rescue nature. The planned expansion of Basingstoke has seen the excavation of a hillfort and several lesser settlements (Smith 1977, Oliver and Applin 1978, Millett and Russell 1984), and the position is remarkably similar at the London overspill town of Andover, with a hillfort excavation (Wainwright 1969; Donaldson forthcoming), if that

indeed is what Balksbury is, and several excavations of smaller sites (Champion and Champion in prep, Davies 1981). Andover is in the northeast corner of the Danebury survey area. The third area where there have been considerable investigations is on the M3.

In terms of sheer area of Iron Age site cleared, planned and excavated, there can be few counties in Britain where a greater area of Iron Age settlement has been exposed. With hindsight it is very easy to say that the resources would have been better spent in concentrating on the fullest possible examination of one area, presumably around one of the urban centres rather than on the linear motorway, and working to a vigorous and constantly reviewed project design for all aspects, both practical and theoretical, of the scheme. In the late 1960's or early 1970's, a policy should have been hammered out to produce a strong research design to examine social, economic and functional relationships of settlement and activity sites of the last millennium BC in one area, with, in light of the likely available resources, a positive and conscious abandonment of all rescue archaeology in the other areas. No blame can be attached for the absence of this policy as the speed with which towns were expanded meant that the full archaeological implications could not be absorbed. There was not time to sit back and reflect maturely on the situation amid the emotional scene of sites being destroyed almost daily, and it is debatable whether the local politics and the local and national funding would have allowed a single comprehensive programme to have emerged. There was no single body with either the authority – moral, academic or financial – or the willpower to implement a policy. Had such a policy been developed and acted on it might have produced answers to many of the queries and problems raised about the infrastructure supporting Danebury, and there would have been a useful framework into which the M3 sites could have been placed, assuming the policy allowed for their excavation.

There has been much good and valuable work into Hampshire's Iron Age, but so much more could have been achieved. There was an attempt in the early 1980's to establish an Iron Age project in accordance with the policy document of the then Wessex Archaeological Committee (Ellison 1981). The project was designed to study the catchment area of Quarley Hill, where there had been minimal excavation in the hillfort campaign of the 1930's (Hawkes 1939), and to relate to the neighbouring studies in the Danebury area. Unfortunately, the project was proposed at a time when project funding was being introduced and the limited public money available was for a handful of rescue projects. On a smaller scale, it was possible to establish a programme of work at Brighton Hill South, Basingstoke. The programme was threat-led but it was possible to instigate a series of excavations in advance of a 100 hectare housing development to examine the relationship of four cropmark complexes (Fasham 1986b, Fasham and Keevill forthcoming). It seems

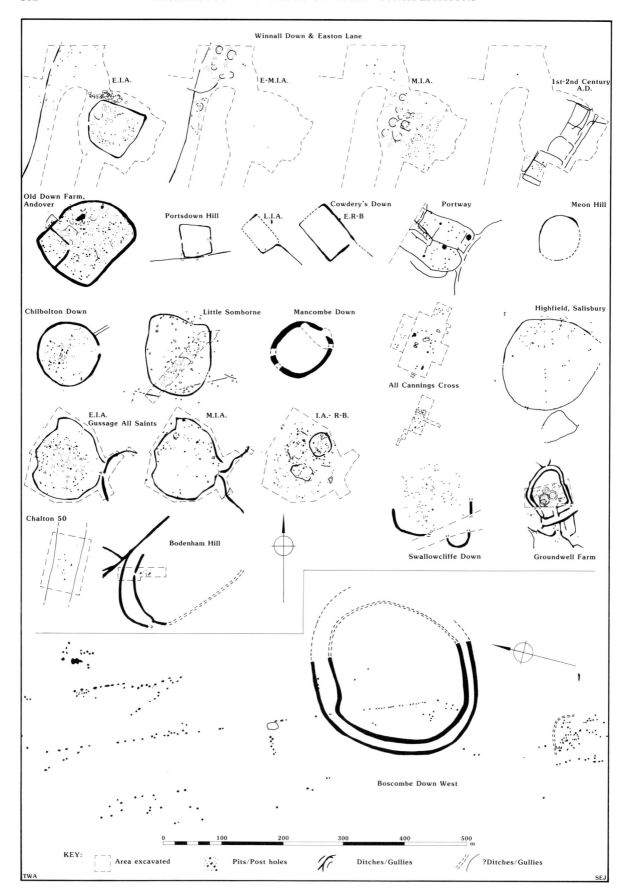

Fig 67.   Plans of various excavated Iron Age sites in Wessex.

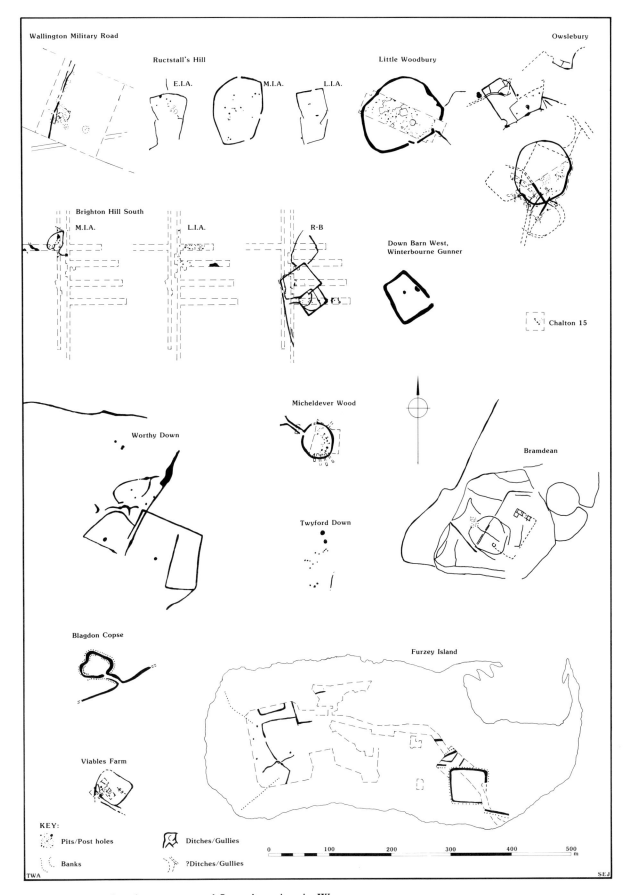

Fig 68. Plan of various excavated Iron Age sites in Wessex.

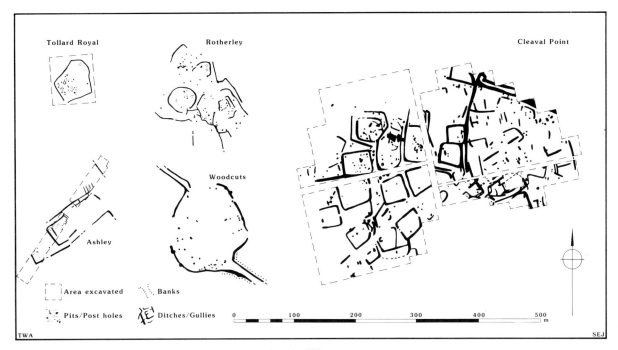

Fig 69.   Plan of various excavated Iron Age sites in Wessex.

likely that the development area and the number of sites will expand in the near future.

The archaeological work on the M3 does, in many ways, reflect most of the trends of archaeology in England over the last two decades. The individual excavations produced much useful data, but the constraints on resources meant that the wider integration of those data has not been possible, even though very desirable.

Finances

In the five years before the project started, the amount of funds available nationally for rescue archaeology had increased at a tremendous rate and it was expected that all rescue archaeology should be funded out of the public purse. Some people were concerned that this approach would lead to a lessening of money available for non-rescue, research, excavations. It led to a different form of archaeology. Even after the great increase of public funds, there was still not enough money available for every threatened site and selections had to be made, usually on the regional and national importance of a site. The idea that the developer, the destructive agent, should be responsible for funding rescue excavation was a long way from many people's thoughts and even further from being a practical proposition.

For national road schemes, the principle of developer pays is still not fully established, although the Department of Transport does now make provision for archaeological investigation on trunk roads in England. Some local authorities pay for archaeology on their road schemes. Dorset County Council have paid for archaeological investigations on at least

two road schemes. The By-Pass at Wareham went through a Romano-British pottery producing site (Cox and Smith in prep), and on a different part of the Wareham By-Pass the excavation of a section of a Roman road was also funded by the County Council. The level of funding may not have been as high as the field archaeologists wanted but the developer was funding the work. On the Western Link of the Southern Dorchester By-Pass, which was a county road scheme, Dorset County Council provided about half of the £60,000 required to do the archaeological work. The rest of the Dorchester By-Pass was a national road scheme and English Heritage will have spent in the region of £300,000, with a contribution from the Duchy of Cornwall across whose land the road runs, for the archaeology of six kilometres of road. The archaeological response that can be made out of a budget of that size is adequate but far from ideal. An original estimate for the scheme, without detailed proposals for post-excavation, was a shade over £500,000. The Department of Transport's annual provision to English Heritage for archaeological work on all national road schemes was raised in 1990 from £100,000 to £500,000.

The total cost since 1973 for the M3 project has been £392,177 for 17 kilometres. This figure has not been adjusted to produce a current day value for the earlier costs, but between 1974 and 1987 government figures show that the retail price index rose by almost four times. Neither the M3 nor the more recent Dorchester By-Pass was a complete package, as the quoted costs were not always for the entire costs including display, storage and publication nor, necessarily, were they the costs for the ideal archaeological work. The archaeological programme was fitted to the resources available.

Concern for the archaeology of motorways did not

materialise in France until the late 1970's, but the scope of subsequent progress has been considerable. In 1953 the first section of French motorway, Lille-Fresnes les Montauban, was constructed without any archaeological input and indeed without any reported archaeological find. In 1987 dozens of archaeologists were at work on at least eight auto-routes. The first archaeological work was in 1977–79 during the construction of the A40/42 and the A71. The Ministry of Transport published in October 1978 a document recommending that the archaeological heritage should be taken into account for road schemes, to reduce the serious site difficulties brought about by an accidental discovery. There now exists a mechanism which allows for impact survey, followed by a summary of that survey leading to a contract between the relevant Société d'Autoroute and the regional Direction des Antiqués Historiques, subject to annual revision, and which deals with the selection of sites for preservation, the attendant adjustment to the route and, eventually, the excavation of selected sites well in advance of construction, a watching brief during construction and the subsequent presentation by display and written word, both popular and academic (Aubin 1987). The work is financed by the various private road companies, local and national government, and is administered by the regional archaeological centres. In the Rhône-Alpes area sites have not been excavated where they are going to be buried under embankments without the topsoil being removed, and the selection process for excavation depends on the ability of the site to produce scientific results in good conditions. Less rewarding sites are dealt with by a watching brief. Discoveries during watching briefs have been rare, perhaps four in ten years in Rhône-Alpes, and usually because of alterations and unplanned modifications to the scheme (Vicherd pers comm).

In the case of the A40–A42 autoroutes from Lyon and Macon to Geneva, the impact study was done in 1977–78. The agreement for the 160 kilometre route was concluded in 1980 with Société des Autoroutes Paris-Rhin-Rhône and route modifications were made. A permanent team, ranging from two to three in 1980 to five or six in 1987, were maintained for the period of intensive excavation. The budget increased regularly from 1980 to 1985, when it levelled out at about 2 million francs. The total budget to 1987 is about 12 million francs over eight years, of which 40%-45% is from local and national government, the remainder presumably from the developer (Vicherd pers comm). The popular booklet is now a well established part of the rescue archaeology scene in France (Vicherd 1987). The problems of post-excavation are just being faced, as are all the familar, related problems of professionalism, continuity of employment and salary scales. However, the benefits of the French system lie in the provision of adequate time to survey and make a selection of sites, and then to be able to excavate them, still with adequate time and with a reasonable and confirmed financial package.

The archaeological response to the proposed construction of the M3 was appropriate for its time. The establishment of a full-time professional organisation to deal with a road threat was the logical continuation of the working methods used on the M4, M5 and M40.

The ideal response for any road scheme involves a number of steps most of which have been mentioned above and are summarised in a nine stage sequence below:

1. A desk-top assessment of all known sites on or near the route, including a place-name study. An aerial survey may be needed at this stage. The assessment can be commissioned as soon as a corridor for the route has been selected.

2. Fieldwalking to locate and record upstanding features of archaeological interest, to record in arable areas surface scatters of archaeological material, and to identify areas of paleaoenvironmental interest such as colluvium and peat.

3. Geophysical survey either by detailed survey of the entire route, or more reasonably, by a form of scanning with selected areas being subject to detailed survey. Since stages 2 and 3 are non-damaging they can usually be done well before compulsory purchase.

4. Test pit digging of areas indicated by the geophysical survey as being of archaeological interest, and test pits positioned at regular intervals along the rest of the route. Engineering surveys also include the digging of holes for a variety of purposes and they are usually undertaken before acquisition. It seems reasonable to assume that these could be observed and their results incorporated with those from the stage 4 archaeological test pits.

5. Assessment of results to date and determination of archaeological priorities with a timetable for excavation of selected sites and deposits.

6. Set-piece archaeological investigation of sites within an agreed programme. Set-piece excavation can take considerable time and there are two possible ways in which the problem of access for archaeological work several months before construction could be resolved. The archaeological body could negotiate entry directly with the owner and agree compensation for loss of crop or grazing, or the Department of Transport could purchase the land early, well before the construction date. To leave the arrangement of a set-piece excavation until after the normal time for compulsory purchase would probably not provide adequate time for the archaeological investigation.

7. Watching brief during construction, particularly during the topsoil strip, but to include all peripheral areas used by contractors.

8. Preparation of archive, post-excavation analysis, report writing and deposition of finds and archive with relevant museum and/or record office.

9. Dissemination of results in scientific and popular form.

The arrangements for the funding of rescue archaeology in the 1970's enabled the Department of the Environment to recognise the M3 project as 'of national importance' and thus to fund the project in its entirety. In the 1980's different attitudes to rescue archaeology, tighter funding for an increased volume of rescue projects, and the movement towards developer funding would have made the single, integrated organisation of the M3 project, as in fact occurred, increasingly unlikely. The archaeological work on the Dorchester By-Pass for example, although largely financed by English Heritage and designed as a comprehensive piece of work, benefited in scope from two earlier English Heritage survey projects: the Dorset Ridgeway Project of 1977–84, and the Maiden Castle Project of 1985–6 (Woodward forthcoming, Wainwright and Cunliffe 1984). The main fieldwork and excavation programme for the By-Pass was under way by January 1987 and, as a separate exercise, observation record work was undertaken during the construction period from late 1987 to 1988 (Woodward and Smith forthcoming).

Returning to the prospect of running a 1970's style M3 project in the 1990's, it is conceivable that with £500,000 per annum a similar project could be arranged, but the altered circumstances of excavating bodies suggest otherwise. It is interesting to note that the southern portion of the M3, to the east of St Catherine's Hill, will be funded fully by the Department of Transport as a cost additional to the usual allocation. English Heritage invited the Trust for Wessex Archaeology to undertake the fieldwork programme. The least damaging route of all those proposed, from an archaeological viewpoint, would have been that which used a tunnel under St Catherine's Hill, an undertaking in which the engineers involved with the M3 project in 1973 privately expressed interest.

The M3 project investigated a 17 kilometre long, 60m wide, strip of central Hampshire at a cost of £392,717, which is about 38.5 pence per square metre. At an equivalent rate it would be possible to complete the remaining 11,500 square kilometres of the Wessex region for £4,447,135,000.

Chapter 10

The Archive

The archive consists of field records, in the forms of notebooks and individual context sheets, field drawings, computer records, post-excavation drawings and ordered files on the different classes of artefact and feature types. The majority of these records are on microfiche.

The material is ordered by site code: these are unique sets of numbers and letters from two sequential systems. Those with an R prefix were organised by the M3 Archaeological Rescue Committee, those with a W prefix by the Trust for Wessex Archaeology. For a full list of sites in code order see Table 23 (this volume).

The archive is housed at Hampshire County Museum Service. A copy of the microfiche is with the National Monuments Record.

References

The abbreviations used are generally those suggested in *Signposts for Archaeological Publication* (CBA 1979). Bold numbers indicate volume or series numbers.

Addyman, P V and Hill, D 1969 Saxon Southampton: a Review of the Evidence, Part Two, *Proc Hampshire Fld Club Archaeol Soc* **26** 61–96.

Addyman, P V and Leigh, D 1973 The Anglo-Saxon village at Chalton, Hampshire: second interim report, *Medieval Archaeol* **17** 1–25.

Akerman, J Y 1853 An account of excavations in an Anglo-Saxon burial ground at Harnham Hill, near Salisbury, *Archaeologia* **35** 259–278.

Alexander, D 1983 The Limitations of Traditional Surveying Techniques in a Forested Environment, *J Fld Archaeol* **10** 177–186.

Allen, M J 1985 *Land mollusca from the multiperiod site at Easton Lane and a cursory review of the Prehistoric environment of a downland block in central Hampshire*, Ancient Monuments Laboratory Report 4626.

—— 1988 Archaeological and environmental aspects of colluvation in South-east England, in Groenman-van Waateringe and Robinson (eds) *Man-Made Soils*, Brit Archaeol Rep S410, Oxford.

Ambrosiani, K 1981 Viking-Age Combs, Comb-Making and Comb-Makers in the light of Finds from Birka and Ribe, *Stockholm Studies in Archaeology 2*, Stockholm.

Ammerman, A J 1985 Plow-Zone Experiments in Calabria, Italy, *J Fld Archaeol* **12** 33–40.

Andersen H H, Crabb P J, and Madsen H J 1971 *Arhus Sndervold. En byarkaeologisk undersogelse*, Copenhagen.

Anstee, J W and Biek, L 1961 A Study in Pattern Welding, *Medieval Archaeol* **5** 71–93.

Archer-Thomson, J 1987 Hedgerows, in Keen and Carreck (eds) *Historic Landscape of the Weld Estate*, Dorset.

Arrhenius, O 1963 Investigations of soil from old Indian sites, *Ethnos* **2–4** 122–136.

Aubin, G 1987 Experience Française en Matiere D'Autoroute, paper presented to the Council of Europe Colloquium on Archéologie et Grands Travauxs, Nice, November 1987.

Baker, H 1937 Alluvial Meadows: a Comparative Study of Grazed and Mown Meadows, *J Ecology* **25** 408–420.

Baldwin-Brown, G 1915 *The Arts in Early England IV. Saxon Art and Industry in the Pagan Period*, London.

Barker, G W W 1975 To sieve or not to sieve, *Antiquity* **49** 61–3.

Beedham, G E 1972 *Identification of the British Mollusca*, Hulton, Amersham.

Bell, M 1981 Valley sediments and Environmental change, in Jones and Dimbleby (eds) *The Environment of Man: the Iron Age to the Anglo-Saxon Period*, Brit Archaeol Rep **87** 75–91.

—— 1983 Valley sediments as evidence of prehistoric land use on the South Downs, *Proc Prehist Soc* **49** 119–150.

Benson, D G 1973 A Sites and Monuments Record for the Oxford Region, *Oxoniensia* **37** 226–237.

Berry K J, Mielke P W, and Kvamme K L 1984 Efficient Permutation Procedures for Analysis of Artifact Distributions, in Hietala (ed) *Intrasite Spatial Analysis in Archaeology* 54–74.

Bersu, G 1940 Excavations at Little Woodbury, Wiltshire, *Proc Prehist Soc* **6** 30–111.

Biddle, M 1972 Winchester: The Development of an Early Capital, *Vor- und Fruhformen der europaischen Stadt im Mittelalter*, Teil 1.

—— 1976 *Winchester in the Early Middle Ages*, Winchester Studies 1.

Biddle, M and Emery, V W 1973 *The M3 Extension: An Archaeological Survey*.

Bowen, H C 1975 Air photography and the development of the landscape in central parts of Southern England, in Wilson (ed) *Aerial Recconnaissance for Archaeology* 103–118.

Bourdillon, J E C 1983 *Animals in an urban environment*, unpublished MPhil thesis, Department of Archaeology, University of Southampton, 1983.

—— nd The animal bone from the Abbot's Worthy site, Report to the Ancient Monuments Laboratory, March 1985.

Bourdillon, J E C (ed) in prep *The environment and economy of Saxon and medieval Southampton*, Southampton Museums.

Bourdillon, J E C and Coy, J P 1980 The animal bones, in Holdsworth *Excavations in Melbourne Street, Southampton, 1971–6*, Counc Brit Archaeol Res Rep **33** 79–121.

Briscoe, T 1981 Anglo-Saxon Pot Stamps, in Brown *et al* (eds) *Anglo-Saxon Studies in Archaeology and History 2*, Brit Archaeol Rep **92**.

Burdy, J 1985 *Autour de Lyon Les Aqueducs Romains.*

Butser, K W 1982 *Archaeology as human ecology*, Cambridge.

Carruthers, W J 1989 The Carbonised Remains, in Fasham *et al*, *The Archaeological Site at Easton Lane, Winchester.*

—— in prep Mineralised Plant Remains from Potterne.

Carver, M O H 1986 *Bulletin of the Sutton Hoo Research Committee* **4**.

Case, H et al 1965 Excavations at City Farm, Hanborough, Oxon, *Oxoniensia* **20** 1–98.

Champion, S and Champion, T C in prep Excavations of an Iron Age Site at Portway, Andover, Hampshire.

Chowne, P 1987 Interim Report on the Western Link Road, Bradford Peverell, Dorset, *Proc Dorset Natur Hist Archaeol Soc*, **109** 125–6.

Clapham A R, Tutin T G, and Warburg E F 1962 *Flora of the British Isles*, Cambridge.

Clark, A J 1974 Magnetic Scanning, in Fasham (ed) *M3 Archaeology 1974.*

—— 1977 Geophysical and Geochemical Assessment of Air Photographic Sites, *Archaeol J* **134** 187–193.

—— 1983 The Testimony of the Topsoil, in Maxwell (ed) *The Importance of Aerial Reconnaissance to Archaeology*, Counc Brit Archaeol Res Rep **49** 128–135.

Clark M J, Lewin J, and Small R J 1967 The sarsen stones of the Marlborough Downs and their geomorphological implications, *Southampton Research Series in Geography* **4** 3–40.

Clarke, D L 1972 A provisional model of an Iron Age society and its settlement system, in Clarke (ed) *Models in Archaeology* 801–869.

Colley, S M in prep The Hamwic Pit Project, in Bourdillon (ed) *The environment and economy of Saxon and Medieval Southampton.*

Collier, C 1878 On an Unexplored Roman Villa at Itchen Abbas, *J Brit Archaeol Ass* **34** 233–34 and 501.

—— 1879 no title, *J Brit Archaeol Ass* **35** 109–110 and 209.

Collis, J R 1968 Excavations at Owslebury, Hants: an interim report, *Antiq J* **48** 18–31.

—— 1970 Excavations at Owslebury, Hants: a second interim report, *Antiq J* **50** 246–261.

—— 1977 *The Iron Age in Britain – a Review.*

—— 1978 *Winchester Excavations 1949–1960 Vol II*, Winchester.

—— 1985 Review of Danebury: An Iron Age Hillfort in Hampshire, *Proc Prehist Soc* **51** 348–349.

—— 1986 Review of the Prehistoric Settlement at Winnall Down, Hampshire, *Archaeol J* **143** 380–381.

Cook, A M and Dacre, M W 1985 *Excavations at Portway, Andover, 1973–76*, Oxford Univ Comm Archaeol Monograph **4**.

Cook, S F and Heizer, R F 1965 Studies on the Chemical Analysis of Archaeological Sites, *Univ of California Publications in Anthropology* **2** 1–102.

Cox, P W 1985 Excavation and Survey on Furzey Island, Poole Harbour (SZ 011871) – An Interim Note, *Proc Dorset Natur Hist Archaeol Soc* **107** 157–158.

—— 1986 *Norden Roundabout: Preliminary Archaeological Assessment* Trust for Wesseex Archaeology Report for BP.

—— in prep The Roman road at Stoborough Heath.

Cox, P W and Farwell, D E 1987 *Wytch Field Oilfield Development: F–D Flowline. Archaeological Assessment* Trust for Wessex Archaeology Report for BP.

Cox, P W and Smith, R J C in prep Excavations on the Wareham By-Pass.

Coy, J P 1975 Iron Age cookery, in Clason (ed) *Archaeozoological Studies*, Amsterdam: Elsevier, 426–30.

—— 1980 The animal bones, in Haslam, Excavation of a mid-Saxon smelting site at Ramsbury, Wiltshire, *Medieval Archaeol* **24** 41–51.

—— 1982a The animal bones, in Gingell, The excavation of an Iron Age enclosure at Groundwell Farm, *Wiltshire Archaeol Natur Hist Mag* **76** 68–73.

—— 1982b Woodland mammals in Wessex – the archaeological evidence, in Bell and Limbrey (eds) *Archaeological Aspects of Woodland Ecology*, Brit Archaeol Rep **S146** 287–96.

—— 1984a The bird bones, in Cunliffe, *Danebury: An Iron Age Hillfort in Hampshire: Vol. 2 The Excavations 1969–1978: The Finds*, Counc Brit Archaeol Res Rep **52** 527–531.

—— 1984b *Animal bones from Saxon, Medieval and Post-Medieval phases of Winchester Western Suburb*, unpublished Report to Ancient Monuments Laboratory.

—— 1985 Assessing the role of pigs from faunal debris on archaeological settlements, in Fieller *et al* (eds) *Palaeobiological Investigations*, Brit Archaeol Rep **S266** 55–64, plus tables.

—— 1987 Animal bones, in Fasham, *A 'Banjo' enclosure in Micheldever Wood, Hampshire*, Hampshire Fld Club Monograph **4**.

—— nd 1 *Animal bones from Wraysbury, Berks*, unpublished report to the Ancient Monuments Laboratory 20/87.

—— in prep, Wild vertebrates, ecology and diet, in Bourdillon (ed) *The environment and economy of Saxon and Medieval Southampton.*

Coy, J P and Maltby, J M 1987 Archaeozoology in Wessex: vertebrate remains and marine molluscs and their relevance to archaeology, in Keeley (ed) *Environmental Archaeology: a Regional Review Vol II*, 204–251.

Craddock P T, Gurney D, Pryor F, and Hughes M J 1985 The Application of Phosphate Analysis to the Location and Interpretation of Archaeological Sites, *Archaeol J* **142** 340–360.

Cunliffe, B W 1971 *Excavations at Fishbourne 1961–1969*, Rep Res Comm Soc Antiq London **27**.

———— 1976 *Excavations at Porchester Castle. Volume II Saxon*, Rep Res Comm Soc Antiq London **33**.

———— 1978 *Iron Age Communities in Britain* (2nd edn).

———— 1984 *Danebury: An Iron Age Hillfort in Hampshire*, Counc Brit Archaeol Res Rep **52**.

Cribb, R 1985 The analysis of ancient herding systems: an application of computer simulation in faunal studies, in Barker and Gamble (eds) *Beyond Domestication in Prehistoric Europe*, New York, 75–106.

Dacre, M W in prep The Early Anglo-Saxon Habitation Site at Charlton Link Road, Andover, Hants.

Davies, S M 1980 Excavations at Old Down Farm. Part 1: Saxon, *Proc Hampshire Fld Club Archaeol Soc* **36** 161–180.

———— 1981 Excavations at Old Down Farm, Andover Part 2: Prehistoric and Roman, *Proc Hampshire Fld Club Archaeol Soc* **37** 81–163.

Dauncey, K D M 1952 Phosphate Content of Soils on Archaeological Sites, *Advancement Sci* **9** 33–36.

Dennell, R W 1972 The interpretation of plant remains: Bulgaria, in Higgs (ed) *Papers in Economic Prehistory*, 149–159.

———— 1974 Botanical evidence for Prehistoric Crop Processing Activities, *J Archaeol Sci* **1** 275–284.

———— 1977 Prehistoric Crop Cultivation in Southern England: a Reconsideration, *Antiq J* **56** 11–23.

DoE 1975 *Principles of Publication in Rescue Archaeology*, London.

Donaldson, P forthcoming *Further Excavations at Balksbury Camp, Andover, Hampshire, 1973 and 1981*, English Heritage Monograph Series.

von den Driesch, A 1976 *A guide to the measurement of animals bones from archaeological sites*, Peabody Museum Bulletin **1**, Harvard University.

Driver, J C 1984 Zooarchaeological analysis of raw-material selection by a Saxon artisan, *J Fld Archaeol* **11** 397–403.

Dunning G C, Hurst J G, Myres J N L and Tischler M 1959 Anglo-Saxon Pottery: A Symposium, *Medieval Archaeol* **3** 1–78.

Edlin, H L 1949 *Woodland Crafts in Britain*.

Ellis, A E 1969 *British Snails*, Oxford.

———— 1978 *British Freshwater Bivalve Molluscs*, Synopses of the British Fauna 11, Linnean Society, London.

Ellison, A B 1981 *A Policy for Archaeological Investigation in Wessex 1981–1985*.

Engelmark, R 1981 Carbonised plant material from the Early Iron Age in North Sweden, *Wahlenbergia* **7** 39–43.

Evans, J G 1972 *Land Snails in Archaeology*, London.

Evans, J G and Jones, H 1973 Subfossil and modern land-snail faunas from rock-rubble habitats, *J Conchology* **28** 103–129.

Everitt, B 1980 *Cluster Analysis* (2nd edn), London.

Fasham, P J (ed) 1974 *M3 Archaeology 1974*.

———— (ed) 1975 *M3 Archaeology 1975*.

———— (ed) 1976 *M3 archaeology 1976–77*.

———— 1979 The excavation of a triple barrow in Micheldever Wood, Hampshire, *Proc Hampshire Fld Club Archaeol Soc* **35** 5–40.

———— 1980a Excavations on Bridget's and Burntwood Farms, Itchen Valley Parish, Hampshire, 1974, *Proc Hampshire Fld Club Archaeol Soc* **36** 37–86.

———— 1980b Archaeology in Wood and Field, in Hinchliffe and Schadla-Hall (eds) *The Past Under The Plough*, 95–104.

———— 1981 Fieldwork and excavations at East Stratton along the Roman road from Winchester to Silchester, *Proc Hampshire Fld Club Archaeol Soc* **37** 165–188.

———— 1982 The excavation of four ring-ditches in central Hampshire, *Proc Hampshire Fld Club Archaeol Soc* **38** 19–56.

———— 1983 Fieldwork in and around Micheldever Wood, Hampshire 1973–80, *Proc Hampshire Fld Club Archaeol Soc* **39** 5–45.

———— 1985 *The Prehistoric Settlement at Winnall Down, Winchester*, Hampshire Fld Club Monograph **2**.

———— 1986a Approches de la prospection systématique, in Ferdière and Zadora-Rio (eds) *La Prospection Archéologique: Paysage et Peuplement*, Documents D'Archéologie Française, **3** 19–28.

———— 1986b Before the Fringe, in Hughes and Rowley (eds) *The Management and Presentation of Field Monuments*.

———— 1987a The Medieval Settlement at Popham, Excavation 1975 and 1983, *Proc Hampshire Fld Club Archaeol Soc* **43** 83–124.

———— 1987b *A 'Banjo' Enclosure in Micheldever Wood, Hampshire (MARC3 Site R27)*, Hampshire Fld Club Monograph **4**.

Fasham P J, Farwell D E, and Whinney R 1989 *The Archaeological Site at Easton Lane, Winchester*, Hampshire Fld Club Monograph **6**.

Fasham, P J and Hawkes, J W 1980 Computerised Recording Systems and Analysis in an Archaeological Unit: Some Observations, in Stewart (ed) *Microcomputers in Archaeology*, MDA Occ Paper **4**.

——— 1983 *Reading Abbey Rediscovered*.

——— 1986 *Reading Abbey Waterfront*.

——— 1987 Computerised Site Archives: A Response, *Archaeol Computing Newsletter* **12** 1.

Fasham, P J and Keevill, G forthcoming *Excavations at Brighton Hill South, Basingstoke*, Hampshire Fld Club Monograph.

Fasham, P J and Monk, M A 1978 Sampling for Plant Remains from Iron Age Sites: Some Results and Implications, in Cherry *et al* (eds) *Sampling in Contemporary British Archaeology*, Brit Archaeol Rep **50** 363–371.

Fasham, P J and Ross, J M 1978 A Bronze Age Flint Industry from a Barrow Site in Micheldever Wood, Hampshire, *Proc Prehist Soc* **44** 47–67.

Fasham P J, Schadla-Hall R T, Shennan S J and Bates P J 1980 *Fieldwalking for Archaeologists*.

Fasham, P J and Whinney, R J B 1985 *Roads to the Past. The Prehistoric Site at Easton Lane, Winchester*.

Faussett, B 1856 *Inventorium Sepulchrae* (Smith, C R ed), London.

Fenton, A 1983 Grain storage in pits: Experiment and Fact, in O'Connor and Clarke (eds) *From the Stone Age to the Forty Five*, Edinburgh.

Fell, C 1984 *Women in Anglo-Saxon England*, London.

Ferdière, A and Zadora-Rio, E 1986 *La prospection archéologique. Paysage et Peuplement*, Documents d'Archéologie Française **3**.

Freestone, I C 1982 Applications and potential of electron probe micro-analysis in technological and provenance investigations of ancient ceramics, *Archaeometry* **24** 99–116.

Fiches, J-L 1986 *Les Maisons Gallo-romaines d'Ambrussum (Villetelle-Hérault). La fouille du secteur IV. 1976–1980*, Documents d'Archéologie Française **5**.

Fiches, J-L and Roux, J-C 1982 *Recherche dans le quartier bas d'Ambrussum, 2. La Fouille de Sauvetage*, A R A L O dossier **3**, Caveirac.

Fisher, P F 1977 *Phosphorous Concentrations in the Soil of Archaeological Sites*, undergraduate thesis, University of Lancaster.

Fowler, P J 1972 Field Archaeology on the M5 Motorway 1969–1971; Some Provisional Results, Analyses and Implications, in Fowler (ed) *Field Survey in British Archaeology*.

Fowler, P J and Bennett, J 1973 Archaeology and the M5 Motorway, Second Report, *Trans Bristol Gloucestershire Archaeol Soc* **92** 21–81.

Fowler, P J and Walthew, C V 1971 Archaeology and the M5 Motorway, First Report, *Trans Bristol Gloucestershire Archaeol Soc* **90** 22–63.

Gallant, T W 1986 'Background Noise' and Site Definition: a Contribution to Survey Methodology, *J Fld Archaeol* **13** No **4** 404–418.

Gilbertson, D D 1984 *Late Quaternary Environments and Man in Holderness*, Brit Archaeol Rep **134**.

Gill, T and Vear, K C 1980 *Agricultural Botany. 1 Dicotyledonous Crops*, London.

Gingell, C J 1975–6 The excavation of an Early Anglo-Saxon cemetery at Collingbourne Ducis, *Wiltshire Archaeol Natur Hist Mag* **70–71** 61–98.

Goodall, A R 1984 Non-Ferrous Metal Objects, in Rogerson and Dallas, *Excavations in Thetford 1948–9 and 1973–80*, East Anglian Archaeol Rep **22**.

Goodman, D 1975 The theory of diversity-stability relationships in ecology, *The Quarterly Review of Biology* **50** 237–266.

Gower, J C 1975 Goodness-of-fit criteria for classification and other patterned structures, in *Proc 8th Conference on Numerical Taxonomy*, 38–62.

Graham-Campbell, J 1980 *Viking Artefacts. A Select Catalogue*, London.

Grant, A 1981 The significance of deer remains at occupation sites of the Iron Age to the Anglo-Saxon period, in Jones and Dimbleby (eds) *The Environment of Man: The Iron Age to the Anglo-Saxon Period*, Brit Archaeol Rep **87** 205–214.

——— 1984a Animal husbandry, in Cunliffe, *Danebury: An Iron Age Hillfort in Hampshire. Vol 2: The Finds*, Counc Brit Archaeol Res Rep **52** 496–548.

——— 1984b Animal husbandry in Wessex and the Thames Valley, in Cunliffe and Miles (eds) *Aspects of the Iron Age in Central Southern Britain*, Univ Oxford Comm Archaeol Monograph **2** 102–119.

——— 1984c Survival or sacrifice? A critical appraisal of animal burials in Britain in the Iron Age, in Grigson and Clutton-Brock (eds) *Animals and Archaeology: 4, Husbandry in Europe*, Brit Archaeol Rep **S227** 221–8.

Green, F J 1979 Phosphate Mineralisation of Seeds from Archaeological Sites, *J Archaeol Sci* **6** 279–284.

——— 1981 Iron Age, Roman and Saxon Crops: The Archaeological Evidence from Wessex, in Jones and Dimbleby (eds) *The Environment of Man : the Iron Age to the Anglo-Saxon Period*, Brit Archaeol Rep **87** 129–153.

―――― forthcoming Landscape Archaeology in Hampshire: The Plant Macrofossils, *Proc 7th Symp IWGP*.

Greig, J 1984 The palaeoecology of some British hay meadow types, in van Zeist and Casparie (eds) *Plants and Ancient Man* Proc 6th Symp IWGP.

Griffith, N nd Animal bones from R27, M3 Motorway Excavations, unpublished Ancient Monuments Laboratory Report, 2647 (1978).

Groube, L M and Bowden, M C B 1982 *The Archaeology of Rural Dorset*, Dorset Natur Hist Archaeol Soc Monograph **4**.

Gunner 1849 no title *Archaeol J* **6** 397–398 and 408–409.

Halstead P, Hodder I, and Jones G 1978 Behavioural archaeology and refuse patterns: a case study, *Norwegian Archaeol Rev* **11** 118–131.

Harcourt, R A 1979 The animal bones, in Wainwright, *Gussage All Saints: an Iron Age Settlement in Dorset*, Department of the Environment Archaeol Rep **10** 150–60.

Harris, E C 1975 The Stratigraphic Sequence: A Question of Time, *World Archaeol* **7** 109–121.

Haselgrove, C 1986 An Iron Age Community and its Hillfort: The Excavations at Danebury, Hampshire, 1969–79. A Review, *Archaeol J* **143** 363–369.

Haselgrove C, Millett M, and Smith I (eds) 1985 *Archaeology from the Ploughsoil*.

Hawkes, C F C 1939 The Excavations at Quarley Hill 1938, *Proc Hampshire Fld Club Archaeol Soc* **14** 139–164.

Hawkes, S C 1973 The dating and social significance of the burials in the Polhill cemetery, in Philp (ed) *Excavations in West Kent 1960–1970*, 186–201.

Hawkes, S C and Gray, M 1969 Preliminary Note on the Early Anglo-Saxon Settlement at New Wintles Farm, Eynsham, *Oxoniensia* **34** 1–4.

Hedges R E M, Housley R A, Law I A, and Bronk C R 1989 Radiocarbon dates from the Oxford AMS system: Archaeometry datelist 9, *Archaeometry* **31** 207–234.

Helbaek, H 1952 Early Crops in Southern England, *Proc Prehist Soc* **12** 194–233.

Hillman, G 1981 Reconstructing Crop Husbandry Practices from Charred Remains of Crops, in Mercer (ed) *Farming Practice in British Prehistory*.

―――― 1984 Traditional Husbandry and Processing of Archaic Cereals in Recent times: the operations, products and equipment which might feature in Sumerian Texts. Part 1: The Glume Wheats, *Bull Sumerian Agriculture* **1** 114–152.

Hinton, D A and Welch, M 1976 Iron and Bronze, in Cunliffe, *Excavations at Porchester Castle Volume II Saxon*, Rep Res Comm Soc Antiq London **33**.

Hoffman, M 1964 The Warp-Weighted Loom, *Studia Norvegica* **14** Oslo.

Holwerda, J H 1930 Opgravingen van Dorestad, *Oudheidkundige Mededeelingen* **11** 32–96.

Hooper, M D 1971 *Hedges and Local History*.

―――― 1974 Hedgerows, in Fasham (ed) *M3 Archaeology 1974* **11**.

Hodder, I 1986 *Reading the Past*, Cambridge.

Hubbard, R N L B 1975 Assessing the Botanical Component of Human Palaeo-Economies, *Bull Inst Archaeol Univ London* **12** 197–205.

Hughes, M F 1986 The Excavations of a Roman and Saxon Settlement and Cemetery at Shavards Farm, Meonstoke, 1984/85, *Archaeology and Historic Buildings in Hampshire* Annual Report for 1984/85, Hampshire County Council, 2–8.

Hurlbert, S H 1971 The non-concept of species diversity: a critique and alternative parameters, *Ecology* **52** 577–586.

Jessen, K and Helbaek, H 1944 *Cereals in Great Britain and Ireland in Prehistoric and Early Historic Times*, Copenhagen.

Johnson, W 1978 Hedges – a review of some early literature, *Local Hist* **13** No 4 195–204.

Jones, D K C (ed) 1980 *The Shaping of Southern England*, London.

Jones, M 1978 The Plant Remains, in Parrington, *The excavation of an Iron Age settlement, Bronze Age ring-ditches and Roman features at Ashville Trading Estate, Abingdon (Oxon) 1974–76*, Counc Brit Archaeol Res Rep **28** 93–110.

―――― 1981 The Development of Crop Husbandry, in Jones and Dimbleby (eds) *The Environment of Man: the Iron Age to the Anglo-Saxon Period*, Brit Archaeol Rep **87**.

―――― 1984a Regional patterns in Crop production, in Cunliffe and Miles (eds) *Aspects of the Iron Age in Central Southern Britain*, Univ Oxford Comm Archaeol Monograph **2**.

―――― 1984b The Plant Remains, in Cunliffe, *Danebury: an Iron Age Hillfort in Hampshire*, Counc Brit Archaeol Res Rep **52** 483–495.

―――― 1985 Archaeobotany beyond subsistence reconstruction, in Barker and Gamble, *Beyond Domestication in Prehistoric Europe*, 107–124.

Jukes-Brown, A J 1908 *The Geology of the Country Around Dover*, London.

Kay, Q O N 1971 Anthemis cotula, *J Ecology* **59** 623–36.

Keeley, H C M 1985 *Itchen Abbas Road, Hants, Watching Brief – report on the soils*, Ancient Monuments Laboratory Report 4617.

Keepax, C A 1977a Identification, Preservation and Interpretation of Wood in Archaeological Deposits. Ancient Monuments Laboratory Report 2277.

—— 1977b MARC3 Charcoal Identification: Interim Report. Ancient Monuments Laboratory Report 2362.

—— 1979 Further Charcoal Identification for MARC3: R 17 and R 27. Interim Report. Ancient Monuments Laboratory Report 2726.

—— 1985 Wood Charcoal, in Fasham, *The Prehistoric Settlement at Winnall Down, Winchester*, Hampshire Fld Club Monograph **2**.

Kerney, M P 1966 Snails and man in Britain, *J Conchology* **26** 3–14.

—— 1968 Britain's fauna of land Mollusca and its relation to the Post-glacial thermal optimum, *Symp Zool Soc London* **22** 273–291.

—— 1976a *Atlas of the Non-Marine Mollusca of the British Isles*, Cambridge, Institute of Terrestrial Ecology.

—— 1976b A list of the fresh and brackish-water mollusca of the British Isles, J Conchology 29 26–28.

King, A 1978 A comparative survey of bone assemblages from Roman sites in Britain, *Bull Inst Archaeol Univ London* **15** 207–232.

Knörzer, K-H 1979 Verkohlte Reste von Viehfutter aus einem Stall des römischen Reiterlagers von Dormagen, *Rheinische Ausgrabungen* **20** 130–137.

Krakker J J, Shott M J, and Welch P D 1983 Design and Evaluation of Shovel-Test Sampling in Regional Archaeological Survey, *J Fld Archaeol* **10** 469–480.

Lapinskas, P 1974 The flotation machine, in Fasham (ed) *M3 Archaeology 1974*.

Leeds, E T 1923 A Saxon Village at Sutton Courtenay, Berkshire, *Archaeologia* **73** 147–192.

—— 1947 A Saxon Village at Sutton Courtenay, Berkshire. Third Report, *Archaeologia* **92** 79–94.

Lethbridge, T C 1931 *Recent Excavations in Anglo-Saxon Cemeteries in Cambridgeshire and Suffolk*, Cambridge Antiq Soc Quarto Pub **3**, Cambridge.

Liddell, D M 1933 Excavations at Meon Hill, *Proc Hampshire Fld Club Archaeol Soc* **12** 127–162.

—— 1935 Report on the Hampshire Field Club's Excavation at Meon Hill, *Proc Hampshire Fld Club Archaeol Soc* **13** 7–54.

Limbrey, S 1975 *Soil Science and Archaeology*.

—— 1978 Changes in the quality and Distribution of the Soils of Lowland Britain, in Limbrey and Evans (eds) *The effect of man on the Landscape: the Lowland Zone*, Counc Brit Archaeol Res Rep **21** 21–27.

Lobb, S J and Rose, P in prep *The Kennet Valley Survey*.

Losco-Bradley, S 1974 The Anglo-Saxon Settlement at Catholme, Barton-under-Needwood, Staffordshire. Interim Report 1973–74, *Trent Valley Archaeol Res Comm Rep* **8** 3–34.

Losco-Bradley, S and Wheeler, H M 1984 Anglo-Saxon Settlement in the Trent Valley – Some Aspects, in Faull (ed) *Studies in Late Anglo-Saxon Settlement*.

Lyne, M A B and Jeffries, R S 1979 *The Alice Holt/Farnham Roman Pottery Industry*, Counc Brit Archaeol Res Rep **30**.

MacGregor, A 1978 Industry and Commerce in Anglo-Scandinavian York, in Hall (ed) *Viking Age York and the North* **27** 37–57.

—— 1982 Anglo-Scandinavian Finds from Lloyds Bank, Pavement, and other sites, *The Archaeology of York. The Small Finds*, Fascicule **17/3**.

—— 1985 *Bone, Antler, Horn and Ivory. The Technology of Skeletal Materials*, London.

Macleod D, Monk M A, and Williams T 1988 The use of the Single Context Recording System on a seasonally excavated site in Ireland: a learning experience, *J Irish Archaeol* **IV**.

MacReady, S and Thompson, F H 1985 *Archaeological Field Survey in Britain and Abroad*, Soc Antiq London Occ Papers (New Series) **6**.

Maltby, J M 1981 Iron Age, Romano-British and Anglo-Saxon animal husbandry: a review of the faunal evidence, in Jones and Dimbleby (eds) *The Environment of Man: The Iron Age to the Anglo-Saxon Period*, Brit Archaeol Rep **87** 155–204.

—— 1982 The variability of faunal samples and their effects on ageing data, in Wilson *et al* (eds) *Ageing and Sexing Animal Bones from Archaeological Sites*, Brit Archaeol Rep **109** 81–90.

—— 1985a The animal bones, in Fasham, *The Prehistoric Settlement at Winnall Down, Winchester*, Hampshire Fld Club Monograph **2** 25, 97–112, 137–8.

—— 1985b Patterns in faunal assemblage variability, in Barker and Gamble (eds) *Beyond Domestication in Prehistoric Europe*, New York, 33–74.

—— 1985c Assessing variations in Iron Age and Roman butchery practices: the need for quantification, in Fieller *et al* (eds) *Palaeobiological Investigations: Research Design, Methods and Data Analysis*, Brit Archaeol Rep **S266** 19–32.

—— 1989a The animal bones, in Fasham *et al* (eds) *The Archaeological Site at Easton Lane, Winchester*, Hampshire Fld Club Monograph **6** 122–131.

—— 1989b Urban-rural variations in the butchering of cattle in Romano-British Hampshire, in

Sarjeantson *et al* (eds) *Diet and Crafts in Towns: the Evidence of Animal Remains*, Brit Archaeol Rep **199** 75–106.

——— nd1 The animal bones from Owslebury: an Iron Age and Romano-British settlement in Hampshire, unpublished Ancient Monuments Laboratory Report, 6/87.

——— nd2 The exploitation of animals in the Iron Age – the archaeozoological evidence (draft for book to be edited by J Collis and T C Champion).

——— nd3 The animal bones from the later Roman phases from Winchester Northern Suburbs 1. The unsieved samples from Victoria Road Trenches X–XVI. Unpublished report to the Ancient Monuments Laboratory 000/87.

Mann, J E 1982 *Early Medieval Finds from Flaxengate 1: Objects of antler, bone, stone, horn, ivory, amber and jet*, The Archaeology of Lincoln, **14–1**.

Margary, I D 1956 *Roman Roads in Britain*.

——— 1973 *Roman Roads in Britain*.

Massy, J L 1984 Circonscription du Lorraine, *Gallia* **42**.

Meaney, A L 1981 *Anglo-Saxon Amulets and Curing Stones*, Brit Archaeol Rep **96**.

Millett, M and James, S 1983 Excavations at Cowdery's Down, Basingstoke, Hampshire 1978–81, *Archaeol J* **140** 157–279.

Millett, M and Russell, D 1982 An Iron Age Burial from Viables Farm, Basingstoke, Hampshire, *Archaeol J* **139** 69–90.

Millett, M and Russell, D 1984 An Iron Age and Romano-British Site, Viables Farm, Basingstoke, *Proc Hampshire Fld Club Archaeol Soc* **40** 69–90.

Monk, M A 1978 *The Plant Economy and Agriculture of the Anglo-Saxons in Southern Britain with particular reference to the Mart Settlements at Southampton and Winchester* M Phil thesis, Univ Southampton.

——— 1985 The Plant Economy, in Fasham, *The Prehistoric Settlement at Winnall Down, Winchester*, Hampshire Fld Club Monograph **2**.

——— 1987a Archaeobotanical Studies at Poundbury, in Sparey Green, *Excavations at Poundbury, Dorchester, Dorset 1966–1982. Volume 1: The Settlements*, Dorset Natur Hist Archaeol Soc Monograph **7**.

——— 1987b Evidence from Macroscopic Plant Remains for Crop Husbandry in Prehistoric and Early Historic Ireland: a Review, *J Irish Archaeol* **3** 31–6.

——— 1990 Scientific excavation recording, *Archaeol Ireland* **4** 1.

——— 1991 The Archaeological evidence for Field Crop Plants in Early Historic Ireland, in Renfrew (ed) *New Light on Early Farming*, Edinburgh University Press.

——— nd Wroxeter Plant Remains: preliminary report on the 1979/80 seasons work.

Monk, M A and Fasham, P J 1980 Carbonised Plant Remains from Two Iron Age Sites in Central Hampshire, *Proc Prehist Soc* **46** 321–344.

Murphy, P 1977 Early Agriculture and Environment in Hampshire 800 BC–400 AD unpublished MPhil thesis, Univ Southampton.

——— 1985 The Cereals and Crop Weeds, in West, *West Stow Anglo-Saxon Village*, East Anglian Archaeol Rep **24** 100–108.

Musee Archaeologique de Nimes 1986 *Par-Dela Le Pont du Grand*, Exhibition catalogue.

Musty, J and Stratton, J 1964 A Saxon Cemetery at Winterbourne Gunner, near Salisbury, *Wiltshire Archaeol Natur Hist Mag* **59** 86–109.

Myres, J N L 1977 *A Corpus of Anglo-Saxon Pottery of the Pagan Period*, Cambridge.

Neal, D S 1979 Bronze Age, Iron Age and Roman settlement sites at Little Somborne and Ashley, Hampshire, *Proc Hampshire Fld Club Archaeol Soc* **36** 91–144.

Oliver, M and Applin, B 1978 Excavations of an Iron Age and Romano-British Settlement at Ructstall's Hill, Basingstoke, Hampshire 1972–75, *Proc Hampshire Fld Club Archaeol Soc* **35** 41–92.

Palmer, R 1984 *Danebury. An Iron Age Hillfort in Hampshire. An Aerial Photographic Interpretation of its Environs*, RCHM Supplementary Series **6**.

Payne, S 1975 Partial recovery and sample bias, in Clason (ed) *Archaeozoological Studies*, 7–17, Amsterdam.

Peacock, D P S 1979 Petrology of fabrics A–H, in Rahtz, *The Saxon and Medieval Palaces at Cheddar: Excavations 1960–62*, Brit Archaeol Rep **65** 310–14.

Pearson, G W and Stuiver, M 1986 High-precision calibration of the radiocarbon time scale, 500–2500 BC, *Radiocarbon* **28** 2b.

Pearson, G W *et al* 1986 High-precision ^{14}C measurement of Irish Oaks to show the natural ^{14}C variations from AD 1840 to 5210 BC, *Radiocarbon* **28** 2b.

Pennington, W 1969 *The History of British Vegetation*, London.

Percival, J 1974 *The Wheat Plant*, fascimile Duckworth, London.

Perry, B T 1972 Excavations at Bramdean, Hampshire, 1965 and 1966, and a Discussion of Similar Sites in Southern England, *Proc Hampshire Fld Club Archaeol Soc* **29** 41–78.

——— 1982 Excavations at Bramdean, Hampshire, 1973 to 1977, *Proc Hampshire Fld Club Archaeol Soc* **38** 57–74.

Pielou, E C 1975 *Ecological Diversity*, London.

Poole, R W 1974 *An Introduction to Quantitative Ecology*, McGraw-Hill.

Pollard E, Hooper M D, and Moore N W 1974 *Hedges*.

Powlesland, D 1986 Excavations at Heslerton, North Yorkshire, 1978–1982, *Archaeol J* **143** 53–173.

Preece, R C 1980 The biostratigraphy and dating of a Postglacial slope deposit at Gore Cliff, near Blackgang, Isle of Wight, *J Archaeol Sci* **7** 255–265.

Prummel, W 1983 *Early Medieval Dorestad. An Archaeozoological Study*, Excavations at Dorestad **11**, Amersfoort.

Pryor, F 1974 *Excavations at Fengate, Peterborough, England: the first report*, Royal Ontario Mus Archaeol Monograph **3**.

———— 1980 Maxey, Micros and Myself – A Personal Assessment From The Archaeologist's Viewpoint, in Stewart (ed) *Microcomputers in Archaeology*, MDA Occ Paper **4**.

Qualmann, K forthcoming *The Roman Suburbs of Winchester*, Winchester Museum Service.

Rahtz, P 1976 Buildings and Rural Settlement, in Wilson (ed) *The Archaeology of Anglo-Saxon England*, 49–98.

Read, D W 1986 Sampling Procedures for Regional Surveys: a Problem of Representativeness and Effectiveness, *J Fld Archaeol* **13 No 4** 477–491.

Reynolds, P J 1979 *Iron-Age Farm. The Butser Experiment*, British Museum Publications, London.

———— 1981 New Approaches to Familiar Problems, in Jones and Dimbleby (eds) *The Environment of Man: the Iron Age to the Anglo-Saxon Period*, Brit Archaeol Rep **87**.

Reynolds, P J and Schadla-Hall, R T 1980 Measurement of Plough Damage and the Effects of Ploughing on Archaeological Material, in Hinchliffe and Schadla-Hall (eds) *The Past Under The Plough*, 114–122.

Richards, J C 1978 *The Archaeology of the Berkshire Downs*.

———— 1985 Scouring the Surface: Approaches to the Ploughzone in the Stonehenge Environs, *Archaeol Rev Cambs* **4.1** 27–42.

———— forthcoming *The Stonehenge Environs Project*, HBMC.

Riddler, I forthcoming, Organic Materials, *The Small Finds from Hamwic*, Vol 5, Part **3**.

Roach, F A 1985 *Cultivated Fruits of Britain: Their Origin and History*, Blackwell.

Robinson, M 1979 'Biological Evidence' in Lambrick and Robinson, *Iron Age and Roman riverside settlements at Farmoor, Oxon*, Coun Brit Archaeol Res Rep **32**.

Robinson, M and Straker, V forthcoming Silica Skeletons of Macroscopic Plant Remains from Ash, in *Proc 7th Symp IWGP*.

Rodgers, P 1987 The Utilization of Computerised Site Archives: The Problem of Accessibility for External Users, *Archaeol Computing Newsletter*.

Roes, A 1963 *Bone and antler objects from the Frisian Terp-Mounds*, Haarlem.

———— 1965 Vondsten Van Dorestad, *Archaeologica Traiectina* **7**, Groningen.

Royal Commission on Historical Monuments 1970 *An Inventory of the Historical Monuments in the County of Dorset. Volume II South East. Part 3.*

Royal County of Berkshire, Planning Department 1986 *Review of Berkshire's Structure Plan Submission Document. Draft Replacement Structure Plan 1986.*

Rowley, T and Davies, M 1973 *Archaeology and the M40 Motorway*.

Schadla-Hall, R T 1977 *The Winchester District: the archaeological potential*.

Schietzel, K 1970 Holzerne Kleinfunde aus Haithabu (Ausgrabung 1963–4), *Berichte uber die Ausgrabungen in Haithabu* **4** 77–91, Neumunster.

Schofield, J (ed) 1980 *Site Manual Part 1: The Written Record*, Museum of London, Dept of Urban Archaeology Handbook.

Schoknecht, U 1978 Handelsbeziehungen der fruhmittel-alterliche Siedlung Menzlin bei Anklam, *Zeitschrift fur Archaeologie* **12** 225–234.

Schwarz-Mackensen, G 1976 Die Knochennadeln von Haithabu, *Berichte uber die Ausgrabungen in Haithabu* **9**, Neumunster.

Sharples, N 1985 Maiden Castle Project 1985: Interim Report, *Proc Dorset Natur Hist Archaeol Soc* **107** 111–119.

———— 1986 Maiden Castle Project 1986: An Interim Report, *Proc Dorset Natur Hist Soc* **108** 53–61.

Sheail, J and Wells, D T C E 1969 The Historical Approach to the Ecology of Alluvial Grasslands, in Sheail and Wells (eds) *Old Grassland its Archaeology and Importance*, NCC Symp **5** 62–67.

Shennan, S J 1985 *Experiments In The Collection And Analysis of Archaeological Survey Data: The East Hampshire Survey*.

Shennan, S J and Schadla-Hall, R T 1978 Some suggestions for a sampling approach to archaeological survey in Wessex, in Cherry *et al* (eds) *Sampling in Contemporary British Archaeology*, Brit Archaeol Rep **50** 87–104.

Shott, M 1985 Shovel-Test Sampling as a Site Discovery Technique: a case study from Michigan, *J Fld Archaeol* **12** 457–468.

Shotton, F W 1978 Archaeological inferences from the study of alluvium in the lower Severn and Avon valleys, in Limbrey and Evans (eds) *The Effect of Man on the Landscape: the Lowland Zone*.

Sieveking, G de G *et al* 1973 A new survey of Grime's Graves, Norfolk, *Proc Prehist Soc* **39** 182–218.

Smith, K 1977 The Excavation of Winklebury Camp, Basingstoke, Hampshire, *Proc Prehist Soc* **43** 31–129.

Southwood, T R E 1971 *Ecological Methods*, London.

Sparey Green, C J 1987 *Excavations at Poundbury, Dorchester, Dorset, 1966–1982. Volume 1; The Settlements*, Dorset Natur Hist Archaeol Soc Monograph **7**.

Spence, C (ed) 1990, 2nd edn Site Manual, Dept of Urban Archaeology, Museum of London.

Stephens, G R 1985a Civic Aqueducts in Britain, *Britannia* **16** 197–208.

——— 1985b Military Aqueducts in Roman Britain, *Archaeol J* **142** 216–236.

Stevens, F 1934 The Highfield Pit Dwellings, Fisherton, Salisbury, *Wiltshire Archaeol Natur Hist Mag* **46** 579–624.

Stuart, J D M and Birkbeck, J M 1936 A Celtic Village on Twyford Downs, Excavated 1933–34, *Proc Hampshire Fld Club Archaeol Soc* **13** 188–207.

Stuiver, M and Pearson, G W 1986 High-precision calibration of the radiocarbon time scale, AD 1950–500 BC *Radiocarbon* **28** 2b.

Summerfield, M A and Goudie, A S 1980 The Sarsens of southern England: their palaeoenvironmental interpretation with reference to other silicretes, in Jones (ed) *The Shaping of Southern England*, 71–100.

Sunter, N and Woodward, P J 1987 *Romano-British Industries in Purbeck*, Dorset Natur Hist Archaeol Soc Monograph **6**.

Taylor, T P 1979 Soil Mark Studies near Winchester, *J Archaeol Sci* **6** 93–100.

Tempel, W-D 1970 Zum Umfang des Kammachergewerbes in Haithabu, *Neue Ausgrabungen und Forschungen in Niedersachsen* **6** 218–223.

Tubbs, C 1978 An Ecological Appraisal of the Itchen Valley Flood PLain, *Proc Hampshire Fld Club Archaeol Soc* **34** 5–22.

Ulbricht, I 1978 Die Geweihverarbeitung in Haithabu, *Die Ausgrabungen in Haithabu* **7**.

Vicherd, G 1987 *Autoroutes dans l'Ain et Archéologie*.

van Vilsteren, V T 1983 The medieval village of Dommelen: A case study for the interpretation of charred seeds from postholes, in van Zeist and Casparie (eds) *Plants and Ancient Man. Studies in palaeoethnobotany. Proc 6th Symp IWGP* Counc Brit Archaeol Res Rep **21** 227–321.

Wacher, J 1974 *The Towns of Roman Britain*.

Wainwright, G J 1968 The excavation of a Durotrigian farmstead near Tollard Royal in Cranbourne Chase, Southern England, *Proc Prehist Soc* **34** 102–147.

——— 1969 The Excavation of Balksbury Camp, Andover, Hampshire, *Proc Hampshire Fld Club Archaeol Soc* **26** 21–55.

——— 1971 The excavation of a Late Neolothic enclosure at Marden, Wiltshire, *Antiq J* **51** 177–239.

——— 1979 *Gussage All Saints: An Iron Age Settlement in Dorset*, London.

Wainwright, G J and Cunliffe, B W 1984 Maiden Castle; excavation, education and entertainment? *Antiquity* **59** 97–100.

Wainwright, G J and Longworth, I H 1971 *Durrington Walls: Excavations 1966–1968*, Res Rep Comm Soc Antiq London **29**.

Walden, H W 1976 A nomenclatural list of the land mollusca of the British Isles, *J Conchology* **29** 21–25

Waller, K 1936 Friesische Grabfelder an der Nordseekuste, *Praehistorisches Zeitschrift* **27** 227–251.

Walters, S M 1949 Eleocharis L., *J Ecology* **37** 196–198.

Waton, P V 1982 Man's impact on the chalklands: some new pollen evidence, in Bell and Limbrey (eds) *Archaeological Aspects of Woodland Ecology*, Brit Archaeol Rep **S146** 75–91.

——— 1986 Palynological evidence for early and permanent woodland on the Chalk of central Hampshire, in Sieveking and Hart (eds) *The Scientific Study of Flint and Chert*, Cambridge.

Werner, J 1977 Zu den Knochenschnallen und Reliquiarschnallen des 6 Jahrhunderts, in Werner (ed) *Die Ausgrabungen in St Ulrich und afra in Augsburg 1961–8*, Munchener Beitrage zur Vor- und Fruhgeschichte.

West, S 1969 The Anglo-Saxon Village of West Stow: an interim report of the excavations 1965–8, *Medieval Archaeol* **13** 1–20.

——— 1978 Die Siedlung West Stow in Suffolk, in Ahrens (ed) *Sachsen und Angelsachsen*, Hamburg, 395–412.

——— 1985 *West Stow, The Anglo-Saxon Village*, East Anglian Archaeol Rep **24**.

Whinney, R 1985 Anglo-Saxon cemetery at Itchen Abbas, *FIND* (the newsletter of the Winchester Archaeological Rescue Group) **35**, January 1985, 3–4.

——— 1986 Itchen Abbas Anglo-Saxon cemetery – excavations 1986, *FIND* **40**, September 1986, 3–4.

Wilson, D M 1983 A Bone Pin from Sconsburgh, Dunrossness, in O'Connor and Clarke (eds) *From the Stone Age to the Forty Five*, Edinburgh, 343–349.

Wilson, R 1985 Degraded bones, feature type and spatial patterning on an Iron Age occupation site in Oxfordshire, in Fieller *et al* (eds) *Palaeobiological Investigations: Research Design, Methods and Data Analysis*, Brit Archaeol Rep **S266** 81–100.

Wilthew, P 1986 *Examination of technological material from Abbots Worthy, Hampshire*, Ancient Monuments Laboratory, Report 4779.

Winkelmann, W 1977 Archaologische Zeugnisse zum fruhmittelalterlichen Handwerk in Westfalen, *Fruhmittelalter-liche Studien* **11** 92–126.

Wishart, D 1978 *CLUSTAN User Manual* (3rd edn) Edinburgh Program Library Unit, Edinburgh University.

Woodward, P J 1978 Flint Distribution, Ring Ditches and Bronze Age Settlement Patterns in the Great Ouse Valley: The Problem, a Field Survey Technique and some Preliminary Results, *Archaeol J* **135** 32–56.

—— forthcoming *The South Dorset Ridgeway Survey and Excavations 1977–1983: The Pre-Iron Age Landscapes*, Dorset Natur Hist Archaeol Soc Monograph.

Woodward P J, Bellamy P, and Cox P W 1987 Field Survey of the Ancient Fields and Enclosures at Black Hill, Cerne Abbas, Dorset, *Proc Dorset Natur Hist Archaeol Soc* **109** 55–64.

Woodward, P J and Smith, R J C 1987 Survey and Excavation along the route of the Southern Dorchester By-Pass 1986–87: An Interim Note, *Proc Dorset Natur Hist Archaeol Soc* **109** 79–89.

—— forthcoming, Survey and Excavation along the route of the Southern Dorchester By-Pass 1986–87.

van Zeist, W 1970 Prehistoric and Early Historic Food Plants in the Netherlands, *Palaeohistoria* **14** 41–173.